e

John was born in 1929 in Paisley and brought up in a suburb of Glasgow. He attended Glasgow Academy and Strathallan School before training as a Scottish Chartered Accountant qualifying in 1952. There followed two years National Service in the Royal Corps of Signals at the Army HQ in Germany. He joined the family business in 1956 and remained in the company when it was acquired by the brewer Ind Coope (later Allied Breweries) in 1960.

Nine years were spent in the retail wine trade running a chain of shops owned by the brewery in Scotland followed by ten years in a small Scotch whisky company Stewart and Son of Dundee, producers of Stewarts Cream of the Barley Scotch. The next ten years were spent in Wm Teacher & Sons to be joined later by the Ballantines brand acquired through the acquisition of the Canadian company Hiram Walker. The size of the Scotch whisky business had grown from very small beginnings to be the second largest in the industry. John served on the main board of the group by now called Allied-Lyons incorporating the J Lyons food businesses in UK, Europe and USA until his retirement in 1989.

For some years thereafter he served part-time in a number of bodies including Food From Britain Council, NHS in Scotland and in two financial companies. Hobbies are golf, reading, travel and current affairs. John was awarded an OBE in 1992 for services to the food and drink industries.

To Eusie Stewart

From the Far Haaf to the Sma' Half

A Shetland Family's 300 Years in Fishing and 100 Years in Scotch Whisky

With thanks for your encouragement

JOHN JAMIESON BLANCHE

A great grandson of Peter Blance of Delting

John

Librario

To the wives and families of Peter, John, Willie and John
who provided constant support and put up with
much inconvenience due to the demands of busy business lives.

Contents

Acknowledgements

James R Nicolson is a Shetlander born and bred, who is the doyen of the local writers. I learned a lot from his *Traditional Life in Shetland* and *Hay & Company Merchants in Shetland.* These books enabled me to envisage the background of previous generations of Blances and to understand how they must have struggled but survived due to the native determination and resourcefulness. Having spent part of his career abroad, he has been able to provide readers with a worthwhile perspective of the islands and the life of the people in his many books.

The Commission on the Truck System (Shetland) report of 1872 is a remarkable document and is probably the only detailed record of the life of fishermen and knitters in that period. I am grateful to the Archivist Brian Smith and to Angus Johnson, who offered help with researches and provided me with a copy of the report and the evidence given before the commissioner.

There are many excellent histories of the Scotch whisky industry and its companies. I have referred particularly to Ronald Weir's *The History of the Distillers Company 1877–1939*, *The Making of Scotch Whisky* by Michael S Moss and John R Hume, *The Scotch Whisky Industry Record* by Charles Craig and *Scotch The Formative Years* by Ross Wilson. I also have a number of company histories in my possession and these have been helpful in providing further details of individual companies.

The *Statistical Accounts of Scotland* provide vivid descriptions of life in the islands. I have referred particularly to an account written about Delting Parish by the Rev Mr John Morison concerning life in the period 1791–99 and another somewhat shorter account of 1845 written by the Rev John Paton.

In relating the lives of grandfather John and father Willie, I have referred to one of my grandfather's old-fashioned letter books dealing with his confidential and private mail covering the period 1898 to 1927, when he died. I also have the minute books of annual meetings and directors' meetings of his company, JJ Blanche & Co Ltd, which are remarkably detailed. They deal with the period from 1922, the date the business became a corporate entity, until 1960 when the company was sold to the brewer Ind Coope. After grandfather's death the minutes tell of the frustrations of the second generation as they struggled to find a happy and effective way of working together. They failed to do so but, nevertheless, managed to expand the business and provide a comfortable life for their families.

A great many people have helped me with research and information about the family in previous generations and others have kindly read the early drafts and made helpful comments. I should especially like to mention my late cousin, Sheila Blanche Durham, whose researches into the family tree indicate how our family line has spread from Shetland all over the world. As well as being an avid genealogist, she collected many anecdotes of Shetland life and about members of the Blance families.

Two people read the complete text and made extremely helpful comments as well as giving me encouragement to follow through to publication. My wife Fiona bravely ploughed through the early drafts and continues to give regular encouragement and take an interest in the progress of the work. Without all these friends, I might well have lost heart and spent more time on the golf course and less at my computer! The manuscript would then have languished in a cupboard until discovered by a great grandchild.

Preface

Whatever happened to the people who left Shetland in the 1870s and what did their families do with their lives? This book tells the story of one such family, whose head lived and worked in Shetland for most of his life. His ancestors had lived on the islands for many hundreds of years and like them he raised a large family.

He was Peter Blance, my great grandfather, born in 1832. He and his wife Margaret Smith raised 12 children and nine survived to a ripe old age. He provided his children with an education so far as was possible in those days and saw all of them leave the islands for mainland Scotland to find a new way of life. Their ancestry provided them with the strong Shetland characteristics of self-sufficiency, confidence, initiative and an ability to innovate. These traits are still evident in each succeeding generation and are a source of strength to all those who have settled in so many parts of the world. Shetland remains a strong influence on everyone who has links with it. Peter was a fisherman, who lived in Calback and then near Brae in southern Delting. His days at sea were spent in fishing smacks, which worked on the Faroe and Iceland fisheries where cod was the main catch.

The eldest son, Robert, together with number three son, John, left the islands in their late teens and trained as licensed grocers. They both started their own businesses in Edinburgh but John soon moved to Glasgow where he founded a wine importing and distilling business that was carried on by his eldest surviving son Willie, my father. I joined the business briefly before it was sold to a major drinks company where I spent the rest of my career. Writing the story of the working life of the four of us has been a pleasant experience and one I would recommend others to follow if only to record the events of our commercial history so that lessons may be learned for the benefit of future generations.

In the course of describing the business activities of the four of us I have endeavoured to highlight the differences between the business scene of the late 19th century and 100 years later. The businesses started by grandfather and a similar one by his elder brother, Bob, were able to survive two world wars and provide for several families in some comfort.

Grandfather, father and I were in the Scotch whisky industry for most of our careers and each of us was able to see at first hand major restructuring affecting almost every business. Each of these periods of change had different origins but the underlying purpose in each was the same – greater strength to ensure survival in an ever more competitive world market. The post WWII success of the industry is unique and could not have been forecast given the difficulties faced by producers in its previous history nor could it have been possible without the influence and participation of the major operator, The Distillers Company.

This book offers a contrast between the life of a fisherman and crofter in Shetland and that of a businessman in mainland Scotland. Both involved very hard work but the businessman had opportunities to improve his quality of life denied to his parents in view of the way in which the economy of the islands operated. Happily, such opportunities are available in Shetland today and for quite a few the quality of life is better than the mainland.

The late 19th century was a period of great change everywhere and it had its affect on Shetland. In researching the evidence given to the Commission on the Truck System (Shetland) in 1871–72 I was provided with a detailed review of the working life of fishermen, crofters and knitters and given an insight into the characters of many of them. The harsh regime of former years had begun to improve partly due to outside influences but also to the relaxing of the strict hold the landlords formerly had over their tenants. It is also interesting to see that some families prospered while others lacked the confidence to take charge of their lives. In summarising the evidence I have sought to emphasise the differences between the various parts of the islands.

The figures in the appendices will be of interest as management tools for those who use trends to forecast the future and plan stock and plant and machinery investments. Maybe they will alert top management to the financial commitment needed for building a successful Scotch whisky company in which there is no chance of achieving an early positive cash flow, although the long-term rewards are attractive. I emphasise that these are merely tools and no substitute for a clear expression of objectives and methods. It is wise never to become a slave to figures, as they will let you down before long! Looking at the situation and making up your mind what to do is far better than taking cover behind figures. Their only purpose is to help you to express what you have seen or wish to do.

This is more of a biography than an historical work and attempts to describe what four people saw around them in their working days. The story starts in Shetland and, after travelling the world on the back of Scotch whisky, returns appropriately and timeously to the news of the building of the new whisky distillery at Catfirth in Shetland. This is the first to be built in the islands and I wish it well as it will expand the scope of the economy at a time when new industry is most welcome.

Many of the families of my grandfather's cousins continue to live in Shetland and use their talents there and I have had enormous pleasure in meeting and talking with them. One of my cousins is a writer and broadcaster and another is building a business converting seaweed into garden fertiliser, a successor to the 18th and 19th century kelp industry, which produced potash for a similar purpose.

Rather like designing an aircraft, there is always some further improvement that can be made. I kept remembering yet another incident, anecdote or view to express and would have gone on and on until a kind person suggested that in that case I would never finish it!

John Blanche
Delting, Boquhan, Balfron, Scotland
January 2011

Introduction

I found myself led into researching and writing this book after I read of my family's origins in the family tree compiled by my cousin Sheila Blanche Durham. She had begun with the family of Peter Blance and Margaret Smith born in 1832 and 1835 and traced their ancestors back to a marriage in 1754. Thereafter, all the descendants were researched to the present day and the record is being updated on a regular basis. I thought I would like to know something of the lives that my ancestors had led in Shetland and began to collect any information I could lay my hands on. I started to read about contemporary life in the islands and this helped me to build a picture of the life led by Peter and Margaret and their children.

My interest was captured but I wondered what made the children leave Shetland. I had of course known that my grandfather had started a business in wine importing and retailing as well as Scotch whisky distilling. It had been carried on by his children and latterly was run by my father. The fact that I had spent 20 years in the Scotch whisky industry persuaded me to dig deeper into the story. One day I was given a very good start when my cousin Andrew Ballantyne sent me a cutting from the *East Lothian Courier* column 'Peeps into the Past'. The date was 28 January 1994 and the piece was from the files of the *Haddington Courier* of January 1894 reporting that Mr JJ Blanche, Peter's second son, and Mr William Hardie, a licenceholder at 4 Picardy Place, Edinburgh, had recently addressed a meeting in North Berwick. It had been called to propose the formation of a Defence Association to counter the efforts of teetotallers in the town. It continued: "Mr Blanche addressed the meeting at some length, pressing upon the audience the benefits of being organised and putting themselves in a position to show a united front to an unscrupulous foe. Mr Blanche said that what the so-called Temperance Party aimed at was not for the total annihilation of a particular form of licence but the total abolition of all licences." The meeting agreed to form a local Defence Association and Provost Whitecross was elected chairman.

The previous week, on 20 January 1994, I had chaired the regular monthly meeting of the Scottish Veto Investment Company (Scottish Veto), which had originally been formed to insure licenceholders against loss of licence as a result of a Veto Poll. The formation of Scottish Veto was a direct consequence of the legislation brought in, in 1913, to satisfy the temperance movement and provided for local community polls to be called to vote for the abolition of licences in the parish. In the years between these two events grandfather, father and I had all been involved in the wine and spirit business as retailers, wholesalers and distillers during our respective careers. As my board colleague Paddy Thompson commented, "This job (chairing Scottish Veto) has been waiting for you for 100 years". I began to think of all that had taken place in those hundred years and resolved to record some of what had happened and what the family had seen of the distilling industry in that time and what had persuaded all Peter's children to leave the islands. I soon discovered that great grandfather Peter had been the first, in a sense, to be involved in the spirit trade as he had been caught smuggling on his way back from fishing near Faroe with a consignment of tobacco and brandy!

Peter's ancestors had lived their lives in Shetland for several hundred years. There were dozens of Blance families and most were concentrated in an area known as Calback Ness, part of Delting parish. Delting is derived from old Norse words – 'dell', a valley and 'taing', a neck of land jutting out into the sea. Other Blances were to be found in Northmavine and Yell. Their lives were devoted to fishing in the stormy but richly endowed waters off Shetland. They also grew a little food and grazed their animals on the 'ness' or common grazing ground. The quality of the land was not good and today it is the site of the Sullom Voe Oil Terminal where the North Sea pipelines land the oil from the rigs prior to loading it onto tankers.

Over the centuries the population of Delting was only a few hundred but by the second half of the 18th century it had begun to grow faster and during this period increased from 956 to 1504. There were 223 families giving an average family of between six and seven. The increase seems to have arisen due to landlords seeking to have as many men as possible on the cod and ling fishing. The young men were encouraged to marry young and start families in order to increase the numbers available to fish. I suppose this was a real example of long-term manpower planning. By 1845 the population had increased to over 2,000 and in reporting this fact the Rev John Paton in his *Statistical Account for Delting* noted presumably with some satisfaction, that there had been only one illegitimate birth in the previous three years! The 1871 census estimated the population of Shetland as a whole at over 31,000. By 1971 it had declined to 17,500. However, the coming of the oil industry and other smaller activities has reduced emigration and brought immigrants to the islands resulting in an increase to around 22,000. In 1971 there were 900 living in Delting and by 1981 it had increased to 2,200 due to the influx of oil industry workers.

The Origin of the Blance Name

The family name Blance (now with spelling variations, Blanch and Blanche) has been inherited unchanged and is not a patronymic name. The origin, therefore, did not appear to be Norse. Recently, however, a California man descended from a Shetlander has set up a DNA project. I have taken part in this research and my Y-DNA demonstrates a likely link with the west coast of Norway. Further tests are in hand but the speculation on the origin of the name is now centred on the possibility that it was Bljan, an old Norse personal name leading to the patronymic Bljanson. A version of it, Blanx, appears in references to Fetlar in 1577 and there was a Blans in Fetlar in 1616 as well as in Yell in 1628. There is another record of a marriage in Rotterdam on 18 November 1747 of a James Blans of Shetland to Janet Foster. Given the Dutch fishing activities off Shetland and the many trading connections, it is more than possible that some Shetlanders moved to Holland. It seems possible that the Norse DNA signature supports the Bljan origin. On the other hand, there is a possibility that the Blances came from France and a Blance woman had a child by a Norseman and the Blance family adopted it! This was quite a common arrangement in those days. This leads to the possibility that these Blances came over as adherents named Blanc to one of the Norman nobles who arrived with William the Conqueror in 1066. A number of them were persuaded to settle in Scotland and help the monarch to unify and control the country. At any rate, there is certainly no connection with sailors wrecked as the Spanish Armada escaped around the northern isles or with the emigration of the Huguenots. The name was in Shetland long before these events.

There are regular references to the name Blance from the late 16th century and it remained unchanged until the 19th century. Then Peter changed it to Blanch before his marriage to distinguish himself from several other Peter Blances in Calback Ness and Northmavine. Later the name became Blanche and, indeed, the Ordinance Survey sheet for North Mainland has reference to 'Blanches Geo' on the Eastern shore of Northmavine. I like to think that this may have been a tiny inlet or chasm where some of the family landed contraband goods and avoided customs duty – an activity better known as smuggling! This was a regular occupation for the people in the more remote parts of the coast throughout Britain after excise taxes began to be levied.

Attitudes to Alcohol

My grandfather's work for Licensed Trade Defence in his early days made him very conscious of the need to use alcohol sensibly but he and his contemporaries felt strongly that the temperance movement was totally unnecessary and, indeed, that it was pointless to campaign to ban alcohol altogether. The trouble began when governments started to tax alcohol seriously in the early part of the 19th century. In Britain one of the first moves was to licence distilleries in order to control the tax opportunities from the start of the process. There followed excise taxes on consumption, which proved very lucrative as consumption increased. The rapid industrialisation from the 1850s onwards changed society completely. People flocked to the cities to work in huge factories in appalling conditions. The housing was of poor quality and life was a hard grind. To make things bearable, the men turned to alcohol which they had money to buy, and families found they had to do without sufficient food and clothing. Frankly these men over-indulged and could not always be controlled by their wives. Major social problems resulted and those in political power did little to solve them. Consumption taxes were raised but not sufficiently to restrict drinking to excess, rather to fill the Treasury's coffers.

Various movements sprang up in a number of industrialised countries (though not in France, Spain or Italy!) for the purpose of developing temperate habits with the eventual aim of bringing about the total abolition of the sale of alcohol. These bodies were strong political movements. They gained popular but not unanimous support and the issue of drink polarised views. There was pressure on governments for action and many brought in legislation to try to satisfy these demands. In Finland, Sweden and Norway there was prohibition and in Canada the government controlled distribution and retailing. These countries still have government control over the production, importing and retailing of alcohol, although the regimes have been relaxed considerably. In Germany and France the distillation of plain spirit is government controlled.

The complete prohibition of the production, sale and consumption of alcohol was introduced in the United States under the Volstead Act. It was in force from 1920 to 1933 and was a complete disaster. It gave rise to huge crime syndicates, which purchased liquor from overseas suppliers offshore and then ran it in and distributed it to individuals and 'speakeasies' or illegal bars. The policing of this activity was half-hearted at best and it was with some relief to all, except the syndicates, that Roosevelt repealed the Act. Although prohibition was ended, strict controls remain over the distilling, manufacture and importation of alcoholic products. In addition, 18 of the states have some form of state government control including state-run liquor stores.

In Scotland, where social problems were the greatest compared with other areas of the United Kingdom, the Temperance League and others mounted a strong campaign for the abolition of all liquor licenses. Naturally, those who earned their living by selling alcoholic beverages were determined to counter this attack. Between the 1880s and early 1900s, there was a constant battle to gain the upper hand between the temperance movements and the producers and retailers of alcohol. In those early days my grandfather played a significant role in the fight against abolition in the 1880s. He was the National Organiser for the Licensed Trade Defence in Scotland. The response by the government was more measured than in the Nordic countries and the USA. The campaigning for and against prohibition had been equally successful and a compromise was introduced in Scotland in the form of the Veto Poll legislation of 1913. In addition, the sale of alcohol was controlled by government in areas, which were important centres of military activity such as Invergordon and Carlisle.

The Temperance (Scotland) Act 1913 provided for local veto polls or referendums enabling communities to vote for the abolition of licences to sell alcohol. Parishes were known as 'wet' for licences being allowed and 'dry' for abolition and no licences. Each parish in Scotland was able to seek a poll for the abolition of licenses in its own area on application by a minimum number of persons on the voting register. A number of them did vote to be 'dry' but generally the activity under the Act was not great. After a few decades of inactivity, the Act was repealed in 1977 after the Clayson Committee Report recommended the abolition of the veto in 1970.

When it was introduced the Act was a threat to individual licence holders, who would lose their businesses in the event of a 'dry' vote in their area. As a means of providing some compensation, not available from government, a company was formed in 1914 to insure licence holders against the loss of their liquor licences. The company was called The Scottish Veto Protection Co. Ltd. An example of what could occur is to be found in the *National Guardian* of 24 February 1945, which reported a Local Veto meeting of the St Giles Ward of Edinburgh. It had been 'attacked' four times with a requisition for a veto poll but each time the attacks were repulsed. The St Giles Ward was an important one as it contained most of the important historical buildings of the city and, maybe more importantly, the Caledonian and North British Hotels as well as two theatres! In the same issue, there was a report and some correspondence about an article by Sir John Stirling Maxwell Bt KT, who had proposed that the retailing of alcohol should be run by a state monopoly along the lines of the system in Carlisle. There the brewery and the pubs were owned and run by the government but not to the satisfaction of the customers. Mr Robert Milburn of the Royal Hotel in Kirkcudbright demolished Sir John's case completely.

When the Act was repealed Scottish Veto found itself with considerable funds accumulated over the previous 60 years. The claims record had been small and Douglas Williamson of Hardie Caldwell, who served as Secretary and later Chairman, thought that the only claim was from Whiteinch in 1922. I have Licenceholders Policy number 79 for 12 Fort Street, Broughty Ferry taken out for £600 and subsequently increased to £1500 at an annual premium of £3-7/6. On the repeal of the Act it was decided that Scottish Veto should continue to manage its funds as an investment company. It was renamed Scottish Veto Investment Company and re-registered some years later as an unlimited company under the Companies Act 1982. Scottish Veto in both its guises was managed by Hardie Caldwell Ker & Hardie, Chartered Accountants of Glasgow throughout its existence. This firm also acted for my grandfather in his later years and provided me with a good basic training in accountancy. In 1991 I was invited to become a Director by Douglas and on his retirement I became Chairman. Thus a family connection was re-established and I was once again involved with the firm that had been connected with our family for most of the 20th century.

I was looking forward to renewing my acquaintance with Douglas but he sadly died at the relatively young age of 80 years. Shortly before his death he was heard to say that when a man reaches 80 he should be sent on his way! He was a man of strong convictions and no compromise but one of the kindest you could meet. He kept Hardie Caldwell going as a small to medium sized firm when all about him were merging into very large worldwide operations full of specialists and little opportunity for client contact. Furthermore he has managed to recruit other partners who have the same philosophy and find that they have many appreciative clients.

Nowadays the attitude to drinking alcohol has become more sophisticated. On the one hand my old company's booklet 'Alcohol Issues at a Glance' states that moderate consumption of alcohol may have tangible health benefits according to research. On the other hand it goes on to warn of the dangers of excessive drinking and a combination of drinking and driving. Most companies now have strict rules about drinking during working hours, particularly where machinery is being operated. In addition, where employees suffer from drink problems, it is normal for employers to give them assistance in bringing their excessive habits under control. This is a huge change from the situation 100 years ago.

In the last century the temperance movement has almost disappeared, as society generally does not tolerate drunkenness to the same extent. Also, the various temperance groups failed to agree a common approach to alcohol-related issues and their combined strength was never harnessed. Some exaggerated the risks of drinking and thus discredited the entire message. In the early 1930s in Britain, the temperance movement celebrated its centenary by predicting that alcohol would be consigned to the museums within 50 years.

In the years ahead, the benefits and risks are bound to be researched in more detail and the parallel question of drugs looked at in a more rational way. Both alcohol and drugs have been used throughout history but in ancient times their use was held in balance by cultural and social habits. The greater availability in modern times has led to problems of over consumption. The alcohol industry has mostly adopted a responsible attitude over the last 200 years and government has been conscious of the need for a framework of control, which attempts to provide room for enterprise while laying down limits, which give some protection to the consumer. In addition there is a regular contribution to tax revenues few governments can do without!

There are signs that social problems are again making an appearance with the availability of alcohol to young people. The questions of under-age drinking and 'binge' drinking are reaching crisis point and may require some action unless the industry takes steps to stamp it out. Binge drinking is clearly unwise despite its arguably fashionable and macho image among the young. There can be no enjoyment during and certainly not after such a drinking session.

I think that one of the contributory reasons for the lack of control is that licenceholders no longer seem to refuse to serve customers whom they judge to have had sufficient to drink. On the contrary, they offer incentives to consume more by having 'happy hours'[1] and other special offers in order to maximise turnover, particularly in quiet periods. Pubs are now mostly controlled by large specialist chains that began to build up their businesses by buying up outlets sold by the big breweries, which came out of pub ownership as a result of government legislation in the late 1980s. Brewers had a long-established understanding, dating from the 19th century, with government that they would run their establishments in an orderly manner. In return, so it is said, government would resist the pressure from temperance organisations for severe restrictions on the consumption of alcohol. As the threat from temperance organisations waned, the responsibility for control was vested in the licensing legislation. Local licensing courts have powers to withdraw a licence if they consider a pub is not being properly run but in recent times they have not been very strict in exercising their powers.

In the mid 1980s The Monopolies and Mergers Commission was asked by the government to carry out a third investigation of the brewery industry as it was regarded as a quasi-monopoly and thus able to charge higher prices to consumers. The report of the Commission recommended that brewers should be required to divest themselves of most of their pubs and retain only a small proportion. Most brewers decided to exit the trade entirely and sold them to a new breed of entrepreneurs. At about the same time there was a move to liberalise licensing hours and leave the market to run the pub sector. Naturally these pubs were not sold cheaply and furthermore large borrowing

[1] The Licensing (Scotland) Act 2005 which came into force on 1 September 2009 banned 'happy hours' and other promotions considered irresponsible.

very often financed the purchases and obliged the new owners to seek quick profit growth from turnover increases. Doing this by increasing prices was not an option as government had achieved its objective of creating a competitive market. So lower prices combined with more liberal licensing laws and the improved earnings of young people have produced a social problem. It is hardly practical to expect the police to control it, as they can never be everywhere at closing times, which vary from 11pm to 3am and later. A change in habits is urgently required but how to bring this about? The first thing is for licenceholders to exercise their powers to refuse to serve those who have consumed enough alcohol and for licensing courts to take action against licence-holders, who do not run their establishments in an orderly manner.

There are signs that pub chains will start to control consumption levels on their premises by cutting out 'happy hours' and 'all you can drink' offers and to stop price-cutting. The Yates Group are the first to make the move and, if others follow, the binge fashion may go into decline. However, it is vital that those in charge of licensed premises refuse to serve customers, who have consumed sufficient alcohol, otherwise the trouble will continue. The licensing courts must not hesitate to take action against pubs that do not control drinking levels, which result in disorderly conduct, by giving warnings and, as a last resort, removing their licences.

CHAPTER 1

Shetland Life and The Blances

Some Background to the Islands

Shetland, Hjaltland to the Vikings, is a group of 100 islands and the most northerly point of the British Isles. It lies 60 degrees north of the equator and one degree west of the Greenwich meridian and is approximately level with St Petersburg, Helsinki, Oslo, the southern tip of Greenland, Anchorage and the northern end of the Kamchatka Peninsula. It has a warmer climate than these places but can suffer from violent storms, particularly in winter. The scenery offers panoramic views of moorland and pasture framed with strips of water cutting in from the sea to form the unique voes. The result in bright sunshine with the blue of the water and green of land is spectacular. The Gulf Stream has an important influence on the climate keeping it fairly moderate compared to Newfoundland at 50 degrees, which is subject to the south-flowing arctic current. The population of over 22,000 has fluctuated up and down by around 20 per cent depending on the economy.

The earliest settlers probably arrived about 3,500 years ago and there is evidence of continuous human habitation through to the Picts, whose circular fortresses known as brochs can be seen around Shetland. The Vikings began to appear in the 8th century as they started to explore the seas West of Norway. They used the route through Bluemull Sound, which was safer than round the north of Unst with its rough stormy seas. Besides, the ten mile stretch of sheltered water gave them a chance to beach their ships and augment their supplies. The Shetland Islands provided staging posts for the great explorations and ventures across the oceans and as time went on migrants settled and provided more permanent facilities for the sea-farers. Many of these settlers were only too glad to find some flat land they could cultivate, as the supply at home was small and much in demand. It was a constant worry that some aggressive neighbour would take possession of your land from you.

The Nordic settlers, therefore, found the prospect of life in a new land a little more promising and were able to escape from the constant fighting for land and from the restrictive rule of their king. They were a little foolish, however, as they were continually raiding their old homeland for supplies not available in Shetland. Eventually the Norwegian king, Harold Fairhair, landed a force in Shetland to subdue the settlers and thus took an interest in the ruling of the islands.

Later Shetland featured in the Dutch Wars of the 17th century. For a long time seamen from the Netherlands enjoyed the free use of the fishing grounds and used the land facilities of Shetland at will. When Cromwell found hundreds of Dutch fishing vessels occupying Lerwick harbour, he ordered a fort to be constructed but the Dutch burned it down in 1673. They remained in control of the fishing for decades afterwards and the fort lay derelict until it was renovated in 1782. It has been rather frustrating for Shetlanders over the centuries to find that neither the Scottish nor the British governments have regarded fishing as an important economic resource and have never taken effective steps to protect it. The 21st century is no different from the 17th or 18th as the European Union now controls the Shetland fishery and vessels from other countries still have as good access as they had then.

Periods of emigration reduced numbers in the late 19th century and again in the post WWII years. However, it increased again with the arrival of oil and as a result of some enterprising people setting up small businesses, which are not affected by distance from markets. Undoubtedly it is a much more attractive place to live and raise a family than many inner city areas.

Shetland was in the front line during the sea battles of both World Wars. In the early 1940s a fleet of small boats known as the Shetland Bus maintained contact with the Norwegian coast throughout the war. As well as helping people at risk in Norway to escape the Germans, many operations were carried out to disrupt the German war effort. The crews were all Norwegian and they ran tremendous risks of being captured and executed as spies. They had to sail in bad weather to reduce the chances of being captured. Their first base was at Lunna and the churchyard there has a stone commemorating those who lost their lives. The second base was at Scalloway, where repair facilities were available and there is memorial to the Shetland Bus on the seafront.

The wildlife is a key feature of the islands. There are large breeding colonies of all the principal sea birds including gannets, guillemots, kittiwakes, puffins, fulmars, shags and the Great Skua (called Bonxie in Shetland). Shetland has about half the world population of the Bonxie. These birds must be watched carefully during the nesting season as they will dive bomb walkers. The main observation points for birds are at Hermaness, Sumburgh Head and the island of Noss. Birds eggs were often a source of food for the crofters and fishermen in the nesting season and many brave men were lowered down the cliffs to retrieve them. Common and grey seals can be seen around the coast and if you are lucky the odd otter, which do come out to feed during the day. The presence of seals will attract orcas inshore and it is also possible to sight other types of whale. On the land the Shetland pony is famous all over the world and is still bred and in demand by enthusiasts. They are very friendly and can be seen grazing on the moors. In the early days of the industrial revolution they were used in coal mines to haul wagons from the coal face to the lift shafts. In earlier times they ran wild over the moors but could be harnessed and used to bring peat to the cottages and to ride into the town with goods for sale.

The traditional occupations of fishing, crofting, knitting and other craft work are still carried on. Fishing continues to be the largest contributor to the economy in spite of reduced stocks and the sharing of the catches with other European Union countries. Reduced fishing activity has been replaced by fish farming, the oil industry and many small high and low tech businesses. The gradual improvement in communications has encouraged a fledgling tourist trade and it has the potential to grow in the years ahead.

The first oil was piped to a brand new terminal at Sullom Voe in Delting Parish in 1978. The construction and the ongoing operation and servicing of this facility improved the economic prospects of the islands and provided substantial funds for community development.

The oil is expensive to extract but since the 1970s the international price has been at a much higher level making North Sea oil viable. The reserves are limited but further exploration is underway in the Atlantic and this will provide a reasonably secure future for this activity.

The Shetlanders are a very hospitable people and very industrious. Traces of the original settlers are long gone and it may be very difficult to establish any remaining connections with the Celts, Picts and the Scotties from Ireland. The majority of the population are descended from immigrants starting with the Vikings followed by the Scots, Normans and people from England, Europe and even Asia. Today there are many people who have moved to Shetland because it offers a peaceful environment and a good place to bring up children and they find that they can carry on careers using modern electronic methods.

Hidden History

There is plenty of evidence of settlement several thousand years ago. One advantage of remoteness for archaeologists is that the evidence of habitation remains undisturbed by constant changes over time. In Glasgow or Edinburgh it is possible to envisage the lives of those of a few hundred years ago from the remains of their buildings many of which still stand intact or have been adapted to modern uses. It is rare to find anything older simply because old buildings are usually demolished, their materials re-used or something else has been built on top of them. This is not so in Shetland where most of the ground has remained undisturbed under the blanket of peat. A good many sites of dwellings and other buildings have been excavated and dated prior to the Early Bronze Age. Undoubtedly the most interesting buildings for the layman are the Brochs. These are defensive structures and can be found in various parts of Scotland. They date from about 600 BC and were developed over the following 900 years.

The design of the Broch was a brilliant solution to the problem of families needing a safe haven at a moment's notice. They were shaped like bells wide at the bottom and tapering about half way up. There are inner and outer walls allowing for a stairway to various chambers on several levels. There is normally only one very narrow entrance easily defended and the walls were impossible to climb. The dry-stone construction has lasted for hundreds of years and supports a height of over 30 feet. The best known and preserved one is the Broch of Mousa on a small island off the southeast mainland. It dates from the start of the first millennium AD and has survived in remarkably good condition. The Vikings mention it in an *Icelandic Saga* as a place of note where one noble successfully escaped the clutches of another until they both decided to negotiate a settlement to their dispute. The remains of other Broch sites are often identified by the place names containing 'brough', 'burgh' or 'bur', which are derived from the Norse word 'borg' meaning castle or fortification.

The archaeologist is to be admired for his skill in combining research, instinct for sites, careful excavation and imagination in interpreting his findings. Opinions obviously can differ but it is clear that the people who originally settled in Shetland were migrants. They had moved north to escape the harrying of warring tribes or to find more space for hunting and farming. Important among these were the Picts, from the Armorican tribes in northern France and the Celts or Keltoi as the Greeks called them. The 'K' gives a clue to why the hard 'C' is used when referring to 'Celtic' peoples or 'Celts' as opposed to the soft one used in Celtic Football Club.

Farley Mowat's Theory

More recently Canada's famous author Farley Mowat has written a book about the Albans using his knowledge of archaeological research in Shetland, Iceland, Greenland and the Canadian eastern arctic. He paints a picture of a people who inhabited Britain along with the Celts and Scots and who originated as far east as Asia Minor. They were a peaceable people, although quite prepared to defend themselves but they were often faced with the overwhelming forces of warriors, whose lives were devoted to pillaging and capturing of slaves rather than farming. They moved to Britain ahead of the others and for a time the country was known as Alba. They gradually moved north and settled in what is now Scotland and the name Alba is still sometimes used for the country or part of it. Latterly they were forced into the highlands above Glen Albyn as the Romans, Picts, Celts and then the Scotti from Ireland pressed them northwards.

The Albans were attracted to the northern isles by the presence of thousands of walrus, from which they obtained meat and oil and whose tusks proved really valuable for trading with merchants as far south as the Mediterranean. Farley Mowat in his book *The Alban Quest* (entitled *The Farfarers* in Canada) weaves the archaeological evidence into a fascinating story of how the Albans then began to follow the walrus to Iceland, Greenland, Labrador and eventually Newfoundland. These animals were hunted almost to extinction over many centuries and it is sad to note that the process continues today with many fish species and wild animals being hunted at such a rate that they can no longer be regarded as renewable resources. One wonders why man can never learn from past mistakes. When the Romans left Britain the Albans were able to hold their own with the other migrants until the appearance of the Vikings around the 7th century.

What little is known of the Vikings in Shetland has been gleaned from archaeological research and the few mentions in the *Icelandic Sagas*. It did not take them very long to gain complete control of the northern isles. The people there probably escaped the horrible fate of some, as they were likely to have been useful servants where they were rather than be shipped off as slaves to Norway or elsewhere. Most writers about Shetland refer to the Norwegian historian AW Brogger, who claims that the Vikings came to a deserted land as settler farmers. Farley Mowat disagrees and concludes that there was a good deal of bloodshed before they settled down to a more normal and permanent life.

The Viking Period and Norwegian Rule

There are two contrasting sources of information on the Vikings and their escapades. There are the graphic descriptions of the raids on monasteries detailing pillage, destruction, killing and theft. That happened often enough for the whole coastal population to be in a perpetual state of fear of a raid by these fierce sailors. If they were not killed, they were shipped off to be enslaved and separated from their families forever. By contrast, the *Icelandic Sagas* describe the glorious deeds of the Viking venturers in sailing to many lands and gaining great wealth. They do also describe the harsh life in Iceland (or Tilli, as it was known then) where no rule of law existed. If your neighbour did you a wrong you simply gathered the male members of the family together and went off and killed him and his family. Thereafter that family's cousins would come and avenge the murders.

So the Vikings were a fearsome and ruthless people but there was a form of discipline for those who became uncontrollable. They were simply banished for a period or permanently. This happened to Erik Rauda (Erik the Red), who after several killings, was banished from Iceland to Greenland (or Crona as it was then called). Erik thought he should have some company and persuaded a group of people to come and settle with him. He told them that Crona had more pastureland than Tilli and called it Greenland. This form of encouragement must rank as one of the earliest examples of successful marketing. Eric may have been right about the green pastures if you read *1421 The Year China Discovered the World* by Gavin Menzies. He claimed that at that time Greenland had wonderful pasture land and that the sea around it was easily navigable to within a couple of hundred miles of the North Pole. Incidentally, Farley Mowat concludes that this migration by the Vikings led to the Albans making a further move west. They must have been rather disturbed later when, having settled in their 'New Jerusalem' in Southwest Newfoundland, they heard of a Viking settlement at L'Anse aux Meadows in the northwest. The Norwegian, Helge Ingstad, excavated this site in the 1960s and it is thought that the leader was Erik's son Leif Eriksson. Fortunately the Vikings did not stay long and neither did anyone else until the settlement of Irish and English immigrants in the early 19th century.

From the Shetland point of view the drama was over quite quickly and before long a population of over 20,000 lived and prospered there. How many of them were indigenous people is impossible to say but very likely there are a good many Shetlanders who are descended from the original settlers. In some respects the Viking influence has remained strong manifesting itself in place names and words in the language. If a comparison is made between a map with old Norse names and the modern version, all the names will be recognisable and many will be exactly the same such as Haroldswick (Haroldsvik), Lerwick (Leirvik) and Sandwick (Sandvik) all named after bays (vik in Norse). Others are different because Norse letters of the alphabet have been replaced. There is a similarity in the layout of the typical crofter's home, which was used until the early 20th century. When they settled to farming the Norse devised a layout, which was functional and consisted of three rooms. The first was for animals, the next for the family to live in with a central fireplace and a hole in the roof for smoke to escape, and the other for sleeping. The only improvements over the years were the inevitable glass windows, a proper chimney, slate roofs and mortared stone walls, which made it unnecessary to stuff turf into the gaps to make them windproof. These dwellings were quite crowded as most couples had large families.

Norway's Problems in Controlling Its New Settlement

In Norse times an assembly called 'althing', which was really an early form of parliament, carried out the government. Tingwall not far from Lerwick was one of the sites and there were others. All the freeman or landowners were required to attend the meetings to carry out the administration of the area. In the early days under Norse rule the farmers were fortunate to hold land under the Norwegian 'udal' system of tenure. It was different from the feudal system in use elsewhere in that the grant of the land did not carry any obligation of personal service and the land was completely freehold. It was the property of the first improver and it was valued on the basis of its ability to produce crops. This system would have been welcomed by tenants of a later period under Scottish and British rule, when improvements carried out by the tenant often resulted in an increase in the rent.

It is not certain how long the udal system lasted but it is likely that some changes were made when Harold the Fairhaired came to power.

He united Norway and decreed that all land belonged to the crown. Furthermore, he became the supreme authority and appointed earls or jarls to help him govern the provinces. The freemen were henceforth required to render service to maintain and protect the realm. Thus the partial introduction of a feudal system, used throughout Europe, took place but the udal system lingered on until Scotland gained control of the islands. It had the disadvantage that on the death of the owner the land was divided among the children equally. Thus the plots became smaller and smaller and some ruthless dealers would buy them up for next to nothing thus re-creating sizeable farms. Then families found themselves becoming tenants-at-will with no long-term rights of tenure.

There was a good deal of dissatisfaction about the changes brought in by Harold and the protests led to Shetland freemen raiding the Norwegian coast to plunder and disrupt life there. In 874 Harold had had enough and set off to deal with the rebels. He annexed the islands and planted loyal subjects and peasants to colonise the place so that it could become a stable base for expeditions to the south for plundering the coasts of Britain, Ireland and beyond. Shetland was put under the control of a newly appointed Earl of Orkney, the first 'jarl' being Rognvald. He had a son Hrolf who was outlawed for the theft of cattle on the coast of Norway and went off to France and helped to found the kingdom of Normandy around AD900. His descendant William invaded and took control of England and proceeded to grant extensive lands to his friends.

Later the Scottish king sought help from Norman barons to control the country and gave them estates as a reward. A harsh feudal regime was introduced in both Scotland and England by these newcomers with the result that the people suffered a period of oppression for several hundred years. However, life in Shetland remained settled and by the late 10th century Christianity was firmly established. A number of impressive churches were built and the islands were organised into parishes whose boundaries have changed little in the intervening years. The peace was shattered in 1194 when the Earl of Orkney and others plotted to unseat King Sverre. A large force sailed to Norway and engaged the king's troops but they were defeated at the battle of Florvag near Bergen. The Earl made his peace with Sverre, who then separated Shetland from the earldom and governed the islands by direct rule from Norway. This probably accounts for the somewhat stronger ties between the two.

Scotland was becoming very impatient with the Vikings and their constant harrying of coastal communities. As a result King Alexander III decided to take action and took on Norway's King Haakon at the battle of Largs in 1263. This was described in the *Sagas* as minor and inconclusive but Haakon died later that year subsequently a treaty was signed in 1266 providing for Norway to retain Orkney and Shetland but giving up all other territories. Thus the battle was significant from the Scottish point of view.

During the next hundred years Norway lost much of its influence in the northern isles and elsewhere and as a result became subject to Denmark in 1397. This brought the three Scandinavian countries under the Danish king for a while. Relations between Scotland and Denmark were not good and, as so often happens, the solution to the problem was a royal marriage.

Scotland takes control in 1469

In 1472, Scotland annexed the islands, following the royal marriage between Margaret of Denmark and James III. The Danish King did not have sufficient funds for an adequate dowry and instead pledged the islands of Orkney and Shetland in 1469 in lieu of cash. After the transfer to Scotland the people acquired new landlords. James, the Stewart King, allocated the land to Scottish barons, only a few of whom ever appeared in the islands. They fell heir to the economic benefits previously enjoyed by the Norwegians and Danes. Even at this early date, the fishing off the Shetland coast was very lucrative. It has been the principal economic activity ever since although there is now a broader base with oil related industries particularly contributing to a more secure and higher standard of living.

The Norwegians attempted to redeem the islands several times but the Scots never seemed to be authorised to discuss the matter when these meetings took place. Delegates were told to deny any knowledge of the claim and 'gif na ansuer thairto'. It is thought that it may still be possible for Denmark or Norway to redeem the islands if they chose to do so. They might well have been restored to Norway at a later date as Adam Robson relates in his excellent book *The Saga of a Ship – The Earl of Zetland*. Early in the Second World War, Hitler planned to take over Norway and was informed that the British also had a plan to occupy the country and thus protect their North Sea flank. In the event he forestalled the British and he is reputed to have declared that "To Norway will be restored the northern islands (Orkney and Shetland) as 'living space' when they have been liberated from the yoke of Britain." It is interesting to note that Denmark controlled all the other North Atlantic islands until Iceland became independent in 1944. Faroe and Greenland are still part of Denmark.

Little changed after Scotland took control of Orkney and Shetland. Gradually Scottish immigrants appeared but not in sufficient numbers to alter the Norse way of life. The legal system remained in force and slowly the language absorbed some Scottish and English words and produced the Shetland dialect used today. There was little contact with Scotland but, more importantly, the trade ties with Bergen, Germany and Holland remained strong and the link with the Hanseatic League towns continued including Danzig, Bremen, Hamburg, Lubeck and Rostock. Trade covered a variety of goods but the main export was fish, which was the key to the wealth of the islands. In time Shetlanders developed a sizeable trade with Bergen and many made their base there. This provided stiff competition for the Hansa merchants, who were none too pleased at this intrusion into their sphere of influence.

The first major change took place when Mary Queen of Scots granted her half-brother Robert Stewart the lands of Orkney and Shetland in perpetual feu. King James VI subsequently made Robert the Earl of Orkney, the old Norse title, and his son Patrick succeeded him ten years later. Both took a keen interest in the islands and built homes in Shetland. Robert held the title of Sheriff (formerly the Great Foude) and administered Norse law with the help of deputies. Although the names of the officials have changed, the structure remains the same.

Indeed the under foudes continued to function with the Scottish name of 'Baillie' and this term is still used in the Scottish cities today. When King James VI came to the throne he replaced the Norse law with a feudal system a rather harsh regime which did away with the last vestiges of an independent Shetland. There is currently some doubt being expressed about whether the udal system has ceased to exist. Some say that even modern statutes have failed to repeal the old system. If this were so then salmon farmers would not have to pay rent for the use of the seabed.

The Dutch Take an Interest in Shetland Waters

Shortly after Scotland gained control of Shetland, Dutch fishermen began to appear in great numbers, although they had first begun to arrive in 1260AD. The herring, which they had caught in the Baltic, had suddenly disappeared and the Dutch set out in search of them. They eventually found huge shoals around the Shetland archipelago and hundreds of 'busses', as the Dutch boats were called, began to fish around the islands. They made their summer base on the mainland opposite the island of Bressay, which provided wonderful shelter from the violent storms that blew up from time to time. Gradually the fishermen and some locals from Scalloway, who traded with them, erected huts and small houses. The modest village was given the name of Leir-vik, which grew in a rather disorganised way.

The major commitment to the fishing off Shetland by the Dutch meant that the Netherlands was the principal beneficiary of this resource. 'The Great Fishery' as they called it was responsible for the growth of Holland's wealth much more than its colonies in the East and West Indies. The Dutch were the first to develop the best techniques for the capture and curing of herring. Their boats came in hundreds and had a free run for several hundred years. Dutch fishing reached its height in the mid-17th century when up to 20,000 Dutch seamen were coming each year. They continued to appear for another hundred years before others came to share in the action.

The Dutch Government provided a state subsidy to encourage

their fishermen. Supplies for the voyage were put on board free of export duty and the early catches (as little as ten barrels) were given a premium. The fish were considered a food with medicinal value and the first appearance of the herring was a very special event and still is. I have been in Utrecht with Dutch friends when the herring arrived and we had a mini banquet that evening on herring and Geneva gin. After the first few weeks the fish were caught and cured at sea and the boats went home only when fully laden.

In addition to all the fishing activity many boats from Hamburg, Lubeck and Bremen came each summer to trade all manner of goods in return for woollens, knitted stockings, sealskins and fresh produce. The main purchases by the Germans were cod and ling caught by the locals in their small boats. The fish were landed at the booths, which the Germans had set up and the catches were then prepared for shipment to Germany. Although there was a lot of barter, foreign coins circulated in Shetland and sometimes these were old and devalued. This meant that ultimately they were of little value to the Shetland merchants and people would not accept them. Having gone the rounds, they tended to end up in the collection plate at church and the clergy were left with the problem of what to do with them.

Little effort was made by successive British governments to maximise the benefit of the fishery for the islanders. The ordinary Shetlanders did not share in the fishing bonanza unlike Icelanders do today. When Iceland became independent from Denmark in 1944 they extended their fishing limits to two hundred miles. This enabled them to conserve the stocks and the fishery has given them a high standard of living for the first time and on a sustainable basis. There was, of course, resistance from other nations used to sharing the catches. Notable among these was Britain and a number of skirmishes occurred during what became known as the 'Cod Wars'. No shots were fired but Icelandic fishery protection vessels rammed many of the British trawlers.

The Press Gangs

For the Shetlanders, one of the dangers of gaining experience as seamen was to find themselves 'pressed' into service with the Royal Navy. The Press Gangs were the scourge of the young and able men but they were operating under the law of Great Britain and there were wars to be fought! The law supporting the Press Gang system was a form of compulsory service similar to that brought in for the two world wars of the 20th century except that it was selective, not comprehensive and there was no appeal for those qualified to go to sea. The law stipulated that anyone with at least two years experience of the sea could be pressed. If the Press Gang picked up a man who had less than two years sea experience, he was entitled to appeal to the sheriff and would be released. At the height of hostilities during the Napoleonic Wars there were about 3,000 Shetland seamen serving in the navy. This represented a high proportion of the young male population over 12.

One of these boys may have been Arthur Anderson born in 1792, who did a tremendous amount for Shetland in later life after he had become a successful businessman. His greatest achievement was founding the Peninsular & Oriental Steam Navigation Company. He put some of his wealth back into the community by promoting the finely knitted Shetland shawls and other knitwear. Also he started the Shetland Fishery Company, which made it possible for locals to escape from the tie of the feudal system and fish for their own account. He sponsored many other activities including education and the major secondary school in Lerwick is named the Anderson High School.

All the pressed sailors came home after the end of the Napoleonic wars only to find there were very few jobs and not enough land to cultivate. Arthur Anderson's venture came at a good time allowing young men a chance to go it on their own. For the first time fishing became an important activity in the Shetland economy and the people had the opportunity of enjoying the benefits of this wonderful resource. All of the Blance families were involved in fishing and many also became experienced deep-water seamen.

In the 19th century there was little need for large armed forces unlike the previous century when Britain fought a series of successful wars, which resulted in tremendous gains in territory mostly from the French. The loss of the American colonies was the only setback and the successes brought unity to Great Britain as well as vast commercial gains for many but not the islanders. It is no wonder that the establishing of the passenger shipping service between the islands and mainland Scotland gave young people the opportunity to escape the tied life of crofting and fishing and find work elsewhere in the newly conquered territories overseas.

Shetland's Two Towns

Scalloway, where Earl Patrick built his castle, was the early capital but it went into decline in the 17th century. By the 19th it had began to recover and expand significantly as a result of the growth in the fishing for cod, herring and haddock. The road to Lerwick was constructed in 1847 and it began to take considerable traffic. There was a shipping service to both towns and the road made it possible for merchants in each place to send goods to the harbour that expected the next vessel. However, the basic facilities took a long time to come and it was 1932 before a proper sewerage plant was installed, followed by electricity in 1939.

Over on the North Sea side the rough dwellings at Leir-vik on the shore grew into a motley collection. With so many fishermen coming every year, the Dutch Fair evolved to provide entertainment. Also many Dutchmen set up homes for their use during the season. Gradually the town of Lerwick expanded but the vast majority of the residents were itinerant fisherman, whose families were back in Holland. In their spare time they enjoyed themselves and the town became a den of iniquity and representations were made to the authorities for action to be taken to control the excesses. Eventually the situation became so bad that the government in London ordered the place to be destroyed and it was burned to the ground in 1625. This provided the opportunity for the building of Lerwick as we know it today and in time it took over the role of the capital from Scalloway.

The Dutch wars sparked off by their fishing fleets invading Shetland waters marked the beginning of the end for the fishermen from Holland. Although they kept coming for some time they no longer had free unfettered use of the fishery. The Dutch boats were sometimes kept at home to avoid destruction. However, the fishing still expanded in spite of some of the fleet being caught and destroyed by British or French warships. This brought the Dutch fleet out to protect the busses and resulted in further battles. Cromwell's construction of the fort, the first stone building in Lerwick, was not an effective deterrent as the Dutch simply burned and partially destroyed it in 1673. The fort lay derelict for over 100 years until it was renovated in 1782 at the start of the wars with France. The Dutch Navy gained some temporary victories but the British usually regained control over the seas for a period. In spite of this the Dutch continued to enjoy the benefits of the fishing for decades afterwards as the British had commitments in other parts of the world, which had more at stake than the fishing in Shetland.

The Union of Parliaments in 1707 resulted in the introduction of the unpopular salt tax in 1712 and as a consequence the lairds took on the responsibility for organising the fishing using their local tenants to fish for them. Their control over the fishing increased their influence over the tenants, who then found themselves totally tied to the landlord. However, the landlords and merchants developed the fishing into a major activity employing more and more people. Shetlanders gained experience in sailing further out from the coast and became skilled seamen. This meant that they were a valuable source of men to crew the warships during the Napoleonic wars. In the remainder of the 19th century the fishery continued to expand and with it the town of Lerwick. Some fine dwellings were built and a new Town Hall was opened in 1882. By 1905 trade reached a peak of over one million barrels and most of the trade and curing was centralised in Lerwick where a new quay and fish market had been built.

Surprisingly some of the old buildings on the seafront, known as Lodberries, have survived intact in spite of having foundations in the water. In the old days boats could come right up to the houses and unload into underground storerooms. From there the cargoes would be taken by underground passage to be loaded onto transport for delivery elsewhere. These passages were extremely useful when smuggling of dutiable goods was a popular and respectable activity. All the merchants were at it and the customs officers were unable to control the flow of contraband goods. They came from the Faroe Islands and from Dutch fishing vessels, which enjoyed a regular trade not only with Lerwegians but also with families around the coast.

Housing

Dr Arthur Mitchell described the dwellings in Shetland in 1860. They were very unpleasant by our modern standards but the Commission on the Truck System, in reproducing what Dr Mitchell had written, commented in their report in 1872 that the homes had improved enormously by then. I quote the description in full, because it is so graphic and provides the reader with such a vivid picture of various aspects of life up to 150 years ago and more:

> The Shetland cottage or hut is of the rudest description. It is usually built of undressed stone, with a cement of clay or turf. Over the rafters is laid a covering of pones, divots, or flaas, (varieties of sod) and above this again a thatch of straw, bound down with ropes of heather weighted at the ends with stones as a protection against the high winds which are so prevalent. Chimneys and windows are rarely to be seen. One or more holes in the roof permit the escape of the smoke, and at the same time admit light. Open doors, the thatched roof and loose joinings everywhere insure a degree of ventilation, without which the dwellings would often be more unhealthy than many in the lanes of our large cities. To this, there is no doubt we must attribute the comparative absence of fever, the occasional presence of which, I think, is greatly due to that violation of the plainest law of nature, the box-bed. This evil is often intensified in Shetland by having the beds arranged in tiers one above the other, in ship fashion, with the apertures of access reduced to the smallest possible size.

Drainage is wholly unattended to, and the dunghill is invariably found at the very door. As the house is entered, the visitor first comes upon that part allotted to the cattle, which in summer are out night and day, but in winter are chiefly within doors. Their dung is frequently allowed to accumulate about them; and I was told that this part of the house is sometimes used by the family in winter as a privy. Passing through the byre, the human habitation is reached. The separation between it and the part for the cattle is ingeniously effected by an arrangement of the furniture, the bed chiefly serving for this purpose. The floor is of clay, and the fire is nearly always in the middle of it.

In some respects, however, the Zetland dwellings stand a favourable comparison with those of the Western Islands. There is a bareness and desolation about the misery of a Harris house that is tenfold more depressing. It is a poor house and an empty one – a decaying, mouldy shell, without the pretence of a kernel, whereas in Zetland there is usually a certain fulness. There are bulky sea-chests, with smaller ones on the top of them; chairs, with generally an effort at an easy one; a wooden bench, a table, beds, spades, fishing-rods, baskets, and a score of other little things, which help, after all, to make it a domus. The very teapot, in Zetland always to be found at the fireside, speaks of home and woman, and reminds one of the sobriety of the people – that very important difference between them and the inhabitants of the Hebridean Islands. I think the Zetlanders, too, are more intelligent, and more inclined to be industrious, and give greater evidence of the tendency to accumulate or provide.

Instead of describing the house occupied by each patient, I have given this between them and have spoken of the special houses as of, above, or below the average.

Infrastructure

Apart from the route from Lerwick to Scalloway there were no proper roads over most of the islands and travel and movement of goods was done by sea. This presented no problem for the Shetlanders, who had sailed all over the seas for hundreds of years. However, the coming of steam made a tremendous difference to the speed and efficiency of transport in the islands. The most famous vessel to provide this service in Shetland was the *Earl of Zetland.*

From the late 19th century communications were improved with the arrival of the '*Earl*', as she was affectionately known. She provided a cargo and passenger service for smaller islands off the north east coast of the Shetland mainland for nearly 70 years. F. Fullerton & Co. built her in Paisley under the direction of James Howden and Company as co-ordinating contractors. The dimensions were length 121ft and beam 20ft and the two engines built by James Howden in Glasgow had a combined horsepower of 50. On her trials, which took place in April 1877 some eight months after construction started, she achieved a speed of 10½ knots. By 1883 the trade served by the *Earl* had increased substantially and the ship was a little too small. The decision was taken to lengthen her by 23ft and at the same time to install a new boiler. It was not until 1922 that she was equipped with electric light for the first time.

The *Earl* continued her service through two world wars and remained unscathed, although she had some near misses in WWII. She also took part in numerous rescue and salvage operations. One of these early in the war involved a Norwegian craft, which subsequently returned to Norway and was the forerunner of the 'Shetland Bus'. However, the building of roads made the coastal vessels redundant and, since the arrival of oil, the road system has been extended to cover all areas supplemented by the inter island car ferries.

My family – the Blances

The traditional home of the Blances was Calback Ness now the Sullom Voe Oil Terminal. They could well have been there for several hundred years but genealogical research can trace nothing before 1725 when a John Blance married Jean Blance at 'da kirk'. This would be the local church which was reputed to be the site of a mediaeval chapel. Andrew, the eldest son of John and Jean, was married the same year as Peter Blance and Barbara Hendries daughter and it is likely that the two families were related, although there is no record to confirm. Peter was my 4th great grandfather but little is known of the family until his great grandson and my great grandfather. Sheila recorded all the families from that generation and gathered a lot of information about their lives.

The people in Calback and other parts of Shetland had to be self-sufficient. This was a real necessity due to the remoteness of the islands and when times were hard with poor fishing and failed crops the people came near to starvation. Governments were sometimes slow to respond to problems of this sort as was evident during famine periods in the 18th and early 19th centuries when food aid was not readily available. The uncertainty of life persuaded those with initiative to leave the islands or go to sea. Later the navy recruited many and others joined the whaling ships. As shipping services to the mainland improved emigration increased. Many went no further than mainland Scotland, arriving initially in Aberdeen and Leith but from there others spread throughout the United Kingdom and overseas to Canada, United States, Australia and New Zealand. Our family is typical and it is a constant delight to find a new cousin now and again. These overseas Shetlanders are much better at keeping contact with their 'homeland' mainly through the Shetland Family History Society. It is reckoned that two per cent of the population of New Zealand is descended from Shetlanders some of whom arrived as late as the end of the 1940s. Recently a large number of families were added to Sheila's records from North America and New Zealand where there are equally enthusiastic genealogists. The number recorded to date is over 1600.

Blance was a common name and naturally there are regular references in various records. Some are not very laudable but they throw some light on the life of the times – a witness in Voxter, a marriage in Weathersta', sons and daughters baptised, members of the Kirk Session, payment of rent in Hardwall (4.50 merks) to Thomas Gifford of Busta. Also there are several mentions of Blance women receiving poor relief, presumably widowed wives of fishermen lost at sea. The Blance families spread out over Shetland including Lerwick. They married local girls from Delting, Northmavine, Olanforth, Scatsta as well as Calback. These girls' names are equally well known in

Shetland – Henderson, Mouat, Simpson, Smith, Gifford, Williamson and Johnson. Large families were quite normal and in the next three generations the child count was seven, nine and twelve. It is also interesting to see the same Christian names cropping up quite frequently. Over the same four generations 135 people have been researched and 60 per cent were given only twelve names. The most common were Peter (11), John (8), James (7), Robert (7), Barbara (7), Margaret (7) and Mary (7). Two sons, two generations apart, married an Ann Johnson, and one of Peter and Barbara's sons married a Williamson, a name that was to appear three generations later when Helen married John Williamson and founded another large family. Other families had their own favourite names. For instance, I was looking at the ancestors of another Blance and they were either named John or William John over eight generations.

Peter and Barbara's grandson Peter Blance born in 1798 was pressed in 1815 and, it is said, was taken to the Battle of Waterloo. It is not clear how the navy managed to land him there! He served in warships for seven to nine years then came home and married Barbara Simpson. They had eight children but lost two: Bruce, a sailor, was drowned at sea and Robert, also a sailor, died of smallpox. There is an entry in Lloyds Register for a Robert Blance born in 1828 stating that he voyaged to the Baltic, Mediterranean, West Indies, and USA. A Captain's certificate, no. 9410, was granted to a Robert Blance at Shields in 1854, the year of son Robert's death from smallpox. Sheila Durham compared notes with Bert Simpson of Shetland about the Simpson-Blance connection. He can trace his line back to Robert the Bruce via the Stuart kings by way of the Earl of Orkney, an illegitimate son of James V. To date the family Peter married into has not been reliably connected with Bert's.

The start of a regular census in 1841 helps in following the lives of some of the Blances. Bruce Blance, aged 78, was living in Calback and three of his children and their families appear in that first census. Bruce's wife, Mary Mouat, had presumably died, as her name is not recorded. Peter and Barbara with their eight children were also living in Calback as were John and Lillias with three children. Thomas and his first wife Elizabeth were in Mossbank with seven children together with an elderly Peter Blance aged 70, whose connection is not evident. By 1851 Peter and Barbara had only five children left at home in Calback: Bruce, Robert and Henry having moved out. Sadly, Bruce and Robert died in 1854, as mentioned above. John and Lillias were living in Calback with four children, all in their 20s. Two, Bruce and Ann, had not appeared in the 1841 census and Arthur was not recorded in 1851. In 1861 only Mary aged 35 was with them.

Great Grandfather Peter was born at Calback in 1832 the fifth of Peter and Barbara Simpson's eight children. He was married in 1857 to Margaret Smith at the age of 24 and settled in Calback near the rest of the family. Most of the families in the parish were occupied in crofting and fishing, although some had other trades such as tailors and shoemakers. They created wealth for the landowners and had little freedom to move away unless they were obliged to do so. A crisis for families occurred in the 1860s when the land owner Major Cameron's agent and factor, the infamous John Walker, introduced new rental agreements offering long leases but with conditions that many of the tenants found difficult to accept.

John Walker was an Aberdonian, who had made money gold prospecting in Australia. He arrived in Shetland in 1860 and immediately concluded that the land tenure system linked to fishing was inefficient and did not bring the best out of the people. He became factor to Major Cameron and proposed to reform the whole system. He appears to have talked his employer into giving him a free hand. At the time the Highlands of Scotland had been largely transformed into big sheep farms and the people had been evicted. Walker planned to do the same and started in Calback. He claimed at the Truck Commission that he was offering 14-year leases with conditions designed to improve the land and make the crofts more productive but did not have much response. Nobody was certain that these improvements would be for the benefit of the tenants and many were suspicious of the motives behind the proposal.

Wendy Gear has recently published an excellent book on John Walker's life and describes the proposals presented to tenants by him.

One of the examples she quotes is great grandfather Peter. He was offered a lease for ten years at a rent equivalent to the agricultural value. Grazing of animals on the scattalds (common grazing enjoyed by tenants for hundreds of years) was reserved for the land owner only. This denied tenants access to the peat for fuel and thatching material. Any breach of the rules in the lease would result in loss of the croft. It is clear that Peter and others found the terms of these leases unacceptable and left the area in the latter part of 1866. Peter relocated to a cottage near Brae called Hardwall, which he rented with land from Miss Mary Elizabeth Irvine for £4-11/. By 1885/86 he had taken on more land with a rent of £20. The cottage is still standing but is unoccupied and in poor condition.

The position in Unst was different. Major Cameron, maybe a little sceptical of Walker's abilities, gave a 12-year lease in 1868 to Alexander Sandison, a partner in Spence & Co, with the improvement conditions attached. Sandison claimed at the Truck Commission that he had wide acceptance for the conditions and after some time the tenants began to appreciate the benefits. The ideas were, on the face of it, very sensible but Walker had an arrogant manner and the tenants did not trust him. He also wished to change things quickly without any consultation and this was not something the Shetlanders could accept.

In his *The Lands of Garth* Jonathan Wills tells the story of one Jimmy Blance, told to him by Brucie Henderson, who died in 1975. Jimmy attempted to lead resistance to the enclosures and clearances organised by Walker. Brucie said that 'Walker made them work the worst piece of land in Calback and dig out stones to make dykes. He forced the crofters to improve the land with dykes and lime and then raised the rents for their trouble.'

Jimmy was a sailor and was the eighth child of Peter Blance and Barbara Simpson and my great granduncle. At any rate, he arrived home and did not like what he saw and said, 'I'm going to grip the bugger and twist his head off. I can do it lovely. And I don't care if I'm hanged for it da moarn for the life we've had with him is no worth living!' Brucie continued, 'He lay in wait for Walker and jumped on him. Man, it took seven strong men to haul him off. He was like a deevil. Mister Walker never showed his face outdoors again while Jimmy was home." Jimmy married Ann Johnson in 1865 and probably emigrated with her after his abortive attempt on John Walker. Jimmy died in 1881 in the USA and would have been in his 20s at the time of this incident. When Walker gave evidence to the Truck Commission in 1871 he said that people had begun to shoot at him and he had carried a gun himself for a few months but never had occasion to use it.

Peter's Work

Great grandfather Peter was one of many Shetlanders who had plenty of initiative and this led him to join the Faroe fishery and skipper a fishing smack. The *Shetland Times* printed an interesting obituary on his death in 1910, aged 77, and stated that he "for many years commanded one of the many smacks, which sailed from here (Shetland) to the cod fishing of Faroe and Iceland. Afterwards he captained more than one large barque sailing from Liverpool and other ports to the West Indies, South America and the coast of Africa." Peter would have gained experience in deep water sailing from an early age as it was a way to earn more money. Fishing was a young man's job starting at about the age of fourteen. By the late teens the better seamen were skippers. The smacks were decked sailboats, which were fast replacing the sixareen, because they were more comfortable and they had a longer range. From this time a Shetland fisherman could be full-time, make more money and control his own life. It may not have been our Peter but in the *Shetland Advertiser* in 1862, it was reported that Blance of the *Robert Duncan* landed 12,000 salt cod at Scalloway.

The principal fishing craft used for centuries in Shetland for what was called the 'home' or 'haaf' fishing was the sixareen, which survived until the early 20th century. The origins of the design can be traced back to the second century AD. It was a remarkably seaworthy craft and was similar to the much larger vessels used by the Vikings. The ends were pointed and the sides flared to the gunwales. They were completely open but were divided into sections by the thwartship rowing benches. They were mainly used in the 'haaf' fishing that particularly interested the landlords, who historically had made it a condition of tenancy that the tenant should fish for him. Latterly the sixareens were used as 'flitboats' for ferrying passengers and cargo from shore to coastal steamers such as the *Earl of Zetland*. The introduction of schooners followed by steam trawlers in the late 19th century improved the fishery enormously and turned it into an international activity.

Peter was away at sea for much of his 20s but found time to marry and have three children before he was 30. The sea continued to claim a large part of his life and Margaret had to look after the croft as well as the family. There would be plenty of work in the house and outside looking after the animals and growing hay, wheat and potatoes. Later the children would help until they in turn went off to find a new life on mainland Scotland. When the 1861 census was taken Peter was absent and only Margaret and two young sons, Robert and Charles, were recorded. The cottage at Hardwall had four rooms on two floors, which was regarded as a large house at the time. It certainly would not be thought large enough today to accommodate up to eleven persons at various times. The house is still standing about three miles North of Brae but is uninhabited.

A common activity throughout the country, and particularly in Shetland, was smuggling and it is clear that Peter was 'in the business'. The *New Shetlander* in 1987 featured an article on 'Gin, Tobacco and the Exciseman', which quotes from the Customs Report of 1861 about the regular practice of Shetland fishermen trading with the Dutch fishing fleet for tobacco and spirits. There were a few informers, who expected some reward for information. One such person wrote to the collector of customs in Lerwick:

> Mr Gatherer (his name was John Gatherer), when you get this, send an officer without delay to Peter Blance in Scatsta and Peter Mouat, Laxo for they have come from Faro with a lot of gin and tobacco and is selling it without fear.

Scatsta is the nearest village to Hardwall. Nothing was discovered on that occasion but later the Revenue cutter *Eagle* intercepted a Peter Blance, then skipper of the *Dryad,* and found 81 gallons of brandy on board.

There is no mention of Peter being charged on that occasion but in 1866 there is a record of, quite definitely our, Peter being charged for 'a Breach of the Revenue Laws' and fined £67-17/- and costs of £16-1/1. He was on his way back from Faroe where he had been fishing regularly since 1860. The information in the Lerwick Jail Record gave some physical characteristics namely, dark hair and eyes, height 5'9" and weight 152lbs. His occupation was described as 'Master of Fishing vessel' and he was found to be able to 'read and write well'. He was bailed and did not serve an eight day sentence in jail. His cousin William Blance, a member of the crew, was charged with him and fined £12 with costs of £1-15/4. He was not so tall at 5'6½" and weighed 144lbs. He also could read and write well. The religion of both was the established Church of Scotland. John Gatherer was the man who apprehended them and so he got his man in the end!

The Census of 1871 listed the family of Peter and Margaret living at Hardwall in Delting Parish. Peter was described as Master Mariner and farmer and was 39 years old. By that year they had seven children, having lost a son in 1870, and they also had living with them their father-in-law Charles Smith and a servant, Bruce Tait. Eleven people in four rooms was pretty crowded even if they had windows! Standing in the house some years ago, I wondered how they used the space. Privacy was not a feature of life in those days and even the very large merchants' houses were not big by mainland standards. In the 1881 Census Peter and Margaret had nine children living at home. It appears that 11 people was the maximum the house at Hardwall could accommodate as by this time Robert and John had left for Leith and Edinburgh to start a new life. Peter seems to have given up the sea to concentrate on his land, leaving the fishing to younger men. As he had built up 11 acres, he probably could be reasonably self-sufficient and have some surplus produce to sell for cash.

The 19th century saw a tremendous expansion in shipping services all around the world made possible by the new steamships. Although sailing vessels continued to be used for coastal services and fishing, the longer distances were taken over by steamships, which could complete voyages in a fraction of the time. A regular service between Lerwick and Leith was established. This service improved the trading prospects for the Shetland merchants but also encouraged emigration. Thus in 1874, Robert, aged 17, was put on board a ship bound for Leith, where he was apprenticed to a licensed grocer. A few years later John followed Robert to Leith and took up the same occupation, lodging with Jane Gosman.

Peter had started spelling his name Blanch before his marriage and by the late 19th century this version was used a lot, although Blance remained the most common spelling as it is today. Later an 'e' was added and this addition gave a French emphasis and had the advantage of distinguishing them from the many other Blances in Delting. It was certainly convenient for son John. He became an importer of French wines from Bordeaux and he bottled them in Glasgow under the name 'Blanche Pere et Fils'!

Many sons of Shetland families joined the Merchant Navy as a career and as a result each generation of the family gained knowledge of the world outside the narrow community life of crofting and fishing. Peter must have had many contacts outside Shetland made from his sea-going experiences and they would have helped his children when they decided to find a life for themselves on mainland Scotland. At least six of them settled in Leith and Edinburgh and two of the daughters married Merchant Navy officers, who served in the Great War. Later the parents themselves moved to Edinburgh and were buried in Morningside cemetery. Peter was an educated man and, as in many island communities, the parents were always keen to give their children every chance in life by making sure that they had some schooling. Shetland was no exception and Peter sent his children to school, taking advantage of the early provision of education in Shetland. This undoubtedly helped them to establish themselves so quickly in a strange new environment. By 1845 there were four schools in Delting and according to the Statistical Account two more were "very greatly required". The parochial teachers were paid a small salary and were able to charge the parents a fee for each pupil. Shetlanders still take education seriously. In 1997 *The Scotsman* published a survey of unauthorised absence from schools throughout Scotland. The record of the 32 education authorities varied enormously and went as high as 37 half days on average. Shetland's was nil.

Robert obtained his first licence in 1881 at 216 High Street, Portobello. He must have been one of the youngest to take such responsibility. Two years later, he and John were in partnership as Blanche Bros at 34 St Leonard's Street, Edinburgh. Robert married Annie Ayer in 1884 and continued to take responsibility for his brothers and sisters. Agnes and Mary lived in his home and he found homes for Helen and Margaret. All four sisters married and settled in Edinburgh. Peter, Laurence and Arthur came to Edinburgh and Robert helped them to set up in business. In 1884 Robert's business moved to 31 Bruntsfield Place, later renumbered 155–157, where it remained until the 1960s. Robert continued working in the business until he died at the age of 88, thus he was probably the youngest and certainly the oldest grocer and wine merchant in the country. He was also the most respected and worked tirelessly for various trade associations becoming known for his robust speeches, which fired the members into action. He traded at Bruntsfield Place, Edinburgh for 60 years and of course saw many changes. In his 'old days' the price of a bottle of Whisky was 2/- and by the time of his death it had 'soared' to 25/9.

Blanche & Co. of 155 Bruntsfield Place, Edinburgh was one of the leading licensed grocers in Scotland and it is significant that it continued to be a well-run and profitable business through to the 1960s, 75 years after it had been started by Robert. It was still run along the same lines but he must have been alert all through the years to the need for change, otherwise it would not have survived. One of his typical initiatives was the use of a pair of Shetland ponies to deliver goods in the early days around Morningside. Molly and the Marchioness were a marvellous advertisement trotting back and forth to customers' homes. An order boy visited each customer once a week to take their order and the goods were delivered the next day. Delivery proved to be too costly when supermarkets began to cut prices and drive the independents out of business. Ironically, these big outlets are starting to introduce delivery services once more as their trade stagnates and they have difficulty in taking market share from competitors on price alone.

Robert and Annie enjoyed a varied life. They were both keen bridge players; Robert played golf at Barnton Golf Club; The Royal Burgess, to give it its grander name, and they had a holiday home at Lundin Links in Fife. They continued to help others in the family and stepped in to provide a home for their daughter Dorothy, who, sadly, had been widowed in India shortly before her own daughter Sheila was born in 1917. The experience for Dorothy was traumatic but she obviously took it in her stride. Special permission had to be granted to allow her and her new baby to sail home from India in wartime. Her husband Robert Strachan had been a railway engineer and probably had good connections with the authorities. Dorothy's plight would be known and as soon as there was a ship with some free space they were permitted to leave for Scotland.

By 1890 Peter and Margaret were finding it a little hard running Hardwall. They were in their late 50s when they too decided to move to Edinburgh with the remainder of the family and again Robert provided the solution by arranging for his father to manage the iron-monger's shop, which he had started in premises next to the licensed grocer's business. My father told me that another contributory reason for the move was the increasing cost of hospitality in Shetland. Peter's home was near the manse and when mourners returned from funerals with the minister they always stopped at the house and expected to be offered traditional Shetland hospitality on such occasions. Even in those days, whisky was expensive and a lot was consumed! It is interesting to note that the family name was changed for the second time when they all moved to Edinburgh. They all became Blanche instead of Blanch, formerly Blance!

The two old folks settled into Edinburgh life surrounded by most of their family, who had also made their lives in the city. The exception was John, who moved to Glasgow. Two of the others were retailers and one was a commercial traveller. Peter played an active part in St Cuthbert's Church as an elder. He usually took his place as head of the family and sat at the end of the family pew. It is recalled that after 'snibbing' himself in with the old-fashioned doors attached to the ends of the pews, he stood for a few seconds surveying the congregation before finally taking his seat beside his wife, sons and daughters.

He was friendly with the Very Rev Dr James Macgregor and the Rev Dr Andrew Wallace Williamson. These two came together in 1883, when the 26 year old Williamson joined the experienced Macgregor. They were a team of two equals for 27 years and remained friends in spite of being of different generations. They both served as Moderators of the General Assembly of the Church of Scotland. Quite recently I visited the church and found it to be a magnificent building erected in 1894. Peter must have come to Edinburgh just before the old 1775 building was demolished except for the steeple, which still stands. No doubt he took part in the fundraising for the new building.

There is an anecdote about Peter and St Cuthbert's, which may be apocryphal but has a familiar ring to it. This was the time of the growing strength of the temperance movement and inevitably one Sunday the minister preached a sermon about the evils of drink and those who sold it. Without waiting until the end of the service, Peter gathered his family together and walked out of the church. Presumably that ended a good friendship!

Robert was clearly close to his father and was probably the son Peter respected most of all. However, if you read Peter's letter of 14 December 1885 (see below), you may wonder if any of the children reached the standards looked for by the old man. It was probably quite difficult for the sons to adjust to the appearance of their father settling in to be head of the family once more when they must have thought that they were well clear of parental influence.

Hardwall House
(Near Brae, Delting, Shetland)
14th Dec 1885

Dear Robert,

Although you seem to have forgotten the way of writing me for this very long time, yet I must not forget to write you now and again believing that there is no ill feeling on your part but simply either want of time or what is far worse laziness – tell Annie we were very glad of her letters to H and M. Maggy was very proud of her letter indeed I think Annie deserves all our best thanks for kind attention in writing. I am quite sure it is not her fault you do not all write often. However do not run away with the idea that I want to complain of anyone at 35 B Pl. I have greater reason to complain elsewhere. I have written to John three times but not a word of reply as yet. We sent him a small box with a little mutton etc. a good while ago but he never told us he had got it but I hope he did get it notwithstanding.

I meant to send your small cask of beef by last steamer from Brae as it was all ready but was sorry we could not get to Brae either by sea or land – the road was so blocked up with snow and then the voe was frozen up so that we could not get out a boat but I will try to be sure and send it by first turn of the little steamer. As the snow is all away now, it has been extremely cold and very boisterous with this last snow, the freezing was intense – do you know I have never yet been in Lerwick settling but I will have to try and get sometime through this week by any means I can.

Tomorrow Monday is our Poling day at Sussetter Betty Smith of the Seatter was proclaimed today with a cousin of her own from Collafirth North Maven. His name is John Johnson a nice lad I do think. I have never been there this season as I could never get from home in May. I ask you again to send an invoice of Mrs Johnson's things also of Scordies dram. I will send you and Peter a Special Edition of the Shetland News in which you will see a short account of all or nearly all Mr Dundas's Meetings in Shetland but of course there can very little if any of the speeches by any of the electors. It will be all over with you by this time and you need not care.

I was very glad to hear you are keeping busy at the new shop and I am always wishing you may get still busier. Tell Annie she will have to take me to help her with the books as I am not so strong now for the hard work I have here and besides it cannot pay. I am getting quite sick of it of course this is an exceptional bad season all over Shetland in very many ways.

The lasses are all out at the Sunday school as the hour has been changed to 1PM. Some of them will write Annie soon and I also will try to write myself. I know of nothing more worth writing about at this time tell Peter I expect a long letter from him by first post.

With kind love to all in which we all join
I remain your Loving Father
Peter Blanche

John, Peter's second surviving son, was my grandfather and, like his brothers and sisters, left Shetland to find a better future in Scotland. As already mentioned, he followed his elder brother Robert into the licensed grocer's trade in Edinburgh and was in partnership with him for some years. After a while he moved to Glasgow and became the Organiser for the Licensed Trade Defence. He travelled throughout Scotland canvassing support and setting up branches of the association to counter the efforts of the Temperance League, whose objective was prohibition. The *Haddington Courier* report in 1894, mentioned earlier, about his addressing a meeting in North Berwick to encourage them to set up a branch was one such effort.

Later John was in several businesses including property, a restaurant, licensed grocers and wine importing. However, his major step in building a lasting business was the purchase of Glen Elgin distillery near the town of Elgin. As John had started business with no capital he quickly learned the techniques of borrowing from banks to finance his ventures. His purchase of Glen Elgin was financed by a bond from the seller paid off over the following years out of profits. It was highly profitable and provided a good cash flow for building a retail business, which was to survive independently until 1960. The distillery still produces its excellent make and is now owned by United Distillers and Vintners, part of Diageo.

He appears to have been a fairly strong and opinionated character, although, when in ill health in the last ten years of his life, he was remarkably indecisive in dealing with his managers. He was generous to many but was very hard on his family. He would give a poor man he met in the street a five pound note and yet keep his wife short of cash to buy food. The sons of his second family were at work in the business at the age of 12 and by the time he died, the eldest, William, my father, was 27 and had considerable experience. John built up a business, which succeeded in weathering the economic storms of the late 20s and 30s. His personality led him to take risks, some of them rather rash, whereas William, his elder son, was a cautious type. He was, therefore, well suited to keeping the business going in difficult times after his father's death and providing for three families and John's widow.

John had tragedy in his life at an early stage. He married Jean Brown in 1884 and lived at 2 Melville Street, Portobello and had four children. Jean died in 3 January 1892 just seven days before her newly born fourth child died. The remaining three children also died, Jessie in 1899, John in 1912 and Robert in 1920 from an injury received in the army. John was married again in 1895 to Isabella Davidson of Aberdeen and shortly afterwards moved to Glasgow. However, tragedy followed him there and his new family suffered loss. The first born, Norman, died in 1897 aged six months; James born in 1898, died in 1916, and Ewan born in 1903, died in 1913. A further three children survived and lived to old age. William born in 1900, died in 1992, Lawrence born in 1905, died in 1988 and Isabel born in 1907, died in 1981.

After his move to the west, John and his family lived at 5 Blairbeth Terrace, Burnside, Rutherglen and later at 26 Park Circus, Glasgow. John kept in touch with his cousins from Shetland and in 1906 his second cousin David was christened at Blairbeth Terrace, his parents having been abroad for some years. The house at 5 Blairbeth Terrace, Burnside was leased in the early summer of 1920, when the family moved to Park Circus. By this time John was not in good health, suffering from what would be called stress today and diabetes. The tenant had some trouble making John put the place in order and repairing leaks in the roof! Looking at the correspondence it appears that the property was in poor condition but also that the tenant Mr Arthur Wainstein was, as John put it, 'a quibbler'. The lawyers were eventually involved and there was further difficulty about tradesmen not obtaining access to carry out work. Wainstein must have given up and a Sydney Redwood took on the lease in March 1923. Wainstein had to be chased for rent arrears.

Helen, Peter and Margaret's eldest daughter, married John Williamson in Shetland and they too made their home in Edinburgh. John was in the Merchant Navy and became a captain with Curries. He was interned in a German port at the beginning of the war in 1914 and Robert and Annie helped Helen and her family during his absence. Peter, who married Isabel McDuff, was a retail grocer, like his brothers, and also worked as a commercial traveller. The next sister in Peter and Margaret's family was Margaret and she also married a merchant seaman in Shetland. He was Andrew Brown, who served as a captain with Cormacks. He was interned at Riga in 1914 for the duration of hostilities. Sadly, Andrew and Margaret's only son Laurence, a commissioned officer in the army, was killed in action in 1917 and was awarded the Military Cross.

Laurence, born in 1870, was the fourth surviving son and, like others in the family, attended Scatsta School. His education was supplemented by lessons from the local minister Rev William Boag at Voxter Manse. He followed his brothers to Edinburgh where he also entered the licensed grocer's trade and was apprenticed to his brother Bob. He learned his trade well and was an expert tea blender in the days when retailers had to do their own packaging and satisfy customer tastes. He set up his own business and became active in the community. His recreations were reading and walking and his nieces have fond memories of expeditions with him, learning something of the wildlife in the Pentland hills. He enjoyed fishing and regularly returned to Shetland for this purpose. He was a member of the Merchants Company and involved in local politics. During World War I he became a special constable and continued serving through the General Strike in 1926.

Laurence married Grace Adams and they had two daughters each of whom produced two new families and ten great-grandchildren. In his earlier years, Laurence served as president of the Ninety Burns Club of Edinburgh. On one occasion he took 100 gentlemen on the annual picnic to Callander where Provost Scott welcomed them. They travelled on to Loch Katrine before having lunch. It must have been quite a party. Of his sisters, Agnes married Thomas Tait and Mary married Thomas MacEwan. The youngest son, Arthur, was gassed during the war and never fully recovered, although he lived to the age of 76.

Peter and Margaret lost three of their 12 children during their lifetime. The first was Charles, their second son, who died aged 11 in 1870. My grandfather, John, was only nine and it must have been a shock to lose an elder brother at that age. When his sister Barbara died in 1890 he was 29 and well established in his business. He showed his sadness in writing a touching poem and reading it you can imagine how shattering the experience of losing so many of his own family within a few years must have been. Lastly, William died in 1905 aged 31 when the whole family were living in Edinburgh.

The family was probably typical of many in the 19th century in giving up the secure, predictable but tough life followed by generations over several hundred years and setting out on the risky path to find a better life for themselves and their families. Opportunities were readily available to young men of initiative, as the growth of industry had increased the wealth of the population and thus the standard of living. Like many before them the various members of Peter's family succeeded in creating a new life for themselves. They were undoubtedly sustained by the culture of self-sufficiency learned in Shetland. The photograph of the family is the only one surviving and shows a group of assured and confident members but also, one feels, a family very close to one another. Alongside there is a photograph of some of the descendants and their spouses taken in 1977 on the occasion of Sheila Durham's 80th birthday.

CHAPTER 2

The truck system in Shetland

Gradually, after Scotland took control of Shetland, Norse udal law was replaced with the feudal system, which brought certain obligations on the tenants to serve the landlord by fishing for him. The price paid for the fish helped to pay the rent as well as the food and other supplies required by the families. All men between 18 and 70 years of age were obliged to attend the fishing. This change in circumstances was extremely difficult for a people used to a more independent way of life.

Each family rented a small cottage and a plot of land not quite big enough to grow sufficient food for everyone. The leases were for a period of one year and notice to leave was only 40 days under Scottish law. If a tenant was told to leave he rarely received compensation for improvements to the land or home. Part of the land was cultivated and in a good season tolerable crops of black oats, barley and potatoes were produced together with cabbage or kail near the cottage. Animals were grazed on the remainder and also on the common ground.

In due course the merchants succeeded the landlords in controlling the fishing and they also opened shops to provide supplies for boats and families. It was a convenience having a source of supplies a little nearer to home but there was not enough trade to provide for competition and prices were high and often quality was poor. They equipped their tenants and received their fish at a price fixed at the end of the season. These transactions were entered in the tenants' accounts. The tenants rarely received a copy of the accounts; it was simply read out to them. Settlement took several months before payment of any balance due was made. And if they were in debt, which was common, the debit balance was carried forward until enough income from fishing paid it off.

Haaf (deep-sea or summer) fishing was the main earner for most people and the one, which in good years paid for the rents and supplies. The catch was ling, cod and tusk but ling was the most important. The fishing was carried out during June, July and August but by the mid 19th century it was starting in May. As the oats and barley were harvested in August, this work would often be left to the women and children as the men were out at sea fishing. The tenants were required to fit out boats, which they either built themselves or they were provided by the landlord or merchant, who financed the purchase of materials for construction as well as the equipment for sailing and fishing. The boat used for the haaf fishing was a six-oared open craft called a sixareen or sixern. Its dimensions were 21ft on keel, 9ft beam, 3ft deep and 30ft overall. There was one mast amidships with an almost square-shaped sail 20ft by 20ft and the tonnage would be about 30 tons. The men fished anything from 30 to 40 miles off shore with lines, which stretched out for up to six miles supported by buoys. At regular intervals smaller lines with hooks would drop down and three or four of these long lines would produce hundreds of fish. The stone ballast from the beaches would be ditched to be replaced by fish and the boat would make for home after two to four days. Long line fishing is used nowadays in the South Pacific but unfortunately it has become a major hazard for the albatross who find themselves caught on the hooks as they try to retrieve the fish.

The Faroe fishery was a later development made possible by the introduction of the smack. The smack was a vessel with a deck providing cover below. It was larger than the sixareen with a longer range and always belonged to the merchant or curer. Its dimensions were 64ft long, 18ft beam, depth from deck 10ft and tonnage of 50 tons or more. The crew had a written contract, which defined the season as from March till August. The men cut and salted the fish during the voyage to preserve them until they reached port. On being landed the fish were then dried for sale some months later. The proceeds were divided equally between the owners and crew when settlement took place at the end of the season after the sale of the fish. The catch was cod from around the Faroe Islands and as far north as Iceland. Peter was involved in this activity and he was able to acquire some wealth as cash was paid for the fish after any expenses had been deducted.

Another fishing activity known as inshore fishing produced herring, some cod and other varieties. The men carried this on in the autumn for their own benefit and they were free to sell the catches to any one. Delting was fortunate in having a long coastline off which a great variety of other fish could be caught. The boats were much smaller than the smacks or sixareens, with only four oars. The fish were sometimes cured by the fishermen or sold to merchants of their choice, for goods or cash, paid for at the time. Herring fishing developed considerably in the 19th century although occasionally the fish would fail to appear. As early as 1833 it is believed that 500 boats and 2,500 men were employed and the total number of barrels cured was 36,000.

The Voes (lochs, fjords) produced a good quantity of sea trout and other small fish which could provide considerable quantities of liver oil. This was a wholesome food for the families and any surplus could be sold for anything from 30 to 50 shillings a barrel. Common seaweed was regularly used as fertiliser but landlords began to realise that incinerating various seaweeds could produce an ash, which was an important source of potash. This activity provided some work for tenants and profit for the landlords until what became known as the kelp industry collapsed in the early 19th century. Most families had some animals, sheep or small cattle, which were grazed on the heath without being herded. They were sold to merchants and meal, flour, biscuits, extra barley and other articles were bought with the proceeds. Sometimes the weather in the winter was very severe as in 1784 when thousands of sheep and hundreds of cattle died under the snow. Such a loss could never be recovered.

There were frequent tragedies at sea. In July 1881 boats from Unst, Yell and Northmavine were fishing on the edge of the continental shelf where the seabed drops from 100 to 600 fathoms within a very short distance. In late afternoon a fierce wind suddenly hit the boats and the temperature dropped sharply. It was difficult to keep heading into the wind and some were turned broadside on. For those that survived they had to thank the extraordinary seaworthiness of the sixareen. It was light and could travel with the wind at incredible speeds when other open boats were incapable of moving. One boat had rowed nine hours offshore in a calm sea and covered 34 nautical miles in that time at an average speed of 3.8 knots. When the storm hit this boat, it managed to keep its head to the wind while the men tried to recover the lines and then the reefed square sail was set causing her to set off like a racehorse. In spite of being caught and smothered by the tail of a breaking wave, they raced back to harbour at a speed of over nine knots. The skipper steered ten miles off shore to avoid the dangerous tides and came round Fetlar into Uyea Sound and calm waters. Accounts vary about the number of boats lost but it was at least ten and may have been as many as 25. Those that perished are thought to have been caught in the tides off the north end of Unst.

When the fish were landed they were accepted by the landlord, who salted and dried them for storage until sold. In due course the merchants took over this role on the landlords' behalf and automatically deducted the rent from the fishermen's accounts. Landlords were sometimes merchants as well. The fishermen were not paid on delivery and had to wait until the annual settlement which took place at the earliest in November but could be as late as March of the following year. In the meantime, the merchant supplied families with goods on credit and at settlement the men were either given the remaining balance in cash or, if their supplies exceeded the amount due for fish, the debit balance was carried forward to the following year. This invariably happened when the fishing was poor.

When the fishing was poor the people would be in dire straits, as they had no other source of income to feed their families. In some comments published with the 1851 census the Rev John McIntyre, minister at Olnaforth in Delting parish, summed up the situation:

> The Secretary of State and Her Majesty's government will turn to a salutary account the present census of this parish and of Zetland if they shall bear in mind that Delting is in a pauperised state with the exception of half a dozen families and of three teachers whose incomes are about £25 per annum and that the whole population are not actually paupers because those who are exceptions possess some measure of youth, health and strength.
>
> The potato disease is a blessing to Zetland. At the time that this disease began to commit its ravages the people were sunk almost as

> deep in misery as possible. They had been completely overlooked in their remote and dreary wilderness by the British legislature who, like the gods of Greece and Rome, were too exalted to regard the affairs of a people so low in the social scale or who perhaps were too much occupied in the laudable endeavour to rival in the Senate the matchless eloquence of the Ancients or it might be were too busy in making by means of liberal endowments a numerous race of sturdy paupers. Providence in its wrath or in its mercy sent this potato disease which would have made speedy work in its destructive progress had not the Christian liberality of the people of Scotland been stirred up to help.
>
> The consequence has been that good roads to a considerable extent have been made through the impassable morasses of Zetland and the people have been enabled to take the first step of civilisation and comfort.
>
> This parish is totally destitute of medical aid. The assistance tendered by government for this purpose has been tried and found altogether inefficient. The resident mid-wives are wholly without training, instruction and people experience.

While the men were risking their lives fishing, the women raised the children, looked after the croft and engaged in knitting for themselves, for exchange or for sale. Sometimes the price received would not cover the labour involved but if the material came off their own animals, at least they would have some return for the effort. The Norse settlers brought with them their native sheep, which were a hardy breed and able to live off the sparse vegetation and seaweed. The wool was soft, light and warm and suited to knitting rather than weaving.

They usually bartered the garments but if cash was required then the price was lower to compensate for the lost profit of the merchant on the goods he would have exchanged, usually about 15–20 per cent. In remote areas the merchants' shops sold all the household necessities as well as the produce they purchased from the women such as eggs and butter.

Hosiery and knitted products varied in quality, colour, etc and were probably held in stock for quite a long time before being sold. It was not possible to generate a regular export trade for these goods as it is today with items produced to standards required by the buyers of bulk quantities or expensive unique garments.

One of the popular items in the early days was stockings, which were traded with the Hanseatic merchants in the 17th and 18th centuries. Fine and delicate Shetland lace was also popular with the Victorians. Stockings and particularly shawls became world-famous and much sought after.

Knitting continues to be an important occupation and remains a profitable cottage industry today. Nowadays pullovers and cardigans are the best sellers and are still knitted using traditional patterns and dies. In recent years a number of knitters have begun to produce more modern and fashionable designs, which are proving very successful.

The practice of supplying workers with goods in lieu of wages was widespread throughout Britain and it was not until 1831 that the first of a series of Truck Acts was passed making the system illegal in many trades. This law was extended on a number of occasions to cover most of industry until the end of the 19th century. Interestingly the system survived in Newfoundland until the early 20th century. There, the merchants and landowners controlled the devolved government and they did not wish any change. Newfoundland was too far away from London for complaints to reach the authorities and so there was little possibility of a challenge to the system.

In Shetland the landowners and merchants claimed that they were not infringing the law because the tenant fishermen were contracted to deliver their fish and therefore were not wage earners. They operated independently and delivered their catches to pay for the rent in accordance with their tenancy agreement and were obliged to take goods in exchange as they had no cash. The merchant supplied their working capital to start them off and see them through the year when little or no fish were caught. The result was that the tenants were nearly always in debt. This suited the merchant because he had the tenants tied to him and very few rebelled against the system.

Technically they were probably right but the point had never been tested in the courts. On several occasions lawyers in Lerwick had suggested to tenants that they were to bring an action against the landowners or merchants under the Truck Acts and they might win the right to be paid in cash. However, the tenants always refused to pursue the case as they were worried that they might be evicted from their cottages. The people had simply become used to the system and felt insecure about the possibility of change. It was too risky. Nevertheless complaints began to mount and shortly after the 1870 Truck Act was passed the government decided to appoint a commission to inquire into these practices and report to parliament.

The Edinburgh Sittings

'The Commission on the Truck System in Shetland' began by hearing witnesses in January 1871 in Edinburgh under Mr Sellar. There were two written submissions and five people were interviewed. The first written contribution was a copy of evidence in the case heard in Lerwick of Anderson v. Peterson. Anderson was a merchant, who was suing Peterson for payment of a debt due to him, because Peterson had delivered his fish to another merchant without paying off the debt. Peterson had signed the account in the ledger after it had been read out to him and Anderson said that signified agreement with the balance due. Peterson on the other hand said that he was threatened with court action if he did not sign. At the end of the season he was unable to remember all the transactions there and then without having the chance to study a copy of the account. Although he said he could not agree to the account until he could study a copy none was given to him and he had gone to another merchant after Anderson had refused to supply his family with goods. The decision on the case is not recorded but the story was useful information for the Commission about the operation of the truck system in Shetland.

The next written submission was a report from the Board of Trade written by Mr RGG Hamilton, which contained a devastating criticism of the system of paying seamen after whaling voyages. The Board was responsible for ensuring that the balance of wages due to seamen was paid in cash, deducting only those items supplied to the men by the captain during the voyage. However, they found that the agent, usually a merchant, came with the seamen to the Custom House where he received "the balance of wages due to him before the superintendent, the man has no option but to hand it all back to the agent at once, to whom he is indebted in an equal or greater amount, and I need hardly point out that it is clearly most important in the interests of the man that he should not merely nominally but actually receive his wages in cash and be able to spend them as he likes". The writer concluded that "the truck system, in an open or disguised form, prevails in Shetland to an extent which, I believe, is unknown in any other part of the United Kingdom, and makes a depressing influence on the industrial and social life of the natives".

The first witness to be interviewed was the Sheriff Clerk in Shetland, George Smith. He confirmed the system used for the Greenland whaling and that the chief inducement for the agent/merchant was the opportunity to sell the outfits and equipment to the seamen for the voyage and to supply their families during their absence. In the case of the Faroe fishery, the owners of the smacks, who were also merchants, engaged the crews and provisioned and equipped the boats as well as supplying the families with goods and provisions. The men were bound to bring their catches to their employers because they were the owners and they had to clear the debt for the goods supplied. Mr Smith also said that the women who knitted opened accounts with the merchant and were only allowed to take goods in exchange, not cash. Furthermore, the only goods they were given in exchange for the items they brought in were chiefly wearing apparel such as ribbons, dresses, gloves or other items of women's clothing.

The next witness was John Walker the notorious factor of the Garth and Annsbrae Estates whom Jimmy Blance had nearly killed because of the hard life he forced his tenants. He said he was totally against the tenants being tied for fishing. They became tied to the merchant first of all when they were employed as beach boys and if they were over 12 years old they could open an account and draw a coat so that they could go to church respectably dressed. At the end of the season they were in debt and so they were 'thirled' for the next season. The merchant, who is usually also the proprietor or factor of the land, had a hold over the men firstly because they had been in debt to him since they were boys and secondly because they were the tenants of the merchant and feared 'ejectment'. He was equally critical of the form of trucking used in the hosiery business. He confirmed Mr Smith's statement about how the women were paid. He quoted an example of a shawl which was sold by the merchant for 30s. The wool cost about 2s and the woman was given a nominal value of 9s for the garment but, because the price was paid in goods, the real value was only 4s. He also said that the quality of the provisions and goods supplied was second rate and that he purchased all his supplies in the south.

Walker stated that the merchants had a virtual monopoly and were able to build a profitable business by persuading enough people to run up debts, which they were not able to pay off. They then felt obliged to continue to take all their requirements from the merchants and deliver the results of their efforts in hosiery and in fishing. The prices paid for the fish and hosiery and also those charged for supplies to the families were fixed by the merchants to give them a good profit. He was convinced that if everyone was paid in cash and there was more competition, the efforts of the people would be better directed. He had even suggested to several merchants that they should open work-rooms for the knitters and give them a pattern so that they could produce a standard garment, which could be sold in quantity and for higher prices. When it was pointed out to him that the system, of paying in goods instead of cash, was not strictly illegal, because the people were not engaged as wage earners, Mr Walker replied "it is very improper, and ought to be illegal if it is not". He thought that a special Act for Shetland was necessary "if you value the interests of 28,000 people".

It seems that Mr Walker considered himself to be a bit of a reformer as he offered to give his tenants long leases under certain conditions, which were designed to maintain and improve the properties. He offered leases to tenants in Delting and Yell but the merchants, in his opinion, persuaded about half to refuse them. Although he had no proof of any intimidation, several of his tenants who had taken leases had suggested that they had been approached by merchants who were concerned that they would lose their hold over the tenants.

The leases were for a minimum of ten years but longer ones were available if desired. The longest lease he had given was 14 years and none would take a longer one. Here is a selection of the rules for a ten-year lease:

- no sub-letting in order to avoid overcrowding,
- bound to keep houses in good repair,
- improve the land in the first five years to the value of the annual rent with half the cost borne by landowner,
- rent was increased by seven per cent of the landowner's contribution for the next five years to cover the landowners cost,
- crops must be rotated
- tenants not allowed to keep inferior animals, which if used for breeding, would degenerate the stock,
- no dogs allowed
- minerals and shootings were reserved
- peat, moss, shell sand and seaweed reserved with power to regulate and divide and avoid disputes among tenants,
- accede to local regulations for the orderly management of the property in the interests of all concerned.

Thomas Edmondstone, a proprietor in the island of Unst, agreed that John Walker had given a fair picture of the barter or the truck system in Shetland and that it had a serious and demoralising effect on the people. He also offered leases to tenants but very few would take one mainly he thought through fear that a lease would bind them but not the landlord. His tenants were not bound to fish for him and he made sure that they were never in debt to him by insisting that the rents be paid promptly. He was of the view that giving credit should be illegal as allowing it meant that the people did not manage their resources properly and found themselves in the hands of the merchants. Although his only dealings with his tenants were the receipt of rent, it was not paid in cash by the tenant but rather by the merchant and debited to the tenants' accounts. This seemed to negate his efforts to free the tenants, who simply found themselves in debt to the merchant for the rent as well as other things. The way to change the system was to insist that all transactions should be in cash with no credit allowed.

Preface

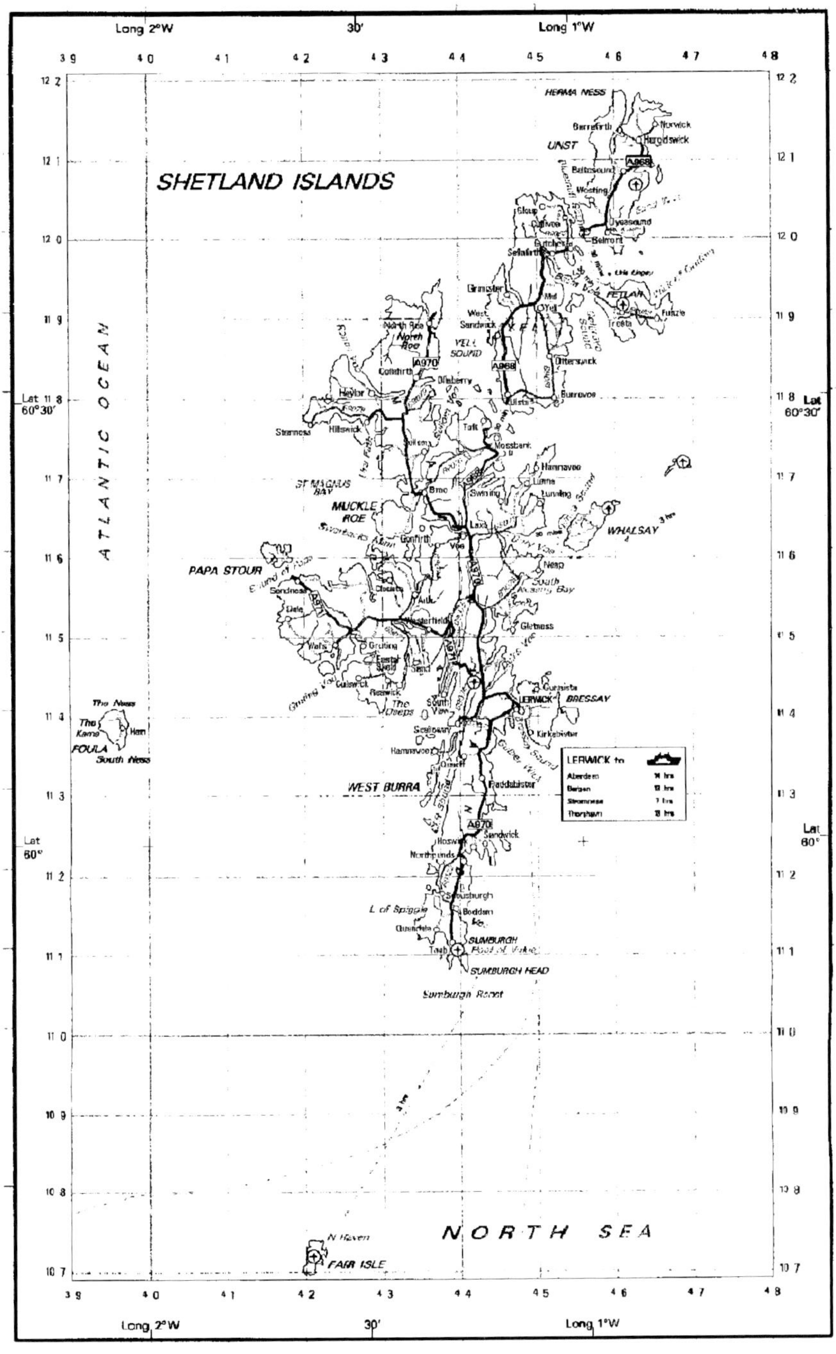

Map of Shetland

Ordinance Survey

A Lodberry in old Lerwick

JJB

Introduction

The Loch of Calback and Calback Village
Shetland Museum

Sullom Voe Oil Terminal
Shetland Museum

Shetland Life and the Blances

Above:
Robert in shop 1945
Family photo

Right:
Peter's obituary in Shetland Times
Edinburgh City Library

Below:
Hardwall still standing but unoccupied
JJB

DEATH OF MR PETER BLANCHE.—Our obituary column last week recorded the death of Mr Peter Blanche, who though for over twenty years has been resident in Edinburgh, where he was associated with his sons in business, took for the greater part of his lifetime an active and intelligent interest in all public matters pertaining to his native land. Born in the parish of Delting in 1832, he like many another Shetlander, chose a seafaring life, and for many years commanded one of the many smacks which sailed from here to the cod-fishing of Faroe and Iceland. Afterwards he captained more than one large barque sailing from Liverpool and other ports to the West Indies, South America, and the Coast of Africa. While resident in Delting Parish, Mr Blanche was a member of the School and Parochial Boards, and an elder in the Parish Church. After coming to Edinburgh, he identified himself with St Cuthbert's Church, and continued in the eldership and took an active part in church work until his death. He enjoyed the personal friendship of the Very Rev. Dr Macgregor and the Rev. Dr Wallace Williamson. He was the father of a family of twelve, nine of whom are alive. Three of his sons conduct an extensive grocery and wine business in Edinburgh. His third son is a wholesale wine and spirit merchant in Glasgow and owns the Glen-Elgin Glen-Livet Distillery at Elgin. His fourth son is a commercial traveller. Three of his daughters are married and resident in Edinburgh, and the youngest is a hospital nurse. His wife pre-deceased him just four years ago. He was very much attached to his many grandchildren, all of whom mourn his death.

To EDINBURGH CITY LIBRARIES Date 7/8/93

WITH COMPLIMENTS

XU92979 - OBITUARY PETER BLANCHE
P/C SHETLAND TIMES, 26 MAY, 1910, P.4

From: John C. Hunter A.L.A. Chief Librarian

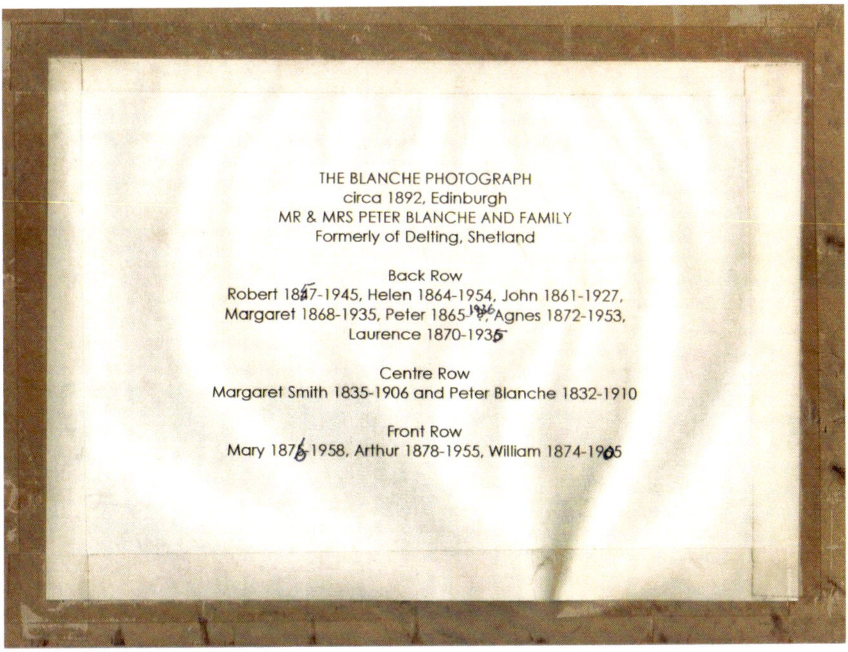

Peter, Margaret and family, c.1890s with names on reverse.

Family photo

PETER BLANCE'S DESCENDANTS (extract)

Dates of Birth, Marriage and Death

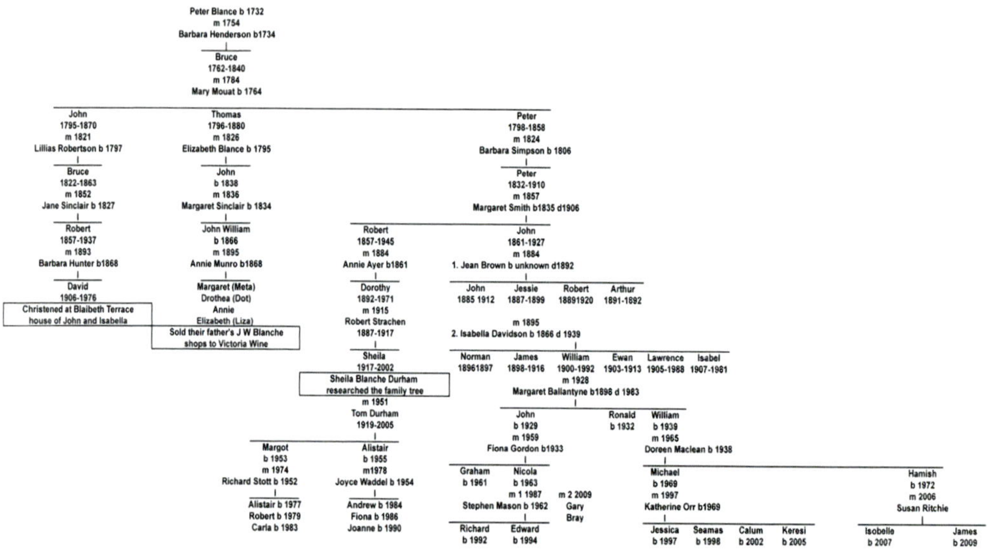

Descendants in late 20th century.

JJB

The last witness in Edinburgh in 1871 was Arthur James Hay a partner of the famous merchant firm: Hay & Company. They were fish curers but also merchants dealing in all manner of goods with suppliers in all parts of the country. They were founded in 1844 and played a major role in the Shetland economy from then to modern times. In 1871 they claimed that they were factors for about a quarter of all rented land in Shetland, most of it owned by the Earl of Zetland. Mr Hay had a different picture of the arrangements for fishing. When asked if yearly tenants were employed as fishermen for the landowner or factors, he said no. Technically this is accurate but later he admitted that yearly tenants did fish for the company, presumably of their own freewill. Leases were available for tenants but very few took them. Most were reluctant to commit themselves to the conditions. For their part the company would probably have very little recourse against people who did not adhere to the provisions of the lease and it would therefore be one-sided. He claimed that most of the tenants paid their rents in cash.

The fishermen were engaged by Hay & Co. and were provided with boats and lines. The fishing lasted from May until sometimes as late as October and settlement was in November the same month the rent was due. The cost of a boat from Hay was £20 plus £10 for the lines and these amounts were debited to the crew, usually six in number. The amount was usually paid off in three years and would cost 33s per annum for each man in the crew. Mr Hay was cross-questioned at some length about the supply of clothes and food to families during the absence of the fishermen and eventually admitted that these goods were supplied on credit until the settlement in November. He confirmed that accounts were usually read over to the fishermen at settlement but that they could have a copy if required. On average the earnings of each fisherman would be £15. In some of the sites rent was included in the settlement and would probably average £4–6. Provisions might cost about £2 making a total debit, including part of the cost of the boat, of £9-10/-. This leaves a profit of £5-10/- on average, which would be paid in cash. In no case did Hay & Co pay this balance in goods. In a bad year the fishermen would be in debt. Mr Hay also stated that he had offered the option of a fixed price for the fish before the start of the season but the fishermen preferred to take their chance with the market. He had not offered this option in recent years however.

This passage involved 30 questions and the examiner was clearly trying to find confirmation of the accusations of malpractice by merchants made by the other witnesses. The questions asked for such detail that it must have been difficult for Mr Hay to be precise in his answers. For example:

About what would be the earnings of a boat's crew for the season?
They vary very much in different districts of the country.
What would they be on average?
You may take the individual earnings of one fisherman with another as ranging from £10 up to £25 yearly.
So that £15 is the average?
Yes, possibly £15 will be about the average.

The questioning went on to consider whaling and the role of the agent, as Hay & Co. was one of four firms engaged in acting for ship-owners. Here again Mr Hay was being asked to provide averages for earnings, which could vary considerably. He did, however, produce answers which gave a reasonable picture of the financial aspects of whaling for the men involved. Hay & Co. received a commission of 2½ per cent and that was their total remuneration. They did not supply outfits to the men but they could obtain a month's advance from the Custom House so that they could purchase an outfit. The families very rarely drew supplies from the firm during the men's absence and when they did the men returned to settle after being paid in cash. Later, he said that while the families were not obliged to deal with the agent who had engaged their men, it was a convenience to do so and 'they do very frequently'. Sometimes the men leave their wages in safe keeping with the merchant rather than risk having them at home. They would be drawn out again when the rents were due. This arrangement was preferable to lodging the money in a bank where the interest was low (1 to 1½ per cent) and the fuss involved was irksome.

The Shetland Sittings

It was clear that the Commission could not pursue its inquiry without taking evidence in Shetland itself. It needed to hear from a wider cross section of opinion and hear the facts presented by those directly involved in the various activities. The Commission began sitting in Lerwick on 1 January 1872. The Commissioner, Sheriff Guthrie, in his introductory remarks said "...that the Act of Parliament under which I am sent here, furnishes me with special and very stringent powers with regard to the obtaining of information." They involved summoning individuals to appear before the Commission, taking evidence on oath and also provision for the protection of witnesses against any intimidation by landowners and merchants. He went on to say that he thought that the people of Shetland had sufficient intelligence and common sense to make it unnecessary for him to use these powers. Reading the evidence it is clear that Mr Guthrie succeeded in obtaining the co-operation of very nearly all the witnesses, although not very many tenants turned up unless they had been summoned. It was suggested that they were worried that their landlord would not like it and give them notice. This seemed unlikely but the attitude was symptomatic of the fears that prevailed among some tenants. It was significant that some of the landowners and officials were very critical of the prevailing system and pressed for change. They had taken no active steps to bring it about but perhaps it showed that the climate was ripe.

Interviewing of witnesses started the same day and after nine days moved to Brae, Hillswick, Mid Yell, Baltasound, Uyeasound, Scalloway, Dunrossness and back to Lerwick before returning to Edinburgh via Kirkwall in Orkney on 9 February. Other witnesses were heard in Edinburgh in April and then Mr Guthrie returned to London to prepare his report. In all he interviewed 282 witnesses and asked over 17,000 questions. The report was submitted to parliament later that year and provides a most comprehensive summary of commercial life in Shetland in the late 19th century. This seems to have been its principal achievement as no specific legislation resulted. However it is evident that things were already changing when the Commission appeared and those who were determined to go their own way did so.

Peter Blanch gave evidence and so did his cousins: Andrew Blance, Gilbert Blance and William Blance. The press gave good coverage and the Archives in Lerwick include reports from *The Scotsman*, *Dundee Courier*, *Saturday Herald* and *Shetland Gazette* as well as the Commission's Report and a transcript of the evidence given by all the witnesses. Mr Guthrie questioned them thoroughly and in great detail. He endeavoured to find confirmation of key facts from several witnesses and even arranged for goods purchased in merchants' shops to be sent to an experienced trader in Edinburgh so that he could check the price and quality.

The tenant witnesses varied in their contributions to the Commission. Some were obviously not confident about being totally frank and some said just enough to avoid being accused of withholding information. Others were very forthcoming and offered opinions about the changes they would like to see. Merchants and landlords invariably offered full answers to the questions and some tabled written submissions afterwards as a result of the discussions with the examiner. There were some who had radical ideas to contribute although they did not seem to have done much to introduce them. The reasons were mostly to do with the tenants' suspicion of changes and the thought that the changes would benefit the merchants and landlords rather than them. It was difficult for them to visualise the advantages and to break with the long-established system of the past.

Undoubtedly there were strong vested interests among the merchants. The current system exposed them to no risk and there was no competition from other traders. In the main they all co-operated in the pricing of fish and in the terms for the supply of boats and equipment for fishing. By the late 19th century the landlords were concentrating on renting their properties and the merchants had taken over the purchase of the fish caught by the tenants and running of shops trading in food and other supplies and purchasing knitted garments, eggs and butter. Often they would also deal in animals the tenants wished to sell. The vast majority of transactions were settled in goods. The landlords usually had an arrangement with a merchant to collect their rents.

Although the tenancies were for one year and the period of notice to quit was only 40 days, it seems that very few tenants were evicted. Many tenants were well behind with rent payments but landlords were usually sympathetic when they knew that the fishing had been poor. The merchants took the same attitude in supplying tenants who were in difficulties; unless they felt that someone was taking advantage of them unreasonably. Both landlords and merchants would often support a widow whose husband had died at sea fishing for them and continue until the children had grown up and could support their mother.

A number of the merchants were in favour of moving over to a cash system but for this to work the fishermen would require to be paid for fish on delivery instead of the end of the season. Even if some tenants had received cash for fish caught on their own account, they tended to leave the cash with the merchant so that they were not tempted to spend it. In any case there was very limited access to banks there being only two in Lerwick at the time and the town was not easily accessible. The merchants therefore acted as bankers and would give out small amounts of cash when asked and debit it to the tenants account.

Dunrossness (South Mainland)

Some landlords and merchants took the view that the people were not capable of looking after there own affairs and needed to be treated like children. One of these was John Bruce of Sumburgh, who was descended from one of the nobles who came over with William the Conqueror. He thought that a change in the system would cause confusion and he was probably right as the people were mostly ill prepared to run their own accounts. Some could not count and mostly they trusted the merchant to keep their accounts accurately. He provided the Commission with a written statement before appearing and it is worth reproducing an extended quotation from it as it sums up the attitude of the more efficient landlords who actively managed their estates:

> The tenants on the property in this parish managed by me are at liberty to go to sea or to the Greenland or Faroe fishing, or to pursue

any land occupation as they please; but if they remain at home and go to the home fishing, they are expected to deliver their fish to me and receive for it the full market value. This is one of the conditions on which they hold their farms and is I consider a beneficial rule for the fishermen. They must fish to some merchant and as I give them as high a price as they could get from another they are not losers, while I provide suitable curing and fishing stations and these stations of mine are the most convenient places for them to deliver their fish.

I am obliged to keep stores at some of the fishing stations for the convenience of the fishermen to supply them with fishing gear, groceries, and other things which they may require. But no fisherman is expected or wished to take anything from these stores unless it is his wish to do so.

Any fisherman can get the full value of his fishing in money from me at any time if he wishes it. I have never once refused to pay a fisherman the full sum due to him in money. And in fact there are many cases in which fishermen take nothing whatever out of my stores but receive the full value of their fishing in cash.

Prior to 1860 the tenants on the property managed by me were permitted to fish to any one they liked and the people were very much in debt both to the landlord and to the various merchants to whom they fished . . . and for the most part could not pay their rents.

The debts to the landlord averaged two years' rents over the whole property.

On account of the general state of bankruptcy I was obliged to take the fishing into my own hands and I consider the people now to be in a much more flourishing state.

For the most part fishermen are quite satisfied with having their accounts read over to them. But those fishermen who ask for copies of their accounts at settlement always get them and the books are always open for them to refer to at any after-time.

With regard to the prices charged at the stores, the goods I keep are in all cases of the best quality and may be a little higher-priced than goods of the same description but of inferior quality but I am not aware that anything is charged unreasonably high.

Many of the fishermen in this country (as indeed many of the poorer classes everywhere) are unable from want of thrift and care

> to manage their own matters in a satisfactory manner and require to be thought for and acted for and generally treated like children and are much better off under the management of a landlord who has an interest in their welfare than they would be if in the hands of a merchant whose only object was to make a profit out of them.
>
> A merchant who has no control over the fishermen may in some cases wish to get them and keep them in his debt in order to secure their custom; but the case of a landlord also a merchant is quite different. It is his interest to have a prosperous thrifty and independent tenantry; and he will use his utmost endeavour to keep them out of debt and to encourage saving habits.
>
> There are no doubt many things in the Shetland system of trade which might be improved but the system has been of long growth and is so engrained in the minds of the people that any change must be very gradual; a sudden and sweeping change to complete free-trade principles and ready-money payments would not suit the people but would produce endless confusion, hardship, and increased pauperism.

The tenants at Scatness, population 500, in the far south of the mainland had a meeting to decide about appearing before the Commission. Only Laurence Mail appeared; the others being frightened that they would be warned out of their cottages. It seems that Bruce was strict but also very fair. He did the fishermen's accounts himself and was very willing to pay cash for credit balances at settlement and to give advances when requested. The prices at the shop were perceived to be high although Bruce maintained that they were competitive given the quality of his goods.

The commissioner was unable to find evidence of anyone being warned out but there was a fear that it was possible if tenants did not conform. Bruce was willing to give ten-year leases and expected the land to be improved. If it were not improved then Bruce would arrange for it to be done and then charge the tenant. No information was produced on the question of security of tenure and certainly the tenants felt that leases offered by landlords were one-sided. Improvements in the land carried out by tenants, it was felt, would be to the advantage of the landlord and they were therefore not motivated to do anything.

From the fisherman's point of view he had no cash at the start of the season and therefore had no alternative to dealing at the landlord's or merchant's shop. This is the critical problem with the system. It was totally inflexible and there was no opportunity for a fisherman to change direction except to join the Faroe fishery where the system was not so restrictive. A man could also leave home and go off on long distance voyages as a seaman and maybe become a mate or skipper after which he would well and truly have established his independence.

Some fishermen cured their fish before selling them to the merchants and thus made a little more money. This practice was not welcomed as the merchant's own curing facilities would then have been under utilised. If a fisherman had time to spare it would make some sense to do this but it was less efficient than using the dedicated facility. Andrew Tulloch of Mossbank was able to demonstrate to the commissioner that he was able to make an extra 1/3 per hundredweight by curing for himself. However, it is doubtful that it was worthwhile earning an extra seven per cent given that the process had to be watched carefully in order to produce a quality result. There was also a risk of damage to the fish from rain and sand.

Brae (North Mainland)

The evidence given at Brae indicated that the situation in the north mainland was a good deal freer and more open than in Dunrossness. Men were free to fish for anyone and to deal with any merchant's shop they wished. In practice most dealt with the merchant for whom they fished as they had an account for equipment and it was convenient to draw supplies for the families during the men's absence at sea. The fishing was obviously better as there was easier access to the Atlantic for ling, cod and tusk and to the Faroe and Iceland fishing grounds for cod. The big operator was TM Adie & Co of Voe, although Pole Hoseason & Co had a sizable business further north at Mossbank. Adie employed over 400 men mainly in the haaf fishing and had a number of curing stations where fish could be landed. In addition to the haaf fishing he had five Faroe smacks. He was a much respected man and did everything he could to make the terms of fishing as attractive as possible. As a result he was able to engage the best and most reliable men.

Great grandfather Peter was 40 years old at the time of the enquiry and gave evidence at the Brae session on 13 January 1872. He had been employed on the Faroe and Iceland fisheries for 12 years and had been skipper of one of Adie's Faroe smacks for five years. Previously he had worked for a Mr Sutherland and George Reid Tait in Lerwick. He usually drew his supplies from Adie's shop but as he was always in credit he was not obliged to do so. When a merchant employed him he considered "it something of a duty, in a moral point of view, to put my money into his shop". Although he always had money to pay his way some others did not and were given credit by the merchant and were then obliged to fish for him. Sometimes cash was advanced if the merchant felt that he could trust the man to repay the debt.

Peter was asked about the system for settlement in the Faroe fishing and replied that he had often thought that it should be changed. They had very little information about the revenue and costs of a voyage and felt that they "don't have that fair play which we ought to have. The present system is almost if not altogether a one-sided arrangement for the merchant". The voyage accounts were never published even to the skippers and the men were simply told what price was given for the fish and the deductions made before the balance was struck. The deductions were £2-10/- a ton for salt and curing, extra fees for the master and mate of so much per ton of fish and score money for the men based on the size of the catch. Most merchants deducted five per cent to cover selling costs and risk. The net balance was divided equally between the merchant (owner of the vessel) and the crew.

Peter suggested that the crews should know the price they were to be given for the fish before the season started. That system was used for English vessels which came from as far a field as Berwick, Grimsby, Hull and London to fish for Shetland merchants. The examiner suggested that the merchant, with his superior knowledge of the market, might fix a price more in his own favour than the crews. However Peter reckoned that many of the skippers would know as much about the market as the merchants. He was more than willing to take the risk of the market fluctuations as it would be a fairer system and more open. As it was, the merchant could not lose as he did not fix the price to be paid for the fish until he had sold them at the end of the season.

The examiner asked for a view on another method where a certain part of the price per hundredweight was paid on delivery and the rest at the time of settlement according to the current market price. Peter thought that would be a far better way because he would be able to see his fish being weighed out and noted down in the records. The merchant would then bear the cost of curing and taking the fish to market. This method would have the advantage of introducing cash to the economy and leaving the men free to manage their own expenditure instead of leaving it in the hands of the merchant thus saving all the extra account-keeping.

Adie had once tried out the system of fixing the price for fish at the start of the season but it did not work out well. The reason was that the price was fixed at too low a level and it advanced during the season. Adie had to increase the price later to satisfy the men. It was stated by others that the price for dried fish tended to be low in the early season and gradually rose as the season advanced. The reason may have been simply the balance between supply and demand. Most of the fish was sold at the end of the season when the demand would tend to be strong in advance of the winter due to the supply being not as plentiful as little fish was being caught. Peter reckoned that it was possible to judge the price trend more accurately than Adie had done on the one occasion they tried the method.

Peter when on the Faroe fishing would sometimes buy salt on his own account for salting the fish during the voyage. In view of the extended time at sea the fish had to be salted otherwise they would be worthless on returning to port. Normally the merchant would supply the salt but Peter was convinced that he was charged too much for it. He claimed in evidence that curing could be done for 37/- compared with 50/- per ton charged in the voyage accounts by the merchant. He said that he had been able to purchase the salt direct from Liverpool for 22/- per ton landed in Lerwick whereas William Adie claimed it was

5/6 more. He also said that the cost of curing, that is washing and drying the fish, was more than the 12/- estimated by Peter. The remaining 3/- was an allowance for overhead cost, making 37/- in all. However that does not explain the difference and Peter probably had made a good point. Better buying was clearly the answer but skippers would not always have the time to negotiate such transactions given the other problems to be solved in preparing for the voyages to Faroe and Iceland.

Peter was recalled later the same day to be further questioned about the cost of curing. William Adie had challenged his earlier evidence but Peter was able to convince the examiner that he had not exaggerated but had spoken from personal experience. He also suggested that merchants should supply the fishing lines as well as the boats. The arrangement was that the men provided their own lines and if they lost them they had to replace them at a high price. They paid 2s. 6d. for a line, which he knew the merchant, was able to buy for 2s. or 1s. 6d.

Adie provided the boats for the men and arranged for them to be built by specialist boat builders. However it was not unknown for some men to build their own if they had the skills. The boats were usually paid for by instalments over five years and generally lasted for between six to 12 years depending on how well they were maintained and how much wear and tear they were exposed to by the weather. Adie paid 3d per cwt extra for the fish to those crews who owned their own boat or were paying it off over a period. This was some compensation for the crews having to take the risk of loss.

Thomas Adie was very fair in pricing his shop supplies. He regularly deducted five per cent from the price of goods bought on credit to make it equivalent to the cash price. He claimed that he wished everyone to have pass books but hinted that many could not be bothered to keep them or were unable to do so. The examiner's questions and the answers were as follows:

Has each man dealing with you a pass book?
No, not all, but the greater part of them have.

But you wish them to have pass books?
Yes; I should be very glad for them all to have pass books, if they

would only keep them regularly. When it is a careful man, his book is kept regularly, and there is very little trouble with him in taking down his account.

James Hay of Mossbank also fished for Adie and had a pass book but admitted that he did not bother to keep it. The following is his exchange with examiner:

How do you square up your account at the shop and your account for fish at the end of the year?
At the end of the year I may have more things put into Mr Adie's hands than my fishing. For instance last year I had that cow and stot, and perhaps some other things, and these and my fishing are all put together to my credit. Then my out-takes and things I have been requiring from Mr Adie are put too, and the amount they come to is stated to me.

Is that read over to you, or have you got it already in your pass book?
Sometimes I have a pass book, and sometimes I don't require one. Sometimes I don't fash with it; that is the truth.

Why is that?
I thought there was very little need for it, because Mr Adie and I never disputed about these things, and when I had a pass book I was not very particular about keeping it.

A cousin of Peter's, Gilbert Blance of Garth near Mossbank, gave evidence. He was engaged in the haaf fishing by Pole Hoseason & Co and dealt with their shop for all his goods. Unlike Peter he was always in debt. However he was able to ask for cash to pay his rent if he required it. He was another of those who did not have a pass book. He said he trusted the honesty of the merchants. Even if he and others had pass books they were often not good arithmeticians and would be likely to make a mess of the accounts.

Gilbert was asked about selling fish to people other than the merchants to whom they are engaged and the questioning went as follows:

When you were out fishing, have you sometimes sold your fish to others than Pole, Hoseason, & Co.?
I have not been in the habit of doing that.

Is it sometimes done?
Perhaps it is by some individuals.

What is their reason for doing that?
I cannot say what their reason may be, unless it is to have immediate supplies.

Or money?
Yes, or money, but it is commonly for something such as refreshments which they wish to take on their way to or coming from the fishing-ground.

Where do you usually meet the people who buy your fish from you in that way?
Sometimes they are met in the course of our fishing operations at the land's end.

On the land?
No; on the sea in a little boat. They will take any small portion of fish we may give them, and hand us refreshments in return.

Do you get a larger sum for your fish in that way?
No; I never knew of any larger sum that was given in that way than the country currency.

Is that practice what you call smuggling the fish?
I suppose so.

The refreshments would be referring to spirits and tobacco duty free!

William Pole of Pole Hoseason & Co appeared at Brae and added a little more information to the picture that was evolving from the hearings. His firm covered North Delting from Mossbank and also operated in the north parts of Yell and Northmavine. He said that all merchants and curers tended to pay the same price for fish at the end of the season and sometimes there would be a meeting to discuss the matter. The price recently had been 8/- for a hundredweight of wet fish. It took 2¼ cwt of wet fish to produce one hundredweight of cured fish, therefore, the equivalent cost for cured fish to the merchant would be to 18/-. The curing cost was 3/- and the fish were sold for 23/- giving a profit of 2/-. That profit had to cover a loss on hiring boats as the hiring charge had remained the same for 20 years in spite of the boats going further out and being subject to more wear and tear.

Pole was not in favour of fixing the price for fish before the season begins as he believes that "under the present system they are getting the very utmost the fish are worth to any merchant". The examiner persevered by suggesting it might be better for the fishermen but Pole responded: "I am not sure about that; I cannot see in what respect they could possibly be better than they are". At least the commissioner knew where he stood! He had a point and if Peter's idea of publishing the accounts for fish trading had been introduced, the men who were after all partners, could see the record and make any recommendations for the following season.

Hillswick (North West Mainland)

Another fisherman cousin of Peter's, William Blance of Ollaberry, appeared at the Hillswick sitting in Northmavine. William was also a brother-in-law having married Peter's sister Elizabeth Beach Blance. In the rather enclosed society of Shetland, it was quite common for first cousins to marry. He was engaged in the Faroe fishing and had worked for Adie for the previous six years. He claimed that he was not fit enough to take part in the haaf fishing and Peter probably took him on his crew to help him out.

He did not seem to be a very confident man and had sometimes hesitated when asked a question. He was warned that he was required to answer all questions put to him. He claimed that when the citation arrived he could not read the writing and took it to the shopkeeper to read to him and explain the purpose of the summons. He was told that he had nothing to fear and that he should tell the truth. He had lived in Ollaberry for four years but said that he knew very few people there claiming to be a stranger in the place. He must have come from Calback where most of the Blances lived at that time until Walker gave some of them notice to move.

William was generally in debt to Adie and took most of his supplies from him as he could charge them to his account. He was not very careful about keeping his pass book and many items were charged which did not appear in the book because he did not have it with him.

This made it impossible to check his account at settlement but he seemed unconcerned saying that he trusted the merchant. The general impression he gave was that he was not very bright but made the effort to keep his family by doing extra work as a tailor for Mr Adie and fishing on his own account near the shore when the Faroe fishing was over.

Another witness at Hillswick, John Sandison, was much more efficient. He was engaged in the home fishing and had worked for John Anderson, a merchant at Hillswick. He also did some boat-building in winter for Laurence Smith. He bought goods from both Smith and Anderson and thus followed the practice of dealing with those who employed him. Although not obliged to do this, he regarded it as a point of honour. The exchange with the examiner was as follows:

> **You said the reason why you went to Laurence Smith for some of your goods was, because you were employed by him: is it a general sort of understanding that when a man is employed by a merchant, he deals with him for his goods?**
> To a certain extent it is.
>
> **He is not altogether bound to do it?**
> No, not in my experience.
>
> **But is it thought fair and proper that he should take a certain quantity of his goods from that merchant?**
> If a merchant gives a man employment, and he has the goods as good and as cheap as they can be got elsewhere, it is generally thought that the man should take his goods from him.
>
> **Do you not forget what quantity of goods you have got from the merchant in the course of the year?**
> Oh no. We can easily remember what goods we have had; and besides, we generally keep accounts of our own; at least I do so.
>
> **Have you got a pass book in which are entered all the goods you receive from Mr Anderson?**
> Yes [produces pass book].

John was not married and lived with his father and mother and appears to have looked after them to some extent. He was very careful in his buying of supplies and constantly checked prices and quality.

Meal, one of the staples, was always given close attention and John had tried buying meal direct from Lerwick. He found that the quality was the same as Mr Anderson's and the price was similar after adding something for carriage. In spite of the absence of roads, there was a regular service for goods and mail throughout the islands by boat. John's father, Alexander, was next on the stand and proved to be an interesting man. He said he was too old to go fishing and had given up three years previously. When he did fish he was free to go with anyone but always stuck with Anderson. He had ceased to be concerned with the fishing practices since he retired from what must have been a very active working life. He had spent 50 years on long voyages from Lerwick to the Davis Straits "and all around the globe" including the odd whaling voyage. He must have been in his 60s when he gave up and turned to the local fishing for four years.

Peter Peterson was a fisherman at Hillyar working for Laurence Smith, a small curer with two boats. Three years previously he had worked for Anderson but had to change. He had a sad tale to tell. His debt had been increasing for the previous nine years and had reached £17, 9s. 5d. At that point Anderson had refused to supply him with goods for his family. The debt was not settled and Peterson put the matter in the hands of a lawyer, Mr Spence. There was no pass book so that it was not possible to agree the account. Mr Anderson did provide a copy of the account for nine years; the first Peterson had been given. The papers were in the hands of Mr Spence. The debt had occurred from the replacement of lines lost at sea due to bad weather making it impossible to take them in. In the last year he had sold fish for cash to someone else in order to feed his family and Anderson stopped supplying him. Peterson further claimed that he was given a boat in his last year with Anderson, which was not fit for sea, and this had made it difficult to catch enough fish to reduce the debt. This case was one of the items of written evidence submitted to the Commission in Edinburgh the year before. Hearing the defender in the case adds something to the story and it is frustrating not to know what the outcome was.

John Anderson gave evidence the same day, immediately before

Peterson, who must have heard all the evidence. When given the opportunity to contradict anything that had been said, he had no comments to make. By this time the examiner was very familiar with the system of engagement and keeping of accounts for the fishermen. However, he was keen to confirm the arrangements and the following exchange summarises them concisely:

> **I presume the way in which you arrange for the payment of your fishermen is similar to that which prevails in other parts of Shetland viz. that the fisherman engages to fish for you for the season at the summer fishing, and to receive payment for his fish in winter at the price then current after the sales have been made?**
> Yes.
>
> **Is it the case also that the way in which you keep accounts with your fishermen is that a ledger account is opened in name of each man, in which the entries on one side consist of advances made to him for the purpose of outfit and lines, boat-hire when the boat is not his own, or for the price of the boat if he is buying it by instalments?**
> Yes.
>
> **And on the other side is entered the price of his fish, and anything else that may be due to him by you?**
> Yes.
>
> **Is there any further explanation you desire to make about the way in which these arrangements entered into and carried out between you and your fishermen?**
> I think that is all, except the inducement I have held out to fishermen to buy their own boats and lines. My practice for several years past has been that when they bought their own boats and lines, and were free of debt, I allowed them 6d per cwt. extra on their fish.

Anderson engaged about 120 men at Hillswick, 60 at Ollabery and others at various stations on other parts of the coast. They fished for ling only, although a few cod and tusk were caught but were of inferior quality. This seemed odd and particularly as he was questioned about the incidence of debt:

Do you find that the majority of your men have then a cash balance to receive, or are they in arrear?
I am afraid I must acknowledge that the majority of them are in arrear.

The fishing could not have been very good and yet Anderson had stations at five sites along the coast, which would give good access to suitable fishing grounds. It is possible that Peter Peterson's criticism of the condition of his boats may be typical thus persuading the men that they could not risk going as far out as the others, who enjoyed good catches. The question of cash payments came up and Anderson gave a standard answer:

Is it ever the case that a man who is in that position gets some payments in cash throughout the season, and is paid the whole balance in cash at the end, and has no account at your shop at all?
I think not. I have never been aware of any case of that kind.

Is that because the man necessarily has to apply to you for an outfit for the fishing at the beginning of the year, such as lines or boats; or is it because he may have an account for necessaries to his family?
He is not obliged to get his outfit or his necessaries from me unless he likes. There is no obligation upon him.

But, in point of fact, he generally does get an outfit from you?
Yes; we are always glad to get them to buy an outfit from us.

He went on to say that his tenants were not obliged to fish for him as a condition of their leases but that it was understood as part of the bargain between landlord and tenant. Although there was no obligation to deal in his shop, if he was in debt that was a different matter:

I suppose you would consider it fair that man who is in your debt should deliver his fish to you rather than to another, in order that he might pay off your debt?
Certainly.

And also that he should take his supplies from your shop, so far as necessary?
Yes, I would expect that.

Is it also the feeling among the men generally, that they are inclined to deal with a person who has advanced them money or goods in a bad season?
I think they would have no objection to deal in that way.

You would probably have rather to keep them within limits in their dealing, for fear they should get too much?
Yes, I think that is quite right.

Anderson was an agent for the Shipwrecked Mariners' Society and confirmed that money for claims made came to him in the first instance. If the man had an outstanding debt for a boat purchased from him, he would put the money to the credit of that account. The examiner goes on:

What is your reason for making that distinction?
I think it is nothing but simple justice to myself. It would certainly be very unreasonable for a man to get remuneration for a boat from the Shipwrecked Fishermen's Society while the same boat was standing unpaid for in my books.

Would the same principle not apply to the case of an account which a man owed to you?
No doubt the man would be entitled to pay me that account; but I would certainly consider it a great hardship if I had to pay that money over to a man who had an account standing due in my books for the very boat for the loss of which the money was given.

Have you ever had any dispute with the fishermen about the payment of that money, or any complaints that it was not settled for in cash?
I don't think I have, within my recollection. I think there was one man who said something about it at one time; but after I had showed to him what I considered to be the justice of the matter, I fancied he was satisfied, and never heard any more about it.

Comparing the Sixareen

The subject of boats was raised and Anderson said that his arrangement was to supply wood to an itinerant boat-builder and pay him £3 for the work involved in constructing a six-oared boat. The commissioner was able to obtain advice about the quality of the boats made in Shetland by comparing them with boats built by Magnus Mowat of Newhaven near Edinburgh. His boats of similar size would cost £22, 10s. for the shell plus another £5, 10s. for fitting the masts, oars and sails, £28 in all. He was examined in Edinburgh on 18 April 1872 and said that he did not think highly of the Shetland boats:

You have seen a Shetland boat: have you any idea whether such a boat as is used there would cost more or less than a boat such as you have been speaking of?
The Shetland boats of the same size would not be half the value of our boats here.
Why?
Because the timber is inferior, and they are lighter. I might have 24 timbers in a side, when they would only have 10 or 12.
Are your boats built in the same style as the Shetland boats? Are they clinker-built?
Yes; but I don't suppose they use the same materials. I think it is Norwegian timber they use; and if that is so, the cost of them would be considerably less.
How long will one of your boats last?
From 17 to 20 years.
Will a Shetland boat, such as you have seen, last as long as that?
It will not last so long, according to my judgement.
Suppose it were used only for three or four months in the summer, would it last longer than it would do if it were more used?
Certainly it would.
But you think it would not last so long in any case its 17 or 18 years?
No. The frame is much weaker: there are fewer ribs in it than in our boats; because, while in a Shetland boat there might be a rib every two or three feet, I might have them 10 or 12 inches apart, and of course the ribs are the strength of the boat.
Would 12 or 14 years be the outside of the life of a Shetland boat?
I would suppose that would be about as long as they could run them with safety.

Mowat estimated the cost of a Shetland boat would be about £20 and the hire for three to four months for the home fishing was estimated at £2, 10s. This estimate was clearly based on the longer life suggested by Mowat of 12 to 14 years. The experience in Shetland was that boats could be unfit to go to sea after no more than six years, which is partly explained by the severe wear caused by the Atlantic seas but, also perhaps, because of a lower standard of design and workmanship.

Hillswick (continued)

Anderson was of the opinion that the situation in Shetland could be greatly improved by the introduction of leases, which gave the tenant security of tenure and provided for the improvements to land to belong to the tenant. He said, "as soon as a tenant here begins to improve his farm, he is very likely to have his rent raised upon him". As this matter had been raised by others the examiner pursued the point and found that Anderson had a very reasonable approach and was making his own contribution to the general improvement of the land:

Have you known cases in which the rent has been raised upon an improving tenant?
Yes. I am not prepared just now to give names, but I think I have met with several cases of that kind.

What is the bar to the introduction of a system of leases in Shetland, which, you say, would greatly improve the country?
There seems to be an unwillingness on the part of the proprietors to give leases. I have known several parties who have asked for leases and have not got them.

Is there a general desire on the part of fishermen-farmers in Shetland to have leases?
I cannot say that exactly. I think there is such desire in many cases, but then they fear that their rent would be raised if a lease were granted.

In the evidence to which you have referred as having been given in Edinburgh, there is a statement that leases were offered on a large estate in Delting or in Yell, but that the bulk of the tenants would not accept of them: do you know the reason of that?
Because, I suspect, they were suspicious of the factor.

The statement was, 'Ten years was mentioned as the minimum length of the lease, because the people were frightened to take leases; but when any one came and asked for a longer lease, I gave it to him. No one would take a longer lease than 14 years, and I have given none longer than 14.' Can you suggest any other reason than that you have named for the tenants declining leases on these estates?

I think it must have been because under the leases, all improvements were to be held to belong to the landlord.

But they belong to the landlord at present?

True; but what I mean is, that that is the great bar to improvements in Shetland.

Do you think it is possible for a man to improve his land much who is employed for four or five months in the year fishing?

I think it is. His time in winter is almost thrown away at present; but if he had the security of getting the value of his labour at the end of his lease or on removing, I think he would work actively and improve his land. There are many, I know, who have regretted that they could not spend their time in that way.

Have you the management of the Ollaberry estate in your own hands?

Yes.

Have you made any effort to induce the people there to take leases, or offered them compensation for improvements?

I have not offered them compensation. I could not do that; but I have told them that the understanding on which they held their lands was this – that if they made improvements, either in cultivating the land, keeping up their fences, or repairing their houses, their rents would not be raised during my lease.

You have only a lease of Ollaberry?

Yes, for 19 years.

Has your intimation to the tenants, that their rents would not be raised if they improved their holdings, had a beneficial effect?

I think it has in some cases; that is to say, they have kept up their fences very well, and I know some parties who have added to their cultivated ground.

Anderson had a written agreement with Adie that they would pay off the debts of men who came to fish for them having left the other because they had been refused supplies due to a high debt balance on their accounts. This was to prevent these men from escaping paying their debts. In general he had a good opinion of the Shetlanders and considered them to have high moral values, to be frugal and sensible in business. His experience in the previous few years was that those in debt had made successful efforts to reduce it. The fact that they spent a lot of time in the winter doing nothing was simply due in his view to lack of employment opportunities. An extension of the fishing into the winter is not possible because of the north Atlantic weather, although some do go out a short distance if the weather permits.

Like Thomas Adie, Anderson comes across as a fair and reasonable man and it is possible that Peter Peterson's sad story may be the result of too little effort on his part or a lack of confidence in tackling his problems. There are many people today, who are quite content to have the security of a safe and easy job, being told what to do and being supervised every day. The job would pay modestly, offer no prospect of advancement and require the man to so organise his life that he lived within the limits of his small salary. A similar option was available in Shetland at the time as the merchant could always be relied upon to bail a man out if he overspent within reason. The man himself had to decide how hard he would work without supervision, other than from his peers in the boat. If he was less energetic than the majority, he could find himself amongst others who were of a similar frame of mind and the result would be poor catches.

One of the more interesting observers of life in Shetland was Rev James Sutherland, who had been minister of the parish of Northmavine for 24 years. He had not been cited but had volunteered to give evidence. In former times ministers were the most reliable reporters of conditions in their areas and *The Statistical Accounts of Scotland* relied on them a great deal. He had some very strong views on the system of payments and running accounts:

Do you think the system of long payments which exists here is a wholesome one as regards the habits of the fishermen?
I think it is most ruinous. I think I have had very good opportunities of judging of the effect of the system upon the people, being intimately acquainted with them, and having received the statements in private of a great many of them; and I cannot conceive any system which could be more ruinous in a moral point of view, apart altogether from its effect upon them in a pecuniary way. In my opinion, the independence of the people is wholly destroyed. There is scarcely a man I know, with very few exceptions, who is not in terror, and terror that I could scarcely describe, of the merchant to whom he is indebted, and I believe that three-fourths of the whole of my parishioners are in debt to some merchant or other, and thoroughly under their control.

The examiner felt that this view was exaggerated but Mr Sutherland managed to convince him that it was realistic. He went on to state that the fishermen imagine that the merchant is taking an undue profit in his dealings and set out to do everything they could against the merchant. As an illustration one of the answers was:

Is it a general impression among the people with whom you come in contact, that the merchant has too large profits?
I will give you an illustration, and that will serve for the whole. There was a gentleman examined today to whose evidence I listened with great pleasure, Mr Morgan Laurenson. I do not mean that what I am now to state should tell against him, but it is rather in his favour; at least so far as I am to use it. At the time he left Ollaberry, there were very considerable sums of money due to him, certainly much more than I would have entrusted to a population such as the general Shetland population. He had to leave rather more suddenly than he expected, and he had not time to collect his debts. A man from Ollaberry came over to me, and I said, 'Are you sorry that Mr Laurenson is going away from you?' He said no. I asked if it was true that the people about Ollaberry were due him several hundreds of pounds? He said, 'No; not we. He has had plenty out of us, he has had his profits which might make up for all that.' I said, 'Then you

> are not sorry?' and he said, 'I am not sorry for it at all.' That is just a consequence of that sort of dealing.

Mr Sutherland went on to say that the statements given by previous witnesses had not been entirely frank as they were afraid to tell the true facts. He would not be specific as people had spoken to him in confidence. He did say in answer to further questioning:

> . . . I put a question to one man concerning a very important matter in relation to what I am to state to-day, and when I asked him to answer that question, the woman of the house, a married woman, seized me by the arms and exclaimed, 'Will that give offence to the merchant? If it gives offence to the merchant, then we won't open our mouths.' That occurred only within the last ten days, and the same dread and terror are over the whole community around Hillswick with very few exceptions.

Mr Sutherland made an important point with regard to individual members of the family having separate accounts with merchant's shops:

> . . . the system is also injurious by leading the husband and wife to have separate accounts and separate transactions, and the children too. The house, instead of being united, is in reality divided against itself. Every member of the family has a separate interest; in that way mutual dependence is destroyed, and that affection, which ought to subsist between children and parents, has in a great measure disappeared from Shetland. A boy gets an account of his own when he is a mere child, or at least in boyhood, and as he grows up he thinks he has only himself to provide for. He has not that dependence or respect or affection for his parents which will lead him, when old age comes to them, to provide for them. I don't know any more prejudicial effect that any system can have upon the community than to see the rising generation growing up and their fathers neglected and despised as they are in many cases here. That feeling is produced very much among the young people by the nature of their early training.

In his view this led to young people ignoring their parents when they become old and in some cases not lifting a hand to help if they were ill or destitute. Another consequence is that the women dress more expensively than they can afford because for some of the items they take to the shops to sell, such as knitting, they are allowed to take only clothing or materials for making clothes in payment when they are in debt for rent on the husband's account.

The examiner raised the question of the fishermen who had attended to give evidence:

> **You were speaking of a system of terrorism which prevails, or is alleged to prevail, here: if that terrorism exists, how do you account for witnesses coming forward and speaking at all?**
> But what have they said?
>
> **We had two or three men who were not cited?**
> I saw one man here who was not by any means a representative of the ordinary tenants. He was not a representative of the class among whom he lives.
>
> **Have you seen many fishermen here during the last day or two?**
> Not very many.
>
> **I have been a little at loss myself to know why fewer people have appeared here than at other places with even less population. Can you give me any explanation of it?**
> They told me beforehand that they dursn't come, and that they would not come; and I will give you an illustration. I went into the house of a man who had been complaining to me about his debts at the shops, and about the misery he was in; and when I got the notice to see what witnesses would come forward and give evidence, I said to myself, 'This man who has complained so much to me will surely come forward.' I went to him, and in presence of his family I asked whether he would give evidence before you. I did not tell him to do so, but said, 'If you are willing now to state your grievances, you have an opportunity of doing so.' The man stood up and trembled, and said, 'Mr Sutherland, it is the truth that you have said! It is the truth that we are crushed; but I am in such a position with the merchant that I dare not do it.'

Most families were secretive about any money they had. If they sold for cash items such as hay they would usually deliver them at night so that their merchant would not know. If they had money in a bank, likewise, they would not wish the merchant to know and would be likely to buy goods on credit rather than use any savings to pay off their debt. They would never know how far the merchant would support them in bad times and so keeping some reserves was a prudent policy. For his part the merchant would look out for any cash due to a customer if he was in debt and try to divert it to pay off the account. Mr Sutherland wanted credit to be abolished as the system encouraged people to go on buying to the limit of their credit without thought of tomorrow. Indeed if debtors were taken to court more often they would learn to be more careful with their spending. He thought that the merchants were too indulgent:

> **Do you think the merchants may be too tender to their customers?**
> No doubt of it, and that for the purposes which are explained by the gentlemen whose evidence I agree with. I condemn the system altogether, apart from the men who carry it on. I don't care who the men are; I defy men to be any better than what I find around me, but the system would make them what they are on both sides.

He had a comment about the high prices for goods in Shetland saying that he had all his supplies sent from the south twice a year, as he could not afford to buy in Shetland out of his stipend. His views were summed up in this exchange:

> **What remedy would you propose for the existing state of matters, and for the evils, which are alleged to exist?**
> My remedy would be to declare the present truck system to be penal.
>
> **What would you desire to be penal?**
> The truck system.
>
> **But the truck system, properly so called, is penal; and the question in this inquiry is, whether other things are to be included within the operation of the Acts which apply to the truck system?**
> Well, I mean that this system of carrying on business in Shetland should be declared to be penal.

> **Do you mean that you would make it penal to give long credit for shop goods?**
> I would make it penal to give any credit at all, and I would admit either party to give evidence against the other party for infringement of that statute, and would be to make all debts so incurred irrecoverable by any process of law. These three things are what I think would form a remedy for the present state of matters. At the same time, I am just as convinced that the merchant ought to live, and must live, and have a reasonable profit, as I am that the people should not pay more for their articles than they are worth.

Mid Yell

John Houston was a parochial schoolmaster in North Yell, who had also some experience in managing property. His views were rather more objective than those who were directly involved like the landlords, tenants and merchants. He had been in Shetland for 15 years and had been appointed by Major Cameron, when he came back from India, to look after his Yell properties. In his first year he had been a little surprised that when rent became due the fishermen had not been paid for their catches. There seemed to be an understanding between Cameron and the fish curer, who was Alexander Sandison, that the latter would settle the rent payment and debit the fishermen's accounts. It was also understood that if some of the men were overdrawing their earnings they would be restricted so that there was something left for the rents. After finishing his evidence he submitted some supplementary remarks in writing, which were illuminating:

> The collecting of rents and arrears of long standing, and the dividing and renting of farms, and other unavoidable accompaniments, placed me as a temporary link between landlord and tenant, and tended to give me a knowledge of Shetland affairs in general, as existing between landlord and tenant, between fish-curer and fishermen, and between merchant and customer. Although the dividing and letting of farms may not be considered relevant to the present inquiry into the truck system, I hold a decidedly opposite opinion. No doubt poverty is the foundation upon which the truck system has been

> reared, and may justly be called its *foster* parent; and the origin may be traced, very clearly too, to the subdividing of farms, it being the interest of the landlord-curer to accommodate as many fishermen as possible. In many districts, and on small properties where the landlord is storekeeper and curer, that system is still upheld, and *fostered* with pious care; while on many of the larger properties the proprietors are endeavouring to abolish it. The islands being over-populated, and the farms so insignificantly small, it follows as a result that the inhabitants have to depend on external aid, and throw themselves, although reluctantly it may be, into the arms of a system which, however honestly conducted, has a tendency to hamper their movements, to bereave them of independence, and to plunge parents and their children into debt, out of which they may never be able to extricate themselves. There is an antidote, but its application would require to be a work of time.

He was asked about the complaints made regularly by fishermen that they were not receiving a fair deal when the price for fish was fixed. It was his opinion that, although fishermen always seemed to be complaining, the origin was in the past. There may have been good cause to suspect the merchant then but the price was now fixed on a fair basis. He did, however, think that the men should be paid much earlier, say at the end of August when the season ends, although he was doubtful if the fishermen would find this acceptable. They may fear that they would not receive the best price as the merchant would not wish to risk losing when he came to sell later in the year.

Houston had some observations about the Edinburgh evidence, which agreed with another witness. He was quite sure that the black picture painted by those who gave evidence in the early stages in 1871 were speaking of the conditions in Shetland many years ago. "The evidence given in Edinburgh contained a great many facts highly coloured, and I may add somewhat exaggerated." He did, however, agree with John Walker that children should not be given credit as it introduces them to a system, from which they rarely escape. He had found, since he came to the islands, that the conditions had been improving regularly and particularly in the previous five years.

Houston expanded his thoughts in his later written observations. They sum up the situation very well about the fishcurers and fishermen:

> In my evidence I stated that at present I considered fishermen were generally well treated, and received as high a price as the curer could well afford; but at same time I *do not* consider the curer is acting judiciously. Under the present arrangement of prices, I can only view the curer and his fishermen in the light of a joint-stock company. The curer supplies boats and lines directly or indirectly. The fishermen give their labour and risk their lives, and when the summer fishing closes, the part the fishermen play in the speculation terminates. The curer prepares the fish for the market, disposes of them, and receives the cash. As the price to be paid to the fishermen is regulated by the market price, I consider it the bounden duty of the curer to lay before the fishermen, at settling, the *missive of sale*, that document being the common property of both parties, and more especially as three-fourths at least of the cash realized is understood to belong to the men. That, however, is not the practice; and hence the fishermen, naturally jealous, and still wincing under the scars of former years, are never satisfied; and I consider the curer in acting thus is reprehensible, and the fishermen justified in complaining, even when the curer is a sufferer. Were it made penal on the part of the curer to treat the bargain so, there would be less injustice done to himself, and less suspicion thrown around his integrity. Since the truck uproar has spread its wings on the Shetland blast, and breathed offensively in the faces even of Her Majesty's Government, it has been suggested by strangers that curers should pay their fishermen each time fish was delivered. That mode would not be advantageous to the fishermen. It would suit their interests better to be paid at the close of the fishing, on the same principle as is done by those engaged in the seal trade. At every station during the summer fishing there is a 'beach price,' and if that price was paid for the summer's catch at the close of the fishing it would put the fishermen in a position of buying with cash instead of being dependent on their curer's store for months after the fishing had closed. The residue of the price, which would be a mere trifle, would be paid them when the fish was sold, and the price known, on the same principal as oil money' in the seal trade. I have no doubt whatever but such a mode, if adopted, would tend to put a stop to

> the present and necessary facilities of drawing so largely upon the curer's store. The fisherman who has neither money nor credit must go to his curer's store, as he has no other alternative; but were he put in possession of his earnings at the close of the fishing, truck for a time would disappear from his individual horizon. I may mention that the hosier referred to in my evidence as having paid £90 in cash in a year to a party in the country for hosiery and yarn was Mr Robert Linklater, Lerwick; and I may further state that I have known Mr Robert Sinclair give £15 once on a £20 transaction of hosiery, etc.

Another cousin of Peter's, Andrew Blance, attended the Yell hearings. He had been on the ling fishing briefly but for the previous 15 years had been at the seal and whale fishing out of Lerwick. He had engaged with Hay & Co as he had "always found them very favourable towards me, and therefore I have always been inclined to go out from them". He was able to confirm that the whalers were paid in cash before the shipping master or the superintendent of customs, the oddly named Mr Gatherer. He would then go and settle his account at Hay & Co for goods supplied to his family in his absence. This practice had been in existence for only the previous five years. He said he did not know why the system had been changed and did not seem to be aware that it was the result of the application of the Truck Acts prohibiting the payment for work in goods.

Baltasound, Unst

The evidence given at Baltasound in Unst, the most northerly sitting, on 19 January 1872 demonstrates the hard work put into this investigation by the commissioner. He interviewed 21 witnesses and asked over a thousand questions. The pace throughout January was hectic. He held sittings on 22 days in eight different locations plus five days for travel. All this time he continued to ask penetrating questions and was able to recall answers by previous witnesses, which confirmed or contradicted those of the witness before him – a real 'tour de force'.

One of the witnesses in Baltasound was David Edmonstone, the father of Thomas Edmonstone, who gave evidence in Edinburgh a year earlier. David was factor to the estate owned by his son. Thomas had read an extract of a letter to the Commission, in which his father had written "the barter or truck system has been and is the curse of Shetland" and hoped that credit would be banned by law thus raising the people "from debt and miserly to comparative comfort and ease".

He again expressed the view that people would be more independent and self-reliant if they were entrusted with cash and had to manage their resources without being bailed out by a merchant from time to time. The man who is independent is usually a more satisfactory customer compared with the man in debt. Breaking the monopoly of the merchants' shops would also create more competition and bring prices down.

He described the houses on Unst. They were 28ft by 12ft, i.e. 336 square feet, and 7ft high with two rooms, built of stone and clay, harled with lime and covered with thatch and turf. Most had at least one chimney and some two. Glazed windows were common, although some of the older houses still had none.

David claimed that the link between fishing and farming was essential as fishing did not produce enough income and was severely restricted in winter due to the weather. Larger boats, which might withstand the winter storms better out at sea, were no good near the coast as they were not as manoeuvrable as the sixareens.

One of David's tenants, Peter Nicholson of Haroldswick, was interviewed. He had fished for John Spence but had given up the sea three years previously. He had since then concentrated on his land and some casual work for John Spence. He was one of the few who dealt mostly in cash and had only a small account with Spence & Co. He charged goods and settled once a year like the fishermen. This man clearly was able to live off the proceeds of his farm demonstrating that farming could be viable at the time.

Later, John Laurenson of Burrafirth appeared and explained that he had for several years fished for Spence & Co and before that for the Edmonstones. His arrangements were similar to other fishermen and he did not feel he was bound to fish for the local merchant or landlord. Like the others he had really no alternative unless he engaged with a merchant some distance away. It was much more convenient to deal with the local man and draw supplies from him also. He was unusual in claiming that, although he did not have a pass book, he could remember the quantities and prices of all the items he had bought from the shop when his account was read out to him at the annual settlement. It is not clear if the examiner believed him!

He claimed that he would like to be paid in cash for his fish so that he could feel free to purchase from other merchants if the price and quality were better. However, he was reluctant to take such a radical step, perhaps unhappy about the risk of leaving the comfortable and secure arrangement with a merchant who would bail him out in a bad season. By contrast Charles Gray, a retired mason in the chromate of iron quarries, was paid in cash and paid cash for all his needs. He was questioned about the general practice and said that many years ago lines were given for purchasing goods in a merchant's shop but so far as he knew the system had almost died out.

Three of the partners of Spence & Co appeared and expressed some forthright views. Alexander Sandison had the longest period on the stand having to respond to 227 questions. From 1868 Mr Sandison had acted for John Walker for most of the properties he controlled on Unst by taking a lease for 12 years. He confirmed that there was no obligation to fish for him as leaseholder and that the tenants were at liberty to deliver their fish to anyone. However, he ran fishing stations, took delivery of fish and had a shop supplying goods. As he was the biggest operator, it was inevitable that he was the first and most convenient choice of merchant to deal with. Furthermore, as Spence & Co were acting for the landlords and had control of the peats, tenants were obviously going to careful about offending them. On the other hand the price given for fish was better than the many merchants in Shetland and, from what Mr Sandison said he appeared to be a benevolent factor and trader. He had been able to persuade all the crofters to improve their land in accordance with the lease conditions and, as the leaseholder, he had power to remove a tenant if he did not carry out improvements under the rules. At that time he had not had occasion to remove anyone or even threaten to do so. The clearing of the ground of stones, draining and introducing crop rotation had benefited all concerned although he confessed that it had been an uphill job. Gradually the people realised that using their spare time in winter was producing results.

Sandison was questioned at length about the possibility of full-time fishing and gave one of the clearest and convincing answers presented to the inquiry:

> **Do you think it would not be possible in Shetland for the men to follow the occupation of fishermen all the year round?**
> I have given that subject most earnest thought. At one time I thought it might, but latterly I have come to the conclusion that it is not possible. In the first place, we have no fresh fish market here, and it is impossible to get the fish into the south market in a fresh state when they would command a high price. Then, in the winter time the weather is so broken, and the seas round this coast so boisterous, that it is almost impossible to go to the deep sea in boats; and the fish that are caught near the shores in the sounds and bays are in such limited quantity that they would not be nearly sufficient to meet the man's daily wants. From the farm, however, he has sufficient potatoes and milk for his family; and even on the smallest farms he has, I should say, six months meal on the average.
> **But if the fishermen were supplied with a different kind of boats, such as are used in other parts of Scotland, say of 32ft keel, such as are used at Wick, could they not go to sea in winter?**
> I am afraid our fishermen would not take very kindly to these boats.
> ***Perhaps* not at first, but would they not do so after a certain period of apprenticeship?**
> I think I would back six of our men against six of the Wick men in their respective boats, and I would expect our men to come on shore when the Wick men would be drowned. I think the Wick boats are much too heavy in a sea, and they are much more in danger of filling than our light skiffs are. I remember on one occasion, on the north of Unst, when some four boats were out, and a gentleman's yacht was near them dredging shells, he thought they could never come ashore, and kindly ran down among them, thinking to render the assistance but when he reached them he found they were far drier than he was. He came in with some of his bulwarks washed away, while they got safe ashore.

Don't you think the weather is just as severe where these Wick and Buckie boats fish as it is in this quarter?
I believe it is as severe, but I don't know if the tides and currents are as rapid and strong, because they have a longer stretch of coast. Off any land end, the current is very strong and the sea runs very high, and I think that nearly three-fourths of all the accidents that have occurred in Shetland have occurred in crossing these springs of tide, strong currents going right against the wind, just inland, as off the point of Unst, or the point of Sumburgh. It is not on the ocean that our boats would be lost, but in taking the land and crossing the tides near headlands.
If it were not for these dangerous tide-ways, would it be possible for the men to go off to the haaf in winter if they had proper boats for the purpose?
They could go off a certain distance, but the day is very short here, and I don't think they would have much chance with the long lines in a day of about eight hours.

He was unusual in claiming that, on average, he paid about two thirds of the price of fish delivered in cash and the rest in goods. However, settlement was still done once a year although he was very much in favour of the men being paid monthly or fortnightly in cash with the price being fixed at the beginning of the season. He had experimented with such a system and found at settling time that he could afford to pay a higher price than that agreed at the start and he paid the higher amount but would not have paid a lower price if the market had gone the other way.

Mr Sandison's main reservation about a change in the system was the problem of some of the families, who had no savings, being in debt at the changeover and being unable to pay them off. He illustrated the point very graphically:

Do you think the fishermen under that new system would not be able to get credit to a certain extent?
I don't see how some of them could. For instance, take the year 1869. In 1868 the fishings were almost a failure. Our total catch in Unst and Yell amounted £1607, which could not average much over

> £4, 10s. to each fisherman. That year we imported meal and flour to the amount of £1824, cost price per invoice; we paid in cash for rents to Major Cameron, Mr. Edmonstone, Lord Zetland, and others, £1600; and we expended on fishing-boats and fish-curing materials £780, being a gross amount of outlay of £4223 against the fishing, the return for which, as said, was only £1607.

The following year, 1869, the crops failed and Spence & Co imported £2300 worth of meal and oat seed and £173 of potatoes and in addition paid about the same amount in rents on behalf of the tenants. This left many families with considerably increased debts. He was pleased to tell the inquiry that these were being paid off quite quickly due to more successful fishing and better crops.

Mr Sandison reflected that, when he was in business elsewhere in Shetland as far back as 1860, debt was a common feature. If a tenant was not given an advance the landlord's agent would threaten to remove him from the fish merchant and place him with someone else. He realised that to go on giving out advances, mainly for rent, he would be ruined. The threat was actually made to the tenant, who then had to approach the merchant to ask for the advance and neither the factor nor landlord had the courtesy to speak to the merchant directly.

This evidence indicates that the situation had been improving albeit very slowly. Many of the more able men had managed to improve their lot, control their affairs themselves and deal with the merchants on an equal footing. Certainly Peter Blanch had established his independence, although some of his cousins were still struggling under the traditional system.

A change from the old system to one of cash payments did not appear to be easy without causing considerable suffering among the families who had no savings. There was no other employment available in Unst except at the chromate ore quarries and there men were employed on an annual basis leaving no vacancies for fishermen in the winter. The only hope, in Mr Sandison's opinion, was to continue to improve the production of crops, which would provide enough food for the population of Unst, at that time about 3,000. He estimated that this would take about another six years. There was another possibility for providing winter work and that was if the government were to improve the harbours and build more roads. This would also ease the movement of goods and make it possible for families to have a greater choice of shopkeepers to buy from, as they would be more accessible.

There was large trade in kelp on Unst employing about 130 women and producing some 40 tons. Spence & Co handled another 20 tons from Yell. They paid a price of 4s per cwt and could sell it sometimes for as much as 5s. The kelp was delivered to the merchant in one or two ton lots presumably by a pony and cart either owned by the family or borrowed from a neighbour. The women usually took goods in exchange rather than cash.

Some useful information was offered about boats and it is clear that the quality of many of them was not good. The work of the carpenters seemed to vary enormously with quite a few boats proving unseaworthy in their first year. A boat cost £20 to build but replacement of sails and other items could take the total cost over its life up to £32. The hire was only 48s a year or 8s a man, which made the hiring unprofitable. The good boats would last for 12 years and sometimes a little longer.

Mr Sandison concluded his evidence in a letter with his strongly held views about the problems of the Shetland economy:

> In all my experience find the best farmer (I speak of the crofters) is never the worst fisher, and is generally out of debt; while the bad and slovenly farmer, though an extra good fisherman, often falls behind, indeed generally so. Of late I have come to the conclusion that the time spent at the winter fishing is a loss to the crofter, as I do think he can be more profitably employed on his farm, at least until he puts it in proper order. Not to enlarge, I consider the land question a more serious one than the truck for Shetland. Get our crofter fishermen to feel and take an interest in the soil they cultivate; induce them to habits of constant activity on their land, when not fully employed at fishing; get them, by whatever way, to take a pleasure in rendering the waste places of their farm productive of food for man and beast; give them better houses; let them have every reasonable encouragement from their proprietors, with patient continuous oversight by those competent to give direction and advice: I would hope for more from this than all the 'Truck Acts' in the world.

The next partner to appear was William Gilbert Mouat. Like Alexander Sandison, he had been in business on his own account until they went into partnership with John Spence to form Spence & Co in 1868. He managed the business at Baltasound, which also included the business in Haroldswick previously run by John Spence before the formation of the new firm. He was questioned at length about the transactions in the ledgers, which he produced for the examiner. Most of his suppliers were in Aberdeen and goods were shipped direct presumably by the ship, *Earl of Zetland*, which serviced the north eastern isles.

John Spence was the last partner on the stand and said that he agreed with everything his two partners said. In regard to the thoughts about changing the system of trading, he read out a letter sent to him by a member of the firm in January 1870, because it expressed the views of everyone in the company:

> Dear Sirs, I have often spoken to you about adopting a cash system in all our dealings with the people but none of you seemed to think it would do. I of course would not press it in the meantime, though I am always more convinced that it would be a much better system than the present, and we should be gainers by it to a very great extent, if wrought as it should be; and, depend upon it, it will have to come in, and that not long to the time, whether we will or not; so I would advise you to consider over it more than you have done. It will take no more capital, but even less than the present system does.
>
> If after further consideration, you still think it would not do, could it not then be possible that the price of fish could be fixed at the commencement of the fishing? Be assured that we will be forced into this, whether we will or not; and certainly it would be the proper way. The price of everything else that we deal in is generally fixed or agreed upon when the transaction is made, and why not do so with fish? We do it with winter fish, and what is to hinder us to do it with the summer ones? In no other part of the world that we know of is there such a system as we have. Look at the herring-curers south: I believe herrings would never keep at such a high price were it not that the price is fixed at the first. If we were to do the same with our fish, I have not the least hesitation in saying that we should have

> them all away and into cash as fast as they could be dried, because we should never keep them on hand when we could get a safe price for them; and the fact that we had got a certain price before we could be safe, would prompt us the more to seek to obtain it, and buyers would come to terms more quickly; indeed, the moment we agreed with the fishermen, we could at same time almost enter into a contract with a buyer or buyers for all our catch. It is often seen what a disagreeable thing it is to keep a large parcel of fish hanging on in the face of a fluctuating market, the chance being oftener against us than in our favour; and fish, in particular, being such a perishing article, the risk is very often great. Many other things could be brought in support of our fixing the price of green fish when the fishing begins. If you do not think we could begin to it alone, it could only be a trial to correspond with all the other curers, and see if they would not join with Hay & Co., Adie, Anderson, Pole & Hoseason, and any other you know of, and make the proposal. Have a meeting of all the curers, say at Voe, or wherever it might be thought best, and try the thing. I am fully persuaded that circumstances, and that not long to the time, will compel us to it, if not to the cash system.
>
> Notice around you even and see how things are tending, and see how opposition is creeping in — of course against us. The old system we keep is the cause of it, to a good extent at least. Mr Sandison should correspond with some of the other curers; or could you not ask Mr Adie to come to Unst? I think we often spoke of doing that before. I suppose he is friendly enough to us. I am almost sure he would join us in the movement, and Pole & Hoseason would do it, also Mr Henderson. I trust you will give this matter your consideration, if it should come no further. Shetland is behind it a long long way, and a new kind of political economy is needed for it; and why should we not make the trial? When we formed into a company, everybody was made to understand that there would be improvements in many things – which I hope there is – but we should go forward, and not stand still.

Here was a visionary who saw that the time was overdue for change. He was a real businessman who recognised that the change he proposed would benefit the firm and also the tenants. It is a pity that

Mr Spence did not reveal the author. Nothing came of this and it is significant that the firm of Spence & Co was wound up in 1874 without taking the opportunity before them.

Mr Spence was very much against having too many small shops. Although they would guarantee more competition he claimed that they would look after their own interests and ignore the interests of the community as a whole. He preferred what he called co-operation and did not regard such an arrangement as a monopoly. He felt that the big firms with less painful disruption could handle the transition to a cash system. The examiner was not convinced and probably had in mind that "he would say that wouldn't he" and continued to question him on the subject. He had not been in good health and his attitude seemed to be that everyone was against his firm. He reckoned that he could sort out the tricky transition from credit to cash if all the tenants traded only with him so that he could work closely with them. He remained convinced that competition would do a lot of harm claiming that the country was too poor to survive it.

Several of the merchants reflected after the event about what they had said in evidence. Spence wanted to put the record straight and in a letter to the commissioner he explained his thoughts more fully, fearing that he had left the impression that he approved of a monopoly, which he undoubtedly had! Some of the passages make a case for his point of view:

> There is nothing in a dealing way I so much dislike as a monopoly. What I wished to be understood was, that no number of small dealers, however willing, working as they do, can improve Shetland as it would really need; but that in order to develop the resources of the country thoroughly, it must be done by quite different means. There is no doubt but that a change is needed, but it should be merged into with caution, or it will do harm to some class. Shetland appears to be so far behind, that the people must serve an apprenticeship, as it were, to any change for their good. It occurred to me that some good might be done by all the dealers in Unst amalgamating, and by their united capitals and efforts carrying on business and the fishings on a sort of co-operative system; but it did not seem to be in accordance with a

free-trade system, and was never tried, though, if properly conducted, I have no doubt it could have done some good.

In reference to the cash system, you would see in the letter I read, and left with you, the views I have held. We have hitherto, for various reasons found some difficulty in adopting it fully, but we trust, ere long, to get it fairly introduced. One hindrance to us getting it fairly wrought is owing to the way we are bound to the proprietors for the fishermen's rents. This also appears to those who do not know the nature of the business, to be a monopoly; because while we are thus bound we are compelled to a certain extent, to restrict such men who, from extravagant habits or other causes, cannot preserve their rents. It cannot be supposed that to such men we can hand over money – perhaps to be made a bad use of; and then, when rent time comes, have nothing to get from them, and often not having got any rent for boats and fishing materials. This is one thing in which there is great room for improvement in Shetland.

As a member of a firm having the principal business in this land, I would beg to state that our mode of dealing seems to be greatly misunderstood by many; and it would be most desirable that an impartial investigation into the books and transactions of every other dealer in the island should be made, when, I have no doubt, matters would look something different. With regard to the fishermen, they are not bound to fish, and they were never told so. I, for one, have urged upon them to improve their farms, so as to enable them to be independent of fishing, which I consider to be a most dangerous employment in such small boats. We pay them cash whenever they want it and have it to get. We do not monopolize our dealings. Could a proper investigation be made in other shops, I can venture to say that, on the whole, we sell cheaper than any other. Besides the other dealers in the island, the steamer runs twice a week in summer, and once in winter, from Lerwick to here; and if the people wish to avail themselves of it, they can get their supplies as easily from there as here. A public roup, advertised all over Shetland, is held once every year for the sale of cattle and ponies, where there is perfect freedom to buy and sell. There are many things we do for the people, which are not generally known. I shall only mention one thing, to show what we have to combat with. 1868 and 1869 the fishings were small,

> and the crops so blighted, that seed and meal had to be imported, and given out on credit to a great many, or else they would have starved. The effects of these two years tell against both the men and us for some time, but such occur occasionally; and it is dealers, standing as we do, that feel it most. We hold, as you are aware, a lease of a large portion of this island, and we are bound to see certain improvements carried out, which, being new here raises a hostile spirit against us by those who are not inclined to see our island made better. We try to introduce any other improvements that can be thought of, feeling assured that if we can get them accomplished, the people will be in much better circumstances than they are. While we are pressing these improvements, small dealers draw away the means of the people, preventing both them and us from getting so fast on as we would otherwise do; and while we are using all reasonable means to try to get the indolent not to sell what, of their own farm produce, they really need themselves, as is sometimes done, the report is often got up that we want to monopolize the business of the island, when there is nothing of the kind ever thought of by us.

Gilbert Williamson appeared during this session and was immediately in trouble. The citation handed to him was addressed to "Peter Williamson, storekeeper, Haroldswick" and he was in doubt that it referred to him in spite of the fact that there was no other storekeeper in Haroldswick named Williamson. On receiving another summons that morning he thought that he did not need to attend as it had arrived too late. The examiner was not pleased and gave him a hard time. He was questioned about hosiery purchased by Mrs Spence at her home and paid for by the issue of notes on the shop run by Mr Williamson. He had been asked in the citation to bring with him the notes for these deals but had not done so. The exchange continued:

> **Why did you not bring them?**
> Because they were not mine to bring.
>
> **Whose were they?**
> Spence & Co.'s.
>
> **Why did you not ask leave to bring them?**
> Because the members of the firm were all here.

Could you not have brought them with you, and asked leave of the partners of the firm here to produce them?
That never occurred to my mind.

Do you make the same answer with regard to the citation to produce all papers, books, and accounts, showing the nature of the company's dealings with fishermen or knitters?
Yes.

You could not bring these here without asking leave of the members of the firm to produce them
I could not ask their leave, because they were here.

Could you not have brought the books here and asked permission then to produce them?
I did not think it was right for me to remove them from the office until I had asked leave to do so. There is one of the books here, the fisherman's ledger, which has been spoken to by Mr Mouat.

How was that book brought here?
Mr Mouat sent for it.

Why did you come here yourself without asking leave of the members of the firm?
Because I was summoned.

Was it not just as necessary for you to ask leave to come yourself as to ask leave to bring the books?
No, I came when I was sent for.

Let me recommend you in future to pay more attention to a legal citation when it is served upon you, or you will get into trouble. I cannot allow you any expenses for attending here, in consequence of the way in which you have behaved.

The following specimen of the lines issued by Mrs Spence was afterwards produced:- 'Haroldswick, 13th Novr. 1871 Messrs. Spence & Co. pay Andrina Boyne the sum of one shilling. 1s. J. SPENCE' The line is crossed, 'Entd. G.W.'

Rev William Smith was summoned to Baltasound. He had been in the parish for three years and was quite convinced that the credit system had a deteriorating effect on the character of the people. He had previously been in Orkney where there was a cash system in operation and it was definitely much better. He saw little evidence of saving in Shetland although he accepted that some had money deposited in the banks. However, they kept that secret so that they could extend their credit with the local merchant without having to pay it off from their savings. In addition people often sold butter, eggs and stock to small traders for cash while still in debt to the large merchant. There has to be some sympathy for John Spence's attitude in view of this evidence, which came up several times. The root of the problem was the embedded lack of trust between merchants and the families, which no one appeared to be able to break down. William Smith stated that, like other ministers, he did not buy his supplies locally but had them shipped in to him from the mainland where he obtained better prices and superior quality.

He went on to agree with David Edmonstone that the quality of housing in Shetland was poor and not as good as in other parts of the country. He was concerned that there was a need to separate the sexes to avoid the amount of illegitimacy and immorality that prevailed. Many houses still did not have windows and maintenance was poor although a cash system engendering a greater self-reliance could result in people improving their dwellings themselves. Another problem with the barter system was the shortage of coins in merchant's shops. There was not sufficient currency in general circulation but no doubt the banks would have supplied it if the system had been changed.

Lerwick

Mr Guthrie, the commissioner, took the last few witnesses in Lerwick at the end of January and then intended to leave for Kirkwall and Edinburgh. In the event he was delayed by bad weather and decided to add a few more witnesses whom he heard on 5 and 6 February. In these sessions he was able to hear from the larger merchants in the islands to complete the picture.

William Robertson was principal clerk to Mr Joseph Leask, who was a landowner, merchant, shipowner and agent and also had large property holdings in Lerwick. He had volunteered to appear to comment on some of the previous evidence. He was obviously upset at the exaggerated statements made in a report by Mr RGC Hamilton of the Board of Trade, which had been submitted to the inquiry in Edinburgh a year earlier. Mr Robertson stated that it was just not true that the truck system in Shetland was far worse than anywhere else in the United Kingdom. There was a lengthy exchange with the examiner about what was meant by the word "truck". Instead of being able to counter the argument that truck existed, he simply resorted to denying the accusation.

Robertson was on firmer ground when he denied that almost every fisherman, his wife and members of his family were in debt and claimed that many had considerable savings in the various banks in Lerwick. He listed these and it is interesting to realise how many there were – the Union, Commercial and National Banks together with the Post of Savings and Seamen's Savings Banks. He also denied Mr Hamilton's accusation that merchants somehow managed to delay payment of the whaler's wages until they were in debt again. He had stated in his evidence, presented in writing in Edinburgh, "when he does pay to the man the balance of wages due to him before the superintendent, the man has no option but to hand it all back to the agent at once". He maintained that the Leask procedures were entirely fair as were those of the other merchants in Lerwick. The examiner played down the significance of Mr Hamilton's statement but received a robust response:

> **You will observe that it is not alleged that any agent in Lerwick does so. All the allegation which Mr Hamilton makes is that the opportunity exists?**
>
> I deny that there is such an opportunity, because Shetland men in general are very intelligent. They are not at all what they have been represented to be. They are a very sharp, acute, intelligent lot of people, and they are perfectly able to take care, and do take very good care, to protect themselves, and to make sure that their accounts are just. I further think they are very provident, as can be proved by the amount of deposits in the banks. I don't think they are an extravagant

> people at all. In my opinion they are a very careful, active, energetic, intelligent people, as a rule, much more so than will be found among the same class of people in other parts of the United Kingdom.

On the question of whether truck does exist in Shetland, the examiner pointed out that workmen in other parts of the country are paid fortnightly or monthly and could spend the money in any way they wanted. In Shetland the practice is for fishermen to have accounts with the merchant to whom they delivered the fish and leave all his money matters to him. He did not think that was a sign of intelligence or independence. Mr Robertson, in response, said that it was utterly impossible for the fishermen to be paid weekly or fortnightly. The exchange goes on:

> **Why?**
> Because the fishermen are in a sort of partnership with their employers. For instance, in the Faroe fishing it is a joint speculation betwixt the men and the owner. The men supply their time and labour, and the owner supplies the vessel and other things, and the men cannot get their share of the proceeds until the fish are dried and sold. It is quite impossible for the fish merchant to settle with them every week or every fortnight unless they have been paid by wages. Of course, if they were paid by wages, the curer could settle at short intervals with the men, or with some one on their behalf when they were away.

This was the justification for the credit system but, of course, the fact that Shetland could not sell its fish fresh was also a major factor. A fresh fish market was available in the highly populated parts of the country but until transport speeded up in the 20th century, Shetland could not supply them with fresh fish.

Mr Robertson also referred to the evidence of George Smith given in Edinburgh in 1871. He was Sheriff Clerk, resident in Lerwick and made some statements about the effect of the barter or credit system in Shetland undermining the independence of the people. Several witnesses had made this point and a number of Shetlanders responded like Mr Robertson:

> Mr Smith says he considers the system of barter to be hurtful to the independence of the people very much. I deny that the people are not independent. I consider them to be as independent as any people in the kingdom. Mr Smith also says, 'they don't know the value of money, and they don't know how to eke it out, or make it last. They are very improvident in that way, and a man's energies are entirely destroyed.' I maintain that the Shetland people know very well the value of money, and they also know how to eke it out and make the most of it. I also say they are not improvident or extravagant, but the reverse.

He was asked if he would be surprised that a large proprietor in Shetland had said that fishermen required to be treated like children (it was John Bruce Jr in a written statement to the enquiry), Mr Robertson said:

> I would be surprised to hear that, and I would not agree with it at all. I have found them all to be very intelligent and very sharp, and perfectly able to take care of themselves.

Robertson must have spent a lot of time reading up the evidence heard in Edinburgh. Having taken Mr Hamilton and Mr Smith to task, he set about John Walker. He was particularly scathing about John Walker's assertion that it cost 8s to 10s to rear a pound of Shetland wool. Declaring the estimate glaringly incorrect, he said that it cost only 2d to 3d on the basis that the only cost is 6d per annum for grazing rent for a sheep divided by 2–3lbs of wool carried by each. He went on to say that he did not want to take up time by going over the evidence any further but said that he had to disagree with almost all of John Walker's statements.

An important point was raised in connection with the role of the agent in finding crews for the whaling and sealing voyages. The Merchant Shipping Act provided that

> if any unauthorised person engages or supplies any mate, seaman, midshipman or apprentice to be entered on board any ship in the United Kingdom, he will be liable to be prosecuted; and if convicted,

> to a penalty of £20 for each offence" and also "the only person authorised to engage or supply . . . are the following: owner, master or the mate of the ship or some person who is a bona fide servant and in the constant employ of the owner; the superintendent of a Government Mercantile Marine Office or an agent licensed by the Board of Trade".

Mr Robertson had the answer! Mr Leask was part owner of all the ships for which he acts as agent except one and the men are always recruited in the presence of the master. What happened before that point, such as buying kit, was a matter between the merchant and the man.

He went on to give a description of the sealing and whaling activities in which Leasks were involved as agents. He explained that at that time the majority of men were engaged for sealing with only about 30 per cent going on to the whaling. This involved seven ships for sealing and four for whaling. The merchant took a risk on the success of these voyages, as they had to lend new recruits money to kit them out. If the voyage was unsuccessful these men were unable to pay off the debts. For that reason the older more experienced men were preferred. These men were also preferred by the masters, particularly for the sealing, although they would take younger ones on the whaling ships. Contrary to Mr Hamilton's claim that the agents favoured giving employment to those in debt to them, they were rarely seen again, although the agents would like to have had the opportunity to find employment for them so that the debts could be paid off.

Mr Hamilton had made a strong point that those who were able to pay for their outfits had to buy them from the agent employing them otherwise they would be marked men from then on not only by the agent but also by others as there were more men looking for jobs than there were berths. Mr Robertson said that that was nonsense and that in his experience over 19 years there was often a shortage of men resulting in ships leaving short-handed. Furthermore, those who bought their outfits elsewhere were usually good men and Leasks were glad to be able to engage them.

James Pottinger appeared in order to inform the commissioner of his displeasure at being charged an extra £1 for peats because he had two chimneys in his cottage. He had refused to pay and Hays, the landlords, charged his father with whom he lived. As it happened he was a useful witness in being able to describe the way in which the Faroe and Iceland voyages were organised. Apparently the Faroe fishing was earlier in the summer and Iceland followed. The smacks returned to Lerwick to reprovision for Iceland instead of going on from Faroe. This arrangement obviously involved much more sailing but the boats were not big enough to take supplies for both voyages as well accommodating the catches.

William Robertson was recalled and produced a sample contract for Faroe fishing. It was for the *Royal Tar*, a smack rigged craft, owned by Joseph Leask. It had a tonnage of 41 and a crew of 10 men and four boys. It was unfortunately destroyed by fire in 1880. If a voyage to Iceland was contemplated, it would start in August after the Faroe trip was over and another contract would be drawn up. For Iceland the crew were paid wages and did not share in the catch. The Faroe document was fairly short:

> We, the undersigned, hereby agree to prosecute the cod and other fishings, in the said vessel wherever required by the master or owner during the fishing season of 1871, that is, from the time we are requested to join the vessel until the end of August if required, it being understood that one half of the net proceeds of the fishing belong to the owner of the vessel, and the other half to be divided among the crew in the proportions set opposite their respective names; the owner supplying the crew with 1lb. of bread per man per day.

The Faroe fishing started around 1852 and after some years it became very popular and the number of vessels increased considerably. The catches were worth more than those from the haaf fishing and this may explain why so many men were able to begin to pay their way, save money and escape the trap of being constantly in debt to the merchants.

Another employee of Leask, Andrew Jamieson, appeared. He was a clerk and had been with Leask for 19 years. This man had been responsible for the engagement and settling with the seamen employed in the Greenland whale fishing. He was questioned at some length about the settlement at the Custom House in front of the superintendent. The examiner clearly wanted to find out if Mr Hamilton's assertions were correct. He discovered that, indeed, some of the Leask accounts were settled at the same time as wages were paid. This was done with the full agreement of the men. The others were settled back at the Leask office. They were not required to come immediately to settle and were left to suit themselves. Later the practice of settling at the Custom House ceased, because the shipping master objected and thereafter all accounts were settled at the office. Mr Jamieson stated that the men did not need to be reminded to settle their accounts as they always did so without prompting.

Mr Jamieson was recalled two days later with further comments on Hamilton's report. There were several points raised by the report that he particularly criticised:

> There was great difficulty in paying off the men in a reasonable time after they were landed. When the men were landed they preferred to go home and come into Lerwick for settlement when it suited them. This was the general practice for the Greenland trade and Hamilton had criticised the agents for breaking the provisions of the Merchant Shipping Act. It provided for the master or owner to pay wages within five days after the men were discharged.
>
> Hamilton claimed that the agents were all shopkeepers and most were landowners or land agents. Jamieson commented that there were only four agents and two did not have a land interest.
>
> He also stated that many of the men are utterly unable to provide themselves with proper clothing and it was common for allotments of wages to be made in favour of the agents. Jamieson denied that this was the case in Leask's business and was fairly certain that it was not done elsewhere and in any case the inability to pay for clothing applied chiefly to the young hands on their first voyages.

Later Mr Jamieson was grilled, quite aggressively, about the possibility that money due to be paid in cash from the Shipwrecked Mariners'

Fund in the case of a loss of a boat was in general practice credited to his account to reduce his debt, which might have included the cost of the boat. After 30 questions on the subject he admitted that it might have been done in the odd case where the man wished to use the money for that purpose and that it was his decision alone.

Dr Robert Cowie was a native of Lerwick and had lived all his life there apart from the time he went south for his education. He was asked first of all about the barter system in the hosiery trade and was adamant that it was detrimental to the health of the people with little means. The knitters, as the inquiry had heard from others, were not paid in cash but had to take goods for the items they sold. Furthermore they were not allowed to take food so their knitted garments were exchanged for fine materials for dressmaking. The result was that the women were flashily dressed but had an inadequate diet. They would also take cotton under-garments in exchange, which were not as warm as the woollen ones they previously made for their own use.

The issue of immorality and prostitution was raised and Dr Cowie reckoned that women of poorer means, who wore fine clothes, were more likely to 'go astray'. He was asked to explain why, if immorality in Lerwick was as bad as other towns, the illegitimacy rate in Shetland was lower than in many parts of Scotland. He suggested that the registration system was not always very accurate partly due to the registrar taking a broad view of what the examiner called 'ante nuptial fornication'. At this point Dr Cowie asked to be excused further discussion of such a delicate matter!

Many of the witnesses had commented on the high consumption of very strong tea by Shetlanders, which was both expensive and not good for them. Dr Cowie, however, thought that most of the country people enjoyed good health compared to those in the town. In the country areas meal, usually in the form of scones, was part of the staple diet along with fish and potatoes, whereas in the town loaf bread was more common. Porridge did not seem to feature at all.

There was considerable discussion about the main disadvantage of the long credit system being the fact that most men do not know from month to month if they had any means. As the merchant handled practically all their monetary transactions, they did not know how much would be owing to them at the annual settlement if anything at all. If they had money in a bank it would be kept for exceptional purposes and would never be used for paying off a debt with a merchant as long as more credit was available. Dr Cowie summed up the effect neatly by saying that "the system fosters a dependent, time-serving, deceitful disposition and cripples enterprise". On the other hand he thought that the people were intelligent and well bred but lacking in ambition to improve their position by producing better crops and improving their house. He praised the character of Shetland men as being sober and steady and commented that shipmasters had a preference for the seamen and often put into an advertisement: "Shetland men preferred".

Towards the end of the Lerwick sessions George Jamieson appeared. He was a farmer in North Roe on the Busta Estate. He had previously been on a Hay & Co property and had fished for them until he refused to go on a boat with some old men. He looked after two paupers and he was paid money for their upkeep. This was paid to Hay & Co's local branch and he drew goods against it. He was intent on portraying Hays in a poor light for he claimed that they would not give him the upkeep in cash and also that he was obliged to fish for them when on their land. He was questioned at length and kept changing his story as the questions became more persistent. The examiner clearly did not believe him and in the end said to him "you have given your evidence in such a manner that I cannot allow you any expenses for attending here".

William BM Harrison was a partner in Harrison & Sons, who were extensively engaged in the Faroe fishing. A few days later another partner, John Harrison, appeared and they were able to give a different view of things as they had no land connections and, therefore, their opinions were slightly more objective.

As previous evidence had informed the inquiry, the proceeds of the Faroe fishing were shared equally between the owner and the crew. More precise information was produced about the deductions from the gross proceeds. In addition to the curing expenses, deductions were made for a master's premium of 10s per ton and the mate's premium of 2s 6d per ton. The men received 8lbs of bread per week and 9d per score of fish caught by each man, the cost of which was shared by the owners and the crew. The owners were entitled to deduct also a five per cent commission on the whole, presumably the gross, proceeds of the voyage. Sometimes the catches were not up to normal and the commission would either be reduced or not taken in order to make sure that the men realised as much as other merchants were paying.

Very few of the men who fished for Harrisons were in debt at the end of the season, although when they were paid as much as £20 at settlement they would almost immediately buy some goods and run up a debt. When asked why they did not use the cash to pay for the goods, they would reply that they preferred to keep the money and let the debt stand for another year. This was very astute but it is astonishing that the merchant accepted it. Harrisons did not charge more for credit and would not sell cheaper for cash and it appears that the profit margins were, therefore, quite generous.

William Harrison considered that a cash system would be better for the fish curers and that was his preference. So far as the fishermen were concerned about two thirds of the men would be able to manage well enough but the remainder would not be able to survive the winter and spring without money. Without a benefit in paying cash it seems hardly likely that the men would see any advantage in the abolition of credit. On the other hand a more productive croft producing income from stock and crop sales would have produced a more regular cash flow and undoubtedly some of the families operated this way. Also, where a cash system was in operation it is likely that the shops would have allowed weekly credit to regular customers, as was the case with independent grocers until the arrival of supermarkets and credit cards.

Harrison had offered some men the chance to be employed on a weekly wage basis but that was not acceptable, because the men thought that they would be missing out on a better return by catching and selling the fish. Those who were good fishermen considered themselves to be in business and their instinct was to maximise the catch and look for the best price for it. What was missing was working capital; a necessity for any enterprise. No business ever has an even flow of income and there are always periods when more cash is going out than is coming in. With working capital these entrepreneurial fishermen would have been able to optimise their profits by carefully controlling their costs and seeking the best price for their fish. In a sense the merchants provided the working capital for the men by giving credit.

The other requirement for a more open and competitive market would have been a fresh fish market. At the time, however, transport was not adequate to bring the fish to the consumers. Nowhere in the evidence given is there any reason given for the cured fish being sold at the end of the season instead of regularly during the season. The only obvious explanation, referred to earlier, is that Shetland was at a competitive disadvantage by being so far away from centres of population compared with the mainland fishing ports. They probably also found that the price rose in the winter when supplies were running short.

Harrison made a surprising statement when he disclosed that, although he had no difficulty in finding men to man the firm's boats, he had found that some men had been hindered from engaging with them as their landlords wished to have their services or those of their sons. The examiner pointed out that previous evidence indicated that the landlord preferred his tenants to go to the ling fishing but if they wished to take part in the Faroe fishing, they raised no objections. John was adamant that the landlord's wishes prevailed as he had the power to warn the tenants off their properties.

He was asked about the relationship between men in debt and their fishing abilities and said that the deciding factor was the opinion of the captains of the vessels. If a man was no good he would not be employed and, if in debt, he would rather write it off than have someone who was not a good fisherman. John Walker, in his evidence in Edinburgh, had stated that merchants liked to have men in debt so that they were obliged to go on fishing for them. This was considered erroneous and John Harrison reckoned that, in his experience, fishermen in debt did not exert themselves so much as the other men who were free of debt. Those merchants who operated on that principle no doubt felt they have a hold over the debtor but it was simply a hold over an unwilling slave.

Harrison confirmed what others had said, that the crofts if properly worked, could support families during the winter when fishing was at its lowest in the year. In this the tenants had an advantage over those who lived in the town, who were dependent on finding casual work in the winter.

The collector of customs in Lerwick was one of the last witnesses to be called on 31 January. He had the rather unusual name of John Gatherer and was the gentleman to whom the informer had written suggesting that Peter Blance of Scatsta had been smuggling gin and tobacco. He was a reluctant witness but wished to say that, although he had not read Mr Hamilton's report about the payments to whalers, he had read the gist of it in the press and had heard criticisms of the accuracy of it. He thought that the report described practices that had at one time been prevalent in Shetland but had, perhaps, not taken into account the practices of recent years. He then went on to make a devastating statement that agents had persuaded the masters of whaling vessels not to appear to pay the seaman, because they invariably ran away home. The men subsequently said that this was incorrect and the Collector did not believe the agents story and reckoned that if the men had believed that they would be paid immediately they would have delayed going home.

John Gatherer went on to suggest that the agents in recruiting seaman were acting in contravention of the Merchant Shipping Act 1854, although William Robertson defended his position by saying that the men were always engaged in the presence of the masters. It is important to note that Mr Gatherer also acted as the superintendent, formerly known as the shipping master, responsible for being present to oversee the paying of the crews. He was quite convinced that the reason the agents wished a delay was to secure the trade for supplying the men. The Board of Trade had been told frequently of the failure to observe the Act in his regular reports.

In John Gatherer's view the agents were able to circumvent the Act by telling the men that they should go straight to the agents' offices to settle their account because he had frequently heard them being told this in the Custom House. In his opinion this made the practice illegal and contradicts William Robertson's statement that they men came of their own freewill without any coercion. He was in no doubt that the supply of goods to the men was the main inducement to acting as an agent and combining the roles of agent and supplier of goods was in his opinion illegal.

The last witness at the Lerwick hearings was another William Robertson, who had worked for Hay & Co for 28 years. He was head of the ship agency business and had appeared in order to lodge a prepared statement about the mode of dealing with men engaged for the seal and whale fishing. The statement was similar to the line taken by William Robertson of Leask & Co and designed to demonstrate that the Act was being adhered to. The masters selected the men without knowledge of any indebtedness to the agent and usually took men they knew to be good seamen and after the voyage a man would come to settle his account at the office quite voluntarily.

The questioning by the examiner was very skilful but Mr Robertson put up a good performance. Reading these differing views of the operation of the recruiting, equipping and subsequent paying of the crews is confusing. The agents are due some sympathy for trying to provide a service to the masters by completing the administrative procedures for them as well as enabling the men to find employment without a great reward. It is a little naïve of the authorities to think that all the administration required in the recruiting process, involving senior clerks, could be worth as little as 2½ per cent of the wages paid. In addition it is a lot to expect another merchant not handling the agency to advance credit for clothing to the men with no guarantee of payment when the men returned. There would be few jobs available and the Shetland crews were well thought of which was why the ships called to complete their crews. The Act was undoubtedly necessary and had the effect of preventing exploitation but there was the feeling that it was badly framed and left too much to interpretation. This much was acknowledged by John Gatherer.

Conclusion

The commissioner, Sheriff Guthrie, submitted his report later in 1872 and in his introduction he laid out the scope of his inquiries, which took in knitting or hosiery, fishing, farm stock and produce, rents, land tenure and the engagement of seamen for the sealing and whaling voyages to Greenland and the Davis Straits. Notices had been posted of all meetings, which were open to the pubic and circulars were sent to out to seek persons to give evidence. Certain others were selected and cited to attend at the seven locations where hearings were held. These covered all areas of the mainland plus Yell and Unst. Fair Island could not be reached due to weather conditions.

The evidence collected covered all aspects of working life in the islands and could be said to provide a comprehensive picture of conditions in the various activities as well as the land tenure question. The whole project had been carried out by Mr Guthrie entirely on his own, which must have been a considerable physical as well as mental effort. He commented that he had not been able to discuss the findings with a colleague and, for that reason, he did not make definite and detailed recommendations. He added that these were questions of policy, which was for government to decide. However, he did observe that it may be possible to frame an enactment, which would leave the fishermen free to contract to fish and share in the profits while requiring payment weekly or monthly of a proportion of their earnings thus obviating the necessity of living on credit. He went on to say that he felt obliged to show what the general result of the inquiry was, what questions arose and how witnesses who were involved viewed these questions.

There was a vast difference between the lives of the merchants, who lived very comfortably and the crofters, fishermen and workers, who struggled to earn enough to feed their families. The so-called truck system had operated for a long time but in the 20 years before the inquiry changes had begun to take place. The introduction of faster and cheaper sailings to the mainland had something to do with it enabling young males to go off and earn cash and return with some savings. Also the introduction of the Faroe fishing and the regular visits of the whaling and sealing ships to pick up crews offered alternative employment to the haaf fishing. In addition some of the fishermen added to their income by improving the output of their crofts and even added more land.

The gradual separation of the various activities of land owning, fish curing and shop keeping allowed the people to run their own lives and choose those whom they wished to deal with. Some of this was apparent in the evidence given, particularly by those who could look back objectively over several decades. The church ministers, school teachers and doctors contributed a lot to broadening the picture in this respect. The landlords and merchants on the other hand demonstrated that they were responsive to change even if they did not take many initiatives to prompt it. The more traditional ones were nevertheless sensitive to the need to support the less able of their tenants and customers, although they put the fear of death into them most of the time!

The tradition of large families was still evident but that presented less of a problem as overcrowding was compensated by emigration. Previous generations had existed at subsistence levels for generations and the life span was curtailed by lack of nourishment and poor housing conditions. The growing population in Lerwick in the 19th century contributed to much poverty as employment was not sufficient or well paid. One of the witnesses, a doctor, suggested that the health of the families in the country was better because they could produce most of their own food for themselves.

The merchants were able to justify the credit system by explaining that the fishermen and the merchants were in a partnership. The merchants supplied the working capital by financing the equipment and day-to-day needs of the families until the fish were taken to market and the men manned the boats and landed the fish. The profits could not be shared until the sale had been made and, although the merchants settled at this point, they did not receive the cash until later as they traded on three-month bills. They, therefore, financed the credit as well.

The introduction of a cash system must have happened gradually and would have obliged those who were not good at keeping track of their income and expenditure to manage their affairs better. An enormous amount of tedious and unnecessary book-keeping was avoided and the costs of running a shop would have been reduced as a result. It was unrealistic to expect families with very busy lives to spend time keeping detailed records in their pass books of all their transactions with merchants. It is as well that, in the main, merchants were trustworthy, although it was in their interests in view of the substantial margins they earned on their sales.

The process of change was difficult to bring about because there was no one to co-ordinate the efforts of the various parties involved. As is clear from the evidence, enough of the landlords and merchants were for change to make it happen but none dared move on his own. There was a role for government but perhaps there were other priorities for the London politicians. Here was a case for devolved government able to give attention to such a local and vital issue.

The question of more competition was raised several times and it may have been naïve to suppose that more shopkeepers would have made any improvement. If the situation is compared with the present day, it is doubtful there are as many shops outside Lerwick today as there were then. In the 19th century the merchants were able to offer a good coverage, selection of goods and extended credit because they had high margins and were able to trade in fish, livestock and other produce. The monopoly was in the combination of land owning, fishing and shop keeping, a form of vertical integration, which left the fishermen and crofters with only one firm to deal with.

The land tenure system was obviously very much out of date and it was interesting to see that tenants were taking out some leases and land was being improved with positive results for the families. Quite a few of the people managing land promoted the ideas expressed by John Walker in Edinburgh in 1871 and had made some headway in gaining the trust of the tenants. It seems more than likely that Walker had borrowed these ideas from others and talked his way into the confidence of Major Cameron. The fact that he failed to make any progress at all indicated that he was not a competent manager. Indeed he was probably out for a quick success in not persevering with leases but going for clearances and sheep farms.

Although there were banks in Lerwick, there was virtually no service outside the town. The merchant, therefore, played an important role in the economy by providing working capital in the form of extended credit. They were the bankers and this was recognised by those who chose to leave money owing to them in their shop accounts. Today, the banking coverage is not very much better but the road system is and it is easy to drive into Lerwick and deposit or withdraw money at the banks.

The major hurdle to overcome was to instil some confidence in the people that change was possible and they should embrace it when the opportunity arose. From what was said by some of the witnesses, the process had begun and what was needed was a groundswell of support to bring it about quickly. Those who would have found it difficult to adjust because they had no savings would have found sympathetic support given the attitude of the majority of merchants and landlords. There was obviously a lack of leadership at the time and I am not sure where it could have come from.

The economy functioned efficiently but was severely restrictive. The inquiry did demonstrate that those who took the initiative could improve their lot and as everyone gained some freedom of manoeuvre, trade flourished. The merchants found ways to adapt and some of the firms of former days are still trading successfully. Emigration increased when fishing was poor but those who moved away often found a new and prosperous way of life.

CHAPTER 3

Building the Family Business

John Seeks a Role

Peter and Margaret's eldest son Robert left Shetland around 1874 and trained as a grocer in Edinburgh and obtained his first licence for the sale of alcohol in 1881 at the age of 24. John, the number three son, also came to Edinburgh probably about 1877 and followed his brother into the grocery trade. Other sons entered the same business but these two achieved the greatest success, although in different ways.

They were quite different characters. Robert was the steadier of the two and was a very good retailer. This is a business, which requires a sustained effort over many years in order to build a reputation for good service and quality products. On the other hand, John was evidently somewhat impatient but he had the flair of a salesman and maybe considered himself a bit of an entrepreneur. He was certainly full of ideas but seemed to lack the skill of selecting or finding able managers to carry out his schemes. Nevertheless, his achievements were considerable.

After training, John started out in partnership with Robert at 34 St Leonard's Place about 1883. In 1884, Robert moved his main business from 216 High Street, Portobello to 31 (later renumbered 155) Bruntsfield Place and the partnership was dissolved leaving each to pursue his own separate career. John set up at 148 High Street, Portobello and married Jean Brown the same year. The shop was not big enough to occupy all his time and he started to take an interest in the work of the Scottish Licensed Trade Defence organisation, which had been set up to counter the efforts of the temperance movement and he became the Scottish organiser. Jean died in 1892 and John married again. He moved to Glasgow after his second marriage in 1895, where he started his own wine and spirit business but continued with his trade defence work.

It is interesting to read the circulation list for his 1897 Annual Report.

It includes many of the notable names in the trade of the day and they were extremely useful contacts for John when he was building up his business. In addition, the people he met up and down the country in his trade defence work provided him with a ready-made customer list. The names of the committee members were:

Robert Usher, 32 West Nicolson Street, Edinburgh
John Watson, 305 West George Street, Glasgow
William Hardie, 4 Picardy Place, Edinburgh
James Wyper, 514 Gallowgate, Glasgow
Harry George Younger, Abbey Brewery, Edinburgh
James Hunter, 401 Victoria Road, Glasgow
James Purves, SSC 32 Queen Street, Edinburgh
JJ Blanche, 180 Hope Street, Glasgow
AG Muir, 19 Waterloo Street, Glasgow
WV Jackson, 4 Carnarvon Street, Glasgow
James MacFarlane, Ely Bank, Broughty Ferry

It was obviously not possible to give much attention to his Edinburgh business now and he arranged for its sale in February 1898 to Messrs Tweedale & Calder. He wrote to the buyer's lawyer in his characteristic peremptory style to arrange stocktaking before the licence was transferred:

> I am arranging for my brother to do the clerking for me and it would be as well for Messrs Tweedale & Calder to be there to clerk for themselves and check quantities, in order that there may be no delay when the auditors come on Thursday morning to make up the valuation. My brother will be at Portobello at 2 o'clock sharp and you will oblige by intimating to Messrs Tweedale & Calder that we will expect them to be there as near that time as possible.

The death of John's first wife Jean on 3 January 1892 and the loss of his fourth child a few days later must have been a severe blow for someone brought up in a very close and caring family. He reacted by throwing himself into his trade defence work and travelled throughout Scotland thus becoming one of the well-known people in the trade.

His fertile imagination produced innumerable ideas for developing new lines of business from the many opportunities he came across. This was a time when the growing industrial economy gave many the chance to try out new things with every chance of success due to the increase in spending power. The unrestrained growth in the economy led to a severe recession in the late 1890s but nevertheless John managed to continue to build his business.

His travels took him to Aberdeen a lot and it was here that he found his second wife Isabella Davidson. They were married on 25 June 1895 and lived in the house in Duddingston, Edinburgh. Isabella was a widow having been married to a man called Bonar; Davidson was her maiden name. Sadly their first child Norman died, aged six months and it was then that the family moved to the west, where they set up house in the Burgh of Rutherglen outside Glasgow. In 1899 they went to live at 5 Blairbeth Terrace, Burnside, a short distance away. The terrace is a fine example of the architecture of the period and is still there looking the same as when it was built. The family lived there for the next 20 years and saw some momentous events unfold. In spite of the very difficult economic conditions, John managed to build a substantial business and to take it through the dangerous years of WWI.

About the middle of the 1890s John joined with others in a challenge to the Distillers Company's (DCL) dominance of grain whisky production by forming Northern Distilleries Ltd. Quite a few distilleries were constructed at this time and grain was in demand as it was cheaper to produce than malt whisky. The demand for grain grew quickly as blended whisky had become very popular in London. However, the capacity introduced by these new openings proved excessive and many were closed down. Some were bankrupt and others were amalgamated and then closed to reduce capacity. The Distillers Company were very keen to see these new plants off the market and orchestrated a programme of mergers and closures. They justified their near monopoly by stating that their customers as well as themselves would benefit from a more reliable supply although at a higher price.

John had a wide circle of contacts throughout Scotland by this time and he claimed that two thirds of those taking shares in Northern were personally known to him and had been influenced to take shares by the fact that he was named as an executive in the Prospectus. He said he had given guarantees to his friends amounting to £6,000 to be repaid if the company failed. It built the Gartloch grain distillery in 1897 at Garnkirk near Glasgow and John took the post of Director and General Manager at a salary of £1,000 per annum and assumed the responsibility for sales. The contacts he made during his service with the Trade Defence Association had persuaded him that he could generate a substantial sales volume by winning business from the established distillers. The managing director of the company was Alex Ferguson and the secretary was George Logan. Offices were opened at 180 Hope Street, Glasgow.

Within a year it was clear that all was not going well. There was a lack of working capital to finance the build up of trade and John wrote to Alex Ferguson in July 1898 complaining that this hampered his selling activities. Shortage of cash obviously prevented the company distilling for stock and offering fillings on demand at a good price. This was one of a number of letters written in his own hand and obviously very private. John resigned in January 1900 saying that there were irregularities in the running of the company. It was very short of money and the sales were not going well due to intense competition. The company could not compete with the more efficient DCL distilleries, which were cash rich and could cut prices below the new entrants. Alex Ferguson tried to persuade John to think again but to no avail. John expressed a willingness to help to rescue the company in the interest of his friends but it is difficult to see what could be done with so much spare capacity around.

John sold his shares in exchange for vatted whisky, which he could trade in the broking market and so came out of his investment with something. Later it transpired that, at the time of the flotation, the vendor 'spontaneously allotted to him 500 vendors Ordinary Shares'. The liquidator took the view that John had made a secret profit, although no arrangement had been made prior to the flotation. There was some acrimonious correspondence, which lasted for some months. The dispute was eventually referred to Counsel, who reported in John's favour.

However, he was advised that it would be prudent to make a payment of £300 to settle the matter rather than face a Court of Session appeal. Northern went into liquidation later in 1900 and the assets were sold to James Calder & Co in 1902. It is not clear if John's friends held him to his guarantee or if there was a deal at all.

The Business of J J Blanche & Co Ltd

In a further effort to become involved in the distilling business John applied in March 1900 to the Dundashill Distillery for the position of representative. He stated that his terms were a salary of £500 plus expenses but he was not successful. This was perhaps fortuitous as this distillery survived for only three years from 1899 till 1902. He decided to become a merchant on his own account, trading in whiskies, imported wines and British wine. He was one of the first customers of Vine Products Ltd, the dominant producer of British wine. This company had been formed by a group of entrepreneurial chemists who created an entirely new market for wine made from imported grape juice. It was very successful and was quoted on the Stock Exchange until acquired by Showerings and subsequently Allied-Lyons.

In March 1898 John had become a member of the Scottish Trade Benevolent Institution. The secretary was Alex Kennedy, Writer, 190 West George Street, Glasgow and the entry fee was £10.18/-. The BEN as it is known is a large organisation, which has substantial funds invested for the benefit of trade pensioners. In recent years it has devoted some of its funds to helping non-trade people, whose lives can be made more comfortable by a small annual grant and regular contact. Anyone who wished to meet others in the trade joined the BEN. It was typical of many such organisations up and down the country. In spite of the growth of Social Services they carry on due to the enthusiasm of volunteers, some of whom give a great deal of time to the work. There is a danger of duplication as a number of them find that their original purpose has become unnecessary and have broadened their scope like the BEN.

In 1900 John's business traded as 'JJ Blanche & Co, Wine shippers and Distillers Agents' operating from 69 Waterloo Street, Glasgow, telephone Royal 06766 and telegraphic address 'Boomerang'. There were cellars at 103 Waterloo Street and 98 Waterloo Lane and a bonded warehouse at 42–54 Wellington Lane. By 1917 the office had moved to 36 Douglas Street. The constant changing of addresses was probably the result of lower rents being available as I imagine, that at this time, there was a surplus of property with the economy in recession. One of the early deals was the business's appointment as Scottish agent of a wine shipper in Bordeaux. In 1901, Glasgow hosted an international exhibition and John met with some Russian officials, from whom he obtained samples of eight wines. He reported that the quality was good and some orders were placed.

John travelled extensively throughout Scotland and made journeys to London to buy wines. Even in those days, communications were really quite good. The mail service was reliable and was fast as a result of the expansion of the railways. A series of letters dated 10-12 July 1900 and written in John's own hand from the Imperial Hotel Aberdeen, demonstrate that it was perfectly possible for travelling businessmen to keep in contact with their offices. The fax and email developments since the mid 1980s have speeded up the process and taken away some of the drudgery for the traveller but, broadly, the result is much the same. In 1900 the mail was sent on by the office and replied to on the move. Letters were copied by a letter press, presumably by the hotel.

On the 11th he wrote to the office from Aberdeen that mail should be forwarded to the Central Hotel Montrose and sent in orders to be entered pending his return. The same day he wrote to John Dewar & Sons offering to sell 1896 grain from Carsebridge, North British, Cameron Bridge and Caledonian for 2/9 to 2/11½ and at the same time wrote to the secretary of Harvey's Yoker Distillery Ltd (grain) the following:

> I must decline to send in any further orders until the matter of price is thrashed out with your Board. It is simply 'rot' for Mr Glen to think that I can sell your stuff at his prices against what other distillers are

> doing in the way of prices, terms, delivery, etc. I can buy grain whisky just now on contract at 1/- per gallon nett and get it delivered and get terms too. Meantime I suspend operations until I hear from you. My journey here is wasted!

It is surprising how quickly a new business could be set up and profitably. Competition was strong but there were few barriers to starting compared with today. The JJ Blanche & Co's wine & spirit list circa 1901 provides an interesting commentary on the extent of the trade and the variety of products available. The agencies for imported wines and spirits included CN Kopke of Oporto (port), Wilson & Valdespino of Jerez de la Frontera (sherry), Peter Melchers of Schiedam (Geneva gin), and wines from Larcher Per et Fils of Bordeaux, Jules Dubois & Cie of Beaune, Heyman Bros of Bingen, Eduardo Vizetelli of Florence, L Issandorfer of Budapest, Sacramento Wine Co of Los Angeles, J van der Dulken & Co of Cape Town, Charles Kinloch & Co Ltd of London (Australian wines) and Blanche Pere et Fils of Rheims and Epernay (champagne). The last named was a good use of the family name for his own label wines.

Australian wines were imported into the United Kingdom in large quantities, as much as 823,500 gallons in 1899. JJ Blanche & Co featured their own Boomerang brand shipped through Charles Kinloch & co from the Australian United Vineyard Proprietors. The wines listed were exclusively table wines and ranged in price from Sauvignon at 13/9 per dozen to Verdeilho at 29/9. The company imported a wide range of Bordeaux in cask but also carried 20 or so wines in bottle. Chateau Beychevelle 1894 was priced at 18/- per dozen, Chateau Smith Haut Lafite 1889 30/-, Chateau Palmer 1878 65/- and Chateau d'Yquem 1891 60/-. Alternatively you could have Chateau Cos d'Estournel 1899 at £15 per hogshead.

These prices were for the wholesale trade but there is no doubt that, if you knew John, he would have been very happy to do business with anyone willing to place a reasonable order, particularly for his Blanche Pere & Fils Dry Royal Reserve Cuvee Vintage 1893 Champagne at 54/- per dozen. The name 'Blanche Pere & Fils' was eventually used as a trade name for all wines imported from Bordeaux and bottled by the company until 1960.

No brands of Scotch whisky were featured on the list. All the whiskies were varieties of vattings priced at from 2/6 to 10/- per original bonding gauge (the number of proof gallons as measured in bond) and usually at proof or up to nine degrees over proof. There were cheaper vattings at 1/6 to 2/3 for up to 10 over. Grain whisky was listed featuring Harvey's Yoker Distillery. Presumably the falling out over price had been patched up. New make was available for orders of not less than 100 butts at 1/1 per proof gallon less ¼d for own wood and ¼d for cash on rail. You received 12 months free rent in buyers' own wood. Stocks of matured grains and malts were available on application.

Wholesalers and many large retailers bought in bulk and bottled the goods themselves. Labour was cheap and non-branded goods were much lower in price. The retailer was able to rely on his reputation for quality and value for money in the products he sold or dispensed and make a larger margin of profit for himself. For a while this practice was abandoned due to higher costs but in recent years the supermarkets have taken a big share of the market for their 'own label' goods produced for them by their suppliers. Imported brands of sherry, port, cognac and champagne hardly appeared in the Scottish trade but branded Scotch whisky was well established and was in regular demand in London by this time, the major ones being Walker's, Buchanan's and Dewar's.

John's business prospered from its early days and the results for the first few years were declared to the Revenue as follows:

Year to 31 May	**1901**	**1902**	**1903**	**1904**
Sales	6,157	16,141	19,341	21,314
Oncosts	1,232	2,879	3,090	3,163
Profits	500	750	212	2000

A prime source of working capital for the business was a bank overdraft and over the next 60 years there was a close association with the National Bank of Scotland at 22 St Enoch Square. It merged to form the National Commercial Bank of Scotland, which was later acquired by the Royal Bank of Scotland. The first recorded contact at the bank was with John Sutherland the manager in 1900. He was asked for an overdraft facility of £12,000 on a temporary basis as John wrote that he was realising some of his securities for the purpose of capitalising his business. Nevertheless, you see below a steady increase in the debt to the bank.

The Balance Sheets for the first three years showed a steady build up of assets:

Assets	**1901**	**1902**	**1903**
Book Debts	1,796	4,026	3,982
Stock Fittings Plant	5,500	8,060	12,742
Cash	7	109	20
	7,303	12,195	16,744

Liabilities			
Bills Payable	763	3,722	4,722
Due to Bank	2,132	3,435	6,610
Due to Open Account	551	750	1,162
Capital Account	3,587	3,837	4,288
	7,033	11,744	16,782
	270	451	-38
Add Drawings	230	299	250
Net Profit	500	750	212

Bad debts were a regular feature of doing business with retailers and hoteliers as they still are. The year 1902/03 was a bad one when they amounted to £1,616. Inevitably the bank had to be reassured that everything was under control. In a letter to John Sutherland in June 1904 John reported that the profit for 1903/04 was over £2,000. He urged the bank to continue his overdraft facility and reminded them that they had been his sole bankers since 1880 although not with the same branch. The family relationship with the branch at St Enoch Square lasted for over 100 years by which time customer loyalty was no longer a consideration in a bank's appeal to its customers.

By 1905 John was writing to the general manager of the bank in Edinburgh. This may indicate that the overdraft was under closer supervision, or perhaps had grown in size beyond the local manager's authority level. The bank now held, as security, parcels of maturing whisky, which were valued regularly and covered 100 per cent of the amount outstanding. The turnover continued to grow and reached £70,000 by 1915. The sales included a high proportion of agency and broking business and the figures were inclusive of excise duties.

The Glen Elgin Distillery was acquired in 1905. This purchase led to increased business for the bank. In 1907 the bank manager was David Watson and he was asked to extend the overdraft limit from £7,500 to £9,500 in order to help to finance the new distillery. The turnover of the business with the bank had doubled in recent months and so how could they refuse! In March 1908 David Watson was told of a record order of 15,000 gallons of whisky from Restells, the London agents. John asked for a £2,000 facility to finance the deal.

The distillery was silent in 1913 as there was a glut in the market and the quality of the barley crop was poor. John Bremner was now manager at St Enoch Square and in March 1914 he was assured that the distillery was back in production and going at full speed. A profit of £3–4,000 was expected. It was not long before the dark clouds set over the business when war with Germany was declared in August 1914. In the event Glen Elgin remained silent for the duration of the war on government orders. Grain was needed for food and there was not sufficient to supply the needs of the Scotch whisky industry.

World War I

During the war there were frequent letters to the bank either to lodge stocks as security for increased overdraft facilities or to withdraw them for sale to reduce the borrowings. It was virtually impossible to obtain supplies, and so it was necessary to deplete stocks in order to carry on the business. When they could be replaced after the war, the cost was five or six times the original. Prices escalated during the war and the sale of matured stocks could have financed the purchase of new fillings but for the fact that the Inland Revenue eagerly taxed the inflated profits. As a result the net of tax profits were not sufficient to cover the cost of replacement stock.

The Baileys retail wine merchants business was started in 1910 by the acquisition of Bailey Clark & Co Ltd at 339 Argyle Street, Glasgow. Argyle Street had become a great thoroughfare and was the prime shopping centre for the retail trade. It has retained this position ever since and rivals Oxford Street in London for the title of the most valuable site in Britain. Retailing eventually became the most important side of the business and proved to be very profitable. The idea was to build up a chain of shops as others were doing around the country. Notable among them was the Victoria Wine Company in London, which eventually owned Baileys. Retailing required more capital but, on the other hand, sales were more secure and there were no bad debts as most of the trade was for cash. The key elements in the business were good siting, the range of products and swift and friendly service.

The next shop to be opened was 68 Renfield Street in 1911. This was also an excellent site and it traded into the 1980s. In an advertisement for Baileys in the *Glasgow Evening News* on 24 December 1914 the claim was made:

> THE CHRISTMAS BOX FROM BAILEYS has now become a household word all over the United Kingdom. Last year the demand was enormous. No wonder as OUR BOXES show 50 per cent better value than any competing house. This year we have excelled all our former efforts.

It goes on with some more hard sell and includes a Christmas box from Russia claimed to be 'strong, vigorous and bracing like the Russian people' and urges customers to 'Support your Allies'.

The early results from the retail business were good and Baileys proved to be an excellent investment. Sales climbed steadily during the war from £5,576 in 1914 to £8,336 in 1915 and £17,269 in 1916. It accounted for most of the business after John's death and was subsequently sold to brewers Ind Coope in 1960. Ind Coope also bought Victoria Wine, the large London chain, about the same time.

It is interesting to compare the contrasting tones of the letters to the bank compared with those to the tax authorities. It appears that there was a certain flexibility in the language used. John was always bullish with the banker and very pessimistic with the Surveyor of Taxes. One of the earliest examples of the technique was a letter dated 17 August 1903 reporting on the results for the year ended March 1903. This was the year of large bad debts amounting to £1,616.

John wrote to E Harris, Surveyor of Taxes:

> We are in receipt of your favour of 14th inst.
>
> We may say that we have practically completed our balance and much regret to report that this year we will have no assessable income owing to the fact that we have suffered serious loss in connection with the defalcation of our Belfast agent. We have had to write off for this loss alone about £1,500.
>
> Meantime, we may say that we purpose getting our books audited by a qualified Chartered Accountant and until this is done we will really not be in a position to state our position accurately.
>
> Last year we overpaid.

Writing to the Assessor of Taxes in June 1916, John explained that things were difficult as very few staff remained who had not been called for military service and certainly there was not enough time to prepare the annual balance. The distillery had been silent for the whole season (September 1915 to May 1916) and so there was nothing to tax there!

The Inland Revenue Solicitor's Department wrote to John about settling an overdue Excess Profits Duty assessment of £250. He promptly suggested that it be paid in two instalments and this was agreed. In May 1918 the Inland Revenue assessed the company for £3,500 for Excess Profits Duty. This was the result of selling whisky at inflated prices compared with the low pre-war cost. John wrote that he was unable, due to war conditions, to get a Chartered Accountant to certify the accounts. He offered to pay by handing over £2,500 of five per cent National War Bonds 1927 and a cheque for £1,000 and the Revenue to arrange the transfer of the Bonds! Again this was agreed.

It must have been very difficult to staff the business during the war in view of the difficulty in recruiting reliable and honest people. There were some instances of crime, devilment and frustration. It appears that John carried on the business almost single-handed, although his son William in his teens was an enormous help on the 'shop floor'. Both sons William and Lawrence were brought into the business as soon as they were legally allowed to leave school. Thus William started in 1912 at the age of 12 and Lawrence in 1917. John's elder brother Bob disapproved of the boys being denied an education but they both achieved a remarkable amount in spite of this disadvantage. William attended night classes and became a widely read man and a very good public speaker. Lawrence was not so coherent but had a charming and extrovert personality. He pursued a career in local government and was the youngest member of Glasgow Corporation when first elected. He became chief magistrate of the city and later chairman of the powerful West of Scotland Region of the Conservative and Unionist Party for which he was awarded the OBE.

In May 1916 a man called James Stocks was taken on as a warehouse foreman with a written reference from Messrs John E Macpherson of Newcastle. This reference was subsequently discovered to be a forgery. The man also had the good fortune to occupy a company house. Not content with his position and the fact that he was avoiding service in the armed forces, he masterminded the theft of a considerable quantity of wines and spirits including 20 whisky hogsheads. He was found out and charged. In court he was sentenced to 40 days in prison with hard labour and told that he should present himself for military service on his release.

In a desperate attempt to improve the staff situation John wrote to the town clerk to seek exemption from military service for his son Robert Bruce Blanche due to the fact that all his employees had been called up. The alternative was to employ 'the men one gets just now are not worth having – they are simply thieves and shirkers'. The appeal was dismissed and Robert was called upon to report for military service within three days. An appeal to the sheriff also failed. This was a very harsh decision but these were bad times and the forces in France were losing so many men in their futile efforts to drive the Germans out.

When William was called up on 1 February 1919 John wrote to his commanding officer to seek his release in the most heart-rending terms and by August he was back home. Robert had apparently been thrown from his horse in the army and been seriously injured when the horse rolled over him. His leg could not be amputated in view of his weak condition and he had been sent home with little hope of survival. The family was waiting for the end and yet another tragedy. This was obviously a severe blow as John had expected Robert to take over the running of the business. In August he wrote in the most pessimistic terms to James Hay of Adam Thomson & Ross saying his health was poor. He was clearly worn out by the war and the struggle to keep things going. Sadly Robert died in 1920, the last child of John's first family to survive.

Another employee, JF McCulloch, recommended by the town clerk, Sir John Lindsay, was employed on light duties in charge of the women in the bottle-washing department. He was discharged for inefficiency and promptly wrote to the gas company to say that the meter had not been examined for 18 months and suggesting that no gas bills had been paid. When the gas company had checked and found everything in order, John wrote to the man threatening a libel action unless he received an apology, which would be advertised at his expense and also that he should pay £10 to the Red Cross funds. No satisfaction was ever obtained.

It appears that quite a lot of the company's business was with hotels in the north of Scotland. They were supplied with the whole range of wines and spirits bought from a variety of sources at home and overseas. Some of the sources were cut off eventually due to the war activities and others like Messrs T Merritt & Co were chastised by John who advised them in December 1916 to withdraw from their list the wines of Joh. Bapt. Sturm of Rudesheim am Rhein! As John said, quite reasonably:

> . . . the beastly Hun has outraged civilisation and humanity. He has become a moral leper – worse than a Hottentot. Our advice is avoid him, pass not by him, turn from him, and pass away.

A New Dawn

Happily things gradually returned to something like normal after the war and John reckoned that he would try a new venture and go into the catering business. He purchased 2/4 St Enoch Place and on Adams Court Lane on 27 May 1920 for £7063. It consisted of three shops and two upper floors, which were to be fitted out as a restaurant. In 1921 the three shops were offered for lease at £200 per annum. A private company, The Princes Restaurant Ltd, was formed in January 1922 to run the restaurant but it was not until September that George Albert Moss was appointed General Manager and Director. A lot of money was laid out on alterations to the upper floors in order to attract a good clientele. This was not one of John's brighter ideas and having taken nearly two years to start the business, he should probably have aborted the whole idea.

One potential customer, Kenneth Muir Simpson, wrote to ask for permanent partitions to be erected to accommodate the Rotary Club but John said it would not be possible. He said he would like the business and suggested temporary ones would suffice. The restaurant did not make any money and Moss was dismissed in October only a month after his appointment. The venture was a big mistake as John had no knowledge of catering and was cheated by the manager and staff. The restaurant was closed down early in 1923 otherwise John, as he commented rather dryly, 'would have been ruined'. Attempts were made to sell the linen, cutlery, plates, cooking utensils, which were all of the highest quality. Some of this stock was still lying around the business in the 1950s and probably not a lot was ever sold. The property was leased in 1924 and the income from rentals was £1,390. This included £500 per annum for the restaurant known as 'His Lordship's Larder' and £890 for the shops. This went some way to recouping the losses incurred in the restaurant.

In the middle of all this trouble the Surveyor of Taxes surfaced again. In February 1921 he asked for £13,719 4/- in Excess Profits Duty. In his reply, after some comment on his financial position, John goes on:

> We think it is very hard we should be bled dry in this way. If you insist on your pound of flesh, well then, we shall give up business, because to be quite frank with you, it is not worth our while to continue in business under present conditions.

The business had been kept going during the war largely by liquidating most of the stock and not replacing it simply because it could not be obtained. Reference was made earlier to the cost of replacing stock after the war being four or five times the original investment. There were obviously large profits to be made in wartime when prices rocketed but most was taken away by the Revenue, who had no sympathy with the cash flow problem created when replacing the stocks sold. The iniquitous Excess Profits Duty assessment was almost too much to bear.

In the spring of 1924, John bought the assets of The Garngad Bonding Company Limited together with the Risk's Royal Vat Scotch whisky brand. It was a much better investment than the restaurant and proved very worthwhile. This is referred to later together with Glen Elgin distillery.

The Stephen Hardie Era

John still had plenty of ideas and most of the investments made were good ones but the running of the business seems to have been haphazard. With inadequately qualified staff and probably very little time for planning the new ventures, it must have been a case of crisis management on a regular basis. In 1921 help arrived at last in the shape of Stephen JL Hardie (SJL as he was known) of Hardie Caldwell Ker & Hardie, 204 St Vincent Street, Glasgow. He made an instant impression on John and proved to be a good friend and advisor to the family for the next 40 years. On 6 October 1925 having visited a lawyer in Greenock, who was SJL's uncle, John wrote the next day:

> Dear Mr Hardie,
>
> To mark my appreciation of your courtesy and kindness when I called upon you yesterday along with your nephew, I am posting you today a small box of cigars and a box of Egyptian cigarettes, which please accept with my best wishes. The old fashioned courtesy that you and I were accustomed to when we were younger is now so rare that one appreciates it when one comes up against it.
>
> At this point I would like to put on record my appreciation of your nephew Mr SJL Hardie. He is really a fine fellow and one can thoroughly trust and rely upon him.
>
> In connection with the licensed shop in West Blackhall Street, that I inspected yesterday, I think we have nothing to lose but probably something to gain by waiting until the next Licensing Session in April. The position is quite good, but the premises would need to be completely gutted out and brought into line with modern requirements. It follows of course that this would mean a big expenditure and I would not tackle it unless I was getting a lease say from seven to ten years. You are so well known in Greenock that I take it you will know the proprietors or factors and enter into negotiations with them and see what they are prepared to do in this direction.
>
> With every good wish,
>
> I am, yours faithfully.

John had sensibly returned his attention to the retail business, although it took until 1936 for this particular property to be added to the chain and by that time John was dead.

Stephen Hardie had had a successful war, as they used to say after WWI. This usually meant they had survived and been decorated. SJL had done these things and become an important businessman as well as continuing his accountancy practice. He was at Paisley Grammar School with the father of my old school friend Stewart McLennan. His father Harold was very friendly with SJL who was known at school as Stevie but in our family he was always referred to in very formal terms. With a few friends, he started Metal Industries, a ship-breaking company, which took advantage of the need to provide industry with scarce raw materials that could be recovered from redundant ships. The first assignment was raising some of the German warships scuttled at Scapa Flow in 1919. The company subsequently set up a yard at Faslane on Gare Loch and survived for over 40 years in its ship breaking activities. The financing of the early activities was innovative at the time. A ship would be purchased for scrap using a short-term bank loan, which was then paid off quickly by recovering and selling all the non-ferrous metal, which fetched a high price on the market. Thereafter the rest of the vessel was dismantled and sold at a slower pace without the encumbrance of loan interest in the overheads.

In addition, SJL and his friends gained control of the management of British Oxygen Company and they provided its chairman and several members of the board until the 1960s. After their landslide victory in 1945, SJL joined the Labour party, saying with some foresight, 'if they are going to be in power for a long time, they had better have some able people to help them'. His reward was to be appointed to run the newly nationalised steel industry.

In his later years SJL bought Ballathie House at Stanley, Perthshire together with six adjacent farms. He then proceeded to use his business expertise by putting them under a single management and running them as one unit. This meant that there was sufficient volume of output to reduce unit costs and afford all the necessary equipment without renting or borrowing from a neighbour. Hardie Caldwell prepared the annual accounts for the farms and the most notable year was the one in which SJL bought a prize bull at the Perth sales for a world record price of £14,000.

Stephen Hardie became a close advisor and did much to put some order into the administration and finances of John's business. On 12

January 1925 the Accounts for the year to 30 September 1924 were ready in record time but showed a drop in profit. This, John said, was due to higher buying prices combined with price cutting in the trade. Also a high proportion of sales were in low margin wines, which in the depressed economy were the principal seller. John decided to waive his salary of £2,000 in order to provide a dividend of five per cent for the shareholders, who were of course his family.

At the meeting SJL suggested that some of the maturing grain whisky at distilleries should be brought into the company's Garngad Bond in order to save the warehouse rent of 3d per week on each cask. A meeting with John Bremner at the bank was arranged to discuss the use of stock in own warehouse as collateral for the company's overdraft. This practice was not greatly favoured by the bank, as they could not have an independent certificate of the stock.

Old Friends Compare Notes

In July 1921 an old customer, Robert Bell from London, surfaced seeking to buy whisky and to exchange news. The Conservative government was not favoured by either of these gentlemen probably because excise taxes were being raised! John made some comments about his health and said he was suffering from neuritis and diabetes. The following week Mr Bell asked for some cigars to be sent to his hotel in Pitlochry and at the same time recommended a prescription to John for his afflictions.

Another old business friend, John Graham of London, wrote and they brought each other up to date. Health was mentioned again but more particularly, John sadly relates the loss of seven of his ten children. These losses were very much on his mind as he grew older and he must have wondered how he was going to arrange for the succession in the management of the business. Oddly in all these exchanges, he never makes any mention of his deceased wife, Jean Brown, whose four children all died.

A trade acquaintance, Henry Huis, wrote to say that he had been dismissed from Melrose Drover and John was very complementary about his selling skills and his old boss Mr CB Drover. Mr Melrose, now in charge, did not have the same skills as John and Mr Huis 'in rubbing shoulders with the customers outside'. This matches a nice anecdote about John's selling skills related by John Monteith, who worked in the family company from the 1920s until the 1960s when he was an area manager for Victoria Wine. He told me of meeting a customer outside John' office in Waterloo Street one day and after a chat asked him if he was going in to see Mr Blanche. 'No', was the reply, 'he might sell me something'.

John wrote to WE Hughes of W&T Restell and in passing recollected the days when he used to take the night train to London, attend the Restell wine auction and travel back on the following night train. He said that his sons were progressing well and hoped they would be taking over the running of the business soon. It must have been difficult for the boys as my father used to say that John never discussed the key features of the business and on his death he was pitched in at the deep end. Mr Hughes wrote again to recommend a business in Leith to John as a possible purchase but Archd Cowan Mason & Co was similar to John's company and called on the same retailers. There was a familiar comment about dealing with traders who did not pay their accounts and were insulting when pressed.

James C Barr of the company of that name had some discussions with John about their respective health problems and wrote about Spa-Radium. John in turn recommended a preparation of his own. It consisted of foreshots from the distillery taken off ex-gratia and then mixed with American turpentine and olive oil to make an emulsion. He rubbed it on in front of his bedroom fire each night as a relief for rheumatism. He went on to say that he did not drink sparkling liquids in view of a bowel complaint and had not used his two large sparkling machines since before the war as he could not obtain the bulbs. He recommended Natural Mineral Water from Vichy and said he spent time in Vichy and benefited from the water. The Vichy Estate was owned by the French Government and had three springs Vichy Celzefin's, Vichy Hopital and Chateau Robert. He kept a regular stock in the office although he had claimed not to drink sparkling water!

J. J. BLANCHE & CO.,

69 Waterloo Street,

GLASGOW.

Telegrams: "Boomerang," Glasgow.
A B C CODE, 4th Edition.
Telephone No. 16.Y. Royal.

Importers and Exporters of all kinds of Wines and Spirits.
Distillers and Bonders of Scotch Whiskies (Highland, Lowland, and Grain).
Brokers, Blenders, and Valuers to the Trade.

Bankers—THE NATIONAL BANK OF SCOTLAND, LTD., St. Enoch Square, GLASGOW.

AGENCIES.

PORTS—
C. N. Köpke & Coy., Oporto (Established in 1638), Shippers of "Crown Royal," "Victoria," and "Roriz" Ports.

SHERRIES—
John Wilson & Coy., Jerez de la Frontera.

CLARETS—
Larcher Père & Fils Jeune, Bordeaux.

BURGUNDIES—
Paray Fils & Cie., Beaune.
Jules Dubois & Cie., Beaune.

CHAMPAGNES—
Blanché Père & Fils, Rheims and Epernay.

HOCKS AND MOSELLES—
Heymann Bros., Bingen o/ Rhine.

FOREIGN LIQUEURS—
De Martignon Frères, Bordeaux.

TARRAGONAS—
Dalmau Hermanos, Tarragona.

SPANISH PORTS—
Garcia Hermanos, Barcelona.

SPANISH BURGUNDIES—
Garcia Hermanos, Barcelona. ("Clarion Brand.")

AUSTRALIAN WINES—
Charles Kinloch & Co., Ltd., London. ("Boomerang Brand.")

ALGERIAN WINES—
Le Brun Frères, Algiers.

ITALIAN WINES—
Eduardo Vizetelli, Florence.

HUNGARIAN WINES—
L. Issandorfer, Budapest.

CALIFORNIAN WINES—
Sacramento Wine Co., Los Angeles.

CAPE WINES—
J. Van Der Dulken & Co., Woodstock, Cape Town.

COGNAC BRANDIES—
The United Vineyard Proprietors Coy. (J. G. Monnet, Manager), Cognac.
Sonac & Co., Cognac.

SPANISH BRANDIES—
Wilson & Valdespino, Ltd., Distillers, Jerez de la Frontera.

HOLLANDS AND GENEVA—
Peter Melchers, Distiller, Schiedam. ("Juniper Tree" and "Castle Brands.")

JAMAICA AND DEMERARA RUMS—
All the leading Marks.

GRAIN WHISKY—
Harvey's Yoker Distillery, Ltd., Renfrewshire.

MALT WHISKY—
Various Distillers of Highland and Lowland Malts.

VATTED WHISKY—
Own Brands.

With Agents and Correspondents in every Wine-producing Country in the World.

VATTED SCOTCH WHISKIES.

Vattings made in Bond under Buyers' Own Names and Brands. No other Name appearing.

Special Labels and Brands designed, registered and reserved for Customers.

We guarantee the uniform quality of all our Standard Blends.

SPECIAL DEPARTMENT FOR MATCHING SAMPLES.

Mark.		Price. (Original Bonding Gauges.)	Strength.
B	FINE SCOTCH	2/6	9 o.p.
L	FINE OLD SCOTCH	3/	8 „
A	OLD HIGHLAND	3/6	7 „
N	CHOICE OLD HIGHLAND	4/	6 „
C	EXTRA CHOICE OLD HIGHLAND	4/6	5 „
H	RARE OLD HIGHLAND	5/	4 „
E	OLD HIGHLAND LIQUEUR	6/	3 „
S	SPECIAL OLD HIGHLAND LIQUEUR	7/	2 „
Special Liqueur.	CHOICE OLD LIQUEUR	8/	pf.
Ex Spcl. Liqueur.	CURIOUSLY CHOICE OLD LIQUEUR	9/	pf.
King Edward's Special.	FINEST LIQUEUR	10/	2 u.p.

CHEAPER VATTINGS.

Mark	Price	Strength
1	1/6	10 o.p.
2	1/9	9 „
3	2/	9 „
4	2/3	8 „

SPECIAL FACILITIES FOR BOTTLING AND CASING FOR BUYERS.

Shipping and Export Orders for Customers carefully attended to.

JOHN
Peter's third son
Commissioned photo

WILLIE
John's elder
surviving son
Commissioned photo

JJ Blanche & Co and Baileys staff annual dance

Commissioned photo

The Staff at Glen Elgin with Willie (centre right).

Commissioned photo

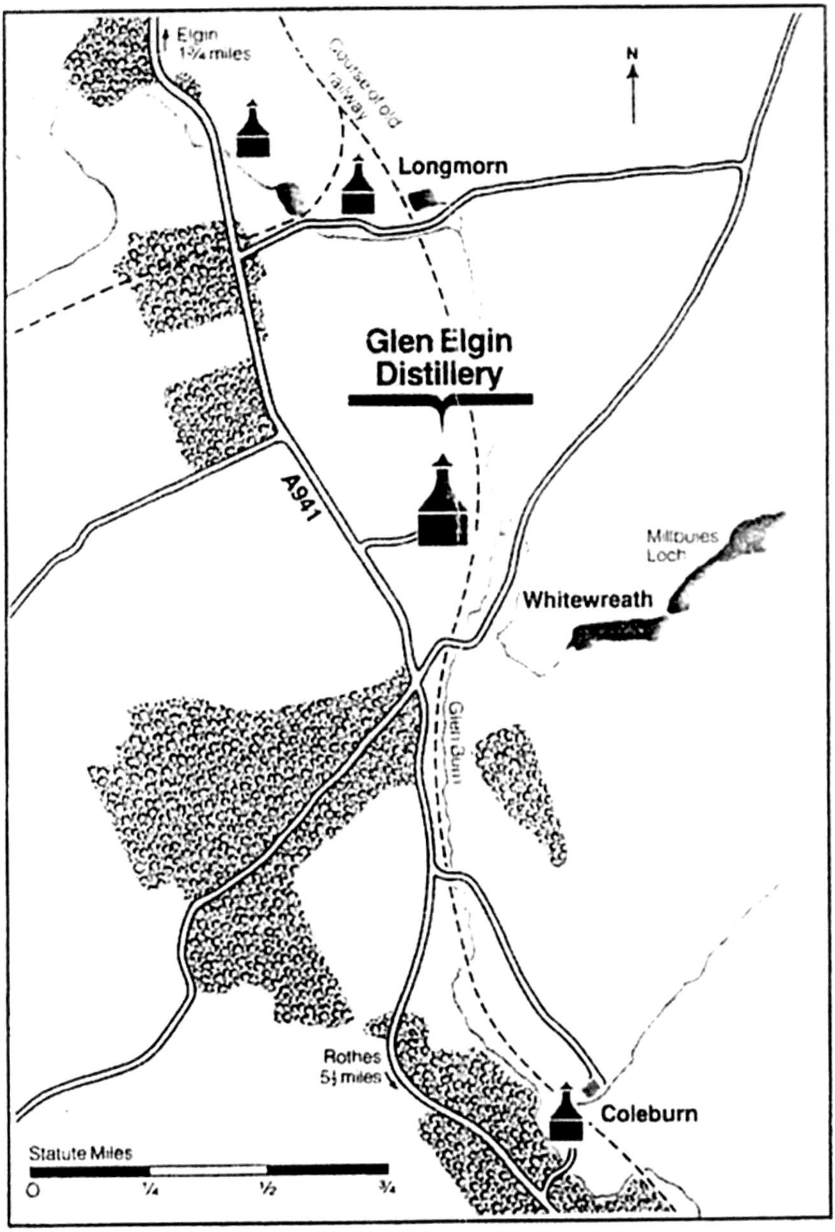

Map of location of Glen Elgin

Unknown

The Growth of the Distillers Company

William Ross the genius behind DCL.
The History of the Distiller Company R B Weir

Plates 1 and 2: Caledonian Distillery, Edinburgh was one of the rare exceptions in the grain whisky trade. It was built in 1855 as a patent still plant rather than as a conversion from pot still, on a seven acre site, adjacent to the Haymarket station. The etching from Alfred Barnard's book, *The Whisky Distilleries of the United Kingdom* (1887), captures the detail of industrial activity (including air pollution). When Barnard visited Caledonian it was the second largest grain distillery in the United Kingdom with a productive capacity of just over 2 million gallons a year, 220 employees and 11 Excise officers. DCL's acquisition of Caledonian in 1884/85 prompted the formation of the North British Distillery Company by spirit dealers.

Caledonian Distillery (Grain) an early acquisition.
The History of the Distiller Company R B Weir

Mergers – A Way of Life

A HISTORY OF GROWTH AND DEVELOPMENT

IN 1839 Alexander Elder set sail from Britain for Australia to found a trading company – a company which, over the years, has expanded its operations to encompass a range of products and services from brewing and agriculture to international trade and finance.

Today Elders IXL's international operations are expanding apace thanks to a sound management strategy of long term international growth and development.

In many ways, the company's recent history is an even more dramatic story than its past.

The story began in 1972 when a management team led by John Elliott took control of Henry Jones IXL, a declining food processor.

Having successfully rebuilt this business and turned around the company's failing brands, the same management team negotiated a reverse takeover of Alexander Elder's business – a company by then in need of a more progressive management approach.

Elders was in turn revitalised and the merged company, Elders IXL, went on to acquire the multinational Wood Hall Trust and the Australian-based international brewing giant, Carlton & United Breweries.

Other acquisitions have been made within this framework. Each has been different. But the companies acquired have all increased their productivity and their profits under Elders' management.

Hardly surprising when you look at the strength of the senior management team. Of its eight members, four have Masters Degrees in Business Administration. Two, John Elliott and Andrew Cummins, have also had experience with the management consulting firm, McKinsey & Company. Despite their relative youth (most are in their 40's) they have a breadth and depth of experience. Ken Jarrett, Geoff Lord and Peter Bartels were part of the original management team that acquired Henry Jones IXL Limited. Graeme Higginson and Michael Nugent were previously in top management positions in companies that joined Elders through acquisition.

Chairman and Chief Executive John Elliott has built a strong central management team that has made Elders a major international force in its four core businesses – brewing, agriculture, finance and international trade.

The team has matured but has lost none of its vitality.
It's committed to sound performance for its shareholders.
It's committed to a long term view.
It's committed to its employees.
And, above all, it's committed to creating an environment for growth.
Let's look at how it puts those commitments to work.

Elders IXL and Elliott

Elders document

ALLIED–LYONS Its Management

At the head is Sir Derrick Holden-Brown who was appointed chairman in 1982. The team includes Sir Alex Alexander, vice-chairman, and John Clemes, financial director, and is supported by Henry Fearn, heading administration. Together they provide strategic direction for the Group.

Allied-Lyons operates through three divisions each with its own executive Board:

Beer, headed by Richard Martin;
Wines, Spirits and Soft Drinks, headed by Michael Jackaman;
Food, headed by Sir Alex Alexander.

Within these divisions each operating company benefits from a high degree of autonomy with strong local management able to react speedily to market trends and exploit new opportunities.

Each operating company has its own first-class management team so that, overall, Allied-Lyons has a breadth and depth of high quality leadership.

Michael Jackaman John Clemes Richard Martin Henry Fearn
Sir Derrick Holden-Brown Sir Alex Alexander

Allied-Lyons is led by a central management team small enough to be cohesive and decisive, and new enough to have plenty of fresh ideas, many of which are already producing exciting results.

The Allied Top Management Team.

Allied-Lyons document

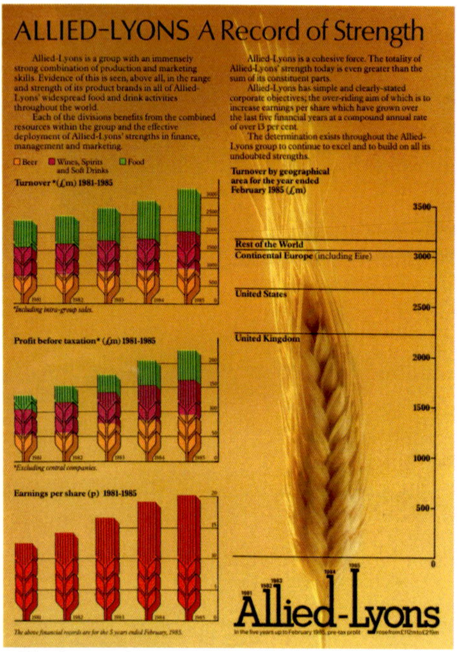

Allied Graph

Allied-Lyons document

More of Allied's brands.

Allied-Lyons document

JJ Blanche & Co – an unlimited company

In 1922 the business became a private unlimited company with a capital of £150,000 and John and his son William were the directors. The assets of the business amounted to £73,000, which included properties £19,656, investments £19,058 and stock £25,376. Trade was good and was continuing to rise, 'going steadily upwards'. The profit for the 13 months ended 30 September 1922 was £8,799 but £5,000 had to be written off the Princes Restaurant property.

The first directors' meeting was held at the registered office at 36 Douglas Street on 7 August 1922. The shares were allotted to: John 1,000, his wife 500, William 500, Lawrence 500, daughter Isabel 450 and confidential secretary Elizabeth Harvey 50. Hardie Caldwell Ker & Hardie were appointed auditors, John E Wilson & Foulis lawyers and The National Bank of Scotland bankers.

The various methods of financing the business were discussed from time to time. In August 1923 a loan of £3,000, secured over the Douglas and Waterloo Street properties, was called in for renewal and the rate was to be increased from 3½ per cent to 5¼ per cent. A competing rate of 4½ per cent was found and Boyds Miller & Thompson acting for the lenders were told to go and get lost in typical fashion.

John's concern about his health proved real when his doctor offered his opinion that he would not have long to live. This made it very necessary to bring in some of the family to share in running of the business. He must have been ill for much of the following 18 months because the annual accounts for the year ended September 1923 were not approved until May 1924.

By that time John was full of optimism again and stated in his report to the shareholders that he was 'feeling considerably better and I am looking forward to the future when I shall be able to take a better grip of affairs than I have been able to do in the past. The will and the desire is there but from time to time physical incapacity makes it very difficult'. The profit had risen to £9,445 but again £5,000 was written off the St Enoch Place property.

Retailing Takes Over

In the meantime, the retail business had been expanded and gradually this was becoming the main activity. An offer was made on 12 September 1923 for the shop at 1293 Argyle Street. It was for £150 for goodwill and fittings with the property being rented. Another offer was made for Wm Hamilton at 950 Argyle Street for £100 for goodwill and fittings. This one was successful and remained part of the chain until closed in 1958 as by then the site was not so attractive, it was difficult to staff and sales were declining.

The same year the Conservative member for Kelvingrove, William Hutchison, pledged himself to the Scottish Temperance and No-Licence League, which incorporated the Scottish Temperance League and the Scottish Permissive Bill and Temperance Association. The fool – he lost the votes of the Blanche family living at 26 Park Circus in his constituency! In 1923 a veto poll was held and John was asked to lend a car to bring out the 'Wet' votes on polling day. It so happened that the Salvation Army campaigned for the 'Dry' vote and in January 1924 John inevitably cancelled his subscription to the organisation. In his letter he commented:

> I claim that I have done more for the cause of temperance than even the Salvation Army or the whole of the pulpit of Scotland put together by pushing and developing the sale of light wines and I am pleased to say that the results are coming in quite satisfactorily to my mind. The public of this country is still drinking on a more intelligent principle.

He had a point, as he was one of the pioneers in the sale of light wines, which provided an alternative to whisky, which was the real target of the temperance movement. These wines were inexpensive and left more money for food in the less well off households. Later, as the standard of living improved, Baileys pioneered the sale of table wines to a wider public.

The car loaned to the veto poll campaign was replaced in December when John took delivery of a 12hp Vulcan at a cost of £400. It seems unlikely that he ever learned to drive as he had a chauffeur for business and family journeys. On one of his car journeys to the distillery John and his wife had an accident in Glencoe on the return trip. It appears that a spring broke causing the driver to lose control and crash into a fence. The chauffeur managed to have the car towed to a small private garage and they spent the night at the Tyndrum Hotel.

In December John sought to persuade Cooper & Co to apply for licences and of course be supplied by JJ Blanche & Co. He sold the idea in what must have been his typical style without holding back:

> There are very few, if any, men in the UK that has a better knowledge of the articles he handles. The best proof of this is found in the fact that we probably handle more wines than all the other wholesale houses put together.

If he was thinking of Glasgow the statement may have been credible, as most of the others would no doubt handle mostly spirits and beer. As we have seen, John sold large quantities of French, Spanish and Australian wines.

John's brother Bob continued his very successful business in Edinburgh and John wrote to him about his growing trade in inexpensive imported wine. He claimed that in 1922 he had sold 1,000 pipes of Ruby Lisbon Red and offered to sell some to Bob at 2/6 per gallon. It was fortified with ten per cent vintage Port to protect it from going off! No wonder the Port Shippers Association in London took him to court for describing this product as 'Lisbon Port'. It was a fast moving low margin business and the overheads were cut to the bone. John's family used to talk of pipes of wine from Portugal being unloaded from the docks onto the pavement outside the warehouse in Charles Street because there was not enough room inside. It was often sold direct from the street and so maybe very little saw the inside of the building.

Christie's wine sale catalogue of 5 June 1997 contained the following lot for sale:

> **Royal Jubilee Port, Vintage 1887** *Bottled by Baileys of Scotland. Metal capsule embossed PORT. Cork slightly shrunken and signs of slight seepage. Labelled* **The Wine of Kings, Vintage 1887, Royal Jubilee Port.**

Excellent level into neck. This bottle has been in the vendor's family for 80 years."

I bought this lot for £300 and wrote to Christie's to ask if they would put me in touch with the vendor. I received no reply, presumably because they never disclose the sources of their sale items. This was disappointing as I was convinced the bottle must have come from the family of an old employee and it would have been nice to make contact.

The wine has not been sampled but it is no doubt authentic. However, there is some doubt in my mind about the claim that it had been in the vendor's family for 80 years. This suggests that the wine was sold no later than 1917. The doubt arises because there is a back label listing the branches of Baileys and the list includes 10 West Blackhall Street, Greenock. As mentioned earlier, John was negotiating for the purchase of this shop with William Hardie in October 1925 and it was not acquired until 1936. At any rate I have an interesting artefact of the business.

The other outlets mentioned are 68 Renfield Street, Glasgow acquired in 1910, 68 High Street, Edinburgh 1930, 13/15 Gilmour Street, Paisley 1929, 158 High Street, Ayr and 139 High Street, Irvine 1938. The label also mentions as agents, presumably owned by the business, 950 Argyle Street, Glasgow. Clearly the back label was added later. This does not entirely destroy the authenticity of the wine but someone has undoubtedly interfered with the bottle dressing.

The profitability of the retail side of the business was becoming more interesting and William Hardie continued to look out for suitable properties on behalf of the company. In March 1926 he found one possibility in Helensburgh but it came to nothing. The West Blackhall Street, Greenock property was considered again without result. FJ & WA Dykes, Cadzow Street, Hamilton offered lease terms for a property occupied by JD McNeill, Licensed Grocer and the company agreed provided that nothing was paid for fittings as £2,000 would be required for refitting. Nothing came of this proposal and it was not until 1947 that a branch was opened in Hamilton.

The result for the year ended 30 September 1924 was a profit of

£2,532, down by £6,913. Trade was depressed due to the state of the economy and there was discussion about dismissing or suspending employees in order to reduce costs – a familiar scene! By 1925 the profits had bounced back to £11,893.

Most of the Blanche family remained in Edinburgh and John kept in touch with them frequently. Family ties were very strong in the generation brought up in the crowded cottage in Shetland. The contrast of their life there with the opulent lifestyles in Glasgow and Edinburgh must have been considerable. Many islanders, who had emigrated from the northern and western isles would have been enjoying the fruits of their energy and initiative in this period and they must all have valued the change in their circumstances, while remembering with fondness the close family life of old. John was clearly delighted on 13 May 1924 to hear that Bob was coming through Glasgow on the 21st, as it was his birthday. They would also discuss some business development, he said, and enclosed with his letter some labels for casks Bob was dispatching for filling at Glen Elgin distillery.

The two brothers were probably quite close. There were only four years separating them in age, they were both in the wine and spirit trade and had been the first of the family to leave Shetland. No doubt Bob helped John when he first came to Edinburgh and I imagine their father would have given them some people to contact in Edinburgh and Leith, who would advise them about establishing themselves.

Although John had been optimistic about his health, he did not improve to any great extent. He kept closely in touch with the running of the business and continued to take all the important decisions but his sons Willie and Lawrie became more involved in the day-to-day work. They took some of the pressure off him and gained some useful experience.

The last private letter written and signed by John was on 18 August 1926. It was to John Bremner at the bank to thank him for meeting him with SJL to discuss the question of the bank accepting whisky in the company's own bond as collateral for the overdraft. It looks as if the meeting had been successful in persuading the bank, because the letter was accompanied by a schedule of delivery orders for whisky to be transferred to the bank amounting to £6,992.

John died on 7 January 1927 and Willie had a very friendly and sympathetic letter from George McNish of Robert McNish & Co Ltd, 56 Washington Street, Glasgow. He replied saying he appreciated the offer of help and advice in the business and suggested that he would call the following week to meet him personally. Willie was 26 years old and had been working since he was 12. His first responsibility for a department had been at the age of 15.

The Next Generation

The annual general meeting following John's death must have been tinged with much sadness at the loss of the founder after 30 turbulent years. To add to the grief the reported profits for the year ended 30 September 1926 were only £458 and no dividend was paid. This was the year of the General Strike, when the country was brought to a standstill for a few months. Businessmen drove tramcars and did other essential tasks before order was restored. Happily the position had improved by the following year when the profit was £3,191. The company changed its status and was incorporated as a limited company on 13 May 1927 just four months after John's death. The name registered was 'JJ Blanche & Company Limited' and the certificate of incorporation was No. 14611.

A very necessary rationalisation of properties took place in 1928. The head office of the whole business was moved out of Douglas Street to 69 Garngad Road adjacent to the bond. This saved the rent and made better use of the site, which had been acquired with the Garngad Bonded Warehouse company. The property backing onto the bond at Charles Street was acquired at the same time and became the duty paid warehouse for wines and spirits. The head office, bond and warehouse were then all concentrated on the same site.

John's sons quickly took control and demonstrated that, although they had not been taken into John's confidence, they had a grasp of the business and were able to continue with its development. A change in strategy was necessary at this time, because the opportunities for expanding the wine importing business were limited. There was less trade being done through Glasgow. The London wine houses were now beginning to take most of it, as shipping services were better and their traditional expertise and range of contacts gave them the edge over importers in other parts of the country.

The national economy was still in recession and very few people saw any rewards coming from taking risks. The one activity that was more or less free of risk was retailing. This had been where the Blanches had started in the 1880s after all and their knowledge of the trade persuaded them to give greater emphasis to this part of the business, which had begun to be developed by John. This policy became the main thrust throughout the 1930s, 1940s and 1950s. The wine importing business continued at a modest level, principally for own bottlings of French wines. In connection with wine bottling by the company, a rather interesting occasion was Willie's 90th birthday. I had saved a bottle of Chateau Margaux 1934 for the meal the family had with him. Afterwards we were reflecting on how good this 54 year old wine had drunk and father remarked "I think I must have bottled that wine myself". It was common practice in those days to import the top Bordeaux wines in cask and the wine would have been delivered in 1936. As a wine of this quality was very valuable it needed to be treated very carefully and so Willie would have done the job instead of leaving it to the cellarman. Shipping in cask for the top Bordeaux wines ceased around the late 1940s.

The Baileys shop at 68 Renfield Street, Glasgow had been opened in 1910 and during the 1920s, 578 Govan Road and 950 and 1293 Argyle Street had been added. 1293 Argyle Street was sold to the manager on the promise made by John before his death. The first move by the sons was the acquisition in 1928 of a business at 13/14 Gilmour Street, Paisley consisting of a public house and an off-licence department with a separate entrance. This was followed in 1929 by the purchase of 68 High Street, Edinburgh (The Royal Mile). The goodwill and premises were bought for £3,000 and the Glasgow Blanche family was back in Edinburgh again.

These moves were a considerable display of confidence in view of the state of the economy at the time. As an indication of the lack of activity in industry the great new Cunarder, *Queen Mary* or number 534 as it was known before naming and launching, lay on the stocks at John Brown's in Clydebank unfinished for three years. I can still remember seeing it towering over the tenements. Its launch in 1934 heralded the revival of the economy and, incidentally, the start of the rearmament programme leading to WWII.

In 1930 there was an attempt to build an export trade and a salesman made regular trips overseas and opened up connections in Nova Scotia and Newfoundland. South America was the next area to be targeted and presumably Australia would have followed, as most export trade was concentrated on the Commonwealth countries at this time. By coincidence, Nova Scotia and Newfoundland were the destinations of the first overseas trip I did when I entered the Scotch whisky business with Stewarts of Dundee.

Management problems

By now Lawrie had been in the business for ten years or so and took an equal share of the workload. He and Willie had quite different personalities and, as neither was senior to the other in the management, friction was bound to develop. Willie, the elder, was more experienced and had had more time with his father to learn how to run the business. Lawrie, on the other hand, had fresh ideas and wanted to introduce them without necessarily thinking them through fully.

The first real sign that things were not going well was when, in 1931, Lawrie announced at a board meeting that he intended to stand as a candidate for the Glasgow Corporation. Willie 'strongly objected' realising that an extra load of work would land on him in the difficult conditions of the time and Lawrie would expect to draw his full salary. This attitude seemed to have stemmed form the fact that the company's shares were left to Willie, Lawrie and Isabel equally and the two boys were to run the business and share the proceeds. So salary, directors' fees and dividends were required to be shared equally but there was no arrangement for equal sharing of the workload and responsibility. Nor was there any consideration given to fixing any differential in salaries to reflect different responsibilities.

When I joined the company in 1956 to fill a gap in the management, Willie was expected to take a reduction in salary to compensate for the extra cost of me! It became obvious that if I were to progress in the company, it would be at Father's expense as the profits were regarded as being shared between families and not just individuals – an odd concept which did not give me much confidence for the future. Investment in new management was not a practice with which the directors were familiar. Lawrie was obviously confident that he could take on outside activities and rely on lower paid staff to cover for him. With the best will in the world things could not be so easy and Willie found himself covering for Lawrie and then being taken to task for interfering. The scene was set for a difficult relationship for the next 14 years when neither brother was able to behave in a cool and rational manner. Sadly also their sister Isabel was brought into many of the quarrels and suffered as a result. Happily she married a delightful man, Tom Murdoch, whose tact and quiet amenable personality kept the peace until 1945 – more of that later.

Lawrie was elected to the Corporation and was the youngest councillor of his day. He went on to a distinguished career on the Council and ultimately held office as the senior magistrate of the city. Later he took an active part in national politics and served as chairman of the western region of the Conservative and Unionist Party (Tories in Scotland). He was also Deacon Convener of the Trades of Glasgow, an ancient and wealthy craft organisation now devoted to charitable work.

In September 1932 the directors met in the offices of Hardie Caldwell Ker & Hardie, which were at 145 St Vincent Street to consider, with SJL, the future strategy of the company. SJL thought that the wholesale business was not very attractive for development nor was the export trade. The most favourable area for expansion was the retail business and it was decided to follow this policy for the future and not waste resources and time on other activities. The company had a good track record in managing shops and they could produce better and quicker results. For a family business this type of decision was not usual as most family businesses simply carried on without consciously making decisions about its direction. This demonstrates the value of having SJL as an advisor and one to whom the family would listen.

Sister Isabel's name appears in the minutes as a director for the first time in 1932, when she was 25 years old. She was an active young lady and had quite a strong character. She and Lawrie were quite like their father in many ways but without the entrepreneurial flair of the old man. There was no holding her back and she seems to have taken an active part in the management. Keen to learn, she asked to be instructed in many of the procedures of the business, in particular, how to take stock in the duty paid warehouse. This was not a straight-forward task and was sometimes the means by which pilfering was discovered. However, she did not work full time and it was difficult to integrate her into the management.

Early in 1933 a further meeting was held with SJL about fixing defined responsibilities for managing the shops, the distillery, the wholesale department, the bonded warehouse and the properties. Willie took over the distillery, bond, wholesale and properties, while Lawrie was to run the shops. This was a good division and suited the skills of each. It is a pity that it was not possible to appoint a managing director, who could have co-ordinated the efforts of these two and given the company a chance to grow into a much bigger business.

SJL called another meeting in March 1933 to agree the form of management accounts to be prepared and presented by Hardie Caldwell. Very few businesses had such a sophisticated reporting system at this time and again the Blanches had good reason to appreciate the benefits that were accruing from their financial advisor. At the same time a change was made to the management duties to streamline the structure further. Lawrie took over responsibility for the duty paid warehouse in view of the fact that most of the supplies were dispatched to the shops, which were already under his control.

In May 1933 the directors appointed Alex Dickie as Cashier and Company Secretary at a salary of £208 per annum. Alex was just the right man to keep a firm hand on administration and board procedures given that the three family members did not have a very happy relationship. He had endless patience and was a stickler for detail. He served the company faithfully and well until his retirement in the late 1960s. He must have been very young when appointed and proved to be a man of considerable integrity. He latterly worked for Victoria Wine, when Baileys became part of the national chain after its acquisition by Ind Coope. He would occasionally visit Willie at his seaside home in Seamill in the 1930s for a game of golf. He sported the biggest bag I had ever seen in those days. As there were no trolleys at that time all golf bags were carried unless you had a caddie. I think that must have been the reason he had one shoulder that was lower than the other!

The policy of concentrating on the expansion of the retail side of the business continued in 1933 with the acquisition of the bankrupt business of Haddow & Aitken in High Street, Ayr. The price was £130 for goodwill with stock at a valuation of £508. The premises were leased at £180 per annum for five years but they were subsequently acquired. The manager was Mr Keith and his salary was fixed at £4-10/- per week plus a bonus of 5/- per week at the discretion of the management. This bonus was conditional upon good results from the regular stocktaking reports. The purchase brought the shop count to six.

There was continual confusion about the duties of the two full-time directors, Willie and Lawrie, in spite of the agreement entered into with the help of SJL. In January 1934 there was a long argument as to who should do the buying. This was a critical responsibility and should have been included in the Hardie scheme. Willie wanted a clear-cut arrangement, as Lawrie was frequently absent on his Council duties. Quite naturally Lawrie did not want to be left out of this activity, as he was responsible for the sale of the goods purchased. It was agreed that both would be involved in buying with Isabel's help, and each would report to the board. SJL was obviously not consulted in this crazy arrangement and I can imagine that Gerry Robinson, the TV business guru, would have had great satisfaction in offering his advice – 'you really must have one of you in charge'. By coincidence, he became chairman of Allied Domecq (formerly Allied-Lyons).

The Retail Business Strides On

In the review for the year ended 30 September 1933 it was reported that the St Enoch Place property had been sold and the proceeds were sufficient to repay the bank overdraft. This was a good outcome from a very bad investment of John's and, although losses had been made on the trading activities, the cash realised was a bonus in the difficult business climate of the 1930s. Thus, for the first time since 1919, the company was not indebted to the bank. Careful husbandry and rationalisation of properties had resulted in a much stronger company ready to take advantage of opportunities in the depressed market.

In March 1934 there was an approach by Booths Distilleries Ltd with an offer to acquire the whole business. However, the increased confidence in the prospects for the future led the directors to discontinue the discussions in May. It seems an unusual venture for a distiller and brand owner to wish to buy retail shops. Booths was independent at the time and their margin of profit on gin was very low, as they had to cut prices to compete with the stronger DCL. They thought that having their own outlets would help to expand their sales at a higher margin. Eventually Booths was acquired in 1937 by the DCL, who sought 'to remove a price-cutting nuisance'!

In October, Willie's car was replaced. The new car was an 18hp Wolseley Saloon costing £340 with an allowance for the existing Rover Saloon of £132. This car was in turn replaced in December 1936 by a 17hp Armstrong Siddeley at a cost of £395 less £140 for the Wolseley. Later in February 1939 a 16hp Armstrong Siddeley for £380 less £155 replaced that car. The trade-in prices for these cars were considerably higher as a proportion of the costs of the new ones than they would be today due to the fact that now the supply in relation to demand is greater. However, nowadays cars are much more reliable and large repair bills after two or three years are very much rarer now. The 1930s was a difficult period for business but this obviously led to remarkable price stability.

Trade began to improve in the mid 1930s as industrial activity increased and this was confirmed at the 13th annual general meeting in February 1935. Sales at the shops had risen five per cent resulting, it was claimed, from increased advertising during the year. The duty paid warehouse had performed well and had dispatched a record quantity of goods in the Christmas period. All told the report was bullish and it was recommended that more shops should be purchased. The profit of £5,216 was the best for five years and the two full-time directors decided that higher salaries were justified and they were increased to £750.

It is never a good thing to be too complacent and this was brought home to the directors in June when they had a nasty shock from a report of poor results from the stocktakings at the Ayr branch. The deficiencies were totally unacceptable and the manager was replaced. A regular check on branch operations was a key aspect of management and the directors were assiduous in their efforts to monitor results and take action where necessary.

Another difficulty arose in Ayr concerning the licence to sell alcohol. The local magistrates declared that every licenceholder must have an address in the burgh and the idea of someone from outside the town holding a licence and carrying on the business was not acceptable to them. Lawrie came up with the answer to the problem. He suggested that if the company granted him a loan of £1,000 at five per cent, two per cent below the market rate, he would build a house in Ayr to qualify him to hold the licence on behalf of the company. Not all Licensing Courts took the same view as Ayr but multiple licenceholders were frowned upon in most places.

When Victoria Wine took over the Baileys shops in 1960 they naturally wished the licences to be held at the Head Office by the company secretary, which was the practice in England. The liquor licensing system is quite different there and the Scottish Courts would not accept this practice. However, it was decided to spread the licences around the management so that no one person held more than four or five and this proved acceptable. By that time Ayr magistrates had moved into the 20th century and accepted that large chains of shops provided a trustworthy management control from the centre.

The company's financial year was changed from September to March in 1935 and the Annual Meeting was held that year in August.

Some interesting developments were reported. The sales were up 11.5 per cent, the Govan Road branch being the only poor performer. A new shop front had been fitted to the Renfield Street branch and it was recommended that the other branches should be given the same treatment. Robert Kemp attended on behalf of Hardie Caldwell and he was now the regular advisor in place of SJL. He was a fine accountant and became the senior partner of the firm.

The Glen Elgin Distillery was sold in 1935 to Scottish Malt Distillers Ltd, a subsidiary of The Distillers Co Ltd. This must have been a sad day for my father as he had nurtured the distillery since his father's day and had created order out of chaos. However, he told me that the rest of the family wanted to extract some money from the business and Father had said with remarkable objectivity that the only asset that could conveniently be realised without undermining the work of the previous years was Glen Elgin. The price was £15,000 plus £3000 for rents and stock at valuation, which gave total proceeds of £37,805. The inflow of cash was used to return £28,210 to the shareholders. They invested this capital on their own account and did quite well from their investments over the next 20 years. It is worth commenting that within 10 years Scotch whisky distilleries were at a premium as the industry sought to increase production to meet the pent-up demand after WWII and Glen Elgin-Glenlivet was one of the better makes. However, the value of the stock market also increased due to the boom in the manufacturing. Factories were going all out to meet the strong demand for goods in a booming post-war economy.

After the capital reorganisation the shares were held as follows:

SJL Hardie & Trustees of JJ Blanche	2,040
Mrs ID Blanche	1,710
WD Blanche	3,228
LS Blanche	3,228
Miss ID Blanche	1,614
St Enoch Square Nominees	270
Total	12,090

The purchase of the bonded warehouse, referred to earlier, proved very successful and the turnover grew steadily in the 1930s. The company began to cooper its own and customers' casks and bottling for outside clients had increased primarily due to the end of prohibition in the United States. There was a rush to establish new distribution outlets by many of the smaller companies before the bigger ones had re-established their links with their former importers. Later this trade declined as many of Garngad's customers were taken over by the DCL. On the other hand the company was able to sell its mature whisky stocks at good prices inflated by the sudden demand from North America.

The retail business continued to expand and in October 1936 the goodwill of the Greenock business was purchased for £850. The property was purchased some years later. In those days most small businesses rented their shops in order to keep the capital cost low. The Blanches eventually bought all the properties that could be purchased as an additional investment and this proved a successful policy given that bricks and mortar have a tendency to appreciate over time. New self-service stores, with larger selling areas, provided very stiff competition and the smaller shops could not compete against the lower prices of the growing number of self-service chains that began to appear. However, the small independents with good situations found that their properties were becoming more valuable as multiple retailers began to look for High Street sites. Gradually these small traders found that the value of their businesses was more in their properties and less in goodwill. Therefore, those who owned their shops were able to realise their investments at satisfactory prices.

An interesting item appeared in the board minutes at this time. The directors decided to approach two brewers for quotations for the supply of own label (Baileys) carbonated beer and were willing to place an order for 25 dozen. Own label beer never became a feature in the retail trade simply because the margins are so low and bottling small orders was not economic. Baileys eventually did a substantial trade in own label wine, sherry, port, cocktails, whisky, gin and brandy for exactly the same reason as supermarkets do today – increased margins of profit from lower buying prices.

Another branch was added to the Baileys chain with the purchase of the licensed grocery business at High Street, Irvine in August 1938. The price paid was £2,325 for goodwill and property, which consisted of two shops, a house and garage. This new addition meant that the chain of shops had more than doubled since John's death and so the three children had done very well despite not having a happy working relationship.

In November 1938 Tom Murdoch, Isabel's husband, was elected to the board in her place. This probably helped to keep things on an even keel, as Tom was charming, relaxed and mild-mannered and a successful businessman in his own right. Isabel was an extrovert and quite excitable and must have found it difficult to hold the balance between her two warring brothers. Tom served as chairman until the business was sold in 1960 and the family owed him a debt of gratitude for putting up with the strife and yet helping them to steer a straight course. He was a good listener and sensitive to the troubles being faced by the business in the mid 1950s, which stemmed from the growing competition from the multiple grocers, who were becoming interested in the wine and spirit trade as well. He was instrumental in persuading Willie and Lawrie that they should sell if they were not willing to invest more capital to modernise the business.

Another World War

Early in 1939 the country was actively preparing for war. There was no doubt that everyone anticipated conflict after the Munich Agreement. Neville Chamberlain's controversial policy of appeasing Hitler had the advantage of giving the nation time to prepare. In April the company approached the Glasgow Corporation for permission to build an air raid shelter on the ground they owned adjoining the Garngad Road property. Although Glasgow was at the extreme range of German bombers, some preparations were thought necessary to protect employees. Steps were taken by the company to arrange for staff training in Air Raid Precautions (ARP as the organisation became known) under the provisions of the Civil Defence Act of 1939.

In the face of the great threat to the country, the company continued to expand its retail chain. In April 1940 the wine and spirit business at 257 Argyle Street, Glasgow was acquired, the price being £3,800 for goodwill. This shop was under the Central Station railway bridge and was one of the busiest sites in the city. It was known in Glasgow as the Heilanman's Umbrella as it was cheap shelter from the rain! The purchase brought the number of outlets to ten, seven having been added since John's death. The shops were run on true multiple lines and, in spite of the somewhat random top management practices, produced good results. Each of the two working directors tended to turn their hand to anything that took their fancy if the other would let them and so things did get done. Neither seemed confident that the other was entirely competent and yet they each had their skills. Lawrie managed the shops well and Willie turned out to be a good financier, buyer and taster. He was prepared to devote himself to the business and was frustrated at Lawrie's frequent absences. He would step in and cover for him rather than risk problems arising.

The company increased its stocks of imported wines at the outbreak of the war and was in a good position to supply the shops, which were given priority over outside customers. By August 1940 supplies from Germany, Holland and France had ceased and shipments from Spain and Portugal were becoming difficult due to lack of shipping capacity. However, it was hoped that the Commonwealth routes would remain open and that supplies from them would help to maintain the momentum of the business. The position deteriorated during the following year and a system of customer quotas had to be introduced. No imports were arriving and stocks in London were at prohibitively high prices. Wine supplies were, therefore, likely to run out in about 18 months.

The Govan Road branch was closed at the start of the war, as it had not been doing well for some time. Govan was a run-down industrial area and would have been difficult to staff adequately. Furthermore the loss of staff to the armed forces meant that the more successful shops were given preference for the services of the remaining experienced and trustworthy managers. By the summer of 1941 all but three of the male managers had been called up for military service.

Here was the same problem, which faced old John in WWI, but by this time women were working and the situation was never as bad as it was in 1914–18.

In October 1942 the licensed grocery business of James Welsh, Troon was purchased for £3,920 for goodwill and property. This branch completed a string of shops along the coast of the Firth of Clyde, which turned out to be good investments. One of the ways Willie would entertain his children during school holidays was to take them on a 'run down the coast'. This was popular and often Margaret, his wife and our mother, would come too. The purpose was for Willie to make his regular visits to the shops and deal with any problems the managers were encountering. On the way a stop would be made at the Promenade, Greenock, known as the 'Tail of the Bank', to view the great assembly of ships of all sorts – passenger and cargo ships together with warships ready to escort the North Atlantic convoys. They would include the *Queen Mary* and *Queen Elizabeth* in their grey wartime liveries. The convoy system was introduced to combat the German U-boats which were operating across the Atlantic between Greenock and Halifax, Nova Scotia. The warships to be seen included destroyers, cruisers and large battleships such as the *Hood*, *Rodney* and *Warspite*. The other bonus for Mother was that the family usually came back with some extra supplies of food 'off the ration' including butter, cooked ham and eggs.

Management Changes and an end to the War

During 1944 Lawrie bought a public house in Airdrie to the east of Glasgow without consulting the other directors. In addition, he began to supply this pub from the company's warehouse, which was still under his control. Supplies were at a premium and the other two directors took a poor view of these precious goods being diverted to Lawrie's own business and denying the established customers of the shops. Also, Willie objected to Lawrie continuing to hold his 'full-time' post of Joint Managing Director, while running another business.

Relations between the two became steadily worse and the strains of running the business under wartime conditions had affected both. Lawrie claimed that his health had suffered and an attempt was made to persuade him to sell the Airdrie business to JJ Blanche & Co Ltd and take some time off to recuperate. A meeting, chaired by SJL, was held on 17 February 1945 and the proposal was approved. However, Lawrie declined to accept and the meeting was adjourned after it was agreed that the managing directors should devote their whole time to the business.

At the adjourned meeting on 26 March SJL was again appointed chairman. The discussion lasted all morning with no agreement about how to deal with the conflict of interest between Lawrie and the company. SJL adjourned the meeting again for a few hours. On resuming, a resolution was proposed which involved terminating Lawrie's appointment with the company forthwith with compensation of £6,000 for loss of office. He would retain his seat on the board and the right to a director's fee and of course the dividend. Fortunately Lawrie agreed and a difficult situation was resolved without recourse to the courts. Tom Murdoch was appointed chairman and the business then settled down to a more normal life.

The next shop to be acquired was Port Glasgow in January 1946. The business traded as Dunlop and Sons and was set up as a partnership with Duncan Shaw the experienced manager of the Greenock branch. This acquisition brought the total to 11 branches, all of which were profitable. A little over a year later, in April 1947, the Hamilton shop of W Fletcher was purchased and proved a good outlet for a number of years. It was known for its cooked ham, which in those days was produced in the back shop. It was a traditional licensed grocery business and fitted into the Baileys chain very well, although its days were numbered. Competition from the multiples was now beginning to affect trade at many of the company's shops.

The directors were concerned that the lease of the largest branch, Renfield Street, would not be renewed and purchased a shop in Hope Street as a precaution for £15,000. In the event, the opportunity arose to acquire premises a few doors down the street at number 64 for £20,000 and it was taken up. The Hope Street shop was subsequently sold for £16,700 but it is worth commenting that the company was back in Hope Street when the licensed grocers at number 200 was bought in 1959 for £24,000.

In March 1951 another two shops were purchased in Edinburgh at Nicolson Street and Middlefield, Leith Walk for a total price of £26,400. Then in 1958 Andrew Jardine's business at 400 Duke Street, Glasgow was acquired. Andrew was one of the characters in the retail trade and took a liking to the company otherwise he would not have sold his business. It was a pleasure to deal with such a likeable gentleman. The purchase of 200 Hope Street in 1959 mentioned above brought the number of branches to 15.

The early 1950s saw improvements in supplies and business was rapidly returning to normal peacetime conditions. The directors had been pleased to report for the year ended 31 March 1949 a record turnover of £320,589 and a record profit of £42,648. The balance sheet was equally strong with net assets of £120,755. From this, the company's best performance, a slow but steady decline started as the pressures of competition began to impact. Willie, the managing director, was somewhat dispirited by the mid 1950s and he tried to persuade the directors to increase the capital base of the company to enable it to expand faster but he received no support. He had carried on an expanding company covering all aspects of the business with the help of only one other executive, Alex Dickie, the company secretary. His rewards were modest for his efforts and all he could persuade his fellow directors to do was to increase his salary to £2,750 in 1953 after several years of seeking an increase to £3,000. It was to stay at the same level until the company was sold.

A Third Generation?

In 1956 I was persuaded to join the business and I agreed as I was really not sure what I wanted to do after qualifying as a Scottish Chartered Accountant and serving my National Service as a subaltern in the Royal Corps of Signals. I was largely unaware of the tensions in the business and thought naïvely that the energy of youth combined with some more investment would produce new growth. After a period of familiarisation with The Victoria Wine Company in London, I was given the unusual post of Sales Manager and Accountant! A board post was not offered, as this would have disturbed the balance of power among the three shareholders. It was not long before I realised that there was no likelihood of the shareholders agreeing to new capital and I found working with the directors was not a stimulating experience. An outright sale appeared to be the only solution and this seemed to be what the directors really wanted.

Stephen Hardie was called into the picture once more. Although he was retired, he was still a trustee of old John's estate and, along with Willie, controlled the shares owned by the trust on behalf of Isabel. He chaired an Extraordinary General Meeting of shareholders on 10 August 1960 for the purpose of appointing Hardie Caldwell Ker & Hardie to find a buyer for the business. Like so many good advisors, SJL was extremely loyal to his clients, especially those acquired in early life. He had first acted for John in early 1920s and here he was still helping his family almost 40 years later. In the intervening years he never failed to answer the call to smooth things over when disputes between John's three children had become deadlocked.

There were several old-established businesses for sale in this period and word spread quickly probably helped by Lawrie, who had a political friend in Manchester. Harold Cluff had been asked by one of the brewers to look out for licensed outlets for sale and passed the word immediately to B Grants & Co Ltd, a subsidiary of Ind Coope. He had already sold his own business to them and Grants obviously thought highly of his knowledge of the retail trade.

Derrick Holden-Brown was then managing director of B Grant and recently recruited to build the business. He wasted no time in visiting Glasgow and coming to terms with remarkable speed. Although not a shareholder, I was allowed to sit in on the meetings, presumably to demonstrate that there was some management succession. During the discussion I was asked about my plans and offered a job as assistant accountant with Grants at Burton-on-Trent. I said I wanted to stay in general management and it was eventually agreed that I would remain in the company as a regional manager. There was a chance that being part of a larger company would offer some prospects for the future. The deal was completed on 15 November 1960 and a new era dawned.

The last full year's accounts to 31 March 1960 recorded total assets of £212,940, net assets of £146,780 and net profit before taxation of £7,693. Profits had declined in the preceding few years due to static turnover and increased costs. It is likely that the company would have been making losses before long and the sale was a welcome solution for all. Lawrie had wanted to realise his investment for several years and so had Isabel. Willie was happy to retire too although he would have liked to see the business continue as an independent after having served it for 48 years.

I had eight years of exciting development of the Victoria Wine chain in Scotland and gradually was given more responsibility. After an interval of a couple of years I was fortunate in being able to report directly to Derrick Holden-Brown or DHB as he was known. After Derrick took on more responsibility in the group, Brian McGrath appeared as boss and he was a charming and supportive superior. These two were among the leaders of what became the Allied-Lyons group, later Allied Domecq. Derrick became group chairman and Brian served as a main board director for many years before retiring to become the Secretary to Prince Phillip. I think Phillip and he suited each other and as I write Brian is still there although now in his late 70s.

The chain of 14 off-licences plus a pub was rapidly expanded and at one time the company was taking over a new shop every month. Among these were three shops owned by the Misses Blanche. These ladies were the daughters of JW Blanche, who was a third cousin of Grandfather John and his brother Robert, and a contemporary of Robert's in the licensed trade in Edinburgh. I well remember driving DHB and Brian to see the ladies to negotiate the purchase. I was not allowed to take part but Margaret and Dorothy (Dot) told me later that the two bounced in full of jollity and proceeded to charm them into selling the business. I had never met or even known of these ladies before but they were a delightful pair. Sadly I lost contact with them after a while. Having taken over 15 outlets in late 1960 the chain had expanded to 36 off-licences by Christmas 1962, an increase of 21 branches in 24 months.

Opportunities for introducing new ideas were frequent and the top management always encouraged them. There was plenty of room for innovation and, for example, I remember starting the trend in the trade for open display of table wines with specially designed slanted metal wine racks. Bringing the wines out into the open increased sales dramatically as customers could browse and then make their own selection without the embarrassment of appearing ignorant in front of a counter assistant. I suppose this was the modern equivalent of John's early efforts to promote the sale of light wines some 50 years previously. Another move was to change the shop fascias from Baileys to Wine Market. Resale price maintenance was beginning to break down even before the law permitting manufacturers to set retail prices and enforce them was repealed. Victoria Wine was determined to hold on to RPM as long as possible to protect their profit margins. In some areas in England, where they were under competitive pressure, they had introduced a new concept called 'Wine Market' offering a more limited range all at lower prices. I was permitted to introduce the idea in Scotland in exceptional circumstances but I could see that we would simply lose trade if we did not take more drastic action. After long discussions I was allowed to go ahead across the whole chain and it proved to be our saviour.

The 1960s was a period of dynamic expansion in the off-licence trade and Victoria Wine was the first chain to become really national. It remained the largest but struggled to make money, as supermarkets broadened their range to include alcoholic drinks in the 1970s. Nevertheless, the multiple off-licence chains survive, because they have adapted by improving staff training, improving layouts, extending hours and moving to sites away from supermarkets. The latter have become much bigger and they have fewer outlets than the traditional wine merchants do. Wine merchants have stabilised their market share and still have a role to play.

Glen Elgin Distillery and Garngad Bond

For 30 years from 1905 Glen Elgin was an integral part of the Blanche business but John did not spend much time there. The excitement of the deals to be done in the City was what seemed to motivate him. He obviously thought that by simply appointing a manager and leaving him to run the place 200 miles away was all that was required. The reality is that all businesses need regular and proper supervision particularly if they are in remote locations. The skills for running a malt distillery are simple and easily acquired but it is essential to have someone, who is completely trustworthy, because there are many opportunities for stealing, fraud or diverting materials and supplies for personal benefit or simply taking to drink. John had been lucky at the beginning to have such a person in William Simpson but later had frequent trouble. When his son Willie was old enough he made regular trips north and on John's death took full responsibility for Glen Elgin. He once told me that he would have samples of each day's make sent to Glasgow by train and would examine them the following day. If he was not satisfied, he would take the night train to Aberdeen and board the milk train for Elgin the next morning for the distillery and discover what was wrong. This attention and regular interest in the operation and the chance to give praise when deserved made all the difference and Glen Elgin proved a good profit earner even in the depressed years of the late 1920s and early 1930s.

The distillery was sold in 1935 and, together with payment for outstanding cask rents, the amount realised was £37,805. The original cost in 1905 was £7,000. The intervening 30 years had produced mixed fortunes for distillers of Scotch whisky. In the early part of the century the economy was depressed and then as trade was building up, along came the war. Most distilling was stopped as no barley could be spared for mashing. In the post war period production increased rapidly to meet the pent up demand but growth was hindered by prohibition in the United States, which lasted until 1933. However, shipments to North America continued, or rather to offshore islands, notably St Pierre et Michelon from which the goods were run in by small boats for distribution to the illegal bars.

The timing of the sale of the distillery was quite good because, although sales were beginning to rise after the end of prohibition, WWII brought a halt to distilling once more. After the war production resumed but was restricted by the slow growth in supply of grain. By 1950 the industry began to forge ahead but it was not until 1955 that output exceeded the 1899 level. By that time Glen Elgin, one of the best malts, would probably have been worth about £1m and with hindsight one wonders if the decision to sell was wise. Father was not keen on the sale and I often wonder what Lawrie and Isabel thought about it later when they saw the growth in value. At the time the DCL was a willing buyer and they took every opportunity to acquire anything that came on the market. They were also the largest customers and the family may have felt a little vulnerable.

John had no starting capital when he began his business and used bank overdraft facilities until he could reinvest profits in hard assets. Even then he preferred to invest in stock, which could be sold at a profit. His method of financing the distillery was to take out a bond from the sellers at a competitive rate of interest to be repaid later when he had produced some profit from the venture. The maturing stocks he had bought with the distillery were paid for when they were sold and thus he did not have to lay out cash at the start. Admittedly, the prevailing conditions favoured these methods but lessons could be learned today by managements of very much larger companies about how to think in terms of conserving cash and cutting the cost of capital.

The Scotch whisky business is a combination of finance and marketing and success lies in getting the balance right. New whisky stocks have to be tied up for anything from 4 to 15 years depending on what part of the market you are in. This involves a considerable investment, which will increase if the product is successful. It is obvious that cash flow will be negative in the early stages and will become worse if volume increases. The faster the growth the greater is the increase in the capital requirement. Aged whiskies, which succeed may not produce a positive cash flow for decades. In addition funds will be required for advertising and promotion and bottling facilities.

The Scotch whisky industry was in some difficulty in the late 1890s and the early part of the 20th century. Many distilleries had closed for lack of orders and some were for sale. John saw an opportunity to enter the industry at a reasonable cost and began looking at several prospects. At this time there were many attempts being made to start new grain distilleries to offer the trade an alternative to the giant Distillers Company. Earlier mention was made of John's part in the Northern Distilleries Ltd, which built Gartloch. It was under capitalised and he withdrew after two years. In his days with the Licensed Trade Defence Association John had made many contacts among distillers and after his affair with Northern, it was natural for him to start trading in whiskies on his own account. In the process, John kept in touch with events in the industry with a view to buying a malt distillery rather than grain. Most of the new grain ventures folded under the relentless pressure from the DCL, who controlled almost all the production and supplied all the important blenders.

One of the first attempts to buy a malt distillery was in August 1898 when John was in touch with George Sellar of Kingussie regarding the acquisition of Strathspey Distillery. It had recently been built and was in voluntary liquidation. Also known as Dalwhinnie, it was sold in 1900, passed through several hands and was eventually acquired by the DCL in 1928. In June 1903 John was proposing to bid for Knockando-Glenlivet Distillery built in 1898 and being put up for sale by J Thomson & Co. He discussed the rate of interest on a bond and suggested that the five per cent proposed was 'a pretty tall rate of interest ... I am of the opinion that a lean could be got for at least two thirds of the purchase price at probably 3½ per cent to 4 per cent'. A price of £4,000 was offered in July but W & A Gilbey Ltd bought it.

Eventually he settled on Glen Elgin and set about improving the sales with great energy. W & T Restell of Mark Lane and J Travers & Son Ltd of Cannon Street were appointed London agents. This was a good way of attracting the custom of the large English brewers, who were offering Scotch whisky in their pubs on a regular basis by then and liked to do their own blending in order to earn a higher margin than was available from branded Scotch whiskies.

The brewers continued this practice until the 1960s when they stopped investing in bulk stock and started negotiating lower prices with brand owners. In 1933 Messrs William Walker & Co Ltd were appointed agents for England with a commission of 3d per gallon on all filling orders for new Glen Elgin that were accepted by the company.

In the early days the bank was helpful in the financing the purchase and in processing one of the first major orders, a quantity of 15,000 gallons. A few good years followed but conditions in the market deteriorated as a result of a growing surplus of stock, which became critical in 1913. The following year things improved and Glen Elgin had started production again with many orders. However, the war obliged all distilleries to cease production, as barley was not available for distilling.

In January 1915 John wrote to Adam Thomson & Ross, solicitors of 2 Union Terrace, Aberdeen, from whom he had bought Glen Elgin, about converting the distilling business into a separate limited company. He said his health was poor and he must 'devolutionise' some of his work. He was considering raising £50,000 from a five per cent debenture, £20,000 from six per cent preference shares and £20,000 of ordinary shares to be issued to him.

In February, he tried to persuade them not to press for repayment of the £3,000 bond over Glen Elgin. In the course of the correspondence on the subject of settling the deal John mentioned that three investors had pulled out due to a prohibition scare. The prohibition legislation in the United States came into operation in 1919 and had a depressing affect on exports. Nevertheless, John remained optimistic and eventually he transferred the shares in the distillery to the family as follows – John 50 per cent, his wife 25 per cent and Robert Bruce Blanche 25 per cent. Robert was the second son of his marriage to Jean Brown.

The characters in the Scotch whisky industry were often colourful and so were some of their actions. One anecdote I had related to me in the mid 1950s concerned my grandfather's efforts to resume production at Glen Elgin after the enforced shutdown during the Great War. His warehouses at the distillery were full of customers' stock and most of it was owned by The Distillers Company, who had purchased it before the war. Unless they removed it John could not start distilling, because there was no space to store the new whisky. He asked them to remove it either for blending or to one of their many other bonded warehouses. They refused and there was a 'nasty' thought that they wished to keep at least one competitor off the market for as long as possible. John was having none of this. He loaded the whole lot onto a train and sent it off to them! He had no further orders from them during his lifetime but he did sell a great deal to other buyers. An example of one of the efforts to build up the filling trade is an early offer to David Blanche of G & J MacLachlan Ltd (no relation) for 100 hogsheads of new make at 5/- per gallon nett free on rail at the distillery if removed to own bond and payment by a six months bill. The distillery had been operating in 1914 and several deals were done for that year's make in 1922. This mature stock would have brought in a good profit.

Problems with Managers

In April 1923 new warehouses were planned, which may indicate that production was increasing. They were given the go-ahead and in addition a cooperage was to be constructed in the old stable. This would provide proper storage for the casks that Mr Bisset, the manager, had left out in the open thus exposing them to weather damage. He was reprimanded in no uncertain terms for not at least putting them under cover in the old stable.

Bisset wrote to John on 20 March 1922 seeking a war bonus in addition to his salary of £150 per annum. He was given a good lecture by the old man but a few days later John wrote to him again enclosing a cheque for £40 and all seemed well between them. However, when the accounts were prepared there was no profit and Bisset was put on a year's notice of dismissal unless things improved. By November John was seeking a replacement for the man, who seems to have been totally incompetent.

Some of Bisset's failures were important for the smooth running of the distillery. For example, Glen Elgin had a filter bed for effluent but it sometimes did not work too well. There were frequent complaints from a neighbour, William Ramsay of Longmorn House. John did not accept these and suggested that Mr Ramsay would have to prove that they were justified. Clearly John was not going to pay any compensation! Nevertheless, he asked Charles Doig, the architect, to look at the problem, which had been allowed to go unattended for about a year, and suggest a solution.

John's health was not good and it is evident that the pressure of business over the years combined with shortages of staff and the deaths of a number of his children had begun to take their toll. On 20 July 1923 John had just returned from one of his rare visits to Glen Elgin and wrote to Bisset to confirm discussions. He said he was exhausted after the journey and feared he would not be able to travel up again. He wrote to an old friend William Shanks shortly after his return and said he had enjoyed his visit to Elgin but he had been ill in the last few weeks.

For some reason Bisset survived but was still committing acts of folly. Having been given a new warehouse, he was still leaving casks outside and furthermore had failed to fill them with water, which would have prevented the staves from opening up prior to refilling. The casks were described as being 'gisened' whatever that meant. It appears that there was no cooper employed, whose duties would have included tightening the staves in preparation for refilling. Bisset had really no excuse, as there was sufficient room in the warehouse if only he had stacked the filled casks more efficiently.

On another occasion Bisset was informed in no uncertain terms that he must not employ any member of his family on pain of dismissal. It was pointed out to him that he had a good billet but that his performance was not satisfactory. There had been a burglary and a case of arson. A private detective agency was employed to watch the employees as an insider was thought to be responsible. The number of employees was 11, including Bisset, but only five were to be seen on John's visit. One wonders if this long letter (three pages) was to confirm points raised during the visit and was a warning letter such as is now the law or if John did not want to confront Bisset face to face. He was ill and not feeling well at the time. It is clear that there was not sufficient supervision and Bisset felt that he could do as he wished. It is surprising that a member of the family did not go and live in Elgin to look after what was a major asset and profit earner.

Bisset was written to on 9 October 1923 and asked to explain a deficiency of 940 gallons between the weekly production returns and the spirit put into warehouse. Also the cost of the make had risen to 5d more than other distilleries. Why? Bisset was obviously never going to improve and it is astonishing that he lasted so long. John was probably lacking in energy due to his illness but he did not help the situation by making frequent threats to dismiss the man and then not carrying them out. Bisset was playing him along and taking advantage of the fact that he was on his own and accountable only to Glasgow 200 miles away.

On 7 November John wrote to Charles Doig to ask if he could recommend a replacement as he was convinced that Bisset was drinking. The post was advertised and in the meantime Bisset had a breakdown and was off work. Writing to William Simpson of Winchester on 27 November 1923 John mentioned that the distillery was compulsorily closed for three years. Simpson was a former manager and his successor was killed at the front. Both were good men and John had become used to the distillery being run without any trouble. Bisset was maybe all that was available during the war. John related an attempt to set fire to the warehouses and that fortunately the fire was spotted by old John Grant just in time. The police chief, Mr Mair, was convinced two men named Hay were responsible and they were married to Bisset's daughters. It was assumed that they had started the fire out of spite but there was not sufficient evidence for a conviction.

John told Simpson that there was no difficulty in selling all the production and he could have sold more in spite of the fact that excise duty on spirits was by then 72/6 per proof gallon and home consumption was half the pre-war level. All the matured stock was sold and so was the new make. He sent a sample of the Old Blended Glenlivet (Glen Elgin-Glenlivet) and offered to supply for personal use only as stocks were too low to canvas for orders.

Happily a new manager was appointed, Mr A B Marshall. It must have been a great relief as John said to Marshall that he was in a 'very critical state of health and worry would be fatal'. I am not sure of the psychology of this tactic with a new manager, but it may have been designed to engender a sympathetic attitude and a willingness to help. Coincidentally Bisset resigned and was shocked when a new manager appeared. John went on in his letter to Simpson about his experiences with Bisset and mentioned that his son Willie had wanted him to be dismissed. John, however, was sympathetic and not tough enough. Marshall was quite old but would, he thought, be good for another five years. Simpson offered to come up and help but his offer was declined with thanks.

It appears that Bisset had been supplying coal to outsiders and had not put the sales through the books. However, Marshall seems to have been getting a grip of the situation in spite of Bisset causing trouble at every turn. Arrangements were made for him to be evicted from the distillery manager's house as soon as possible.

About this time it was discovered that some petrol cans had been used to block the effluent pipes and this was the cause of the system malfunctioning. Before long Marshall found himself displeasing John. In March 1924 he was ticked off for organising a chimneystack repair without referring the matter to head office and then to Charles Doig. The chimney repair was a bad job and John would not pay the account. An action was raised against him and Mr Doig confirmed poor workmanship and was asked by John to appear in court as a witness.

The Innovative Doig Family

Charles C Doig was named after his father, who had made a notable contribution to the design of malt distilleries. In the late 19th century, architects were engineers as well as designers and provided technical support for the distillery owner. They thought up and designed the improvements and were able to fine tune still design to improve the spirit produced. Nowadays there are specialist engineers both independent and employed in-house and the role of architect is a more conventional one. Charles Doig's most famous contribution was the invention and design of the Chinese-style pagoda roof ventilator for the building that dries the malted barley. It has such delightful proportions that it has survived and has become a recognisable feature of a malt whisky distillery. Even if the distillery does not produce its own malted barley it will no doubt have a pagoda roof somewhere. The old man died in 1918 but he undoubtedly played an important part in Glen Elgin's working. His son followed him in the Elgin practice and this explains why John would always turn to Charles Doig when in any sort of difficulty. He and his firm were the best-connected people in the Scotch whisky industry north of Perth.

In April John received a letter from a distilling friend in the north to say that Marshall was drinking and he again asked Mr Doig for help in confirming the accusation. He also sent Willie up to Elgin where he found that Marshall was 'hopelessly intoxicated and quite unfit for duties'. Willie took immediate action by removing the keys and handing them to W Shiach, who was installed as temporary manager. At a board meeting on 22 April 1924 it was decided to dismiss Marshall without further ado. His successor, Andrew Paterson was appointed later that month at a salary of £350. He was from Glenfyne Distillery, Ardrishaig, owned by Highland Distilleries. However, by September 1926 Paterson was in trouble, had been dismissed and there was discussion about laying criminal charges against him. From this point on the distillery must have been in Willie's hands because John did not write any letters on the subject and things must have been stabilised over the following period.

Mention was made earlier of the distillery being silent in 1913 and this is still a standard practice when times are hard. If sales are slow there is no point in producing more whisky simply to keep people occupied as this ties up precious capital. The resumption of production in 1914 until war broke out was useful in providing stock for sale after the war ended but it must have been frustrating to have to close down again when hostilities started. The depression of the early 1930s caused further interruptions to production when Glen Elgin was silent for the whole of the 1932/33 season. The warehouses were full of customers' stock and there was thus a good income from rents. The total outstanding rents payable at September 1933 amounted to £4,450. Rents were charged to customers when they withdrew their stock and could cover many years of storage. Nowadays, they are usually invoiced annually, as the distiller does not have the margin to cover the cost of financing the debt.

During the season 1933/34 the distillery planned to produce 62,000 gallons, of which 84 per cent was to be sold to outside customers. In the event the output was 48,259 gallons of which 9,495 were for the company's own account. The 38,763 gallons sold to outside customers produced a turnover of £6,930 equal to 35½d per gallon. This performance was regarded as very satisfactory and yet a little over a year later the directors were prepared to sell. One explanation might be that most of the orders came from, as the AGM Report said, 'principally one buyer'. This buyer was probably The Distillers Company, who eventually bought the distillery!

In 1994 Christie's had one of their regular Scotch whisky sales in Glasgow and it included the following lot:

> **RARE OLD GLEN ELGIN**
>
> **'KOSB 25 year old Pre 1930**
>
> Kings Own Special Blend JJ Blanche & Co, Distillers, Glasgow and London
>
> Driven cork and lead capsule 1 bottle per lot £300–500
>
> The Glen Elgin Distillery, Longmorn, Elgin, Moray, as purchased by John J Blanche, Whisky Merchant, Glasgow in 1907. The company became JJ Blanche & Co in 1921 and incorporated as JJ Blanche & Co Ltd in 1927.'

The heading 'RARE OLD GLEN ELGIN' and the description above implies that the product is a single malt. In fact the label states quite clearly that the contents were 'Highland Malt Whisky' and the word 'blend' appears in the translation of KOSB (King's Own Special Blend). The modern term used for a mix of malts is actually 'vatted'. In spite of the inaccuracies I bought this artefact of the family business. It is not for drinking but rather as an investment to be offered at Christie's again when this record has been published. I hope to make at least the purchase price of £567. It would be interesting to know the seller's name but Christie's would not divulge it. It must have been someone with a connection to the business, who was able to give some background information. Perhaps it was the seller of the Royal Jubilee Port purchased from Christie's in 1997!

As always, John could not resist a bargain. The Garngad Bonding Company Limited came up for sale and it was agreed the JJ Blanche & Co would buy it as it neatly complemented the distillery business. William and John Risk, owners of Moses Risk & Sons Ltd and Provanmill Lowland Malt distillery in Glasgow had incorporated Garngad on 16 June 1914. With this purchase came the Moses Risk Scotch whisky labels including Risk's Royal Vat, which was the house whisky in the Baileys shops until 1960.

Garngad had been run in conjunction with the distillery for ten years until it was sold to John in 1924 for £9,000. John Risk had died in 1918 and his shares were transferred to his son William. One of John Risk's trustees was James Denny, the shipbuilder in Dumbarton and another was Hugh Osborne, provision merchant, Glasgow. William Risk died in 1921 and the directors, James Findlay and young William carried on the business for a few years.

The minute book records that the audit fee was £1-1/- in the first year and it was raised in 1918 to £5-5/- and again in 1923 to £8-8/-. The profits averaged around £1,400 but no dividend was paid until the last meeting before the sale of the company. Then £20 per share was paid out free of tax amounting in total to £2,000.

The first directors meeting under the new owners was on 8 July 1924 and William (24) and Lawrence (19) were appointed directors but were not authorised to sign cheques! A number of staff were given one month's trial at reduced salaries. The registered office was changed to 36 Douglas Street, Glasgow, which was the head office of JJ Blanche & Co. On the death of John, Willie was appointed chairman at the AGM attended by Willie, Lawrie, Isabel, Stephen Hardie as trustee of John's estate and Elizabeth Harvey, secretary. The company became a department of JJ Blanche & Co and no separate books were kept after 1931.

On reflection, it seems that John was interested in distilling and would have been unlikely to sell Glen Elgin and one wonders what he would have thought of his children's decision to sell. It would not have been allowed! On the other hand his two sons seemed to be more comfortable in retailing and life in the city rather than in a country town like Elgin. When the record of the industry between 1900 and the early 1930s is considered, maybe they were right. No one could have forecast the tremendous boom in exports after WWII and the subsequent growth in the highly profitable malts. At the time the Blanches had the alternative activity of retailing whereas the other independent distillers who hung on had no other course to follow.

The story of the Blanches in distilling might have been tidier if there had not been a gap between 1935, the sale of Glen Elgin, and 1969, when I was asked take charge of Stewart & Son of Dundee. I spent the next 20 years in the Scotch whisky industry, a period of dramatic changes more far reaching than those of the 1920s when The Distillers Company arranged their merger with Walkers, Dewar's and Black & White.

CHAPTER 4

The Growth of the Distillers Company

Early Days

In the early 1800s some distillers began experimenting with the faster and more reliable continuous distilling. Among these was the Stein family and their patent still was installed by several companies around 1830–33. This new equipment produced spirit much faster and at lower cost but the economic benefits of the early operators were not forthcoming. The reason was overcapacity, which caused several companies to go into liquidation.

The curse of overcapacity has plagued the Scotch whisky industry to this day, although its effects have been mitigated by the creation of large vertically integrated companies capable of owning grain capacity and thus matching output to requirement.

About this time Aeneas Coffey of Dublin perfected an improved patent still to be known as the Coffey still. It was designed to produce grain whisky and, although expensive to install, it was cheap and simple to operate and could also produce gin, a highly rectified spirit. Several were installed in Scotland in the 1830s and the Coffey still became firmly established.

Provided a company was sufficiently capitalised, it was easy to enter the distilling business and before long several new distilleries were opened. The output of patent still grain whiskies expanded enormously and was sustained not only by local demand but also by exports. The mildly flavoured grain whisky compared to malt was popular in mixed drinks in the hotter climates. By 1856 output had climbed to 6.5 million gallons of grain spirit and competition was intense. Many companies became vulnerable and it was only a matter of time before all but those with a long purse risked bankruptcy. This situation prompted six patent still distillers to agree to a co-operative for one year during which they would share the trade between them. The arrangement worked well but it was not renewed at the end of the year.

A new trade arrangement was entered into in 1865 when eight distillers agreed to join together for a little over a year. However, the consortium continued with a fluid membership. Some were not satisfied with the percentage of trade they were allocated and thought they could do better on their own. Now known as the Grain Whisky Association, it was dissolved and then re-formed from time to time. It appears that there was a continuous demand for a quasi monopoly in order to earn higher profit margins. Given the situation, it was perhaps the only sensible commercial course to follow. Eventually this led to a more formal arrangement in 1877 when The Distillers Company was formed.

The shareholders of the new company were the owners of the grain distilleries of Port Dundas, Carsebridge, Cameron Bridge, Glenochil, Cambus, Kirkliston and finally Caledonian, which joined some years later. Most of these distilleries had been in the Grain Distillers Association, whose purpose was thus given a much more powerful backing. The new company dominated the market for grain and beat off the threat of new entrants by the use of competitive pricing from a strong financial base. The DCL, as the new company became known, continued to dominate the grain whisky supply for the next 80 years.

The only successful alternative supplier of grain whisky in that period was The North British Distillery Company Limited formed in 1885 by 35 gentlemen, who were non-aligned blenders and purveyors of their own brands of Scotch. All the capital was subscribed by members of the trade and a new distillery was constructed at Roseburn near Gorgie railway station in Edinburgh. It cost £142,000 to build and had a capacity of 25,000 gallons per week compared with the largest, Caledonian, which could produce 40,000 gallons. The key characters in the early stages were John Crabbie (ginger wine), Andrew Usher, William Sanderson (VAT 69), Alexander Murdoch, John Sommerville, James McLennan and George Robertson, all of whom were already successful businessman in the trade. The board of directors continued to be composed of members of the trade, who supported the alternative source of supply and no further competition to DCL appeared until WWII. The business was run for the benefit of the trade and guaranteed the continued existence of an independent source of supply of grain whisky.

Although the concept of the DCL was protectionist and monopolistic, it was a stabilising influence for the industry, along with The North British (NB). Like The North British, it was formed by like-minded people who were brought together by force of circumstances. However, whereas the NB was composed of merchants who bought from the one source, the DCL was a grouping of several distillers each of whom wished to maximise the output from their own distillery. The management was carried on by allowing the participants a great deal of freedom in running their own businesses. This devolved form of management was controlled by a committee, which agreed the share of business for each distillery. This meant the board was in constant negotiation but it worked because the alternative was a return to the previous chaotic market conditions. At first sight this sounds like the modern philosophy of empowerment, where individuals are encouraged to do their job as they see fit to produce the best results. Not so, for today every one knows who the boss is and under whose authority they carry out their duties. Under the DCL system each operation had a say in top management decisions and they usually made sure that their own businesses were not threatened by the others. It was management by committee and the system survived until Guinness acquired the DCL in 1986.

During the next 20 years the DCL quietly bought up a number of small distilleries as they became available and continued to supply the trade with large quantities of grain whisky. As well as being used for blending with malt, grain whisky was also sold unblended in pubs and benefited from its Scottish origins as far afield as London. But soon its principal appeal was as an important ingredient in blended Scotch whisky, which rapidly found favour as a popular drink due to its lighter character compared to malt.

It should be appreciated that Scotch whisky was really regarded as a product made in batches of fermented malted barley and using a pot still. There was no statuary definition but this was the traditional method until the introduction of the Coffey still, which operated on a continuous basis, using only a small quantity of malted barley, the remainder being other grains. Also, around the late 1870s, the government had carried through the Sale of Food and Drugs Act and the Merchandise Marks Act, which sought to protect consumers from shoddy goods being passed off as higher quality items. The malt distillers had for some years been trying to persuade the authorities to define Scotch whisky as exclusively made from malted barley in a pot still. They had so far failed.

In 1905 someone (cynics say the malt distillers) prompted Islington Borough Council to test out the application of the Acts to grain and blended whisky and to take out a summons against some retailers for selling 'an article not of the nature and substance demanded'. This was a direct challenge to the grain distillers, who were supplying a growing market at good margins. The threat to employment was serious and the huge investment at distilleries would be lost if grain were not allowed to be called Scotch whisky. The early stages could have been described as comical if the issue had not been so serious. The Magistrates Court decided in favour of malt and the grain distillers, who were defending the case, appealed to the Quarter Sessions. Here the bench was equally divided and the matter could not go to further appeal.

The Royal Commission on Whisky

After much public debate, the government agreed to appoint a Royal Commission and it was formed in 1908 under Lord James of Hereford. The Commission took submissions from a cross section of the trade, including wholesalers as well as malt and grain distillers. Among those who gave evidence was my grandfather, who as we have seen, was involved in the 1890s boom in grain whisky earlier in his career. There was also a contribution from William C Teacher, whose family business was one of the more successful of the new brand owners of blended Scotch whisky.

William Teacher was clearly for blending and did not think it desirable to place restrictions upon the manufacture of Scotch whisky, considering it a good wholesome article. He could not understand why some people approved of one kind of whisky and some of another (meaning grain and malt). He found that tastes varied and gave as an example the following statement:

> The public taste has changed very much during, I might say, the past 20 years. My firm's style has always been a very malty one, but 12 or 15 years ago we had to introduce lighter and less pronounced whiskies to suit the changing taste. I might also mention that till about 20 years ago a large licence holder in Glasgow whom my firm supplied sold at 4d a glass, that is half a gill, only pure malt whiskey, but finding the public taste changing, he had 20 per cent of old grain whiskey added, and some years later he increased that to 25 per cent. I just mention that because I think it is an important point. This licence holder was noted for the quality of the article supplied.

He was asked further questions regarding the age of Scotch whisky and the record relates the exchange as follows:

> Now I want to put to you one point with regard to the statement in your précis that the average age of Scotch whiskey is greatly increasing, and that you give that as a reason for taking no administrative action. Is there not likely always to be a demand for the cheapest whiskey that can be supplied? – Yes I might mention that in the Scotch mining districts the miners would not thank you for an old whiskey. They must have something ... Something with a bite in it? Yes, with – a bite.
>
> I may take it the gist of your evidence, if I may summarise it, is that the public is to take all Scotch whiskey on trust without any means of control over the statement of the blender? – I think they might safely do so. I think that is as regards Scotch whiskey. As regards any spirit used as Scotch whiskey otherwise I have a different opinion.
>
> I take it from your evidence that you have it in your mind chiefly to produce a cheap whiskey for the labouring man? – Yes. They require it.

Grandfather John's evidence was somewhat controversial when he suggested that whisky could be made from a wide variety of materials and not simply malted barley. Whereas we now know Scotch whisky as a blend of malt and grain whiskies produced in the traditional manner, there was absolutely no control over what was sold as Scotch whisky at that time. Indeed, what he said then has proved to be true for other countries, who now produce whisky of their own.

This line of questioning was concluded as follows:

> Looking to the history of the word 'whiskey,' perhaps your evidence might be summed up by saying this, that it was originally spirit distilled from malted barley in a pot still, but that by evolution it has become a generic term, and has become applicable to spirit distilled from other materials by other processes? – Yes, I do.

His next contribution was perhaps a typical piece of lateral thought:

> You make some statements about the intoxicating effects of taking heavy pot still spirit. What are those statements based upon? – They are based upon actual experiments made upon myself. I have taken what we would call, a good skinful of patent still spirit, and gone to bed, and I have got up the next morning with a perfectly clear head. I have done the same with pot still whiskey, and I have got up the next day with a fearful head. It is accounted for by the essential oils that are contained in the Spirit. The one, the patent still, is a light spirit.
>
> 'This is a very important experiment, and we must go a little more into detail. Are you sure the skin was just as full both times? – Perfectly. I should rather think that the balance would be in favour of the patent still.
>
> (Chairman.) 'What constitutes a balance in favour – little or much? – I took sufficient of each spirit to believe myself that I was intoxicated, and I went to bed and I had, what would be called, a sleep, not a very refreshing sleep. I judged by the effect upon me the next day.
>
> 'Which do you think began to have effect first? – The patent still, but it ended very much sooner. It is easily explained, because the patent spirit, being light, is evanescent, and goes to the head at once, but it gets out of your system quicker.

> 'With the patent still spirit you could not detect any headache whatever? – That is so.
>
> 'I want to get at any possible differences. Were the experiments quite parallel? Did you take them at the same time of day? – I took them at the same time of night – immediately before going to bed. I did not want to be knocking about.
>
> (Chairman.) 'You took it lying down? – Yes.
>
> 'You think it is simply a matter of difference in the amount of essential oils? – I do.
>
> 'The essential oil is probably about half as much in the patent still spirit, I take it, as in the pot still spirit. That is the general run of things – that there is about a half to a third as much of the essential oil in the patent still as in the pot still spirit? – I really could not say.
>
> 'Were the experiments on successive evenings? – Yes.
>
> 'Which experiment came first? – The patent still spirit I took first.
>
> 'I am afraid I cannot accept that as evidence? – Possibly not. I am not prepared to repeat the experiment.'

His evidence finished with a discussion on wrongdoing:

> 'I suppose you also would agree that the freer we allow trade to be done uninterfered with by the State the better, except for the purpose of checking the evildoer? – That is so.
>
> 'According to your opinion, where does the evildoer come in the whiskey trade? – I am not acquainted with any evildoers in our trade. I only recollect in 30 years experience one case where a certain blender – not mentioning names – in Leith was using methylated spirits for diluting his spirit. That is the only instance, and it was so unique that it was spoken about for a very long time. I should say that he was singular.
>
> 'In the first place, you have the check of public taste, which represents public opinion, where the customer chooses his own source where he deals – that is, apart from legislative check? – That is so.
>
> 'There is no doubt, is there not, the evil of a man buying very cheaply and selling very dearly? – Yes.
>
> 'Do you know personally of any instance where the State has ever interfered to prevent that being done? – I am not aware of any.

Definition of Scotch Whisky

The recommendation of the Commission when it reported in 1909 was that malt, grain and blended whisky could be described as Scotch. The question of a minimum maturing period for Scotch was discussed by the Commission in the context of public health but it was thought that there was not sufficient medical evidence to come to a conclusion.

Subsequently, in 1916, a three-year minimum period of maturation was introduced. Much later it is interesting to note the J J Blanche & Co directors minute of 7 July 1933, when Willie reported that the provisions of the Finance Act 1933 section 24 required that only spirits distilled in Scotland could be described as Scotch whisky. Hitherto it had been possible to use grain produced in other parts of Britain to blend with malt. The company had a large stock of Watney grain from London presumably bought at a lower price.

The 1933 Finance Act included the first formal definition of Scotch whisky. It had to be 'obtained by distillation in Scotland from a mash saccharified by the diastase of malt and had been matured in bond for a period of at least three years'. Much later the Scotch Whisky Act 1988 contained a wider definition including a minimum strength of 40% alcohol by volume. The European Community also adopted this requirement. The Act prohibits the production in Scotland of whisky other than Scotch whisky.

The position of the DCL was immeasurably strengthened by the Royal Commission's decision and enabled the industry to promote a high quality product worldwide. The DCL led the way and they continued to build up their cash resources from an excellent profit record. Even during World War I they averaged over £250,000 in spite of distilling being curtailed due to shortages of materials.

The Distillers Company Aims to Restructure the Industry

The Royal Commission's decision not only secured the position of the grain distillers it also changed the shape of the Scotch whisky industry. Blended Scotch whisky proved popular and enabled the blenders to expand their businesses through promotion of their proprietary brands.

Three were outstanding in the early 20th century, Dewar's, Buchanan's and Walker's, known as the Big Three. Their market share was 12 per cent in 1910 but their share of the branded business was probably well over 50 per cent. These three began to discuss a merger in 1909 motivated by the desire to limit the 'excessive' expenditure on sales promotion. They were a little naïve in thinking that they would not have to disclose financial information or in the case of Walker's, that the merger could be based on the figures of the best years. The negotiations were complicated by the intervention of the DCL, who wanted to set up a holding company for all four operations and allow each to continue as before. This was their well-tried formula, which had been introduced in 1877 and lasted until 1986. The three brand owners were suspicious that DCL might dominate and they were not ready for that, although acknowledging that they would eventually join with them.

Until this point the DCL had been a grain distiller primarily and had sought to expand in the general industrial field following their major contribution to the 1914–1918 war effort. They had formed the United Yeast Company in 1899 to supply their own needs and those of others. As the war progressed, it became obvious that with supplies from the continent being cut off, the bread supply would be in danger. The DCL, therefore, filled the gap in supply and all but cut out production of Scotch whisky to compensate. They were also involved in industrial alcohol used in the manufacture of explosives. In addition they introduced a motor fuel named Discol distilled from molasses. It was innovative but oil eventually won the day as it poured out in ever increasing quantities at ever lower prices.

The merger discussions progressed when all were persuaded to divulge their figures but no satisfactory method of valuing the businesses on an equitable basis could be found. Walkers were a stumbling block and were ruled out but White Horse came on the scene and appeared keen to join the talks but they too were left out. That left Dewar and Buchanan and they came together by forming Scotch Whisky Brands in 1915. Later it changed its name to Buchanan-Dewar Ltd. It was a powerful combination and much bigger than the DCL with a more exciting profits performance. Its management structure consisted of committees for finance, purchasing, UK sales and exports and the individual identities of the two companies were retained.

In spite of their failure to arrange a merger with the Big Three the DCL were keen to expand in the Scotch whisky industry if possible. Indeed their aim was a wide restructuring by creating a vertically integrated company, which would be self sufficient in grain capacity and include all the major blenders and brand owners. They could exert a powerful influence as the dominant supplier of grain but at the same time they were vulnerable because the Big Three accounted for 20 per cent of their grain whisky fillings. On the other hand they had restrictive agreements with two 'independents': the Cork Distilleries in Ireland and J & W Nicholson in England. The North British remained completely independent to its great credit.

The DCL's first major acquisition was John Haig in 1919 and later in 1923 Haig & Haig, a separate business but owned within the Haig family. The DCL did not use this brand believing that there were enough brands already on the market. This was in spite of the fact that it had been the top brand in the US before prohibition and therefore a front runner in the smuggling trade. They were to regret this decision later when others threatened to introduce a Haig brand and compete with their John Haig business. Indeed the threat involved some of the participants in the plans for a major merger who took their eye off the ball slightly.

In between these two acquisitions an approach was made to William Teacher & Sons but without success. The purchase of the Tanqueray Gordon gin company followed in 1922. Gin is made with plain spirit from a continuous still and this made a nice fit with the existing plant capacity. Tanquery's Gordons Gin was to become the world's leading brand and a big earner for the DCL.

At last in 1925 the long discussed idea of a major amalgamation came to the surface and talks began in an atmosphere of gloom. Whisky stock prices were falling and world trade was not buoyant. There was prohibition in the United States, although some trade continued through 'middlemen'. At the same time there were discussions about the acquisition of White Horse but they were not progressed and that company carried on independently until 1927 when it was acquired by the DCL.

This time the DCL, Buchanan-Dewar and Walker were serious but that did not make the discussions easy. As Buchanan-Dewar was the biggest company according to published results, they reckoned it should become the new holding company for the merger. DCL felt that they should take over the others by issuing new shares, because they had been quoted for almost 50 years and were Scottish registered. There was a comment that the London brokers were not so interested in handling a Scottish registered company and would prefer Buchanan-Dewar, which was English registered. This arrogant attitude angered the DCL and by a quirk of fate became a central issue when Guinness was proposing to merge with the DCL in 1986.

A central character in the negotiations was William H Ross, the DCL chairman, originally employed as a clerk in 1878. He became company secretary in 1889, general manager in 1897 and one of the first non-family directors, appointed to the board in 1900 as managing director. Over the years he had gradually increased his influence, because he was able, had a non-family independent background and had a vision unencumbered by pricing and share of trade questions, which obsessed most of the others. In the early days after his board appointment he took a firm line on tackling the problem of vendor-management referred to by Ronald Weir in his excellent history of the DCL. You sold your business to the group on the condition that you would continue to manage it, while having the benefit of having realised the capital tied up in your company. You could still regard the business as yours without having the final responsibility for the results. To compound the problem the heirs of the vendors were regarded as natural successors and it was a problem that never left the DCL, although the influence of these heirs and their descendants gradually declined.

Ross was keen on rationalising the Scotch whisky industry and that became his major achievement. He also took DCL into industrial alcohol and chemicals and made direct investments in Canada and Australia to circumvent tariffs. He was a clear thinker and he was the one who came up with solutions to problems and schemes for new profit opportunities other than defending margins and looking for price increases. He could recognise these and develop strategies to maximise their potential. My favourite example of his skill is, I think, the yeast business, which became a DCL moneyspinner. Yeast is a by-product of the mashing process in distilling and had been sold by Scotch whisky distillers for many years. However, the quality was variable and the bakers, who were the big users, preferred to import yeast from the continent. When Dr W S Squire, a consultant chemical engineer, approached them with a new process, the DCL entered into an exclusive agreement with him and in 1885 the new yeast went on sale.

The economics were exceedingly attractive. Although the production of yeast reduced the yield of spirit, the margin on yeast was large enough to compensate and to produce an additional profit. Gradually other distillers followed suit and foreign suppliers stepped up their efforts to recover some of the market share lost to the new higher quality producers in Britain. The generous margins were declining as prices dropped. Ross responded by organising the acquisition of many independent dealers and formed the United Yeast Company (UYC), which then set up a national distribution system capable of providing the fast delivery service necessary for a short life product. In addition UYC introduced tinned dried egg for bakers and distributed other products required by wholesalers to the food trade. A whole new business had been born out of a distiller's by-product.

As well as the difference of opinion on the domicile of the merged company, there was disagreement on the value of the Buchanan-Dewar and Walker businesses in terms of the DCL shares. At this point Ross produced his trump card by disclosing the true financial position of DCL as opposed to the reported position. He was conservative in his reporting and it is inconceivable to the modern businessman that it was possible in those days to understate profits and asset values.

The DCL disclosure of its true value suddenly concentrated the minds of everyone and the terms were agreed quite quickly. Buchanan-Dewar people were glad to be part of the merged group, because it gave them a security in grain whisky supplies and the DCL's strong finances were a comfort in a difficult market. The DCL was to be the holding company with the head office in Edinburgh. The DCL would issue 6.75 million new shares and Buchanan-Dewar and Walker would have a majority in the merged group. The new board had 21 members, ten DCL, eight Buchanan-Dewar and three Walker. Ross was appointed Chairman and Managing Director in recognition of his patience in carrying through the negotiations and as the only truly independent member of the board.

The William Ross Philosophy

It is interesting to read Ronald Weir's description of the policy adopted by the DCL in conducting themselves in an industry they controlled so tightly after the merger. Lord Dewar, in praising Ross, said that he was 'their new Moses to take them out of strenuous competition and lead them into the land flowing with respectable dividends'. Ross was conscious of the risk of public opinion rising against the threat of monopoly. He gave assurances that all customers would be treated alike. He foresaw that the rise in whisky stocks would lead to price competition and result in small firms going out of business. He therefore developed the concept of 'organised competition'. He saw the DCL not as a profit-maximising company but one that would govern the industry and help it through difficult times. From what I have heard and experienced in recent times, this principal did influence their actions at the top but there were those in the field who took full advantage of the DCL strengths in overseas agent selection and in pricing. However, I am not aware that they deliberately set out to destroy a small competitor. There were occasions when they helped those in trouble by supplying some stock in short supply or acquired a business at a reasonable price, which would otherwise have folded. Looking back the Ross philosophy was a remarkably responsible view to take and it is inconceivable that businesses today would adopt such a policy. The cynics no doubt take the view that it was a cunning plot to secure domination and self-interest.

The years since WWI had ended had been difficult economically and the Scotch whisky trade had suffered likewise. Output, which had peaked at 35.8 million gallons in 1899 dropped to 27.4 million gallons in 1924. There was a real threat of a substantial surplus of stock if sales did not increase. Some hard decisions were needed to cut capacity and, as DCL controlled the largest proportion, it required to make the largest cut. Having been dominant in grain for some years, the working capacity was reasonably well balanced with demand but action had to be taken with malt capacity. Between 1925 and 1930 the number of working distilleries in Scotland fell from 124 to 94. Taking stock of their inheritance, the DCL in its merged form found itself controlling 60 per cent of the industry, a share, which they came to believe, was their sovereign right.

The board of the DCL was large and Ross set up a committee system to take day-to-day decisions and to spread the load. Although families still influenced some of the new appointments, it is evident that the old 'vendor-management' practice was finished. Expertise and achievement were the major factors in recruiting top management. The committees covered finance, grain distilling and research, malt distilling and blending and sales. The system was tested early on by a proposal from Ross that advertising should be cut now that DCL owned brands accounting for more than half the industry's sales. The blenders were sufficiently strong to counter this move and advertising rose steadily over the years in order to strengthen brand loyalty. In time the blending and sales committee was split into home and export sales each with representation on the board. Ross's successor formed a management committee to take responsibility for all group activities but no one was appointed chief executive. Thus the strategic vision supplied by Ross as the managing director ceased to exist and this was to prove its undoing.

This basic structure lasted into the 1980s because it fitted the situation and the personalities. However, it did not offer the opportunity for the further rationalisation necessary in the pre and post-WWII years, nor did it recognise the growing importance of the industrial side of the business. Major projects were undertaken but no one in top management took a close interest in the problems. The brand owning companies continued to operate independently albeit under the supervision of the two sales committees. Sadly Ross became blind in

1932 but continued as chairman for another three years. In 1933 he asked for a review of blending and sales functions as no benefits had accrued in this activity since the merger. He was denied this change and it took another 53 years for rationalisation of blending, sales and marketing to be achieved under Ernest Saunders.

William Henry Ross's establishment of the policy of benevolent stewardship of Scotch whisky was responsible for the growth of a strong, profitable and economically beneficial industry. DCL made critical contributions to the national effort in both world wars and the industry's export performance is a major contributor to the United Kingdom's balance of payments. Being a large undertaking in the industry naturally obliged the DCL to take all possible steps to protect its 60 per cent share of market at all levels. At times it was higher and efforts were required to counter the possibility of public criticism of its quasi monopoly position.

Ultimately, this defensive strategy resulted in a decline in market share, because new entrants with good financial backing adopted the more profitable course of building their brands aggressively and succeeded in capturing key markets from the DCL notably the United States. The paradox is that this was exactly what Walker, Dewar and Buchanan did to establish their brand franchises in the first place. Nevertheless, the DCL's methods established a strong consumer image for the Scotch whisky category simply by selling a good product efficiently and regularly meeting demand. The fact that their market strength protected them for so long resulted in the image of Scotch being stronger than the accumulated strength of the major brands. In white rum and vodka the reverse is true, where Bacardi and Smirnoff dominate their categories by virtue of brand strength.

The acquisitions of smaller businesses continued throughout the '20s and '30s and included the Glen Elgin distillery owned by the Blanche family in 1935. By this time the DCL was controlling about 80 per cent of the industry in all its levels and as a result was able to set the price levels for the market.

The period between the two world wars was also significant in that much of the export trade was in supplying the North American markets where prohibition was in force. Normal marketing methods were of no use and the business was done through a series of middlemen. The ending of prohibition in 1933 saw a surge in trade interrupted by WWII. During the war, as in the 1914–18 conflict, there was very limited output of new whisky and the DCL, with large stocks, were able to take advantage of a seller's market. Shipments were restricted only by shortage of shipping space particularly from 1943 onwards.

A More Competitive Market

Thus at the end of WWII the DCL had very little experience of competitive marketing, although they owned all the big brands. These were built in the market by the original owners but the DCL people who succeeded the original pioneers had never acquired brand building skills simply because they were not needed. They were also discouraged by the efforts of Ross in the late 1920s and early 1930s to reduce advertising.

The post 1945 period was again a seller's market with strong demand from the USA. Scotch whisky became the front runner instead of Bourbon and consumers paid premium prices for supplies. It was a dream period for those with whisky stocks and even the small operators made many a fortune. However, the big DCL brands had the backing of large stockholdings and they naturally dominated the market without much effort.

Gradually a number of smaller companies began to invest in distilling capacity and stock and to spend increasing amounts of time on selling trips overseas. In addition two US companies, Paddington and Buckingham, made deals for the supply of stocks from independent distillers and began to build brands with the support of their controlled distribution networks across the country. New York was the trendsetter but much of the thrust came in California, which was developing at a fast rate. New consumers there were keen to find a prestigious drink, which would set them apart from their elders, who thought Bourbon was the supreme experience.

Paddington with J&B and Buckingham with Cutty Sark forged

ahead in the United States and claimed increasing market shares. Teacher's were busy in Canada, Australia and England and Bell's captured a dominant share of the Scottish market. Seagram introduced the supreme brand to the international market in Chivas Regal. This was the brainchild of another pioneer, Sam Bronfman, who had begun planning the stock build up for this new 12 year old brand well before the war. Hiram Walker had acquired control of George Ballantine & Son Ltd in 1937 and the following year had built the Dumbarton grain distillery. William Grant & Sons built a new grain distillery at Girvan and invested in the Glenfiddich distillery and brand. This brand eventually competed in volume terms with the major blends and was a money-spinner for this fiercely independent family company.

Suddenly things were becoming difficult for the DCL. No longer could they rely on distilling and market dominance. It was being challenged on all fronts. They had neither the culture nor the willingness to learn the skills of the marketing business, which was being exploited by their new competitors. However, they still controlled or as they saw it, 'owned' a dominant share of the world market including the UK. Overseas, they had contracts with the best distributors in every market and this, combined with skilful pricing, kept the competition in check from the late '60s until the early '80s.

During this period, DCL made a strategic error. The UK market was not as profitable as the export market and the competition was becoming quite intense due to a number of new entrants. The low level of UK margins was largely the DCL's fault in keeping prices low in order to squeeze their competitors. The practice of parallel trading, whereby large overseas buyers would buy in the UK at the low prices prevailing there, was becoming a problem and Johnnie Walker was the main target. The DCL decided to withdraw this brand from the UK and give up a good market share to protect the business overseas. Thereafter they gave priority to overseas markets, where their dominance still worked for them.

In spite of the pricing tactics, several brands made dramatic progress and the DCL share of market in the UK dropped from 80 per cent to

20 per cent, partly due to Johnnie Walker's withdrawal, and their share of world sales dropped below 50 per cent, although they owned the largest brand, Johnnie Walker. In the UK the DCL's Haig and Walker brands had dominated the market but by the mid 1970s Teacher's and Bell's accounted for over 30 per cent. In the USA Cutty Sark, J & B and most of the DCL brands were declining. The exceptions were the DCL's Dewar's and Walker brands. They were holding volume in North America but not growing. In Europe, Ballantine's was vying with J & B and Walker's for market leadership. Meanwhile Gordons gin had become the DCL's biggest brand, much of it bottled in local markets, and together with Johnnie Walker accounted for over half the total volume of sale. The competition from other spirits was strong and came from two big brands Bacardi white rum and Smirnoff vodka.

The lack of a strategic response to the emerging competition in Scotch whisky and in spirits generally was not the only reason for the DCL's decline. In the early days of the merger in 1925 they had decided upon diversification as a means of providing better growth for their shareholders. They had assumed that Scotch whisky would not grow significantly and had invested in various industrial products including alcohol, yeast, methylated spirit, carbon dioxide and animal feedstuffs. These all used existing expertise in grain distilling and some were by-products, which improved profitability of the distilling operation. Later they invested in glass bottles, motor fuel, synthetic resins and a range of chemicals. In the post war period they invested heavily in petrochemicals and pharmaceuticals and saw themselves as a major industrial concern and not simply a Scotch whisky marketer.

The Thalidomide Crisis

In the event the management found it very difficult to give sufficient attention to a totally new industrial sector. The 'blenders' were always in the majority on the board and in controlling the other operations they often relied on outside advice instead of having highly qualified people in powerful positions within the group and on the board. Furthermore, the pace of development in these new sectors was staggering and competition was intense. Huge sums of investment monies were put at risk for equally huge rewards if successful. Ultimately they could not keep pace with the competition. In addition, their only major pharmaceutical product, Thalidomide, prescribed for pregnant women as a sleeping pill and to treat morning sickness, was destroyed overnight when it was found to produce thousands of deformed babies.

The man who was obliged to deal with this crisis as Chairman, Alex Macdonald, was perhaps the wrong person. He was a Scottish Chartered Accountant with a brilliant mind and a flair for complex problems. As a partner in the well-established Glasgow firm of Moores, Carson, Watson, he was for many years the auditor of DCL. It was said that their accounts were so complicated that he was the only one who understood them, including the directors. It was natural that he should join the board in mid-career and ascend to the chairmanship when critical financial decisions were being taken. He was also a domineering character but unused to communicating with outsiders. Both these traits made the handling of the situation much more difficult for him and the company.

This event, tragic for the families affected, set the DCL back on its heels and diverted the attention of its senior management for many years. The DCL were obliged to set up a large compensation fund for those unfortunate families who suffered from the experience.

To make things worse, it was followed by the major oil crisis of 1973/74, which halted the long period of growth in export sales of Scotch whisky since the end of WWII. The company still had the same structure carved out between 1925 and the early 1930s with the addition of an industrial division. The various companies acquired had been allowed to continue as before, usually with the owners being left in charge until they retired. The more powerful owners had been offered places on the main board and their successors retained authority over the individual brands. The series of committees co-ordinated distilling, bottling and sales in the home and export trades. The industrial products were eventually sold off thus relieving the company of the drain on its capital resources and the diverting of management attention.

The Twilight Period

Several attempts were made to restructure the company along modern lines as an integrated business but these involved no more than tinkering and did not succeed in taking cost out of the operations to compensate for the drop in margins. In the seventies, markets varied from static to volatile and it was impossible for the defensive tactics used by DCL to improve volumes. Robin Cater succeeded Alex Macdonald. Macdonald had been involved at the centre of the company's strategic decision-making for so long and had honed the investment policies, production and administrative machine into a superb operation. Now Cater, another strong man but more outgoing and experienced in selling all over the world, set out to rejuvenate the business and give it some bizazz.

However, there was not sufficient time to achieve a dramatic change, because events in the developed world economies were changing fast. A second oil crisis and a further recession masked some fundamental changes in consumer preferences and Scotch whisky brands needed attention. This was a period when the industry realised that branding was an art and attitudes of consumers changed from one generation to another. The old names of Walker, Haig and Buchanan, magic to the ears of the fathers, meant 'old-fashioned' to the sons. Paradoxically the original pioneers, Walker, Dewar and Buchanan had realised this in the early 1920s when they saw alcohol taking a smaller share of consumer expenditure. Their response was defensive leading them into mergers and cutting advertising. Sixty years later alcohol consumption had grown substantially but so had the choice of products. Scotch no longer had it all its own way and had to cope with declining market share. Other companies had broadened their range but not the DCL. Even within the Scotch whisky industry they had resisted the growing popularity of single malts, as this was contrary to the original philosophy and interests of the blenders. The result was that the DCL was vulnerable to changing tastes and stuck with its narrow range. Their Scotch and gin were the best and they had the leading brands in each category. However, others could compete with them but also had big brands in sherry, Scotch malt whisky, coffee liqueurs, vodka, cordials, champagne, cognac and tequila.

The profits were showing no growth and shareholders were becoming restless. The company had to acquire new and profitable businesses to broaden its range or merge with another group, which could benefit from the DCL's strengths and give it the security of participation in a wider sphere. The scene was set for one of the most hard-fought take-over battles of the 20th century, involving a long and well-discussed build-up and dramatic and fast-moving events when the race started. To give the story added spice, there followed a series of criminal trials under the new regulatory regime designed to control excesses in stock market dealing. Many of the issues raised at the time of the merger in 1925 reappeared but this time the mastermind of William Ross was absent.

CHAPTER 5

Mergers – A Way of Life

I do not pretend that this is a complete history of the development of Allied-Lyons. It is simply the view I had of the group from where I was at any given time. The group was built up over a period of 40 years to become the number two drinks business in the world and the number two Scotch whisky distiller.

The Development of Brewery Companies

In the 18th century breweries sprang up all over the country and built up a strong local following. Competition was keen in the larger cities big enough to support more than one company but the range of distribution was quite short relying on the horse and cart. In the mid nineteenth century the railways arrived and beer could be dispatched to most places but shelf life was short and advertising was not yet in regular use. After WWI motor lorries came into use and the combination of these and the railways speeded up the distribution system. Advertising was regularly used and when combined with good distribution the development of national brands was a profitable business. The ownership of pubs provided secure outlets for these brands with the result that several companies became very big through a combination of larger breweries, large chains of pubs and national advertising.

For the first time the local breweries, with their strong local franchise were faced with fierce competition. Over the years the market share for their own brands declined and they found that they had to sell more and more of the national brands. With smaller sales for the local brews, their owners were left with spare capacity and thus uneconomic breweries. Most of these local breweries were family businesses and they had usually made a lot of money in previous generations. They were quite happy to trade on with static profits and a comfortable existence. In time however, family members not actively involved in the business became restless and wanted to sell and reinvest their capital in more profitable companies. This gave the big brewers their chance and they were able to buy out the family businesses by offering a premium to attract the non-active family members. In due course the smaller breweries were closed and production concentrated in larger ones thus making them more efficient. The local brews became scarce but the popularity of the national brands increased and satisfied the demand for a consistent brew, which was always served in good condition.

By the time the 1960s arrived five large companies – Bass, Ind Coope, Whitbread, Courage and Scottish Brewers dominated the market. Nevertheless, many local breweries survived and made a name for themselves over a wider area by offering beers with more flavour. Their appeal grew and eventually demand, fostered by the Campaign for Real Ale, forced the big brewers to introduce similar beers in addition to their national brands, with which consumers were becoming bored. The market became more complex as a result and more difficult due to the steady albeit slow decline. This was a recipe for more rationalisation.

Over the next 30 years Bass reigned supreme until the 1990s when Scottish acquired Courage and became the largest brewer with a 30 per cent market share. It has been the only one to remain true to its origins and is now investing overseas to achieve growth. There was early activity in Scotland with the formation of Caledonian United from a number of smaller breweries but they too eventually fell to Bass together with the long established Tennents in Scotland and Charringtons in London. Many of the regional breweries in England fell to the big companies until these giants were constrained by the competition authorities. Being primarily in the hospitality business they began to diversify into hotels and lodges and over a period both Bass and Whitbread found these much more profitable. The result was that they came out of brewing altogether and Bass having controlled the Holiday Inn and Intercontinental hotel chains have sold their breweries and split themselves into Intercontinental Hotels and Mitchells & Butlers owning pubs. Likewise Whitbread have sold their breweries and now control roadside inns and a chain of theme restaurants.

'ICTA' to Allied Breweries

Ind Coope, a long-standing competitor to Bass, its near neighbour in Burton-on-Trent, acquired Taylor Walker in London and then merged with Ansells of Birmingham and Tetley Walker in the North of England to become, unbelievably, Ind Coope Tetley and Ansells. After an interval common sense prevailed and the name was changed to Allied Breweries. The merger was the first major step in consolidating the industry and was masterminded by Sir Edward Thomson. He managed to persuade these very independently minded brewers that the gradual decline in the beer market in Britain required some consolidation as a defensive move. His team had all served in WWII and was composed of some pretty strong characters. It took an even stronger one to keep them together. Rather like the DCL, the group was managed as a series of independent fiefdoms, which worked well but did not exactly encourage moves for greater efficiency by rationalising the major facilities. However future events forced changes helped by retirements and shifts in power through further mergers and acquisitions.

In the meantime the larger groups were diversifying their activities and investing in wines and spirits. This sector was showing promising growth as it came out of the post-war period when supplies were difficult to obtain. Retail off licences were a natural extension to the public house chains and the consumption of wine was growing fast as more and more people travelled abroad and acquired a taste for it. Scotch whisky was also enjoying rapid growth as production in the post war period recovered to meet increasing demand from overseas as well as healthy growth in the home market fostered by an increase in spending power.

Ind Coope was the first to appreciate the opportunities and was pleased to acquire The Victoria Wine Company, through its purchase of Taylor Walker. Victoria Wine dominated the London trade with 400 branches and was long established with a reputation for a good range of wines and spirits. Smaller chains were bought up in Birmingham, Manchester and ultimately Scotland. There in 1960 Ind Coope bought my grandfather's family business with 15 outlets and I found myself working for Victoria Wine after having done a short period of training with them as a 'guest' in 1957.

The control of more outlets boosted the profits of Allied Breweries and the profitability of these new businesses also improved by giving preference to the group's own brands as well as being able to negotiate better prices from suppliers due to better buying power. Although the investment in property was high, the asset base had growth potential, as many of the properties were High Street sites always in demand from national chains in all trades. The chain eventually exceeded over 1,000 outlets and was the leading wine merchant in the country. It did not have it all its own way however. Other brewery groups caught up and the High Streets had several wine merchant chains represented in all the large towns in the country. In addition, the self-service shops of the 1950s expanded into supermarkets in the 1960s and began to expand their range of goods to include not just food and household items but also clothing and wines and spirits. To begin with, the licensing controls restricted them to separate counters, which could be closed during the hours when alcohol could not be sold outwith the licensing hours. Gradually these controls were relaxed and the alcohol displays could be accommodated on the normal shelving thus increasing the opportunities to pop a bottle or two into the trolley.

Allied was the first of the large brewers to invest overseas when it bought two breweries in the Netherlands, Oranjboom in Rotterdam and the Breda brewery together with their wine and spirit subsidiaries. In addition the Warninks Advocaat company was purchased in Holland. It had a long connection with Victoria Wine, who had acted as the UK agents for many years and had built the largest market for Warninks. This, however, proved to be the last foray into brewing ownership overseas and the Dutch breweries were eventually sold. The brewery division did however enter into an interesting consortium arrangement with brewers in Canada, Brazil and Belgium under which each agreed to brew and sell Skol lager in their own markets and also overseas. The Annual Report for 1973 states that Skol 'is the fastest growing international brand of lager in the world, and with the continued progress of our partners and franchisees in over 50 countries the outlook is most encouraging.' By 1975 the sales had reached 3.8 million barrels. Gradually our partners lost interest in the arrangement, although Skol is still to be seen in Brazil and the UK. There was also a possibility of expansion in the Pacific area when Allied acquired a 25 per cent stake in an Australian firm Castlemaine-Toohey.

This investment came about through Allied's sale of some Australian assets to Tooheys of Sydney. They subsequently merged with Castlemaine of Brisbane and Allied retained a holding in the new group in order to give it some comfort in the face of threats from other predators. In the event the stake was sold in 1985 to Bond Corporation, which had made an attractive bid and it was felt that there was nothing to be gained by holding on to it. We could not influence the outcome of the takeover by Bond nor could we avoid the value of the investment falling if we remained as a minority shareholder with Bond controlling the other 75 per cent.

Showerings Transforms Allied

In the late 1960s Allied took a major step into the branded wine and spirit trade by merging with Showerings Vine Products and Whiteways (SVPW). This was itself a combination of several businesses acquired by Showerings in an effort to create a company with a broader front than offered by their cider and perry products. Showerings Babycham had been launched in the late 1940s and enjoyed phenomenal success. I can vividly remember in my early days at Baileys trying desperately to gauge its growth when ordering for the Christmas trade. I never succeeded in the estimates and ran out of stock four years in succession. Francis Showering, one of four brothers who ran the family cider business in Shepton Mallet, invented Babycham. In its test market it hit a hotspot in the days when most food products were still rationed after WWII. The launch only succeeded because Francis had the foresight to negotiate with the government for an extra large sugar allocation otherwise the initial demand could not have been met.

Francis was astute and with his brothers took good advice on the branding and launching of the new product. It was targeted to appeal to young women, who were not experienced drinkers but were happy to enjoy the novel post-war practice of going out to a pub with their boyfriends and husbands. The drink was christened Babycham, which gave it a cuddly image and was sold in bottles of 100ml at a strength of 8% alcohol by volume. When served in a suitable glass it seemed quite harmless and the girls could sip away confident that they would not be drunk by the end of the evening. In reality it was not exactly an innocuous drink being twice the strength of beer. However, as long as you did not have more than say three in the evening you would be all right. To pep it up some used to add a shot of brandy to it and that was a different matter! Marketing managers were always in a dilemma wondering if they should emphasis the alcoholic strength or not. On the one hand nervous drinkers had confidence in the innocuous nature of the drink but on the other the experienced women knew it had a kick and could always add the brandy to boost it more as well as adding a bit of sophistication.

There were seven other companies in the SVPW group. Two, Whiteways and Coates Gaymers were traditional cider businesses happy to be under the umbrella of benevolent West Country businessmen as they were in a declining market. Vine Products (VP) manufactured British wine, which enjoyed a preferential rate of excise duty on its products and had been founded as early as the late 19th century. It produced sherry and port style wines and later table wines from reconstituted grape juice. The quality was exceedingly good and the wines sold at very low prices, which sadly sometimes appealed to homeless alcoholics but also to respectable ladies on low incomes. VP had a legendary sales director, who was a real charmer. After I joined the family business he told me that my grandfather had been one of VP's first customers and I believed this until I talked to the managing director after we both found ourselves in Allied. Oh, he said, he told everyone that tale! Wooley Duval & Beaufoys had products produced in a similar fashion but mostly from fruit flavourings. These were mainly sold in supermarkets at the lower end of their price range.

The star of SVPW was John Harvey & Son, which also owned Cockburn's Port and Stewarts of Dundee Scotch whisky. Harvey's

Bristol Cream was a major world brand selling well in the UK and the US. Harvey's range of sherries dovetailed with the range of wines sold by Victoria Wine and the Allied wholesale company, Grants of St James, which had its own house brand of sherry. After this acquisition one of our directors, Brian McGrath, was asked what he thought of the quality of Harvey's Bristol Cream compared with our own brand. This was a tongue-in-cheek question because Brian had spent some years drumming into us the fact that our own brand Regency Cream was far superior in quality. His response was that, surprisingly, Harvey's quality had improved dramatically overnight! Anyway everyone was excited about the possibilities of the export trade and keen to follow the Harvey example.

Things did not start well as each side to the deal had different ideas about the enlarged group and how it should be managed. Four members of the Showering family joined the Allied board, brothers Herbert, Ralph and Francis and nephew Keith, all of whom were strong characters. Furthermore, the Showerings were well regarded in the City in view of their success as a quoted company. They reckoned they could repeat their success with the enlarged group with its larger resources and wished to take control of the management. Their style was direct and confrontational in contrast to the brewers, who plotted behind the scenes but rarely made a fuss at board meetings. Happily one of the younger members of the new board, Derrick Holden-Brown, was quick to develop a rapport with the Showerings and he played an important part in reaching agreement about how the group would be run and plan for the future. Sadly, one of the casualties of this affair was Derek Pritchard, whose term as chairman was curtailed to two years. During the protracted negotiations he became worried that relations between the two sides would break down completely, cause the City to lose confidence in the company and downgrade the shares in the market. Rather unwisely he confided in two of his brewery colleagues and together they planned an approach to Unilever with a view to joining the larger group.

Although a little sceptical about the logic for such a tie up, the stock market was interested in the concept of a successful international marketer taking an interest in the drinks business. Unilever did operate breweries in Africa but had no other drinks operations. The Showerings were distinctly underwhelmed by the idea and proceeded to use all their influence to put a stop to the talks. It was a tense time for those directly involved and the rest of us simply had to keep going as normal hoping our worlds would not be disrupted too much in the end. The problem was resolved by the appointment of Gerald Thorley (Joe) as chairman but only for a fixed period of five years. He was a real tough but genuine character and had the respect of everyone. He was well known for his 'fruity' language but no one minded that and he did not really care what people thought, having seen life in the raw in a Japanese prisoner of war camp in Singapore. Keith Showering of the new generation of the family was made vice chairman with the understanding that he would succeed Joe. This gave the group the opportunity to settle down and allowed the Showerings time to appreciate the different businesses they had become involved with.

For the first time I had a key role to play albeit a very small one. Stewarts was plucked out of Harveys and put together with two other Scotch companies, which had been subsidiaries of two of the brewery companies. They were Curtis Distillery Company of London and Glen Rossie of Liverpool. I became chairman of these businesses under the banner of Stewart & Sons of Dundee. I was a little concerned to learn that one of my predecessors had committed suicide after having perpetrated a whisky fraud by selling in-bond stocks twice when the company was in financial difficulties. Like all such plots, it was to be a temporary expedient until other monies became available. A sorry tale.

Charles Forte v. Allied Breweries

It was not long before a new excitement hit the headlines. Allied made an unwelcome bid for Trust House Forte, a move driven by Francis and Keith Showering. It was an astute move, as Forte had not long joined with Trust House Hotels an established, respectable but rather sleepy company, controlled by a charitable trust. It had strict ideas about how their hotels should be run. Forte had charmed them into a deal by reassuring them that nothing would change. History tells us that such promises are never kept simply because circumstances change and a business has to react and change with them. The Allied profit record had not been spectacular but, with the Showerings aboard, it was reckoned that sufficient support would be gathered to carry the day. The tenacity of Charles Forte's response was both unexpected and impressive. He had come to Britain as a refugee from Italy and after a period in internment during WWII had started a milk bar in Scotland. Having reached the heights of industry more or less by his own efforts, he was not going to be upstaged by a bunch of brewers and West Country cider makers.

Allied did already own a chain of hotels, which had started with the development of brewery inns but had been expanded by the addition of several four and five star hotels. This did not impress Forte and he claimed during the battle that 'he could cut a thinner slice of smoked salmon than Allied Breweries.' Good copy for the stock market but one wonders what his patrons thought! The trustees of the charitable body controlling a sizeable portion of the Trust House Forte (THF) equity were bound to consider selling its holding once the price had risen in case the share price fell after the whole episode was over. To counter this threat and avoid Allied's bid gaining the trustees' support, Forte pledged his fortune and more to buy THF shares in the market and thus acquire enough shares himself to vote down the bid. At the same time Allied was buying in the market too and acquired 26 per cent of the equity. In the end Forte had his way but Allied retained its stake in the hope that another chance would come along. No further opportunity arose and the shares were sold in 1978. The original investment cost £40m for 21m shares at cost per share of 186p. After the 1974 stock market crash the price came down to 40p and the shares were 'bed and breakfasted' and the loss written off. The sale in 1978 yielded £48.4m thankfully showing a nice surplus. A steady nerve was needed in those exciting times.

A Showering at the Top

Keith Showering became chairman in 1975 and in the previous year Tom Boardman returned to the board following the defeat of Edward

Heath's government in 1974, in which he had been minister of trade. He stayed for only a year before becoming chairman of Natwest Bank. In 1976 Keith had his first major success by buying William Teacher & Sons with Allied's shares. This investment complemented Harveys in providing another international brand in a category we already had a small interest in. The Teacher families had kept control of the business when it was floated on 1948 to raise cash for expansion after WWII. The business had continued to grow through the industry's boom times in the 1960s and early 1970s and money had been raised by borrowing. There was a need for a further injection in the 1980s, which presented the family with a dilemma. Increasing borrowings was not an attractive option and raising more money through another share issue raised the question of losing control. Rather than face this the family decided to pick a group to join and Allied moved quickly to grasp the opportunity. It was said that the business had first been offered to Bass, who had declined. In the event we were happy to be chosen!

Keith was determined to expand the group's activities with a view to reducing the proportion of brewing in the business. The Forte bid was the first attempt and although we still held a sizeable stake, it was clear that Charles Forte was not going to let go. In 1978 along came another opportunity in J Lyons & Company. This company had been struggling for some years after encountering a financial crisis as a result of borrowing in hard currency and investing the proceeds mainly in assets in countries with softer currencies. The depreciation of the pound sterling in 1974 obliged Lyons to sell off their hotels in order to cover the extra cost of repayment of the loans. The hotels were the best part of the business, and would have been a very useful addition to Allied's existing hotel chain. The company had some very good brands but growth was static in many of its businesses and others were declining. In the event the City did not approve and this had a depressing effect on the share price. A change of name to Allied Lyons in 1981 had the effect of reminding the City of the acquisition!

By coincidence I had been taking the Senior Executive Programme at the London Business School in 1970 and the programme had included two talks from senior Lyons directors, who explained their philosophy of management. We all had to do a project on one of the Lyons businesses and I was deputed to tackle the bakery shops. As it happened, not only had I been in retailing but I had also been offered a job to run the Rank Hovis McDougall bakery shops in Scotland a few years before. With this limited knowledge of the trade my report was very critical, as Lyons seemed to be run in a sloppy fashion and lacked direction and thrust. Maybe this attitude had permeated the whole group and they had lost their way; what a pity as the owning families had been energetic and innovative in the past and always seemed to produce several bright people in each generation.

An outsider was appointed to run Lyons and prove the City wrong. He was Sir Alex Alexander, an energetic entrepreneur who had built up a frozen food business and sold it to the Imperial Group where he galvanised the management there with his fertile mind. Over the next ten years Alex rationalised Lyons, sold some assets and increased the profits from £16m to over £90m. Unfortunately very few of the businesses had real growth potential and it was clear by the late '80s that an injection of more profitable food companies was necessary if Allied had a future in the sector. A number of possibilities were looked at but none were available and in the nineties most of the companies were sold off with the exception of Baskin-Robbins, the American dairy ice cream business. The acquisition of Lyons had, however, made money for Allied but had not given it a permanent position in a new field.

Keith Showering was knighted in 1981 but sadly died in March 1982. This was a blow and certainly gave the stock market a fright. However, there were three slightly elderly but tough and experienced hands, who were able to fill the gap. Derrick Holden-Brown became Chairman and Francis Showering and Alex Alexander, Vice-Chairmen. This was also a difficult period in the economy as inflation had been soaring during the early days of the new Conservative government. The stock market was in recession and the Falklands war was imminent. There were not many favourable signs around and it was as well that the group had a strong team to lead it.

A minor acquisition was made in May 1982 of the pubs and the London Gin business of J & W Nicholson & Company. The vendors,

Bass chose to retain the gin distillery and supply spirit to us at an agreed price. The gin trade was taken over by Stewarts, which enabled it to achieve a profit of £1m for the first time. This was a great fillip to the morale of the team, who had worked so hard over the previous 12 years starting with a profit of £200,000 mostly made from whisky broking. Bass was not very co-operative in fixing the price of gin spirit and it proved difficult for Stewarts to sell the gin at a profit. Stewarts and Teacher's together decided that the only solution was to produce the spirit themselves and this they proceeded to do. The project demonstrated what sharp decision taking and the successful execution of a clearly defined business plan could achieve. The Stewarts and Teacher's management teams found a suitable consultant to guide them in product formulation and the design of the distilling facility. A small but adequate copper still was installed in the Teacher bottling plant and within months gin was flowing off the still in Glasgow and 'London Dry Gin' at that!

In 1984 Allied acquired United Rum Merchants (URM) from Booker McConnell. It was an old established company with some wonderfully romantic brand names such as Lemon Hart, Lambs Navy and Black Heart, which conjured up thoughts of pirates and ships of the line. The trade was almost wholly dark rum, which was a declining market, although there was still plenty of volume in the UK, Canada and, of course, the Caribbean. There were possibilities of fashion changes, and rationalisation with the rest of the spirit business offered cost cutting opportunities. Also on offer was 51 per cent in Tia Maria a successful coffee liqueur but the minority partner Hiram Walker exercised its pre-emption right to acquire the whole business. Some years later Allied acquired Hiram Walker and was able to add Tia Maria to the group portfolio. The managing director of URM at that time, Harvey Allen, remarked 'can I have my ball back?'

The wine & spirit division was anxious to expand its activities overseas and spirits was an obvious way to do this. Most developed markets had large local brands usually without any great potential for export. The large international brands were few in number and were mainly British with the exception of Bacardi. I spent quite a bit of time visiting companies and merchant banks in North America seeking out opportunities. The alcohol market was in decline at the time but an opportunity to extend our range with a minimal increase in costs made sense. As is often the case the available businesses were rather run down. There were a number of good companies operating in the low margin trade but the owners wanted very high prices to sell out and there was little hope of making anything of that type of business. Allied was looking for good brands with some growth potential but, of course, they could only be bought at inflated prices. We did manage to set up a joint venture company with Hiram Walker to handle all the Allied brands in Canada including Teacher's and Harvey's and they put into this operation some local Canadian products.

DCL Comes to Talk

Quite suddenly we had an approach from The Distillers Company requesting talks with a view to a merger! While most observers in the Scotch whisky industry had wondered how long the DCL could go on underperforming the market when owning two of the world's top four spirit brands, a merger or even less a takeover was not something the DCL board appeared to contemplate. Their long and distinguished history and their dominance of the industry had led them to think that they were secure, although they had realised for some years that there was a need for diversification. Their reliance on spirits was a weakness, particularly as they were not represented in the growth sectors of the market, vodka and white rum. They made a major investment in chemicals, which they had to sell off, as they could not support the large capital investment required for the business. They had a shot at drugs and licensed products from major companies in that industry. This investment ended in total disaster with the thalidomide scandal.

After these ventures the DCL were back to where they started except that they had not changed their marketing methods in the post-war period and found themselves facing several successful brands challenging their dominance. The press began to speculate about the possibility of someone making a bid for them and they had had wind of a specific threat and realised for the first time that they were vulnerable. Their plan was to find an amenable company in the alcohol business, which they felt would let them carry on with their pleasant way of life. Joining with us would have the advantage of widening the business from its rather narrow base of gin and Scotch whisky and they probably saw us as a company operating in the same way as them. They had forgotten that, although Allied devolved the running of its business to its subsidiaries, there was a strong but small team at the centre headed by a chief executive. The DCL did not have a chief executive but preferred to manage through a series of functional committees such as production, sales and finance. The chairman was simply there to chair the board and did not have any executive authority.

It was with some excitement that I joined John Clemes, the Allied finance director and Michael Jackaman, Chairman of the wine & spirit division in early June 1985 for a series of clandestine meetings in London. Bill Forrest, Corporate Affairs Director, Bob Temple, Finance Director and Bob Ball, who acted as secretary to the small group, represented the DCL. Coincidentally, Bob Temple and I had studied for our Scottish CA finals at the same time in Glasgow. He was the brightest student of the year and quite a few of us aspired to match his performance but none of us did.

I took on the task of looking at the trading profiles of both companies and found that they dovetailed beautifully. There was the overlap in Scotch whisky, which offered scope for rationalisation in distilling, blending and bottling and this would need to be emphasised in the plans to be presented to the City. Teacher's had a strong position in the UK market whereas the DCL were weak. The DCL had a major brand in Gordon's gin whereas Allied lacked a white spirit. Johnnie Walker Scotch was the number one brand in the world outside the UK and had a valuable network of the best distributors. On the other hand Allied had a wide range of alcoholic brands strong in the UK but with potential overseas. The combination of a wide range and excellent distribution would give a new group an edge over the competition. The term 'synergy' was fashionable at the time and it soon became part of our vocabulary!

It was important to be able to present sound reasons for merging these two groups, because neither was an outstanding performer in the stock market at the time. Both businesses were in mature product sectors and we realised that new and radical strategies would have to be adopted in order to achieve renewed growth and the market would have to be convinced that the ideas were feasible. Within a fortnight we had a report for the chairmen of the two companies and it was duly despatched to them. The DCL chairman was John Connell, whose background was gin where he had succeeded his father in the same business, as had many of the DCL senior executives. John was a low profile man and had progressed up through the echelons of Distillers without any trouble and was rarely if ever called upon to respond to sudden changes. His job was to preserve the status quo. On the other hand Derrick Holden-Brown had had a full and varied business career and was capable of matching the ablest negotiators with the aid of a keen financial brain.

I did not attend the meeting between the two and only heard second hand reports of what was discussed. However, it was evident that a key element had been the need for a drastic restructuring of top management with clear lines of responsibility – no committees. The DCL committee system had been in operation since the mergers of the 1920s. It preserved the fiefdoms of the original brilliant founders of the various businesses and it seems likely that the DCL wished to retain their autonomy. It may be that the possibility of a poor reception by the stock market influenced the thinking in view of the difficulty that Allied had had after the acquisition of Lyons. Anyway the merger idea was buried without any further discussions or investigation. I was slightly amused during our talks to find that the DCL were still using foolscap paper when the rest of the world outside the US had been using A4 for years. I also remember that we were all sworn to secrecy and no one knew of the meetings for some months. However, as DCL came under more pressure in the City they felt they must demonstrate that they were doing something and mentioned the abortive talks to the Financial Times.

Elders IXL Sets the Cat Amongst the Pigeons

The summer was quiet and pleasant and in the autumn the search for new international businesses was resumed but not for long. Our world was turned upside-down by the appearance of an Australian, John Elliott. He was a former consultant with Mckinsay and had bought into the old established pastoral business of Elder Smith Goldsbrough Mort. From the unlikely base of the wool trade, Elliott had an ambition to build a major international company. He renamed the company Elders IXL and had already acquired Carlton and United Breweries of Melbourne who owned Fosters lager, which was the main competitor to Castlemaine XXXX, owned by our partner Castlemaine Tooheys based in Brisbane and Sydney.

Elders had been buying Allied shares for some months and eventually their holding had reached six per cent and was above the threshold at which disclosure of an interest is required. There was some press speculation about this interest and Allied wrote on 23 August 1985 to the chairman of Elders asking for clarification about his company's intentions. On 5 September 1985 Hill Samuel, the merchant bank advisors of Elders, made an announcement that the finance was being prepared for a bid for the whole of Allied and it was hoped to be able to clarify the situation within six weeks. It appears that the intention was to sell off the food and wine and spirit divisions to other major companies and to retain the beer division.

On 21 October 1985, Elders announced an offer for Allied of 255p per ordinary share and 120p per preference share, placing a value of £1800m on the company. The original plan to join in a consortium had been dropped and Elders made the move on their own. It was well timed as Allied had some six months before reported profits a little less exciting than the previous year showing a growth of only 12 per cent compared with 22 per cent. The chairman in his report had spoken of difficult conditions in the market place after the year- long miners' strike and mentioned the emergence of cheaper own-label brands of Scotch whisky over the Christmas period. The food division had, however, produced an increase of 18 per cent. In my own contribution to the report I had mentioned the fact that UK market share for Teacher's

Highland Cream had dropped one point in the face of own label competition, although our margins and profitability had been preserved. As a consequence of our determination to preserve margins along with other companies in the division, wines & spirits profits were restricted to growth of only two per cent. Our first lesson was to acknowledge that, even if the medium and long-term performance and prospects were good, there would always be a short-term issue, which a predator can focus upon and criticise. The principal argument put forward by Elders to justify the bid was that they could manage Allied's assets better than the incumbents could. With careful choice of elements in our business, Elders were able to create damaging publicity.

Elders were considerably smaller than Allied. Their net assets in June 1985 were A$697m and their gearing was 110 per cent. By contrast Allied's net assets in March 1986 were £1910m and gearing was 15 per cent. Allied was, therefore, over five times the size of Elders. The gearing issue was much discussed in view of the normal conservative attitude, which favoured equity as the main source of finance. In the UK average gearing in 1982 was 32 per cent and in the USA it was about the same at 38 per cent. The idea of a little known small company borrowing five times its net assets to buy another was extraordinary. Improbable as it may sound, the stock market took the bid seriously and so did Allied. S G Warburg's were appointed to advise us as they were known for their robust defence of companies under attack. When shareholders are offered cash for their shares there will always be a proportion who will be willing to sell and they need to be assured that there are growth prospects for the company and that it is well managed. The bid price was 255p per ordinary share, which was almost frivolous as it was 23p lower than the then current market price. This placed a value of £1800m on Allied. At the time this seemed to be only a sighting bid and it was likely that Elders could expect to pay anything from 360p to 400p requiring £2800m.

There was no fixed view on the desirable level of gearing. Much depended on the economic climate of the time and the risk factors in different businesses. However, the Bank of England stated later in its evidence to the Monopolies & Mergers Commission (MMC) that 'they regarded capital gearing of 50 per cent as acceptable whilst a level of 100 per cent would provide some grounds for concern. Similarly, interest cover of 4:1 would be quite normal whilst a ratio of less than 2:1 would on the face of it be unsatisfactory'. Elder's profits before tax for its last full year to June 1985 were A$134m. The combined profits of Elders and Allied would barely cover the interest on the borrowings required for a successful takeover. Little was known about Elders and few details of the bid had been divulged. It seemed certain that Elders would have to sell off considerable chunks of assets to pay off the debt but this could take some time and doubt was expressed about the effect on the business and employment in the meantime.

The excitement level was high and Derrick Holden-Brown motivated the whole management to counter the attack on us. He held several senior management meetings so that we could hear at first hand what was happening and what we could do to support the effort. The slogan '**Allied-Lyons a great British company**' appeared everywhere and was supported by '**Allied-Lyons … going on growing**'. So much fuss was created about the bid that the hoped for reference to the Monopolies and Mergers Commission took place in December. A reference would give some breathing space and reduce the momentum of the Elders campaign. In addition more time would be available for Allied to convince its shareholders to support the company in their own interests. Although much time would be taken up with preparing and giving evidence to the MMC, the rest of the management would be able to redouble their efforts to improve performance.

In the meantime an impressive range of material and advertisements were produced and issued to the press. Also a four-page newsletter was issued regularly for staff to keep them up-to-date. These placed emphasis on the positive trends that were coming through in the group's performance. All the graphs were curved upwards including profits, earnings and earnings per share. For example: 'Looking at all 12 of our immediate competitors in the brewing and distilling sectors with a market capitalisation in excess of £100 million, Allied-Lyons' performance by the same criterion is the best in the sector.' We were able to report that the profits for the half-year before the bid were

£123m, up by 22 per cent including an improved increase of 17 per cent from the wine & spirit division. Elders on the other hand came out with Interim profits to December 1985 of A$74m up 41 per cent! The Elders literature was equally impressive in its damning comments about the Allied performance. Nothing was up and everything was down but improved leadership offering better opportunities for employees would alter this, said Elders. Some of the points were good but there was little but hype to justify Elders ability to deliver a better performance.

An interesting project was set up with the Financial Times in which an FT reporter known as the 'fly on the wall', was allowed to sit in on the meetings of our strategy group known as the Pratt Committee named after Tony Pratt, the head of the corporate affairs department. It met weekly to co-ordinate the various activities of the defence. The 'fly' was sworn to secrecy on the understanding that he would have the exclusive right to publish an article on the discussions of the group when everything had been settled. The piece was duly published in four daily instalments from 24 to 27 September 1986. Going through and quoting from this text is as good a way as any to relate the sequence of events.

There was some impatience to start hitting out at Elders. 'It would help if someone were to give him (Elliott) a bloody nose. It would be good for morale if nothing else.' Sir Alex Alexander, the vice-chairman, counselled 'you've got to be patient,' and the 'fly' commented later of Sir Alex being 'a man not particularly noted for this quality'. Michael Valentine of Warburgs had persuaded everyone that we should hold our fire until the formal offer was published and a target presented itself. Communications with staff from the centre produced some sobering results such as 'confused addressees who claimed never to have heard of Allied-Lyons. Investigations showed that they worked for Tetley or other operating companies.' There was a lot of discussion about slogans and Tony Pratt said there would be a competition for the best one and the prize would be a Becker's horsemeat sausage and the 'fly' was invited to join in! The Office of Fair Trading (OFT) asked the company for a defence plan summary to help it when they interviewed John Elliott. This became known as 'the charge sheet'. It was suggested that about 20 pages would be sufficient but one of the Warburg team commented 'That sounds disturbingly succinct' while holding his forefinger and thumb a good two inches apart. 'I'm an inches man myself.'

There was continuous discussion about the lobbying of government for a reference to the MMC. It was important that Allied was not seen to be openly canvassing for this and personal approaches were thought to be best by a small group of people. Trade Unions, some MPs and ministers and civil servants needed to be covered. 'One divisional MD had reported back from a meeting with his local parliamentarian. The target had written saying 'thank you for the nice lunch. PS. I have just received a letter from Mr Elliott. I think he makes a very good case for taking you over.' 'But he's as thick as two planks,' (meaning the MP) came the disgruntled murmur.' Care in choosing the targets was obviously required.

Sir Derrick was pressed by the Pratt Committee to lobby the trade unions and he was reluctant in view of the risk of them feeling that they had an Allied-Lyons debating ground. Ultimately he agreed to talk to his colleagues on the food and drink Economic Development Council. The 'fly' commented: 'He would do what he always intended to do. Everyone smiled. Putty in his hands.' This is quite common with chief executives. I remember in my early days at Stewarts having a long discussion about an overseas market with Jim Delaney. He wanted to do it one way and I was arguing for another. Eventually he gave up, smiled and said, 'as usual we will do it your way'. After all, the head man has to carry the can if it goes wrong and if he is not happy he has to say so!

Michael Valentine suggested that TV ads should carry a tailpiece identifying the products as Allied offerings. 'Sir Derrick, casting a nervous eye towards Sir Alex, the autonomy-minded head of the food division, approved.' At a later meeting Michael Jackaman protested that it would be expensive and tricky to manage and could cost several hundred thousand pounds. Sir Alex seemed cross. 'I didn't even know the idea existed,' he claimed sitting bolt upright in the chair he occupied a week earlier when the idea was first discussed. No one dared to remind him he had been present when the idea came up. He was outvoted and it happened much to the annoyance of us all, who had to arrange the implementation.

Meantime the committee was preparing for a conference of senior managers to brief everyone on the progress of the defence. Frustration surfaced angrily and some warned that the staff was not in a good mood because they felt that Allied was not being aggressive enough. Tempers were raised about other issues and Warburgs came under fire for their lofty attitude about the front cover of the defence document and changing the end of the video for the institutions. In their absence a further discussion took place and Pratt said: 'It's a matter of opinion and it so happens that Warburgs are wrong.' From the blackness: 'Who's going to tell Warburgs?' Answer came there none. Some better news came with the report that Sir Derrick had had a good meeting with some of his trade unionists colleagues on the National Economic Development Council, who were going to demand a reference to the Monopolies & Mergers Commission.

With not very much happening and Warburgs still holding fire, the Pratt Committee members were even more restless. Warburgs were criticised for their high-handedness. Sir Derrick had to constantly come in and smooth feelings and demonstrated an enormous amount of patience. The pressure was relieved somewhat by the issue of the offer document and it was something for the committee to get their teeth into. Michael Valentine of Warburgs was trying hard to placate the disgruntled committee members and the relationship began to improve. The offer document turned out to be full of irrelevant comparisons seemingly chosen to maximise the charge that Allied was performing poorly. They were so general that they were almost impossible to counter. Closer study turned up some outrageous items, which were easily refuted and everyone felt more cheerful as they began to see the defence taking shape.

The management meeting was held on 'Day 39' (30 November) in Birmingham and the atmosphere was good in contrast to the suggestions earlier that the mood was critical of senior management. Sir Derrick had a great success and received a rousing ovation. Michael

Valentine in his address said, 'You are the top 1 per cent of employees in this group. You are the people described as awful, appalling, tired and antiquated. I don't suppose you like it very much.' This was an attempt to raise our hackles and persuade us that there was work to be done and we would all have to pull together. He said the best defence and the best protection of our own livelihoods was better profits. He told us to come with strong reasons to refute the criticisms levelled at us and to demonstrate that we were innovative and active in dealing with the competition. Gradually a convincing defence took shape and included aspects, which might appeal to the government, who would be considering a reference to the Monopolies & Mergers Commission.

The main elements of the defence plan were:

> The effect on employment from a break up of Allied.
>
> The considerable risk of a collapse of the merged group with a dangerously high gearing and burdened by interest payments and lack of money for new capital investment.
>
> The cost to shareholders, who sold out and found that they were being offered new Allied shares at a higher price as part of an Elders plan to issue new equity to reduce gearing after the acquisition.
>
> The effect on the UK economy on the loss of control and the effect on the balance of payments from dividend and interest payments going to overseas companies.

The announcement came on 7 December that the bid had been referred to the Monopolies and Mergers Commission and there was a sense of great relief on the committee but there was more work to be done. The MMC would require an enormous amount of information, which would need to be gathered from every corner of the group, from managers who were already working hard in running their businesses. Tact and determination and relentless pressure to meet timescales would be needed from the committee members. Sir Derrick held a briefing for shop stewards from all parts of the group similar to the managers meeting. It went quite well but there was no cheering! One TGWU representative asked if there could be more of this type of meeting in the future. The reply was 'We shall give careful thought to what you have said.' Voice off: 'He means no, Jim.'

It was not until September 1986 that the MMC report was published and it recommended that the merger would not operate against the public interest. The government agreed that Elders was free to renew its bid but by that time the scene had changed dramatically for both Allied and Elders. Allied had acquired the Hiram Walker Spirit business and was reorganising its wine & spirit division. Elders had entered into a deal with Broken Hill Proprietary, the large Australian resource company and were about to absorb Courage, the West of England brewers. The bid was not renewed and everyone heaved a sigh of relief and began to set about their normal business.

Hiram Walker – Both Saviour and Prize

The escape was welcome but it was opportune that the chance to acquire Hiram Walker came along. It provided a good way to torpedo the Elders bid by adding considerably to the asset base thus making it more difficult than ever to finance it. Hiram Walker was exactly what we had been looking for in the last few years but it had never occurred to us that this fiercely independent family controlled company would ever be available. It was fortunate that Derrick Holden-Brown took the view that the acquisition would be an advantage and not a distraction during the period when we were under attack. It was also a remarkable tribute to his abilities that he was able to continue the fight against Elders while tackling a fiercely contested acquisition of Hiram Walker.

Hiram Walker had felt vulnerable as a medium-sized operator in overseas markets, although it was a major force in Canada along with Seagrams. They had some marvellous brands in Ballantine's, Courvoisier, Kahlua and Canadian Club. However, the Canadian market was static and their fine brands faced intense competition in the key markets of USA, UK and Europe. They had made an attempt to strengthen their brand portfolio by making a bid to acquire Highland Distilleries in 1979. It was referred to the MMC in January 1980 and the Commission reported in June 1980 that 'the merger may be expected to operate against the public interest'. Hiram thus lost the chance to acquire the Famous Grouse brand, then number three in the UK market. Their response to the threat of takeover was to merge with a gas distribution company in Ontario, Consumers' Gas, which could not be acquired without provincial government approval. They reckoned that their influence with the provincial politicians would safeguard them in the future. There was also a subsidiary engaged in oil and gas exploration and production. The group adopted the new name Hiram Walker Resources. The Hiram Walker management dominated the new group and their proven investment expertise and their knowledge of Canadian business appeared to give them the strength to beat off or discourage anyone who might wish to mount a bid.

They reckoned without Paul Reichmann who headed the very successful Olympia & York (O&Y), the world's largest property developer. They owned large chunks of Manhattan including the World Financial Centre next to the Twin Towers of the former World Trade Centre. The Reichmann family had emigrated from Hungary first to Austria then France, Spain and Tangier before reaching Canada. O&Y was an unlikely predator but the company was highly geared and the cash flow from spirits and gas distribution was attractive. What is more it could be acquired at a discount and parts of the company could be sold off at a profit. The bid looked certain to succeed.

The Hiram management was strong on strategic thinking and they came up with an instant solution. They would sell the spirits business to Allied-Lyons and most of the cash flow would be out of the reach of Reichmann. The deal was done in March 1986. The cost was C$2.6 billion (£1.2 billion at the time) and the Allied shareholders gave their approval on 27 May 1986. The Reichmanns were furious and when they acquired Hiram Walker Resources through their subsidiary Gulf Canada they set about trying to recover the important part of their prize. O&Y brought an action for damages in the Canadian courts and Allied responded by suing O&Y and the stage was set for a bonanza for the lawyers.

The legal cases involved a major time commitment and in addition the acquisition was subject to the approval of the regulatory authorities in Canada, UK and USA. On top of the work involved with the MMC enquiry into the Elders bid for Allied, this represented a workload that might have sunk many managements. It is greatly to the credit of the top management at Allied that very few of us in the operating companies were aware of how much was involved. They seemed to be coping with ease! Sir Derrick was the inspiration and directed the whole business with a clear head. One wonders if fiction could have produced a more exciting story than this one.

It was satisfying to see that some of my recent work with Hiram Walker had been a little helpful. The document to shareholders made reference to the fact that 'last year we entered into a joint venture with one of their (Hiram Walker) subsidiaries to sell wines and spirits in Canada.' This had been entirely my creation sparked off by my concern that our Teacher brand needed a more aggressive effort behind it if it was to make further progress. I have described the project in more detail later.

The various events connected with Elders, the MMC, the O&Y bid for Hiram Walker and our acquisition of Hiram Walker Spirits happened in very quick succession. The MMC investigations were continuous and involved tedious digging for information by the Pratt Committee and the financial people. The Hiram Walker saga moved swiftly. On 19 March Gulf Canada Corporation, controlled by O&Y, made a partial bid for Hiram Walker Resources. This prompted the management to offer to sell to Allied Hiram Walker Spirits and by 31 March the deal was signed. On 2 April Gulf Canada sought a Court injunction to restrain Hiram Walker and its directors from implementing this agreement. The document to Allied shareholders of 10 May 1986 relates that on 9 April the Court ruled that the directors of Hiram Walker had acted 'prudently, properly, reasonably and fairly' and that there was 'no impediment to the completion of the sale to Allied'. Gulf Canada made an increased revised bid and gained control of Hiram Walker Resources. On 21 April O&Y appealed against the court's decision and scheduled the hearing for 23 June. On 2 May Gulf Canada replaced the non-executive directors of Hiram Walker with its own people and stopped supplying information to Allied on Hiram Walker Spirits. The shareholders of Allied approved the acquisition of Hiram Walker Spirits on 27 May.

Apart from our trading connections with Hiram Walker there were other reasons for Allied being able to be seen as Canada friendly. Derrick Holden-Brown had spent some of his early career with Hiram Walker and during this period had married his wife Pat, who was a Toronto girl. He was familiar with the country and a regular visitor. He had friends who would vouch for him. These things helped to balance the considerable odds against Allied in the courts and with the government who protected Canadian companies against foreign ownership to some extent. The battle, for that is what it was, lasted for six months and lawyers were begging to take over strategic control and enjoy themselves. Although not involved in the legal activities, I sat in on a reporting meeting in Toronto on one occasion and listened to the leading lawyer explaining how they had managed to engineer a mandatory court appearance of the other side's leader in the middle of his annual vacation overseas. The idea was to apply pressure, make him mad and perhaps lead him to make some faulty judgements!

This was the moment to settle the case and several meetings took place between O&Y and Allied with Sir Derrick very much involved. These were inconclusive and Allied were becoming frustrated and concerned that the court proceedings would drag on, incur escalating costs and harm the prospects for the merger with Hiram Walker Spirits. It was decided to walk out of the talks and go home but that Derrick would stay behind on the pretext that he was visiting friends in the Toronto area. This was made known to the other side in the hope that an approach would be made to him when the others had left in a very public fashion vowing not to come back. Sure enough Paul Riechmann called Derrick and they met twice over the weekend for frank talks. The outcome was that Derrick travelled back to London happy and with a bit of paper in his pocket, which resolved the dispute.

The new agreement was detailed in a letter to shareholders on 2 October prior to the annual general meeting. It gave Allied 51 per cent of Hiram Walker Spirits with Gulf Canada becoming the minority shareholder. In addition Allied had the right to acquire Gulf Canada's minority holding two years after completion at a price based on the original consideration. The price for the controlling interest was in direct proportion to that originally agreed for the whole business. This deal satisfied our objective of developing our wines and spirits business worldwide, acquiring international brands and having access to a distribution network dedicated to all our brands.

I was a member of the main Allied board by this time and I looked forward to playing a significant part in the integration of the two businesses. Over a weekend I had drawn up a plan for an integrated structure rather like I had done in a smaller way twice before with Stewarts and Teacher's. I took it to Michael Jackaman, Chairman of Allied Vintners, the wine and spirit division and he said we had better take it to Derrick and we went to see him a few days later. The joint control of Hiram Walker Spirits meant that there were a limited number of seats on the joint board. I discovered that the meeting with Derrick was so that he could tell me that there was no room for me. This was a disappointment after 17 years in control of Allied's spirits business but I was within three years of retirement and realistically I could not expect to be involved forever!

Acquisitions Continue

We had a regular contact with Hiram Walker Spirits between October 1986 and December 1987 but the managements naturally remained separate. It was not an easy relationship but some useful things were done in managing our respective overseas businesses. The executives were also able to get to know one another and, as usual in this situation, size up individuals and the threats they might pose for our futures when a complete integration came about. Happily for the sanity of everyone, the opportunity arose to buy out the minority shareholder in Hiram Walker Spirits and this was finalised on 3 March 1988. The price involved the issue of convertible preference shares to O&Y and, when converted, this gave O&Y a 10 per cent holding in Allied. I took no further part in the management of the wine and spirit division but was given the consolation prize of Chairman of Allied

Distillers, the integrated Scotch whisky business. I spent most of the next year and a half before retirement in the enjoyable role of 'co-ordinating the group's trade development in the Soviet Union and China'. This brought me into a little conflict with Alex Alexander, who was never willing for his food division, J Lyons, to be co-ordinated by anyone!

Allied had owned 25 per cent of Chateau Latour for many years through John Harvey & Sons, who were one of the main shippers of this First Growth Bordeaux. In March 1989 Allied acquired from Pearson their 54 per cent holding and later added most of the remaining minority shares. This deal valued Chateau Latour at £104m. The rationale for this considerable investment was that it gave prestige and credibility to the large wine business carried on by Grants of St James's, which was the largest in the country. It was a move that would have been ideal in the 1950s and would have given Grants the authority and authenticity that was so valuable in those days when dealing in wine. Michael was set on the investment and Derrick supported him with good reason. Unfortunately, the asset became redundant in the changed circumstances of the 1990s and it was sold for £86m together with Grants of St James to help finance the acquisition of Pedro Domecq. Domecq had a joint venture with Hiram Walker and there was an agreement that each had an option to sell to the other. Allied completed the acquisition of the various holdings in Domecq between 18 May and 31 July 1994.

The long-term contract to brew Castlemaine XXXX in the UK had been very successful and was cemented by a 25 per cent holding in Castlemaine Toohey. It was a surprise to find in 1985 that the Bond Corporation was bidding for the company. They had already bought the Swan Brewery of Perth, Western Australia. The Allied holding was vital and could have prevented the bid succeeding. This had been the original idea as it protected what we saw as an important part of our business. However, the board took the view that the Allied shareholders would not be too pleased at the group losing an opportunity to sell at a very good price, particularly if the value of the holding subsequently dropped when we were the only minority shareholder.

The holding was, therefore, sold and the brewing contract had to stand on its own unprotected. Needless to say the Castlemaine Toohey management was not too happy but I suppose that's life!

The Bond Corporation had bigger ambitions and thought, like John Elliott of Elders, that they might be able to gain control of Allied itself. During 1988 Bond acquired 11 per cent of Allied's equity and had several discussions with the chairman about an amalgamation. The story was that there was an opportunity to create a worldwide brewing business to match Heineken, Carlsberg, Stella Artois and San Miguel. Allied took the view that the approach was sheer opportunism and refused to discuss the matter further. I remember commenting at the board that, if that was Bond's objective and he was serious, he could make a start by taking up the opportunity to capture the Asian market but he had made no attempt to do so. Bond was not able to hold on to his Allied holding, as it had been bought with borrowed money and the costs exceeded the dividends received.

I retired from Allied in July 1989 and the acquisitions continued in the spirits field. In addition to Domecq there was Beefeater Gin and Long John from Whitbread, which we had previously considered and turned down. I have no idea if we paid more in the end or not but there was a new wave of rationalisation afoot and the opportunity was well taken.

It is tempting to reflect on the purpose, necessity and results of mergers over the decades since companies became the vehicles for controlling and running enterprises. However, it would take another chapter to deal with this issue and in any case many able writers have recorded opinions on the subject. Certainly the stock market influences events to a large extent. Acquiring other companies is a recognised way to keep up growth in a share that is in demand and cost savings are often the main source of increased profit. The disadvantage of acquisitions by quoted companies is that there is usually not enough time to plan and implement the integration of the target with the acquiring company. Some value is inevitably lost and very rarely is there a proper audit of the results of restructuring against the substantial write-offs to cover the costs. When a business has lost its way completely it will inevitably be taken over if it has attractive assets, which would include brands. These assets can be integrated with the existing business and contribute to the overall profit of the acquiring company without the burden of central costs. This makes for a successful merger.

The main thing to bear in mind is that business is not like a golf club, church or rural village life. It is in a constant state of change simply because markets are always changing and those who do not adapt fade away. Against that scene there is the constant of brand franchises, which will survive almost anything and if looked after can continue to produce profit. Their share of consumer spend will decline as choice increases but greater spending power can compensate. An illustration of the interplay between share of spend and absolute spend is the food business. Its share of total spend has dropped substantially and yet we are eating more thanks to greater earning power. Methods of handling brands will change but, as long as the core values of the brands are supported, they will survive and prosper. The prime example is Coca-Cola but Johnnie Walker Scotch whisky and Guinness would also qualify for inclusion in the list. And the food industry is littered with other examples such as Bird's Custard invented in 1837 to mention only one.

CHAPTER 6

The Economics of the Business

The Early Days

The history of distilling goes back many centuries and much has been written about it in many countries. Distilled spirits have been part of the culture of most societies throughout history. In modern times, that is, from the late 19th century, the development of branded Scotch whisky has provided consumers with the additional benefit of displaying a degree of sophistication by virtue of their choice of product and brand. The demand for this benefit is still strong in spite of a decline in per capita consumption. Indeed, the share of the Scotch market for brands may well be greater than ever.

In Scotland the 18th century saw a widespread growth in distilling all over the country and it gradually became a formalised part of the rural economy. Farmers saw it as a sideline, which enabled them to use their own surplus grain and sell the distilled product to the local community. The result was a larger profit compared to selling the grain in the market. A hundred years later the farmer became the distiller and saw his farm as a sideline, which secured his water rights and the distillery fed his cattle with wet draff from the distillery.

The formalising of distilling led inevitably to taxation of whisky and the licensing of distilleries. Illicit distilling continued for a long time and the excisemen had an active life tracking down the illicit distillers, who were very good at avoiding capture by constantly moving their equipment to new sites.

Distilling activity grew enormously in the 19th century and great strides were made in quality control, which encouraged a wider distribution of the better whiskies. These whiskies as they became better known gradually acquired a premium reputation. The introduction of the continuous still and the blending of malt and grain whisky attracted many more drinkers and maturing whisky for several years in oak casks further enhanced quality. Thus a simple rural activity has turned into a complex business involving major investments and the deployment of a whole range of skills.

Negative Cash Flow – An Attractive Investment!

As maturing became an important element in the quality of Scotch whisky, and eventually a legal requirement, distillers had to lay down stocks. Furthermore, the level of these stocks had to be increased regularly to meet the possibility of higher sales in the years ahead. Here then is the principal feature of the industry's financial profile. There is a direct link between capital invested in stock and volume of sale but separated by the maturing period, which can be five or six years for a normal blend to 30 years for a premium malt whisky. Thus, an expanding trade will result in a negative cash flow, as the current sales volume will be lower than the stock investment for future sales.

It will take at least 15 years to reach a positive cash flow for a new introduction or a planned increase in the sales of an existing brand. A good return is possible provided the target profit margin can be achieved in a highly competitive market. This will include covering all the costs of financing the stocks. Resisting the temptation to improve the rate of growth by discounting is difficult and a strong constitution is required to see the project through. This is what Sam Bronfman did when he started filling for Chivas Regal 12 year old in the mid thirties and launched the brand after WWII. He controlled his own business and could take a long-term view without criticism of slow growth from shareholders. Similarly Dewar's and Walkers brands, created and launched in the 1890s, took the medium-term view in building their brands. The maturing period was not so long but the growth rate was high and this put pressure on the sources of funds. In addition, large amounts were spent on advertising in order to capture the leading positions in the British market. Since then only Chivas, Ballantine's and J&B brands have succeeded in establishing a truly international position in the Scotch market.

It is an advantage to own your own distilleries so that stock can be built up at cost thus enabling you to reach a positive cash flow a little sooner. A positive cash flow for a 12 year old would take at least 22 years, which is a long time for a publicly quoted company to sustain the effort. Some companies are tempted to introduce 30 year old brands without realising that the price must cover a very large investment cost. In times of high inflation there is the illusion of fat profits as prices rise above the original cost of the whisky sold. However, it should be borne in mind that these profits will be taxed and that, after tax, there may not be sufficient cash to invest in replacement stock. This problem was particularly evident during the two world wars when taxation was extremely high. On the other hand, if you were destocking at these times, the profits were very good. Even in normal times destocking will produce an excellent return as the investment in stock is declining and not increasing. Such a policy would only be adopted if a company had decided to come out of the business altogether.

Achieving an optimum selling price for the sale of a case of Scotch is often very difficult in periods of intense competition. In order to succeed with a 12yo and achieve a perfectly reasonable investment rate of return of 20 per cent requires a margin of over six times that needed for a normal blend averaging six years old or at least an extra £6–7 per bottle. The consumer will pay more for a 12yo Scotch because it is perceived to be better but is £7 acceptable?

It is quite common for companies that invest in stocks to meet the total future demand for their brands to have a tendency to underprice the final product. Distilling capacity is very flexible and excess output is always a risk. Surplus stock depresses the prices of maturing stocks and robs the stockholder of a proper margin. Occasionally a major company will avoid this investment by contracting for a proportion of the requirement of fully matured bulk whisky ready for blending and bottling. In the first decade of the 20th century, Buchanan's bought 'old' whisky on the market but Walkers bought new fillings and lost a lot of money when the market collapsed and they had surplus. Buchanan's employed less capital than Walkers and achieved a better return on capital. However, it is probable that the stockholder, who sold the matured stock to Buchanan's did not achieve a full price. In recent times, Whyte & Mackay chose not to hold stocks or even own a bottling plant with the result that they could sell at lower prices and yet produce a return similar to their competitors. In the United States, Buckingham and Paddington were able to rapidly grow Cutty Sark and J&B without major capital investment by means of a series of contracts for supply of matured stock and bottling facilities. You have to risk the stock not being available when you want it and for a big brand that is not a policy that can be adopted.

There used to be quite a number of privately owned stockholding companies or brokers, who held stock as a speculative investment. They hoped to cash in when there was a market shortage and the price would rise against a strong demand. You find a similar situation in the Cognac industry in France where the growers will hold key quantities of old cognac for special occasions, such as a daughter's wedding, for selling not drinking! It can be better than money in the bank, which would lose its value over time. This source of supply is not a lot of use to a large blender, who needs regular supplies at stable prices. On the other hand, it could be useful in filling gaps in a stock portfolio at short notice to meet an unexpected demand.

In the main it is not possible for large operators to contract out for matured stock, because it is not likely to be available in sufficient quantity. As companies become bigger they fill most if not all of their requirements themselves. This became obvious when DCL merged with the 'Big Three' in 1925. Later the further concentration of the industry in the 1980s reduced the market for bulk maturing whisky to a small proportion of the total requirement. This has meant that the large groups have to make constant reappraisals of their future requirements and assess the risks associated with their stock investments in terms of pricing, return on capital, sales growth and cash flow. Even a standard brand can take ten years or more before it achieves a positive cash flow. The return will be attractive provided prices are not under pressure. When they are, the investment in stock should be carefully controlled.

As in all enterprises, the use of investment funds is the key to profitability and growth. This is well understood in, for instance, the oil industry but is often not fully appreciated in the drinks business.

New fillings of Scotch whisky are treated as stock and thus current assets on the balance sheet and are not usually subjected to the rigors of sophisticated capital appraisal schemes.

Dichotomy – Sales Forecasts v. Stock Investment

In a large company, the new filling programme will normally be fully considered and the cash flow considerations incorporated in the budgeting process on a year by year basis. The filling proposals are usually put forward by the whisky buying department after consultation with finance and marketing colleagues, who will have done their sales projections usually on an increasing trend. Buyers are responsible for placing the orders advantageously but cannot be held responsible if the stock filled is not sold. The sales people will sell what they can at the price available in the market but volume and price may not match the original forecasts. It will be obvious that no one has taken responsibility for the investment.

Balancing the decisions made in stock investment, product pricing, sales trends and return on capital presents a tricky problem for managements. It is particularly difficult in large companies, which tend to be organised into separate functional divisions. The problem is compounded at the sales end of the business, where heavy promotional expenditure is required to build and nurture a brand. This 'investment' is also a long-term consideration but of a different nature to stock investment.

However, the most important management function in a Scotch whisky company is marketing. Brand building and selling are the key activities in the business and require the best talent available. Marketing has the responsibility for creating the demand for the brand by deploying the considerable funds at its disposal over a period of years. It must make decisions on pricing, distribution, sales force and promotional spend. Logically, it should also take responsibility for submitting proposals for stock investment, which is dependent on the rate of growth achieved from marketing decisions.

In practice such a division of responsibility would not normally be acceptable, although I cannot see why. It would avoid the frustrating discussions about how much to fill. It would give the managing director more room for considering the proposals before becoming directly involved. It would enable a better judgement to be made about the decision on the rate of return target unencumbered by inter-department arguments. These are all too familiar. Marketing expects to have as much stock as it estimates it will need to meet sales projections. Buying will tend not to believe these estimates, as they tend to be over-optimistic. This can often be a classic case of not seeing the wood for the trees.

While the problem of how to allocate responsibilities may be clear, it is not quite so easy to apply solutions in a large multi-product group where marketing is centralised for Scotch whisky, and perhaps Cognac, as well as non-matured products. Marketers are trained to evaluate investments in promotional programmes and judging their results but it is difficult for them to direct their minds also to the stock investment consequences of growing a Scotch whisky brand. You could say that they have enough on their minds without being bothered with the buyer's problems. They can make decisions about pricing, how many salesmen to deploy and the consumer groups to target. They cannot influence the response from the consumer nor can anyone. They can, however, make value judgements about the estimated outcome giving reasoned arguments and not simply taking cover behind a series of sales projections, which may be too high or too low.

Moreover, the field sales forces are strongly influenced by market price levels and achieving volume targets against them. A management needs to focus on the most profitable route for the long term or at least as long as it takes to extract the company from the investment it has made in stock. Unfortunately it will have to make further stock investment decisions before the original investment has been realised and a clear line of responsibility will avoid the inevitable awkward confrontation when the managing director is trying to find out why the company's return on capital is so poor.

Setting Targets and Allocating Tasks

The question is often asked, 'what is the correct rate of return?' and the answer usually is 'it depends!' Obviously the target rate must at least equal the cost of capital plus a surplus for investment in new fixed assets and additional working capital. Sometimes rate of return is not relevant where a company has a low capital base and a high net margin. However, in most manufacturing companies it is very relevant and will vary from say 15 per cent to 35 per cent. There will be an optimum rate, which will promote profit growth and the MD will decide where to pitch the target, depending on how much growth is available in the market for the company's products.

The key responsibility of the MD is growth in profits at the desired rate of return. It is worth listing the essential elements of cost in the business and how they might be managed. They are:

The cost of producing or buying the various whiskies included in the blend make-up.

The cost of maturing the individual whiskies.

The cost of packaging materials.

The cost of handling bulk whiskies from maturing warehouses through the blending and bottling processes.

The desired rate of recovery of overheads.

The rate of recovery of promotional costs.

The cost of storage and dispatch of finished goods.

The profit margin required covering the cost of capital invested in stocks and fixed assets.

These cost elements can be put together as shown in the table overleaf, which will test whether or not the achieved or planned price levels can support the cost of the product and if there is a sufficient return on the capital invested per case sold. Of course, the periodic profit and loss accounts for the whole operation will provide the result of all the transactions but that is history and too late for corrective action on pricing. A budget projection will normally be prepared for the whole organisation and provide a forecast of the period ahead, usually only a year. However, it needs to be translated into terms understood by the sales force that fixes the selling prices so that they will know that they have a chance of meeting the target profit.

General management needs to balance investments in distilling capacity, stocks, blending and bottling capacity and marketing expenditure. It must communicate to the heads of these functions what is expected of them if the company is to reach its target profit. Each function has to understand how its actions will influence the whole and be able to monitor progress and take corrective action where appropriate. Conventionally framed profit and loss accounts and budgets are not sufficient to do this. The management needs to influence the detailed decisions in the interests of the overall performance and must control the balance of the actions of the various functions. The constant monitoring of the cost elements against planned performance is easy although tedious but is essential to guarantee the optimum use of capital.

The aims and motivation of each function head will invariably be in conflict as soon as they are set, simply because each requires to adjust their plans to meet changed circumstances. Therefore, management needs to keep the performance in focus and make sure that the chosen direction is being followed. Without this control there is always the risk of surplus stock investment or spare distilling and bottling capacity each of which will reduce the rate of return and be costly in other ways.

It is worth defining the aims of each function and understanding the bias each has when changes are necessary. This will help to create a suitable management structure, which will assist the company to reach strategic decisions without too much conflict. If the direction is clear and understood, then the difficult matters of judgement will more easily be dealt with by a group of managers pulling together.

Distilling

This is an activity, which has hardly changed since early days except for the introduction of continuous distilling. The process is traditional and that is one of the attractions of the product. However, the methods have been dramatically improved thus cutting costs and increasing reliability. The distillery manager seeks to achieve the lowest unit cost consistent with the quality specification of his 'make'. He can influence the yield in litres of alcohol from the malted barley delivered to him through process improvements and the economical use of fuel. He cannot easily smooth out fluctuations in barley prices unless he can negotiate long-term contracts, which can also help to secure regular supplies of good quality malted barley. The volume of orders will, of course, affect unit costs and he will always wish to maintain planned output levels and have a little spare capacity for sudden surges.

New Fillings

The new filling buyer will tend to support the claims for spare distilling capacity and be able to have all his stock at distilling cost. Most malt and grain requirements for blending can be acquired by exchanging your own make with other blenders who own distilleries. If you wish to buy from a distiller who is not a blender you will have to pay cash and the same will apply if your company is short of distilling capacity. Sometimes there are shortages of matured bulk whisky for blending, which are only discovered late in the day. Other blenders may be happy to release some surplus stocks or the broking community may be able to supply. The price will usually be high but no capital has been tied up in the stock and the effect on return on capital will be positive.

Maturing

Aging of new whiskies absorbs fresh capital each year through the purchase and coopering of casks. From time to time additional warehouses will be required to house increased stocks, although outside storage is generally available at distilleries and in public warehouses for limited quantities. The warehouse management will naturally wish to carry spare capacity and not rely on outsiders but availability of capital may be a constraint.

Packaging

Purchasing of packaging materials is a specialised activity for a major brand-owning company. In an industry that is selling image and consumer satisfaction the lowest cost option is not what is needed. Flair for innovative design and presentation are the key considerations and it is important to find suppliers, who are not only capable but are also reliable. For high volume items such as containers and outer packaging, there are sometimes capacity shortages, when prices escalate and delivery can be problematic. Being an important customer counts in this situation. When prices are dependent on quantity, buyers will tend to want to buy large quantities, which ties up capital and warehouse space.

Bulk Handling

Bulk whisky is transported from storage warehouses to blending and bottling factories by large road bulk carriers and transferred into vats at destination. Small quantities are still moved from distilleries in casks, which are picked up by container trucks going round the various distilleries in a sort of 'milk round'. This is a vast change from early days when casks were loaded onto trains from the north and then horse-drawn carts for conveyance to blenders within easy range. The cost savings have been enormous and fewer people are needed for the work. Marginal savings are always arising where there is growth in volume or when reviews of procedures reveal opportunities for cutting costs. Alert managements will come up with new ideas on a regular basis, which will involve expenditure on vats, pumping systems and vehicles.

Blending and Bottling

The same is true of the whole of the blending and bottling field, which employs the largest proportion of people in a whisky operation. The flow of spirit through blending, reduction to bottling strength with water, filling of bottles, labelling, packing into cartons and storage for dispatch to customers can be handled automatically. The degree of automation will depend on the size of the business, which can vary from tens of thousands to millions of cases a year. Great care is required to avoid high capital expenditure without the consequent gains in productivity. It is easy for a bottling hall manager to present capital expenditure bids for new machines regularly but another matter to trace the benefits from the investments. From a revenue point of view it should be possible to see a constant downward trend in unit labour costs but often there are other changes that mask the benefit and make it difficult to determine if a sufficient savings have been achieved.

A big brand can introduce highly automated plants dealing with long runs. The benefit is that more can be produced in less space at lower cost. The cost advantage can sometimes be eroded by higher overheads often unchallenged by management. A good example of a successful, fast, low cost bottling operation is the German small bottle bitter brand 'Underburg'. It turns out a million bottles per day from a space no bigger than a chairman's office!

The main consideration in bottling Scotch is in the multitude of pack-size and labelling requirements, which are essential to meet consumer demand and government regulations in overseas markets. Here flexibility rather than speed is vital and with care the extra cost can be minimised by operating out of small, low overhead plants.

Occasionally and to the amusement of my colleagues, I would suggest that if I were surrounded with a supply of spirit, bottles, labels and cartons I could produce more cases in a day than the factory could per employee. In fact when I started in the family business I learned to bottle wine in exactly that way. I do not think the method has changed since my grandfather started the business in the early 1900s! I am not sure that I convinced my production colleague but it did prompt much discussion and an effort to prove otherwise by better performance.

To my further amusement I came across an article in The *Financial Times* recently about a Japanese manufacturer of electronic goods, Yamagata, which had recently transferred production of one of its products from low-cost Malaysia back to Japan and found it could produce at a cost 10 per cent lower than the Malaysian supplier. They changed the layout of the factory and the way parts were delivered to the workers so that rehandling was cut by half. Everything needed was placed no further than 75cm from where the person was standing thus reducing the space needed by 70 per cent and the number of workers from 22 in Malaysia to as little as seven or even four. Wage rates were four times those in the other factory. Lead time was reduced and inventories were down from 18 to just three days!

Over the years I had the opportunity to review Scotch whisky blending and bottling operations and, not surprisingly, these reviews confirmed the cost benefit of large inflexible plants for dealing with long runs of the same product and pack-size. Good examples are milk and Nicolas 'planque' wines in Paris. However, they also proved that the spare capacity in these large plants could not handle a variety of products with short runs as cheaply as a smaller plant with less automation and more staff.

Packaging is not a large part of the cost profile but it is one where the cost is controllable. A high unit cost compared to some other bottling operations such as milk is essential due to the quality specification required. Rates of pay have improved over the years as the jobs have become more technically sophisticated. Labour relations are good due to the fact that the work can be programmed evenly throughout the year and a crisis is a rare occurrence. Being a fast moving consumer trade, it is essential to maintain the flow of goods to customers otherwise the consumers will turn to competing brands and I think this is recognised by employees, unions and management alike.

Marketing

The key activity in the business is the marketing function including the operation of field sales forces. Sales activity can be contracted out for some or all of the requirement and out-sourcing and in-house control are equally successful. The major companies have, in recent years, set up their own selling operations in the bigger markets and benefited from the extra profit accruing to this activity. Either way, a very strict control is required over the sales personnel to make sure that the effort is in accordance with the aims of the marketing policy. This is particularly important in the pricing of brands in the market, where aggressive competition can unsettle salesmen and result in over-reaction.

Scotch Whisky is Unlike Other Spirits

It will be appreciated that starting a Scotch whisky company from scratch or even expanding a small one involves a considerable outlay of cash without any flowing back for many years. It is all the more difficult to accept this constraint when you realise that the principal competition, gin, vodka and white rum do not have the same problems as they are not matured spirits. Unless a management is prepared to set a higher price than these competitors and a different positioning with consumers, it might as well forget the idea of running a Scotch whisky company.

The result of the efforts of the brilliant entrepreneurs of the 1890s and early 20th century really established the position of Scotch whisky with the consumer. The Buchanan's, the Dewar's and the Walkers by various means literally transformed the product from a peasant drink to a sophisticated experience. It is not altogether clear that they knew what they were doing or had achieved. They appreciated the fortunes that resulted but when they began to talk of merging their companies they saw one of the main benefits to be saving in advertising. They had captured the British market and they saw no need to continue high levels of promotion if they could eliminate competition by combining their businesses. They reckoned that growth would come from exporting and their next step was the introduction of Scotch whisky to foreign markets taking its existing reputation with it. In most western countries an import is special and can command a premium price. These brilliant salesmen did not appreciate that a brand must be nurtured to keep it alive. If this were not so, Haigs, the largest brand at one time, would still be alive!

Scotch is a drink with certain characteristics, which are unique. Along with cognac, it can offer the consumer an experience not available from other spirits. Together Scotch whisky and cognac denote adulthood, discrimination and confidence. Scotch whisky has an advantage over cognac in that it is seen as the every day drink for many different occasions. It can help younger people to grow up and acquire a worldly image. It demonstrates to their peers that they have made the transition to adulthood and they have acquired the confidence to discriminate between the best and the pedestrian. Consonant with these strengths is the matured element in the make up of Scotch whisky and its traditional distilling process. Variations of this positioning are evident in some foreign markets but the essential strengths of uniqueness are preserved.

There is a lot of talk about the need for Scotch to appeal to younger drinkers. This is true to an extent in that new consumers are not being recruited as fast as is desirable. In earlier generations the fathers unwittingly taught the sons to turn to Scotch whisky usually when they were settling down to a steady job and married life. Scotch whisky was the ideal signal. However, the pattern of life has changed radically and settling down is not quite the major event it used to be. In addition, young people tend not to follow their elders and may move to other drinks or at least another brand. During this change Scotch whisky brands have continued to be promoted in the same way as before. If you look at ads of the 1920s they do not look a lot different from those of today except that presentation and design have improved. They have the same message and I suspect that the younger generation does not see it.

I hope that when there is talk of advertising to young people, brand owners do not make the mistake of trying to appeal to vodka and white rum drinkers. These drinks appeal to first-time consumers of alcohol and they are usually consumed with mixers with which they are familiar from teenagehood. They are also cheaper and their price level would greatly reduce the profitability of the Scotch whisky industry and probably result in its decline. A head on clash with white spirits is a battle that Scotch whisky will inevitably lose.

The Scotch whisky consumer profile is tending towards the mid fifties and it certainly needs to be much younger than that, although targeting the early 20s would certainly not bring real benefit. Matching the price competition from white spirits (not matured) would reduce

Cased Scotch Whisky Profitability

Brand Name: 6 yo blend

			Per cs	Per bot
Age Certificate:	6	Liquid litres:	8.40	
Strength:	40%	Regauge litres of alcohol:	3.36	
Bottle content (cl):	70	Conversion factor	1.15	
		Original litres of alcohol:	3.86	

Product cost per case

Blend		Mix	Price	Ola	Per cs	Per bot
Malt		40%	2.34	1.55	3.62	0.30
Grain		60%	0.95	2.32	2.20	0.18
			1.51	3.86	5.82	0.48
Bottling materials					5.00	0.42
FOB					1.25	0.10
Direct Costs					12.07	1.01
Overheads		**Rate per ola**	**No of years**	**Ola**		
Rent		0.07	6	3.86	1.62	0.14
Coopering	new wood			3.86	0.00	0.00
Wood deprn		0.06	6	3.86	1.39	0.12
Blending & bottling					3.00	0.25
Variable Costs					18.08	1.51
Margin		% FOB	36.98		15.16	1.26
Selling & Administration					3.00	0.25
					36.24	3.02
Promotion					4.75	0.40
FOB Price Check					40.99	3.42
Excise Duty	per rla	19.56	rla	3.36	65.72	5.48
Duty Paid price					106.71	8.89
Distribution Margin		30%			32.01	2.67
					138.73	11.56
VAT		17.50%			18.67	1.56
					157.40	13.12
Investment						
Blend	per ola	1.51			5.82	0.48
Wood	per ola	0.58	ola	3.86	2.24	0.19
Coopering					0.00	0.00
	per ola	2.09			8.06	0.67
Compound value						
Years	Rate	DCF				
6	20%	0.334898			24.07	2.01
Less residual value of wood					0.85	0.1
					23.22	2.08
Margin Required					15.16	1.26

Notes:
1. This calculation is designed to test that the price of a product can recover all the costs associated with its production.
2. The margin is calculated on the capital cost of stock and the rate chosen can be increased to take account of growth in stocks to cover future sales growth if desired.
3. The rate of return should be adequate to cover the fixed assets used in the business.

Calculating the profitability of a case Scotch

Stockbuilding for 6 year old (constant prices millions ola and £s)

Year	Fillings	Stock	Cost per l	Investment	Sales Yr	Growth	Sales mn	Margin	Profit	% Return	CashFlow	Cumulo
1	0.20	0.20	2.09	0.42							-0.42	-0.42
2	0.22	0.42	2.09	0.88							-0.46	-0.88
3	0.24	0.66	2.09	1.38							-0.51	-1.38
4	0.27	0.93	2.09	1.94							-0.56	-1.94
5	0.29	1.22	2.09	2.55							-0.61	-2.55
6	0.32	1.54	2.09	3.23							-0.67	-3.23
7	0.35	1.70	2.09	3.55	1		0.05	16.29	0.81	22.96	0.49	-2.73
8	0.39	1.87	2.09	3.90	2	0.1	0.06	16.29	0.90	22.96	0.54	-2.19
9	0.43	2.05	2.09	4.29	3	0.1	0.06	16.29	0.99	22.96	0.60	-1.60
10	0.47	2.26	2.09	4.72	4	0.1	0.07	16.29	1.08	22.96	0.65	-0.94
11	0.52	2.49	2.09	5.19	5	0.1	0.07	16.29	1.19	22.96	0.72	-0.22
12	0.57	2.73	2.09	5.71	6	0.1	0.08	16.29	1.31	22.96	0.79	0.57
13	0.63	3.01	2.09	6.28	7	0.1	0.09	16.29	1.44	22.96	0.87	1.44
14	0.69	3.31	2.09	6.91	8	0.1	0.10	16.29	1.59	22.96	0.96	2.40
15	0.76	3.64	2.09	7.60	9	0.1	0.11	16.29	1.75	22.96	1.05	3.46
16	0.84	4.00	2.09	8.37	10	0.1	0.12	16.29	1.92	22.96	1.16	4.62
17	0.92	4.40	2.09	9.20	11	0.1	0.13	16.29	2.11	22.96	1.28	5.89
18	1.01	4.84	2.09	10.12	12	0.1	0.14	16.29	2.32	22.96	1.40	7.30
19	1.11	5.33	2.09	11.13	13	0.1	0.16	16.29	2.56	22.96	1.54	8.84
20	1.22	5.86	2.09	12.25	14	0.1	0.17	16.29	2.81	22.96	1.70	10.54
21	1.35	6.45	2.09	13.47	15	0.1	0.19	16.29	3.09	22.96	1.87	12.41
22	1.48	7.09	2.09	14.82	16	0.1	0.21	16.29	3.40	22.96	2.06	14.46
23	1.63	7.80	2.09	16.30	17	0.1	0.23	16.29	3.74	22.96	2.26	16.72
24	1.79	8.58	2.09	17.93	18	0.1	0.25	16.29	4.12	22.96	2.49	19.21
25	1.97	9.44	2.09	19.72	19	0.1	0.28	16.29	4.53	22.96	2.74	21.94
26	2.17	10.38	2.09	21.70	20	0.1	0.31	16.29	4.98	22.96	3.01	24.95
27	2.38	11.42	2.09	23.87	21	0.1	0.34	16.29	5.48	22.96	3.31	28.26
28	2.62	12.56	2.09	26.25	22	0.1	0.37	16.29	6.03	22.96	3.64	31.90
29	2.88	13.82	2.09	28.88	23	0.1	0.41	16.29	6.63	22.96	4.00	35.91
30	3.17	15.20	2.09	31.77	24	0.1	0.45	16.29	7.29	22.96	4.41	40.31
31	3.49	16.72	2.09	34.94	25	0.1	0.49	16.29	8.02	22.96	4.85	45.16
32	3.84	18.39	2.09	38.44	26	0.1	0.54	16.29	8.82	22.96	5.33	50.49
33	4.22	20.23	2.09	42.28	27	0.1	0.60	16.29	9.71	22.96	5.86	56.35
34	4.43	22.04	2.09	46.07	28	0.1	0.66	16.29	10.68	23.18	6.89	63.25
35	4.66	23.81	2.09	49.77	29	0.1	0.72	16.29	11.75	23.60	8.04	71.29
36	4.89	25.53	2.09	53.36	30	0.1	0.79	16.29	12.92	24.22	9.33	80.62
37	5.13	27.17	2.09	56.79	31	0.1	0.87	16.29	14.21	25.03	10.78	91.40
38	5.39	28.72	2.09	60.03	32	0.1	0.96	16.29	15.63	26.04	12.39	103.80
39	5.66	30.16	2.09	63.03	33	0.1	1.06	16.29	17.20	27.28	14.20	117.99
40	5.94	31.67	2.09	66.18	34	0.05	1.11	16.29	18.06	27.28	14.91	132.90
41	6.09	33.10	2.09	69.18	35	0.05	1.16	16.29	18.96	27.41	15.96	148.86
42	6.24	34.46	2.09	72.01	36	0.05	1.22	16.29	19.91	27.64	17.08	165.94
43	6.40	35.72	2.09	74.66	37	0.05	1.28	16.29	20.90	28.00	18.26	184.19
44	6.56	36.89	2.09	77.10	38	0.05	1.35	16.29	21.95	28.47	19.50	203.70
45	6.72	37.95	2.09	79.33	39	0.05	1.41	16.29	23.05	29.05	20.82	224.52
46	6.89	38.90	2.09	81.31	40	0.05	1.49	16.29	24.20	29.76	22.22	246.74
47	7.06	39.88	2.09	83.34	41	0.025	1.52	16.29	24.80	29.76	22.77	269.51
48	7.24	40.87	2.09	85.43	42	0.025	1.56	16.29	25.42	29.76	23.34	292.85
49	7.42	41.90	2.09	87.56	43	0.025	1.60	16.29	26.06	29.76	23.92	316.77
50	7.61	42.94	2.09	89.75	44	0.025	1.64	16.29	26.71	29.76	24.52	341.29
					45	0.025	1.68	16.29	27.38		41.43	382.72
					46	0.025	1.72	16.29	28.06		42.46	425.18
					47	0.025	1.77	16.29	28.76		43.53	468.71
					48	0.025	1.81	16.29	29.48		44.61	513.32
					49	0.025	1.86	16.29	30.22		45.73	559.05
					50	0.025	1.90	16.29	30.98		46.87	605.92

The Stockbuilding and Cash Flow

UK and Top 10 Export Markets 2003 - Shipments and Rank (lpa mn)

	1979		1982		1985		1988		1991		1995		1998		2003	
France	16.32	4	20.58	4	23.23	3	29.47	3	25.68	3	33.24	2	35.48	1	37.43	1
USA	86.02	1	78.82	1	65.94	1	53.16	1	40.88	1	35.74	1	33.79	2	34.33	2
Spain	5.35	11	6.61	8	8.24	6	13.94	5	18.80	4	25.28	4	32.60	3	34.16	3
United Kingdom	52.54	2	44.85	2	46.09	2	45.17	2	38.26	2	31.00	3	28.86	4	31.83	4
South Korea											9.40	6			12.49	5
Germany	9.03	6	8.32	6	7.80	9	7.60	9	9.18	7	8.89	7	11.48	6	11.99	6
Thailand									5.47	11					10.47	7
Greece							5.18	11	8.18	8	8.83	8	8.97	7	9.48	8
Australia			7.94	7	8.05	8	9.28	8	6.85	9	7.49	11	6.89	9	8.46	9
Venezuela	6.02	8	5.55	11									8.51	8	6.87	10
South Africa	5.42	10	6.56	9	8.11	7	9.60	7	5.61	10	8.07	9	6.50	10	6.72	11
Japan	28.62	3	25.78	3	15.35	4	16.80	4	18.02	5	11.60	5	16.17	5		
Italy	12.79	5	11.07	5	13.71	5	11.95	6	8.62	6	8.05	10	6.41	11		
Canada	5.55	9			4.75	11										
Belgium	7.24	7	5.81	10	5.59	10	5.68	10								
UK & Top 10	234.91		221.89		206.86		207.83		185.55		187.59		195.66		204.23	
% of Total	74.58		74.88		76.06		71.38		69.75		64.05		69.12		66.94	
Total	314.97		296.32		271.98		291.14		266.01		292.86		283.07		305.10	

The Top 10 Markets for Scotch 1979–2003

Growth Markets 1958-2050 (lpa mn)

Market	1958	1978	+/- 1958	1988	+/- 1978	1998	+/- 1988	2003	+/- 1958	Est 2050	+/-2003
UK	17.81	48.81	31.00	45.18	-3.63	28.86	-16.32	31.83	14.02	29.00	-2.83
France	0.41	14.45	14.04	29.47	15.02	35.48	6.01	37.43	37.02	35.00	-2.43
Germany	0.94	9.26	8.32	8.02	-1.24	11.48	3.46	11.99	11.05	12.00	0.01
Italy	0.32	11.81	11.49	11.95	0.14	6.41	-5.54	5.82	5.50	6.00	0.18
Spain	0.06	9.50	9.44	13.94	4.44	32.65	18.71	34.16	34.10	32.00	-2.16
Portugal	0.52	0.85	0.33	4.06	3.21	5.97	1.91	4.79	4.27	6.00	1.21
Greece	0.52	2.36	1.84	5.18	2.82	8.98	3.80	9.48	8.96	8.00	-1.48
Belgium/Luxembourg	0.65	7.43	6.78	5.68	-1.75	2.87	-2.81	1.61	0.96	2.00	0.39
Netherlands	0.31	5.78	5.47	4.65	-1.13	4.37	-0.28	2.52	2.21	3.00	0.48
Denmark	0.27	1.32	1.05	1.65	0.33	1.54	-0.11	1.46	1.19	2.00	0.54
Sweden	0.42	3.96	3.54	3.29	-0.67	2.53	-0.76	2.16	1.74	3.00	0.84
Western Europe	**22.23**	**115.53**	**93.30**	**133.07**	**17.54**	**141.14**	**8.07**	**143.25**	**121.02**	**138.00**	**-5.25**
USA	28.10	94.03	65.93	53.16	-40.87	33.79	-19.37	34.33	6.23	40.00	5.67
Canada	2.35	5.61	3.26	3.70	-1.91	3.17	-0.54	3.20	0.85	4.00	0.80
Mexico	0.52	1.29	0.77	1.91	0.62	2.38	0.47	1.97	1.45	3.00	1.03
Venezuela	1.17	11.62	10.45	3.82	-7.80	11.59	7.77	6.87	5.70	8.00	1.13
Paraguay	0.26	2.06	1.80	2.27	0.21	3.27	1.00	0.85	0.59	2.00	1.15
Brazil	0.37	3.27	2.90	4.67	1.40	4.88	0.21	5.02	4.65	16.00	10.98
Argentina	0.47	2.66	2.19	0.12	-2.54	2.81	2.69	1.81	1.34	3.00	1.19
Americas	**33.24**	**120.54**	**87.30**	**69.65**	**-50.89**	**61.89**	**-7.77**	**54.05**	**20.81**	**76.00**	**21.95**
Japan	0.41	26.85	26.44	16.8	-10.05	16.17	-0.63	6.32	5.91	15.00	8.68
Australia	1.53	8.02	6.49	9.28	1.26	6.9	-2.38	8.46	6.93	7.00	-1.46
India	0.29	0.33	0.04	0.47	0.14	1.34	0.87	3.34	3.05	30.00	26.66
China & Hong Kong	0.19	1.10	0.91	1.17	0.07	1.88	0.71	1.72	1.53	40.00	38.28
South Korea	0.00	0.22	0.22	3.2	2.98	3.74	0.54	12.49	12.49	9.00	-3.49
South Africa	1.38	5.29	3.91	9.59	4.30	6.5	-3.09	6.72	5.34	6.00	-0.72
Russia	0.03	0.19	0.16	0.35	0.16	0.54	0.19	1.99	1.96	15.00	13.01
Asia & Others	**3.83**	**42.00**	**38.17**	**40.86**	**-1.14**	**37.07**	**-3.79**	**41.04**	**37.21**	**122.00**	**80.96**
Total Selected	**59.30**	**278.07**	**218.77**	**243.58**	**-34.49**	**240.10**	**-3.48**	**238.34**	**179.04**	**336.00**	**97.66**
Percent of World Total	**87.31**	**86.00**		**83.66**		**84.82**		**78.12**		**84.00**	
Others	8.62	45.25	37.25	47.56	2.31	42.98	-36.77	66.76	58.14	64.00	-2.76
Word Total	**67.92**	**323.32**	**256.02**	**291.14**	**-32.18**	**283.07**	**-40.25**	**305.10**	**237.18**	**400.00**	**94.90**

Guestimate of Growth up to 2050

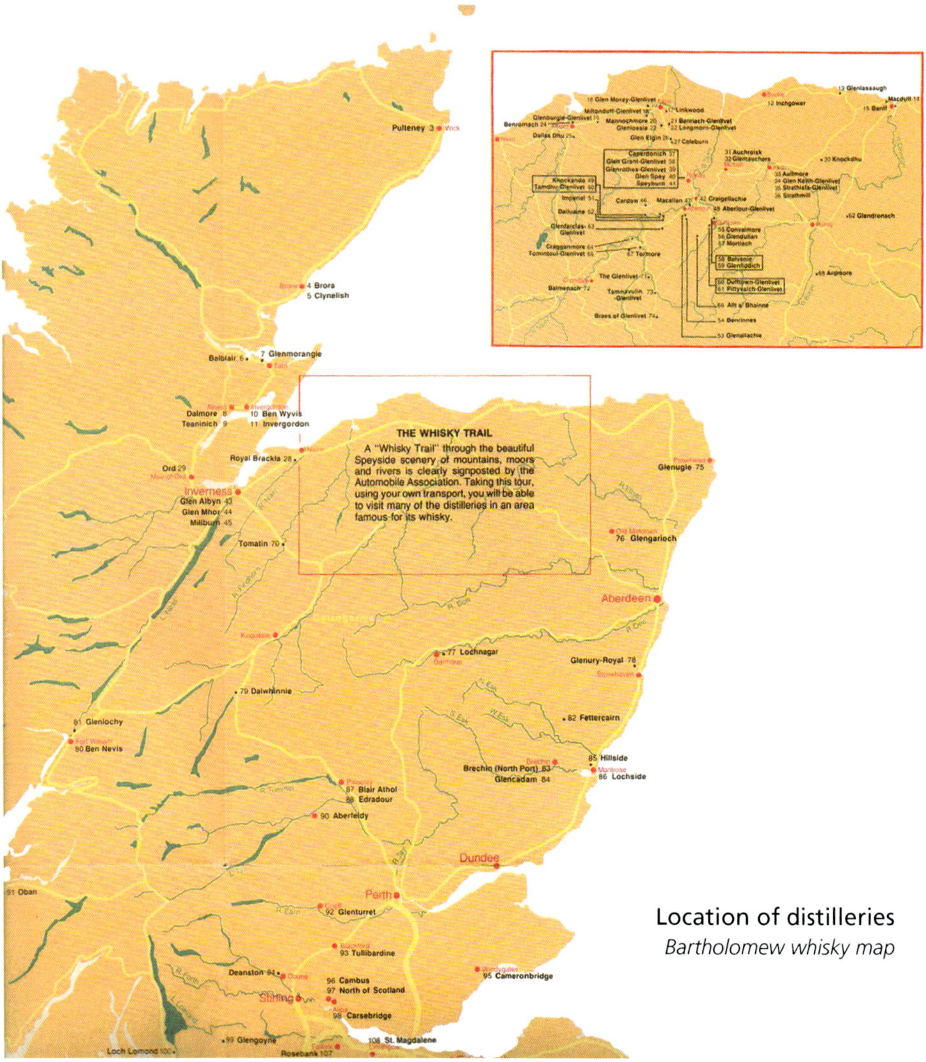

Location of distilleries
Bartholomew whisky map

The Battle for the Distillers Company

Left:
Saunders known at Guinness as 'Deadly' Ernest.
Press cuttings

Right:
James Gulliver a gifted businessman.
Press cuttings

Below:
The Guinness justification for taking on Distillers
Guinness document

Who is the better partner for Distillers?

Qualifications Required	Argyll	Guinness
— A company with relevant brand management experience	×	√
— A company with a good drinks management record	×	√
— A company matching the leaders in its own field	×	√
— A company with significant international marketing experience	×	√
— A company committed to Scotch whisky production	×	√
— A company of significant scale	×	√

× — misfit
√ — fit

TWENTY GOOD REASONS WHY YOU SHOULD ACCEPT THE ARGYLL OFFER.

1. It's A Generous Offer.
2. You'll Be Better Off With Argyll Shares.
3. Distillers Needs Vigorous New Management.
4. Distillers Has Failed To Reward Its Shareholders.
5. Distillers Has Failed In Scotch Whisky At Home.
6. Distillers Has Failed In Scotch Whisky Worldwide.
7. Distillers Has Mismanaged Johnnie Walker.
8. Distillers Has Mismanaged Its Gin Business.
9. Distillers Has Failed In Brand Marketing.
10. Distillers Lacks Vision.
11. Distillers Isn't Changing.
12. Distillers Isn't Growing.
13. Argyll Has Built A Strong, Growing Business.
14. Argyll Has A Consistent Management Approach.
15. Argyll Has An Excellent Record.
16. Argyll Has Rewarded Its Shareholders Well.
17. Argyll Has Revitalised A Major Retail Business.
18. Argyll Has Experience In Drinks Marketing.
19. Argyll Can Revive Distillers.
20. Argyll Is Committed To Scotland.

Argyll's reason for taking over Distillers

Argyll document

The complex story

Financial Times

The Formation of Allied Distillers

Above:

Adam Bergius chairman of Teachers with Alex Gibson.

Right:

Barcardi Deal.

Gordon Black blending director at Stewarts

Jack Oliver export director

Left: Stewarts factory

Above: New packaging for Glendronach

TEACHER'S CHAIRMAN RETIRES

On an evening at the end of July in the opulent surroundings of The Hutcheson's Hall in Glasgow the distinguished career of John Blanche as Teacher's Chairman for the past decade was generously acknowledge on his retiral by a gathering of his peers.

Teacher's Managing Director, Mike Cowman, paid tribute to John's foresight when in the early 1980s at a time of high profitability John was determined to build on this success and seek new directions for the Company. John will be remembered for championing Teacher's operations in Brazil through some up and downs, said Mike Cowman, recognising it as a valuable asset with which to attach that vast, potentially lucrative market.

John Blanche entertains audience with his farewell speech.

Fun at my retiral dinner

PURE BRAZIL!

Tachino — as they say in Glasgow — is pure brill!

Tachino is the new white spirit from Brazil, launched by Teacher's, which has added an exciting new dimension to the existing white spirit range, of white rum, gin or vodka.

From the heart of Brazil, Tachino has brought a fresh international style to cachaca — the national spirit of Brazil which since its test launch in Glasgow last year has created a strong presence in the market.

Tachino is a particularly versatile drink, which can be enjoyed with most mixers, or neat with ice. Either way, Tachino's smooth clean taste and distinctive character guarantees its success.

Helping to build Tachino's success has been the host of promotional activities and events aimed at making both trade and consumers aware of the brand.

Exotic billboard catches the eye.

Tachino Advertising

'Scotland the What?' show their bottle . . . Auchterturra

I AM delighted to report the "Scotland the What?" team are getting into the spirit of the North-east with even more conviction than usual.

They commissioned distillers William Teacher to bottle a special malt for them to give them courage before, and comfort after, a hostile audience.

Teacher's, who have a distillery in the heart of "Scotland the What?" country at Kennethmont, came up with The Auchterturra, named after the fictional scene of so many skits.

The single malt cheerfully admits being distilled "just beyond the back of beyond at Auchterturra, by Rhynie, Huntly, Aberdeenshire".

The Auchterturra, sadly, is not for sale but our picture shows it is more tangible than the town it is named after. And with it are, of course, (from left) Buff Hardie, Stephen Robertson and George Donald.

Above:
'Scotland the What'?

Below:
Fagan and Queen

profitability and will ultimately mean that management will be short of cash to replace stock sold. The consumer profile for white spirits takes account of the fact that young people are taking alcohol for the first time and look for a 'nice' taste, which come from the mixers like cola and fruit juice. The great strength of the appeal of Scotch is that it has always been a drink to aspire to and is something of an acquired taste, which makes it also a challenge. The 25–35 age group is perhaps where sales have been lost and identifying with modern life styles successfully will produce results. This age group has quite different attitudes and habits compared to 50 years ago but they must still have aspirations which Scotch could satisfy.

There are many more outlets for promotion than there were eighty years ago and modern research techniques enable targeting of consumers to be more precise and more effective. Television has come into use in recent years and it could prove effective if used carefully. Major campaigns are not really possible, as the cost could not be met out of the volume and margin available from the sale of even the top Scotch whisky brands. It is also difficult to find a unique positioning for an individual brand of Scotch to make television do its job properly. The image of the category is very strong and certainly stronger than a single brand. Nevertheless, the task of creating a buzz around Scotch whisky once more is do-able and offers the current generation of marketers a real challenge equivalent to that facing the Buchanans, the Dewars and the Walkers all those years ago.

The Scope of Marketing?

There is much debate about the role of marketing people and how they should be trained. Certainly they must be familiar with all aspects of market research, media advertising and selling. They need to be able to judge how to obtain value from marketing spend and be strong enough to change course if a chosen strategy does not work. However, changing campaigns too often can be wasteful. It is claimed that when management are becoming bored with a campaign the consumer has only just begun to notice it. It is a fine judgement.

The question arises: should more be expected of the marketing man? Should he be expected to take responsibility for profits and capital employed in view of the fact that he will have control over pricing? Extending the responsibilities or not is a matter of choice for each organisation. However, if profitability becomes a consideration for the marketing people it is important to make sure that the senior person is properly qualified. One way is to take marketing people and train them in finance or vice versa. Another is to recruit MBAs and train them in marketing. Where the marketing function is limited to deploying the budget, fixing prices and selling the product, someone, like an assistant managing director, should be given responsibility for monitoring performance against profitability criteria. This applies particularly to Scotch whisky, and indeed cognac too, because there is a considerable investment in maturing stocks, which otherwise will literally be forgotten.

A word of caution is worth mentioning. The large companies now operating on a global basis wisely concentrate their advertising on the brands, which are or could be global brands. Globalisation can bring big rewards if the resources for funding the cost of promotion are available. Often the hard choice is to cut the support for the smaller brands and redeploy the money to the larger ones. That is fine as long as the support for the smaller brands is not cut out completely. If it is, they will die quickly and the gross margin earned on them will not be available to help fund the advertising of the larger brands.

The smaller brands have a big share of market and will earn profit if given modest in-store support. Consumer prices can be reduced by passing on the savings in advertising and marketing overheads but watch that the cuts do not go too far. If the brand is to be 'milked' ie closed down, then the price can go even lower as long as the bulk stock used up is not replaced. However, it is possible to keep a small brand going indefinitely by pricing it so that there is sufficient profit contribution.

In a large company that is organised along functional lines, the marketing group will not realistically be able to devote attention to the profitability of these small brands. If the profit contribution is significant, it is essential that they be managed separately, perhaps by the bulk stock group as a profit centre. Provided the return on capital is satisfactory, the activity will add value to the company's operations and thus retain management support. It is reasonable to require the smaller brands to match the corporate return but not be required to equal the overhead recovery, simply because they do not use a high level of overhead costs.

Another way of extracting value for shareholders out of small brands is to sell them with or without a management team. Some say this will increase the competition for the business but if you are not able to build a small brand into a big one it is unlikely that someone else will succeed. The buyer of the small brand will normally be a smaller company with the capacity to keep it going with perhaps a modest rate of growth at most.

The Last 100 Years and the Next?

The introduction of the patent still for producing grain whisky broadened the base of the market. At first grain was produced as a straight drink but gradually blends of grains and malts proved more popular than malt or grain by themselves. Blended Scotch whisky was particularly popular in the south of England and this led to the first major expansion of sales outside local areas. The creation of popular blends helped to formalise the business and hastened the disappearance of illicit distilling and sale of local immature product. Nevertheless the path was not even for everyone, because the new entrants brought excess capacity into the industry and also difficult economic conditions made survival a challenge.

My grandfather started trading in bulk whisky in the late 1890s and planned to acquire a distillery of his own. There were quite a few available at the beginning of the 20th century but it was not until 1905 that he found a suitable distillery in Glen Elgin just outside the town of that name. Three years later he wrote a review of the market in 1908 and it is reproduced below. It is full of platitudes but gives a picture of the bulk trade, which will be familiar to those in the trade today.

'The outstanding feature of the last year's business has been the remarkable appreciation in the value of young grains. These have given the bonder a return equal to that of the best days of the "boom period". The difficulty in obtaining adequate supplies and the high prices ruling is naturally having a reflex action upon the older makes which are now quoted somewhat firmer. With the heavy makes of 1897 to 1899 off the market we may expect to see better terms for this particular branch of the industry.

In malt whiskies young Glenlivets from 1903 to 1906 are coming in for a big share of attention and a marked advance in prices has to be recorded. This is a type of whisky that no blender can afford to be without as it not only gives body but also produces that silky finish known as 'Glenlivet Style' so much appreciated by the consumer. Some of the large houses, believing that these will be scarce when sufficiently matured for the vat, have been quietly picking them up. We believe time will justify their action. The recent return obtained on the motion of Sir John Dewar will have a tendency to still further stiffen the prices of malt, as most people believed that the production of malt was on a much heavier scale than that of grain. The returns show that there is practically little between them. Not the least prominent feature in the year's trading has been the marked depreciation of certain well-known whiskies that used to command 'fancy prices'. Blenders seem more inclined to buy whisky on its merits rather than on a name. This is as it should be. 'A fair field and no favour' is all that any reasonable man can expect. Distilleries have to pay stiff prices for barley this season but they are being compensated to some extent by the increased extract obtained and by the very excellent quality of the produce. The samples we have seen compare favourably with the best makes of former years. In conclusion we are optimistic enough to believe that the dark days of the distilling industry in Scotland are rapidly drawing to a close. Production has been brought into line with consumption. In spite of a period of unparalleled trade depression the demand is still healthy. The quality of the article was never finer. The men handling it were never more fit. Given a revival in trade we may expect an increased demand that will cheer the hearts of these veterans of commerce that have successfully weathered a period of unexampled depression with honour to themselves and credit to the industry.'

It is worth looking at the significant changes, which have taken place in the last hundred years. It has been a period of considerable expansion in consumer spending and with it a dramatic growth in the sales of Scotch whisky worldwide. Output of new whisky can vary dramatically at times due to unanticipated changes in sales levels with the result that surpluses or shortages of stock for blending will result. Quick changes in output levels usually correct the overall position but individual companies may have their own problems if their actions have not been appropriate. Sales projections tend to be too optimistic in every company and often no attempt is made to anticipate what the industry position is likely to be. If only blenders would hold back on their filling programmes early enough when a surplus is expected, then the profitability would be improved greatly.

Production in 1850 was probably about 30 million litres of pure alcohol (lpa) and reached a peak in 1899 at 93m after which it declined steadily to 52m in 1911. It picked up again and remained remarkably steady during WWI although many distilleries were closed due to the shortage of grain. The DCL were the main producer during the war as they had priority for supplies of grain on account of the fact that they produced strategic supplies of yeast. In the 1920s exports helped to keep production at a healthy level until the world financial crisis of the late 1920s and early 1930s. The low point was 1933 when output fell to 15m lpa. Thereafter improving economies helped to encourage increased production and another peak was reached in 1939 at 98m lpa. Virtually nothing was produced during WWII and it was not until 1948 that supplies of raw materials began to flow at a normal rate. From then on output climbed steadily until in 1955 the 1899 and 1939 peaks years were exceeded at 100m lpa.

By that time all the old stagers were gone and the next generation was nearing retiral! However, in the intervening 56 years the character of the business had changed radically. The principal reason was the arrival and subsequent dominance of branded Scotch whisky. The industry had become an international business and the product and its brands were known worldwide.

The period from 1950 to 1978 was one of dramatic growth. Sales increased by nearly ten times, equivalent to an annual growth rate of 8.5 per cent. In the early stages there was a pent-up demand from the United States after WWII, where Scotch whisky became the fashionable drink. Later the accession of the United Kingdom to the EEC gave a further stimulus to exports, particularly in France, Italy and later Spain.

Industry Stocks

The years 1958 to 1978 saw a substantial expansion of distilling capacity and output, which was driven by the growth in exports. Confidence was high and stocks rose from 590m to 2932m lpa. This was a period of explosive economic expansion bringing with it an equivalent growth in earnings. Consumer spending rocketed well beyond basic needs and ultimately leading to what became known as 'conspicuous consumption'. These conditions were ideal for the development of branded goods and they had a field day. Scotch whisky figured strongly among the spending of the high earners and they were able to demonstrate their attitudes and status by their choice of brand, particularly in the United States. A number of premium Scotch whisky brands reached volumes of over a million cases and some over two million. The lead in the market changed from time to time led by fashion. It was said of Chivas Regal, one of the new major brands in the States, that when the chauffeur began to drink Chivas, it was time to change to something else!

There was a hiccup in stockbuilding during the late 1960s. A number of new grain distilleries had been built, including Invergordon by Frank Thompson and Girvan by William Grant. Both these plants are still going and have contributed much to the economies of their areas. Output of new grain more than doubled between 1960 and 1966 whereas sales increased by just 70 per cent over the same period. This prompted the industry to make a precautionary reduction in stock building, which helped to stabilise stocks to a comfortable level. Thereafter production was increased far too quickly and the industry was back in surplus later in the 1970s. Sales declined sharply in the early 1980s with the result that substantial surpluses were built up leading to a dramatic cut in output. As the adjustment was left too late, the reduction in orders for new fillings was cut by nearly 50 per cent over five years. By the mid 1980s sales had levelled off but have never so far returned to the peak of 459m lpa in 1978.

Constant and frequent hard-nosed reviews of stock requirements by individual companies are a management priority if returns on capital are to be preserved. A strong managing director is needed to hold in check an equally strong sales team who do not want to be short of stock to meet the demand they hope to create and a similarly strong distillery team who seek to maintain full utilisation of capacity in order to preserve employment and keep unit costs down. A balance has to be found which will maximise shareholder returns.

Sharks enter the Scene

During the growth period a few optimists outside the industry found that they could obtain supplies of new whisky from distillers, who did not have a large established business with blenders. These 'entrepreneurs' began to offer new fillings to private investors with the suggestion that very attractive returns were possible when stocks matured. In reality there was no ready outlet for these investments simply because blenders had already filled enough to cover their own requirements. Very few were short of stock and established distillers expanded the capacity of their distilleries if they anticipated substantial growth. The investment in new plant offered a good return and it was not capital intensive. Sadly most private investors were left with losses and sometimes failed to find any outlet for their investments.

In recent years this practice has been revived by a few opportunists, who have adopted the hard-selling tactics reminiscent of the time-share salesmen. I contacted several companies to find out if anything had changed. The promotional material was well designed and printed and the arguments used to persuade investors were tempting but fallacious. Lesser or unknown whiskies were offered at two to three times the price to blenders. It was claimed that the whisky could be sold when mature but there was no demand except at distressed prices. Clients, who had paid by credit card, were able to claim on the credit card company, which was unable to realise more than 10 per cent of the original investment.

One of these companies was offering Springbank at £975 per

hogshead, which is £5.87 per original litre of alcohol, compared with a filling price to a blender at that time of between £2 and £2.50. The proposition was that new whisky was very cheap and can be sold for an enormous profit in bottle. Here is a quote from one brochure: 'Early in 1995 a bottle of single malt Springbank distilled in 1965 and bottled in 1994 was sold at Christie's in Glasgow for £190.'

At 30 years old the whisky required for a bottle will be 0.46 lpa at a cost of £2.68 for the spirit plus £1.05 for storage and £0.92 for handling and bottling. Duty and VAT at the time would be £7.25 giving a total cost of £11.88. The number of bottles would be 360, which could probably last an individual anything from 10 to 20 years without giving him any variety. The total outlay would be £4279 without taking into account the interest lost of 74p per bottle if the interest rate remained constant at 5 per cent, which is not very likely. An investment of this sort is not for the private investor. Even if the purchase is made for drinking, it is a major commitment lasting at least for up to 50 years until the investment is liquidated, that is after the last bottle was drunk. Friends could help but they might become tired of the lack of variety and would you all live long enough? Certainly comparing £190 with the cost of a bottle out of the hogshead at £12.62 (including interest) is irresistible but could you sell 360 of them at Christie's for that price? Even if you had bought it when you were 20 years old and were prepared to drink it constantly after you were 60 would you finish it?

In July 1995 I was subjected to a 'don't say no' phone call by one of these companies and it became very acrimonious. In the end I had to put the phone down. I had made an enquiry by post and received an offer to sell a little known distillery make for £1145 and the prospect of an 18 per cent return but there was no external market to realise the investment. *The Economist* ran an article in October 1996 warning of the dangers of these investments but too late for many. It was estimated that 10,000 people invested over £60m. They mentioned that the Metropolitan Police's Fraud Squad was looking into allegations concerning these activities. The outcome was a series of convictions at Southark Crown Court in February 2001.

What of the Future?

In 1958 the established markets for Scotch were the UK and USA, which accounted for 68 per cent of world sales. By 1978 a further 11 export markets had expanded their imports to the point where the 13 markets accounted for 80 per cent of world sales. The total sales had grown nearly five times from 66m to 323m lpa. Scotch whisky became the first choice international drink for upper income groups and world travellers. It provided a veneer over domestic drinks markets, where local spirits still accounted for the vast majority of sales. It was only in the UK and USA that there was any significant penetration. Fashion played a part in the growth in France but in Germany Scotch whisky had a tough time against strong local drinks. Oil wealth in Venezuela produced explosive growth for de luxe brands selling at a substantial premium against standard brands. In Japan, Scotch whisky became the number one gift item among businessmen and the wealthy. Italy followed a similar pattern to France but Spain increased its imports largely to satisfy demand from the huge influx of tourists. Canada and Australia were among the first important export markets and kept their place with the leading ones, although growth was not so spectacular. The profile of each market differed but Scotch was the premium spirit drink in them all to a greater or lesser extent.

After 1980 the established markets for Scotch whisky levelled off and there was no further penetration. In some, the United States and the UK particularly, changing consumer habits began to affect shipments, and indeed other drinks, which brought about a steady decline in total shipments.

However, new markets were still developing and included Spain, Portugal, Greece, Southeast Asia and Brazil. Some were the result of the increase in the tourist business and others the removal of import controls. Whatever the reason, they demonstrated, yet again, that growth for Scotch comes from the opening and subsequent development of new territories. These places either attracted tourists in large numbers or became economically successful and thus provided their people with a higher standard of living. However, the increases in these markets were negated by the decline in hitherto buoyant markets. The UK fell by 40 per cent, the USA by 64 per cent and Japan by 40 per cent. These markets were in former years the bankers for the industry and their collapse has been a big blow. However, the total of shipments dropped by only 13 per cent and value has trebled demonstrating that Scotch is a premium product, which can command a premium price over time.

Whereas the Americas and other areas have declined, Europe has been particularly buoyant. The expansion of the tourist business has brought gains for Scotch in France up 245 per cent, Greece up 380 per cent, Spain up 344 per cent and Portugal up 700 per cent. France now accounts for more than the UK and the USA and is now the largest market.

The future trend in consumption in the developed markets may be downwards due to lifestyle changes and declining populations. On the other hand, countries which are attracting more tourists, may well increase their imports of Scotch whisky. The big question is what is the potential of the developing countries with large populations? China, India, Indonesia, Philippines, Thailand, Brazil, Argentina, Mexico, Russia and Ukraine all have the capacity and resources to become economically successful and thus big customers for Scotch whisky. Many people would like to be able to estimate the timescale and make the right guesses about which will be the winners. There is enough potential for the industry to plan with some confidence for growth but care is needed in judging the pace as well as the places it will occur. Mistakes will result in surplus stocks and distilling and bottling capacity and a lower return on investment. Also, it is tempting to increase marketing expenditure in the established markets, when it might be better to concentrate development on the fledgling ones like Brazil, India, China and Russia.

The ten markets listed above all have large populations and most have the natural resources to enable them to become wealthy economies. Political reform and/or improved economic management in Brazil, India, China and Russia appear to be bringing changes which would favour close attention and the others have ambitions which may take some time to realise. I think that there is a good chance that choosing these four offers the best opportunity at the moment. It should be emphasised that such a choice requires to be monitored and reviewed regularly and managements need to be ready to change tack quickly and decisively when there is good reason to do so.

In the meantime the dozen or so principal markets are likely to decline or remain static and the other new markets can only bring about a modest growth in world sales even if they grow at an explosive rate. In addition to the four selected markets named above, Mexico and Argentina could also be big importers by 2050. Together the six markets might account for sales of over 100m lpa. If the rest of the world markets hold their present level then the industry may achieve a minimum growth of up to 25 per cent over the next 50 years.

This suggests that stock levels could be eased down for the next ten years or so and gradually rise thereafter at a very modest level to 3500m lpa in 2050. Distilling capacity would not need to increase at all. Grain capacity is ample and the improving trend in bottled malt sales can be accommodated by bringing mothballed distilleries back into production and using spare capacity in others. If the trends change then adjustments will be made at the regular reviews. Providing an average cover of seven years stock will enable the surplus to be maintained below 10 per cent without running the risk of shortages.

What Strategy?

It is tempting to conclude that Scotch whisky will remain exactly the same as it has always been and the growth desired will simply appear. Afterall the product and its appeal to the consumer have hardly changed in a hundred years. It is possible that a 'same again' strategy could work but the volume potential would have to be scaled down considerably. Capacity at all levels would have to be cut and Scotch would become a top shelf item in bars alongside the famous French liqueurs.

This approach does not fit well with the history of an industry that has had a successful record in the international market. However, much depends on whether the large companies, which control most of the industry now can see the opportunities that their predecessors did. They are involved in the whole spectrum of alcoholic drinks produced in many countries and will not be very concerned if fashion favours one type rather than another. They will not have the same emotional tie to their businesses that Coca-Cola have for their soft drink or Bacardi have for their white rum. These companies must stick to what they have because it earns most of their profits and it has overwhelming brand strength. In Scotch whisky only Johnnie Walker has a franchise approaching these two but is still some way behind. Two others, J&B and Ballantine's have the potential to build a strong position provided their owners can find a way to stick to the task over perhaps a generation as well as keeping their institutional shareholders happy.

This is the classic dilemma for quoted companies, which are expected to produce short-term as well as long-term results. If a company tries to build a brand over a period of say 15 or 20 years, its share price will come under pressure. If it abandons the project with a consequent effect on the long-term growth it will ultimately come under pressure unless it makes acquisitions. The answer is to explain the strategy clearly and take the 'flack' early on and to deliver honest progress reports during the build-up period. Of course there will be a risk of a predator swooping but if the company makes a good case in defending itself it will either persuade the attacker to go away or will achieve a handsome price for the shareholders.

One of the lessons to be learned from the history of the spirits business is that the first in with a new idea will tend to succeed quite quickly. Hence Buchanan's, Dewar's and Walker's were the first serious brands of Scotch whisky and reached a commanding position in less than ten years. Since then there have been numerous new brands, which have made it to the top but it has usually taken them many years, sometimes as many as 25 years or more. It is a crowded market place now and building a brand is a long haul.

The Scotch whisky category has tremendous strength and new brands continue to appear. They are instantly recognised if they are presented in a proper manner simply because they conform to the known characteristics of the product. They may achieve some early success out of curiosity but their main difficulty is achieving distribution, which is what takes the time and determination. There is no need to lose your shirt in the attempt, as patience will achieve much more. For this reason it is a good idea to have a number of brand projects running simultaneously and at different stages in their development.

Another matter, which requires constant attention, is product quality. The advent of blended Scotch whisky and the introduction of maturing in oak casks in the early 20th century led to a major improvement and the process has continued ever since. The market is much more competitive not only from many more brands but also from the popularity of other quality spirit drinks, notably vodka, white rum and tequila. Innovations in style, taste and presentation will also help to promote growth of premium Scotch whisky, which is a business that will last. Already the market has offered opportunities for bottled malts, which open up a wider range of tastes while enhancing the core values of Scotch. The share of market taken by cheaper blends, which cut down on blend quality and presentation, has been a feature of the Scotch whisky business now for several decades. This business does nothing for the long-term success of the industry but it does thrive on surplus stocks. A more sensible handling of the filling activities and the resultant forcing of blenders to hold stocks will oblige everyone to follow sound stock planning and marketing practices and enjoy the benefits of a thriving Scotch whisky business in the future.

An Historical Perspective

Looking back it is clear that there is a much better approach to balancing the various functional priorities now than there was in the past when each had its dominant phase. Distilling in the late 19th century was the important activity and as whisky was sold at a young age output was easily adjusted to demand. During this period grain distilleries increased capacity and prices declined. Price wars were frequent and were only brought under control when the DCL was formed in 1877. Thereafter new entrants found it more difficult to establish themselves as the new combine had a dominant position.

In the 1890s and into the first decade of the 20th century several brilliant salesmen began to build reputations for their proprietary labels. This was also the beginning of the export trade and its overriding importance to the industry. At the same time brands gained the major share of the Scotch whisky business at home even in a period of declining market sales.

At the end of WWI the brand owning companies were starting to feel the financial pressures brought about by the need to put money into increasing stock investment and keeping up the costly promotion of their brands in the face of increased competition. In the meantime the DCL were cruising along comfortably selling low cost grain whisky at a generous margin with a major share of the trade. They were strong financially and had little need for heavy capital investment.

The logic of putting these two sides of the industry together and creating a vertically integrated business was irresistible. Thanks largely to the brilliant diplomatic and financial skills of William Ross, the DCL managing director; this amalgamation was achieved in 1925. Production, selling and finance were at last able to be co-ordinated in the enlarged group, which must have accounted for nearly 80 per cent of the industry at the time.

The DCL remained the only fully integrated Scotch whisky business for the next 60 years. They managed their dominant position well but did not encourage innovation. If Scotch whisky was to grow and become more profitable the DCL had the major responsibility as they controlled most of the business. They were however a stabilising factor and without this influence Scotch whisky might well have been in straightened circumstances in the depression of the 1930s.

Nevertheless, the DCL made sure that they retained their dominance by clever pricing and capturing all the best foreign distributors. At home the DCL chose to put their strength behind the Scotch Whisky Association (SWA). They provided the chairman and the majority of the members of the SWA Council. It developed a pattern of unwritten rules of conduct of business by member companies. These supported the DCL's own policies and kept the others in line. A couple of examples demonstrate that they were quite restrictive. First, it was considered that selling bottled malt was harmful as it threatened the blended business and of course the output of grain whisky, where DCL were all-powerful as the major grain distiller. Secondly, it was not thought helpful to state the proportion of malt and grain on the label of a blended Scotch, naturally because the DCL were strong in grain distilling and did not want to have to compete by increasing the malt content and the blend cost and also threaten the grain business.

Always fearful of being classed as a monopoly the DCL were very glad to support the SWA as a useful way of demonstrating that there was competition within the industry. I served for eight years on the Council and only learned of the 'rules' when our company breached one of them. On one occasion I was taken to task for a new innovative Teacher product called 'Teacher's 60', which was a blend of 60% malt. Later the principal Teacher brand, 'Highland Cream', which was known for its higher than average malt content, made a declaration on the label that it contained more than 45% malt. By that time the DCL were not so dominant and strong-arm tactics would not have succeeded with an equally large company, Allied-Lyons, backing us. Ironically, some years later the DCL under the control of Guinness did exactly the same thing with one of their brands!

At least the 'independents', as the non-DCL companies were known, represented on the SWA Council were able to share in the control of the industry and this proved extremely useful in providing a co-ordinated approach to some serious threats to trade. The SWA has been able to persuade UK Governments to take a more reasonable view of levels of excise duty and to lobby with its support the many foreign governments who have imposed discriminating taxes, tariffs and quotas, which restricted the imports of Scotch whisky. Through public relations activities the SWA have often changed attitudes and perceptions to the benefit of trade and great success has been achieved in pursuing the many cases of passing off local whiskies as Scotch whisky by various means such as kilted figures on labels.

While there is now healthy competition amongst Scotch whisky companies and their brands, there is still a case for continuing the work of the SWA. Indeed its work is constantly being expanded. In the future it is possible that it might embark on a long-term approach to the preparation of new markets in order to make them receptive to Scotch whisky, which is a strange product to people like the Chinese for instance. Foreigners outside Europe are not normally interested in or curious about Western habits and something more than short-term public relations activity may be beneficial. The Chinese and the Russians are very much concerned with their own way of life and rarely desire anything other than their own local spirit drinks. Travellers have sustained growth in many markets but in the big potential ones of the future; the vast majority of consumers need to know a lot more about the consumer benefits of Scotch whisky.

The new markets to be targeted are not so welcoming to foreign products as those of the last 40 years were. There will be no GIs returning home with a taste for Scotch nor will there be doctors suggesting that Scotch may help the French to avoid heart attacks! These new consumers will need to be introduced to the benefits and the enjoyment to be had from sampling the joys of someone else's culture plus the prestige to be had among their contemporaries by indulging in conspicuous consumption of something foreign and expensive.

Where there is a latent demand, new markets can begin to grow quite quickly. The major advantage that Scotch whisky has is its combination of traditional values and high quality. The target markets already mentioned have nothing to compare with Scotch whisky. They will be likely to produce above average economic growth in the next two generations and, therefore, will be importing large quantities of new products, which their consumers think will enhance their lifestyle. Scotch whisky will be on the shopping list certainly, but will it command wide interest or be a quaint Scottish tradition?

If you take a view of the period 1750 to 2050, one thing will be obvious and that is that each time there is a significant new market opening, there is a step change in consumption. From the early beginnings when farmers sought to use their own resources of barley, water and energy to produce whisky, there has been no stopping the growth. The trade became so good that a tax was introduced. The tax was not popular and illicit distilling was common but gradually the growth of the trade was such that the tax was acceptable. Later exporting, when no tax was payable by the producer made it all worthwhile.

The trade grew up from producing a peasant drink to marketing a highly sophisticated international beverage. The fact that Scotch continues to be produced by traditional methods using traditional materials is a major part of its attraction. It is interesting to look at the Cachaca business in Brazil today, because that is how Scotch began. Everyone drinks it but those who know will buy from a reliable distillery they can trust to produce a quality product, having had a recommendation from a friend. This was the case with Scotch whisky in the early days but now the recommendation comes from the brand but also from the product itself, which has acquired a reputation for universal quality still to be earned by Cachaca producers as a whole.

Quality led the Scotch whisky industry to realising it had something to sell to others outside their own area and it also led them towards higher profitability. The long-term investment cycle needs an increasing input of working capital and the creation of a brand franchise requires a commitment to service the promotional costs on a consistent basis over time. To do this you need a high margin and profitable growth will come only from a high price policy.

Over two hundred years the market has widened and although this has brought more competition for Scotch whisky, it has also given it more opportunity to sharpen its focus and thereby gain a stronger consumer franchise. Scotch whisky is one way of offering consumers the opportunity to demonstrate a degree of sophistication, which might otherwise take them a decade to establish with their peers. The regular recruitment of new drinkers, who would benefit from Scotch whisky in this way, is, of course, essential to future growth and success. However, it is important to be clear about the strengths of Scotch whisky and not try to jazz it up with what some define as 'lifestyle' characteristics, which runs the risks of a head-on clash with white rum and vodka, which appeal to the very young. Scotch whisky's strengths are unique and it is best not to confuse them with what other products offer very successfully.

Although marketing is the key function in the industry, it is worth bearing in mind that the element in the business that makes it all possible is share of distilling capacity. There are now only two major companies, Diageo and Pernod-Ricard, controlling a large proportion of distilling capacity. They must have a secure supply of spirit, which can only be achieved by operating a balanced selection of distilleries and planning stock investment constantly. Shortages of stock cannot be covered by purchases in the open market except in very small quantities. This puts pressure on the stock planning and investment procedures and the need to carry them out frequently in order to conserve working capital and guarantee availability. Even the small and medium-sized companies must do the same otherwise they will run into stock availability problems. In times of shortage your competitors will not wish to bail you out and there will be few independent stockholders.

CHAPTER 7

The Concept of a Third Force

Allied's Start in Scotch

The brewing industry embarked upon a period of mergers after WWII with great gusto. The pub chains grew bigger and the national brands of the largest companies gained market share through the extra distribution offered by the new pubs. At the beginning the pace was gentle and conducted in a very gentlemanly manner and many a deal was done on the grouse moors of Scotland. There the brewers would meet distillers large and small and before long it became obvious that Scotch whisky could be bought from suppliers other than the Distillers Company. Most brewers had small wine & spirit departments and often bottled wines imported in bulk from France. Clearly the same could be done with whisky and, moreover, it could be bought newly distilled and held by the brewer during maturation. Thus all the larger brewers held bulk whisky stocks and bottled their own brands often using names spotted in the Highlands such as Glen Rossie and Invercauld.

Serious diversification into the wine & spirit trade began in the 1960s. Small wine & spirit departments were occasionally acquired with a newly merged brewery and were added to existing businesses. In 1969 Allied took the first step in rationalising various businesses when it found that it had two whisky companies tucked away out of sight in Tetley Walker and Ind Coope. These companies were Glen Rossie Distillers and The Curtis Distillery Company. In addition Harveys, which came in with Showerings the same year, owned Stewarts of Dundee. About a year later a fourth small whisky business was acquired with the purchase of a retail and wholesale wine merchant in Scotland, David Sandeman.

Having joined the family retail and wholesale business and stayed on when it was sold to Ind Coope, I had been in retailing for about 12 years and was becoming a little bored. The business had largely been centralised and my job was not developing at all. I was virtually an area manager, which was interesting for a while but not something I could do for another 20 years. Suddenly the job of putting these four little whisky companies together presented itself and I jumped at the opportunity. My experience in whisky was limited but I had the advantage that nobody in the group knew anything about whisky at all. Just about all I knew was the difference between a butt and a ben! My father and grandfather had been distillers and I was familiar with some of the jargon. The distilling process, blending and marketing were mysteries to me but I was about to learn.

There was a good deal of talent and experience in the new Stewarts, which was the chosen vehicle for the combined businesses. The people in Stewarts had long wanted the freedom to develop the company but Harveys had in recent years controlled most of the activities and direction of the company. It never had enough money to do anything worthwhile. The ideas mooted in those early days were rather over ambitious but maybe they were better for that than the attitude expressed by one old worthy in the trade, Charles Rattray, Managing Director of Macdonald & Muir, who commented that 'there would never be another new brand'. Our average age was quite young and so, with the help of the team, I began to build a profile of the industry and look for a place for Allied-Lyons in it. There was a growing interest in Scotch whisky spurred by the desire to break the stranglehold the DCL had on it. Many brewers and other retailers were fed up with being told what to do and the lack of flexibility in pricing, particularly as many were very large buyers.

Who Were the Big Players?

It was obvious that an acquisition programme was the practical route for building a big enough investment in Scotch whisky to be able to compete on equal terms with the Distillers Company, although not necessarily equal to it in size. However, there were no obvious targets ready and willing to sell unless circumstances changed. It would take years to build Stewarts little brand Cream of the Barley into a major earner if it was possible at all. We were working on that with limited resources with some help from group outlets in the UK but overseas was like climbing a series of high mountains. In 1969 85% of Scotch shipments were to export markets and the DCL probably accounted for two thirds of the total. It had been more in 1945 but two brands had captured a substantial share of the US market. These were Cutty Sark (Buckingham) and J&B (Paddington). Both Buckingham and Paddington were owned by two brilliant US entrepreneurs with access to the complex distribution system in the States, and who wanted to increase their business in Scotch whisky, which had become a major growth market after WWII. Returning US troops had acquired the taste and many, who had not been abroad, had enjoyed the priority supplies that had been shipped during the war to balance the purchase of war materials. Buckingham and Paddington had actually started their operations after prohibition ended in 1933 but had received little encouragement from the DCL, who were unwilling to release large quantities of bulk Scotch to them. They, therefore, turned elsewhere.

Buckingham negotiated a long-term contract with Robertson & Baxter (R&B), a long established distiller and blender to the trade. R&B supplied from their own sources or otherwise acquired stocks and blended whisky to the Buckingham specification. Buckingham then found another partner Bury Bros & Rudd, London wine merchants, who owned the brand name Cutty Sark and it was adopted for the project. R&B then set up a major blending and bottling facility in Glasgow and started to supply. The brand was an instant success benefiting from secure distribution to customers, who were desperate for increased supplies of Scotch whisky with flexibility in pricing. Cutty quickly became market leader and held that position for many years selling over two million cases.

The Paddington case was similar and their partner was International Distillers and Vintners, which incorporated the old wine and spirit business of Gilbeys. Given the large unsatisfied demand, J&B enjoyed instant success in the US and it later also became market leader and the No. 2 brand in the world after Johnnie Walker. Cutty Sark gradually declined and never succeeded anywhere outside the US.

Gilbeys owned distilleries and were also able to acquire stocks in the broking market from holders, who did not have strong brands but were happy to take advantage of the high price offered in a market where demand exceeded supply. There had been almost no distilling during the war and all the stocks of bottled whisky had been shipped abroad, mainly to the States. Production resumed in 1945 but did not reach the 1939 level until 1955. Given that demand for Scotch was stronger in the post-war years, the shortage of stocks for blending resulted in unbelievable prices for bulk Scotch whisky and many fortunes were made by those fortunate enough to hold stocks.

North America had two other well-established spirit businesses in Seagrams and Hiram Walker. Seagram had been started by the legendary Sam Bronfman after prohibition and had expanded very quickly. In the period 1933-39 Bronfman had a joint venture with the DCL and this had given him a start in Scotch whisky. After the war he went his own way and, unlike Buckingham and Paddington, invested in assets in the Scotch industry. He acquired distilleries and set up blending and bottling facilities in Scotland. He was, therefore, able to produce his own stocks as well as acquire others in the market. Sam was a farsighted individual and started to lay down stocks in the 1930s for an aged Scotch. It was to be twelve years old, which meant that the first sales of his new brand Chivas Regal could not be sold until the1950s. As we know this brand has become a major success and is the only new brand of Scotch to have achieved world leadership.

Hiram Walker was a different company having been founded much earlier by some enterprising Canadians to produce Canadian Spirits. They too invested in assets in Canada, the United States and Argentina, where two of them went to buy horses and came back with a distillery. In 1938 they bought a small company called George Ballantine and built a grain distillery and bottling plant in Dumbarton. They also acquired malt distilleries in the Highlands and began to develop their brand. Ballantine's was to become the No. 3 brand in the industry with a dominant share of the European market. These two companies were smaller but strong enough to take on the DCL and appeared to be secure from predators like Allied-Lyons.

The success of these four companies in the USA was quite a shock to the DCL, who had been used to having complete control over the home and export business. If anyone proved troublesome the DCL would have a little word with them and they would fall back into line. In my days at Stewarts and Teacher's I had first hand experience of this treatment on two occasions. It was not malicious but polite and 'helpful' and there were a number of ways in which DCL could help a small company in the industry as long as it was not a major threat to its market share. It was not an unreasonable attitude given that DCL had been the main prop for the industry in the difficult times, particularly in the 1890s, when grain distilleries were going bankrupt and in the recessions of the 1920s and 1930s. Although my grandfather had offended the DCL after WWI, they were generous enough to negotiate with my father to buy Glen Elgin fillings regularly and ultimately the distillery. All the DCL brands lost share in the US, although some recovered. The major casualty was Black & White one of the core brands and it never achieved a strong position in any market again.

The competition that the DCL faced in the US understood the market much better than they did and recognised the changes that had taken place in consumer attitudes. The DCL management was ill equipped for such a battle having been used to controlling markets by dominating the supply of stock and engaging the most powerful distributors. The success of J&B and Cutty Sark demonstrated that the industry needed to orientate itself to consumer needs and a number of the medium-sized companies had begun to do this. They were mostly tightly controlled but lacked the resources for a major drive. Teachers and Bells had succeeded in outselling the DCL in the UK although they were not very strong overseas. By the mid 1960s DCL were under pressure in the two main markets, the USA and the UK, and as the European markets started growing strongly on the back of the tourist trade, Ballantines and J&B gave them a hard time in France, Spain and Italy.

When the UK joined the Common Market another problem confronted them. One of the principles of trading in the EEC was that goods could move freely from one country to another. If prices differed, then buyers were perfectly entitled to buy at the best price and import the goods for resale. Where exclusive agents had been appointed this meant that they were by-passed and lost the sale. One of the DCL tactics used in protecting their market share in the UK was to keep the price to the trade at a comparatively low level. The lower margin put a strain on the smaller but successful companies like Teachers, Bells and Grants, who could not generate sufficient cash to advertise as much as they would have liked. The only trouble was that the big buyers on the continent began to buy large quantities from British wholesalers and ship the goods over. The exclusive importers complained that it was no longer possible to do their job if they were denied the sales revenue from these 'parallel' imports. The brand that suffered most was DCL's Johnnie Walker, which was and still is the number one brand in the world and also the leader in Europe. The DCL decided, rather than raising their price in the UK to match the European level, that they would withdraw Johnnie Walker from the UK market in order to preserve even greater sales abroad. It was a radical step and one that made no commercial sense in the long run. The only justification for this move was that they did not need to raise the UK price and thus continue to put pressure on the successful independents.

The family business of William Grant had invested in grain distilling capacity of their own after WWII to add to their two good malt distilleries, Glenfiddich and Balvenie. They were self-sufficient in the supply of whisky stocks and they adopted a competitive price strategy to compete with the stronger brands. The members of the family, who owned the business, were persuaded to accept very small dividends for many years in order to release cash for stock building and promotion. After all, if you already have enough for a comfortable life and did not have expensive tastes for yachts in the Caribbean, it was a perfectly secure way to build the business and they did this very successfully. They also bought a bulk whisky importing company in New York when the owner wished to retire and found a way to develop sales in the US. To combat the low margin in the UK trade, they had joined with Allied-Lyons, Bass and Whitbread in a consortium, which gave them assured outlets and a vehicle for funding the financing of stocks. My first involvement in Scotch whisky for Allied was serving on the board of this company, Wm Grant & Sons (Standfast), and working closely with its management and that of William Grant. It was good for learning about the industry and gave me a welcome diversion from retailing, which was becoming a little tedious. I was a part-time financial advisor and learned how to manage whisky stocks and find the appropriate finance at the lowest possible cost. I was also exposed to some of the problems of sales and marketing and spent many an hour with Roy Trustram Eve, MD of Standfast, trying to persuade Sandy Grant Gordon, MD of William Grant, to spend more on advertising Glenfiddich Malt, which gave the Grants (Standfast) company a better margin than the blended Scotch.

Bell's had become an important brand in the UK and was particularly dominant in Scotland. The original controlling shareholder had gifted his shares to a charitable trust known as the Gannochy Trust and they felt they had a duty to preserve their money-spinner for the benefit of their good works. As long as the trustees took this attitude it was bid-proof. It was a well-run company and there was a good succession of young managers appointed to push it forward. On the death of the legendary W G Farquharson, or Farquie as he was usually known, after 46 years with the company, it was put in the hands of a maverick character of a different sort, Raymond Miquel. Raymond was an original workaholic and drove his team relentlessly to greater and greater achievements. The brand was the undisputed leader in the UK but Raymond never seemed to be able to motivate his overseas distributors in the same way. For a start they would not have put up with his style of direct management with every detail having to be 'just as I say'!

Teacher's Highland Cream was entirely different but almost as successful in the UK. It was number two not far behind in market share and probably a little stronger in the South East, where it was the respectable 'City' drink. The various families, who controlled the company, were also hard working but their style was more suitable for dealing with customers abroad. Several of the directors travelled overseas regularly. The image of the brand was good and many of the importers were old established houses in such places as Canada, Australia, Italy, USA and even little Malta. The company had placed some shares on the stock market but the directors had retained control and therefore were secure from the threat of a predator unless they were willing to sell.

Teachers, Bells and Grants were the prime candidates for acquisition but there were others, which could be considered to provide additional distilling capacity and extra profitable volume. Matching the DCL for size was not feasible but a more profitable operation with better growth prospects was possible. Among the malt distillers were Macallan and Glenlivet, two of the most favoured malts for blending and Scotch malt brands in their own right. The profitability of bottled malt was much better than blended Scotch and the potential had not been fully exploited. This was the result of a long-established DCL policy disapproving of this business. It seems hardly credible but the theory was that sales of bottled malt would harm the sales of blends and as the DCL owned most of the Scotch grain whisky distilleries they did not wish to see consumers turning to malt and leaving these plants under used. This was an important example of producer-led rather than consumer-led thinking in the DCL, which was eventually to lead to their downfall.

Hill Thomson with their Queen Anne brand and Whyte & Mackay were both old established blending houses with some useful trade in a number of overseas markets and they would add to the range and choice of importers as well as contributing to profits. Hill Thomson had merged with Glenlivet and Whyte & Mackay with Dalmore Distillery. Each sought to become vertically integrated and thus improve profitability but was still quite small and vulnerable to the pressures of competition. Another interesting candidate was Macdonald Martin, who had a sizeable volume of competitively priced blend in the US as well as an attractive malt distillery, Glenmorangie. Like Glenfiddich, Glenmorangie was potentially a bottled malt prospect as it had a good taste and had a following in the north of Scotland.

The North British Distillery was put on the list, as it was an independent grain distillery formed in 1885 to counter the monopoly in grain distilling controlled by the DCL. The shares were held by various individuals and companies in the trade and the 'NB' as it was fondly known, was the only successful supplier of grain to offer an alternative to DCL until Invergordon and Girvan were built in the very early 1960s. Obviously, if there was a chance of acquiring William Grant, who owned Girvan Grain Distillery, there would be no need to take on the 'NB'.

The Difficulties in Making Acquisitions

As most of these companies were fiercely independent or otherwise securely controlled it would be difficult to make any headway unless there was another period of rationalisation in the industry. The prospects looked good for a repeat of the dramatic changes of the 1920s but for different reasons. Then most markets were in recession and distilleries were threatened with closure due to lack of business. In the 1960s demand was strong and sales were growing at a steady 10 per cent per annum. For the smaller companies it was sometimes difficult to share in this growth. Distilleries relied on selling their new whisky to blenders and usually did not have a brand of their own. However, the big blenders and brand owners were often self-sufficient in whisky stocks and were able to exchange their makes for others at no extra cost thus giving them a suitable variety for their blends. The few blenders who were net buyers of new fillings did not have the resources both to promote their brands and to invest in increasing stock levels to fuel growth. As a result their brands did not often match the growth of the bigger companies.

The modest profit levels of the smaller companies were usually sufficient for the needs of family shareholders and there was not much pressure to sell their businesses and realise capital. Even on modest margins, sales of Scotch were enough to provide a comfortable lifestyle. The idea of creating a strategic third force in the industry to compete with the North Americans and the DCL was attractive but it did not look very possible until there was additional pressure on owners to sell. Allied was interested in investing more in Scotch and several of the senior people had begun to acquire knowledge of how the industry worked and felt that there was an opportunity to take some share of it from the DCL.

After completing all this research, I persuaded Derrick Holden-Brown, then managing director of the wine & spirit division, and Tom Boardman, the group finance director, to meet in mid-1970 and consider some ideas about how Allied should go forward. At that time it was assumed that the DCL, Hiram Walker and Seagrams were not vulnerable in view of their size. DCL had leading positions in practically all the export markets and the two Canadian companies had similar positions in the North American markets. Seagrams and Hiram Walker were long-term investors in the industry and had the resources to expand further by acquisition. Allied had the resources but not the opportunity to deploy them in a major way. Teachers, Bells and Grants were obvious first choice candidates and had ambitions to grow. The snag was that they did not seem to be ready for the big idea. Nevertheless, it was useful to map out the best route and await opportunities arising. At least we could be ready and know what we wanted and where we should go.

The DCL were making £53m a year and had net assets of £317m. We picked out Teachers, Bells and Grants, who had good brands and some distilling capacity. Grants were self-sufficient and perhaps had a considerable surplus of grain whisky capacity but the other two were net buyers of new fillings. Including Glenlivet, Macallan, Hill Thomson, Dalmore Whyte & Mackay and Macdonald Martin provided sufficient distilling capacity in both grain and malt together with a sizeable business in blended and bottled Scotch sales. These companies had combined profits of £7.8m, which compared well with Hiram Walker at £5.7m. Combined assets were £45m giving a return on capital of 17.3 per cent, which matched DCL at 16.7 per cent. The seven businesses (Glenlivet and Hill Thomson had merged) would have 14 malt distilleries and one grain distillery.

The advantages for Allied were a greater share of the international drinks business, the high growth rate in Scotch whisky compared with beer and an attractive equity return without a major investment in property, which depressed the return in the brewery. For the target companies, joining in a stronger operation would enable them to counter the dominance of the DCL and the intrusion of the North Americans into the industry in Scotland. In addition they would avoid the strain on cash resources for financing increasing stock levels, would have access to greater funds for promotion, a broader choice of importers and would achieve improved productivity and profitability. The release of family wealth tied up in the businesses would ease its transfer to the next generation and the prices that could be offered were likely to be attractive.

Five of these companies were quoted on the stock market and their market value was considerably lower than the true value. The non-quoted companies were Grants, where shares were all held by the families and Bells, which was controlled by the charitable Gannochy Trust. I calculated that, taking book value for the non-quoted and market value for the others, the total value was £28.9m. Maturing whisky stocks were worth much more than book value and we would require to offer in excess of £55m and maybe more to persuade the shareholders to sell. Not all members of the families were employed in these companies and so it was possible that those not enjoying the benefits of employment would be happy to have their capital released.

While the financing of such a project may have presented problems, they were not insurmountable. The likely cost of between £60m and £70m looks a bargain today but in 1970 it seemed a big investment for a group, whose main earner was beer followed by various British wine products, where margins were relatively slim. Tom Boardman, the group finance director thought that the £25m nine per cent loan flotation, which I had suggested as part of the funding package, would be 'difficult to get away'. Who was to argue with a future government trade minister and chairman of the Natwest Bank? The meeting ended without a conclusion but I was happy with the seeds sown. While at Stewarts we hoped to grow the business, we were never going to be very large without acquisitions and it was obvious that a company as large as Allied had to be large in Scotch if it was going to be worthwhile. We could at least think out our strategy and let events develop in its favour. The objective was clear and the opportunities, when they arose, would be instantly recognised.

It was, in a way, a means of stimulating the thoughts of top management of Allied to think about Scotch whisky. The concept of Allied becoming a 'Third Force' in the industry was fixed in the minds of the top management and various main board directors began to talk about Scotch whisky. Several prospects were discussed notably Long John, owned by Schenley of the US, and Dalmore Whyte & Mackay. By that time Stewarts was doing quite well but finding life hard and adding two other businesses with the same problems was not going to progress our agreed strategy of being big and profitable in Scotch whisky. Whyte & Mackay was bought by young Hugh Fraser and we calculated that the purchase price would give a return of only five per cent. We were well out of that one and it never made much money and lost its owners considerable sums as it kept being sold on to yet another hopeful buyer. Long John was eventually bought by Allied after the major acquisitions and proved a useful rationalisation project as it had a more modern grain distillery.

The Trend of Events

The 'target' companies all began in different ways to deal with the problem of finding enough cash to cover increasing stock investment to meet the expected growth in sales and for advertising in the many new markets, which were developing a taste for Scotch. By the mid 1990s only two remained independent, Grants and Macdonald Martin, and the latter was sold later. Of the seven candidates only Teachers came into the Allied fold but, in a glaring piece of misjudgement, Hiram Walker became vulnerable and eventually joined Allied. After that, all the acquisition problems were solved and in a much easier fashion than anticipated. Nevertheless, we were ready to move fast when these two opportunities came along because we recognised them as the way to internationalise our spirit business and to establish a major position in the Scotch whisky industry.

In the following years the world economy was shattered by two major oil crises. Just as coal had fuelled the growth of the industrial revolution, so oil enabled the developed countries to capitalise on their technological advantages. Markets were opened and expanded all over the world and Scotch whisky followed in the wake of this economic explosion. Suddenly the price of oil rose from 80p per barrel to £22. Every form of economic activity was affected and consumers began to cut back on all but essential things. Scotch whisky shipments stagnated for three years and output of new whisky was cut back sharply. These developments added to the financial problems of the 'independents' and brought forward the forecast change in attitude. It also made companies like Allied more selective in considering investments in the industry, because of the higher cost of capital.

When Teachers approached Allied there was no doubt what our reaction should be! The families had made their decision to sell and wished to choose a partner who would accept their philosophy of brand building. They were in a position to make a choice because they acted as one family and they still had a controlling interest. They looked at two or three candidates and the first to be approached was reputedly Bass, although no one has ever said so. Bass were not interested and Allied, knowing what it wanted did the deal within a few days helped by the fact that Keith Showering, who was now chairman, was from a similar family background and with his uncle Francis controlling the direction of the group.

Teachers brought Allied onto centre stage in the Scotch whisky industry and happily the people in both Allied and its new subsidiary were well matched. During the following eight years the combined Teachers and Stewarts grew the business and improved profitability, outperforming the industry in the process. There was a steady improvement in Stewarts' business and we were able to unlock the full potential of Teachers. In particular, the export team set some good foundations in old and new markets and some began to pay off quite quickly.

Meantime the market for Scotch was having some fundamental problems. The end of the 1970s had seen a return to growth after the economic shocks of the earlier period of the decade. However, it was short-lived and in the following eight years from 1978 to 1986 shipments dropped 13 per cent. This was unprecedented in the long history of the business with the exception of the two world wars. Inevitably these conditions were going to result in another restructuring of the industry on a scale equivalent to that of the 1920s. Allied started to set its sights higher having been satisfied with the results so far. It saw that as a group it had to be bigger in the international spirits business and it had unmatched expertise in acquiring and integrating new businesses. In spite of some critical comments from the financial press after each acquisition, particularly the Lex Column in the *Financial Times*, they had all increased shareholder value. We had gained in confidence enough to look at the bigger companies including the DCL. Before anything could be done, the unexpected happened when Hiram Walker suddenly found itself under threat and turned to Allied as a 'white knight'. So the 'Third Force' came into existence quite suddenly. The method was different from the scenario envisaged some years previously but the strategic objective was reached exactly as foreseen.

CHAPTER 8

The Battle for the Distillers Company

The Distillers Company has an impressive history of 109 years. It started in 1877 as a consortium producing grain whisky and traded in that business for nearly 50 years. Then in 1925, the DCL merged with Buchanan-Dewar and John Walker & Sons to create a vertically integrated company, which dominated the Scotch whisky industry at all levels. In the depressed markets of the 1930s the company began to diversify into chemicals, glass bottles and pharmaceuticals adding to their existing business in yeast and industrial alcohol.

After WWII, the capital requirements for these diversifications escalated to the point where they competed with the need to finance the rapid growth in whisky stocks to meet the rising overseas demand for Scotch whisky. The decision was taken to sell the chemical businesses to British Petroleum in exchange for BP shares. This was an astute move, because the shares produced a steady growth and regular sales provided the capital for investment in more whisky stock.

In the late 1950s the DCL entered into a contract with a German company to licence the sale of a drug called Thalidomide prescribed for pregnant women as a sleeping pill and to treat morning sickness. Unfortunately, the drug proved a disaster as it resulted in the birth of thousands of deformed babies. It was withdrawn immediately. Years of litigation followed before the liability of the DCL was settled. The directors agonised over the dichotomy between the interests of shareholders and the moral obligation to do everything possible to ease the problems of the children and their parents. The experience left a scar on the reputation of the company and it never really recovered its confidence.

Meanwhile, the overseas markets for Scotch expanded dramatically in the 1960s and the DCL benefited enormously from their dominant market share. It was extremely difficult for smaller companies and new entrants to make headway. However, two did succeed in the USA in spite of the dominance of DCL's brands. They were J&B marketed by Paddington and Cutty Sark distributed by Buckingham. Both Paddington and Buckingham were American companies, which had a flair for marketing alcoholic drinks in their own market. They simply licensed the brands and contracted for their supply.

At the same time a number of small brands were making headway in the UK market and threatening the DCL share of over 50 per cent. In order to fuel the growth, they had to find capital to invest in new whisky stocks and cover their negative cash flow. A high profit margin is the normal way to support this type of investment but they were frustrated by the DCL delaying price increases in the UK. This led to a differential between the UK and export prices resulting in parallel trading of DCL's leading brand Johnnie Walker. In addition, the EEC ruled that dual pricing violated the treaty of Rome. DCL decided to protect the export price of this brand by withdrawing it from the UK market. The result was that the company's market share in the UK dropped over several years to as low as 20 per cent in the late 1970s.

Distillers were on the defensive but this was nothing new for them. They were past masters at defending their overseas markets by selecting the best distributors and with skilful pricing and promotion. Their leading brands had been leaders since the 1890s and the DCL strategy was to protect and defend them aggressively. This worked for several decades but once the demand started to take off in the 1960s it was no longer enough. The new entrants deployed more sophisticated marketing techniques, nourishing their brands and building strong images to match those of DCL.

Most consumer advertising contributed to a strengthening of the image of Scotch whisky but did little to enhance that of the individual brands. As a consequence, it is likely that the strength of the Scotch category image was stronger than the cumulative strength of the brands. The DCL relied on the Scotch whisky market carrying them along, which it did until Scotch sales stopped growing in the 1970s.

By 1985 it was too late for the DCL to take effective action, which would turn things around in the short term. Their profits stagnated and they came under considerable pressure from the stock market analysts. They were vulnerable to takeover at a time when funds were readily available for financing acquisitions. The market was at a feverpitch, expecting a new deal every week or so.

The people who had guided the DCL in its long history were able and in some cases entrepreneurial. Even at the end, there was a cadre of able managers, who were however, limited in their actions by the rather conservative and unchanged management structure. There are three key figures, who, I think, made an unusual contribution to that long and distinguished history and they are William Ross, Alex Macdonald and Ernest Saunders.

Sir William Ross was, undoubtedly, the major figure in the early days. He had the vision to take the company from a collection of strong willed grain distillers to the heights of British business. DCL was successful in the expansion of its business and was a desirable investment for its shareholders, paying a regular dividend when others were not so reliable. Ross crowned his career by masterminding the merger with Buchanan-Dewar and Walker in 1925.

Sir Alex Macdonald was chairman in the late 1960s and early seventies and knew the DCL inside out. He started his career as a practising Chartered Accountant and became the auditor of the DCL. It was a diverse collection of more than 100 companies and it was said of Alex that he was the only person who knew his way around every part of the group not excepting the directors! It was he who had the undesirable job of dealing with the Thalidomide affair. He attracted much unfair criticism by refusing to be steamrollered into granting unlimited compensation, which would have been against the interests of shareholders. He eventually worked out a compromise having established the parameters of fair settlements for the families.

Ernest Saunders was never considered for a knighthood, which would have been his had he managed the acquisition of DCL more skilfully. He was one of the few top-flight marketing men in management having learned his craft in J Walter Thompson and Beechams. He rose to be one of the top managers in the giant Nestle food business before he was asked to join Guinness. This company had hit difficult times in the late 1970s and needed some firm handling to sort out the problems. He succeeded beyond the expectations of the Guinness family by multiplying the share price five times and outperforming the stock market more than twice. This success led him to set Guinness on a course to become one of the top companies in the country. Having become a large retailer, Guinness then acquired Bell's Scotch whisky in August 1985 and looked forward to building and expanding these two businesses. However, Saunders was persuaded to take an interest in the problems of DCL, when they came under attack from Argyll almost immediately after the Bell's transaction was complete.

Much has been written about the takeover of the DCL and the subject has been covered from a number of angles. This account looks at the event as an important episode in the history of the Scotch whisky industry, which continues to prosper and still owes much to the founders of the company both in marketing terms and in production.

As mentioned earlier, Allied-Lyons had secret discussions with Distillers in June 1985 but they failed to make headway. The two companies were not producing sparkling growth and a radical restructuring was essential combined with a convincing set of new objectives if the stock market was to be convinced that a combined group could produce real growth.

There was little duplication apart from Teacher's Scotch, which would have dovetailed neatly with the DCL sales profile as it was strong in the UK and the DCL were not. I drafted some notes for discussion, which were designed to lead to a justification for a merger. It will be no surprise that the points made were very similar to those used by both Gulliver and Saunders in their efforts to convince the Distillers shareholders to accept their later offers. It would have been quite difficult, although not impossible, to convince sufficient of the institutional shareholders that Allied-Lyons could do the job. Nevertheless Allied had demonstrated that it was capable of turning round newly acquired companies by slimming and improving managements, cutting working capital and improving sales volumes and prices. The problem we could not crack was persuading the DCL directors that we should overhaul the managements and appoint a chief executive to be responsible for running the business.

In our discussions at the Allied/DCL Working Party I found myself in disagreement with Bill Forrest (DCL Corporate Affairs Director), who was proposing that the DCL would form a separate division (including Teachers) alongside the wine, food and beer divisions. I suggested that it would be more efficient to have only two divisions for beer/food and potable alcohol. I had in mind the need to mix the managements of DCL and our wine & spirit division in order to bring about changes in attitudes and a more dynamic approach to growth and new products. Bill clearly had in mind the DCL being able to carry on as before knowing that they would be supported by their nominees on the new group board. However, it is worth noting that they were prepared to sell the various opulent company offices in central London and other surplus assets something that was never contemplated hitherto. They were clearly being forced to consider drastic measures.

It was also noteworthy, given what happened later in the Guinness bid, that the DCL members of the Working Party insisted that a paragraph in our final report to the two chairmen (DCL & Allied) be inserted, which read: 'The Working Party recognised the "political sensitivity" stemming from DCL's Scottish origin and historical connections and the fact that it remains a Scottish company. A new parent company name and corporate structure would have to have regard to this and to other political pressures.'

Our approach was far too radical for the Distillers directors, who did not yield autonomy for the businesses each controlled. The 'Combine' formed when the DCL merged with Buchanan-Dewar and Walker in 1925 left management control with the individual companies. William Ross had rid the pre-1925 DCL of what he called 'vendor management' and he probably thought that, once the merger was complete, the same thing would happen to management of the new group. Sadly he was too old and in poor health by then and the system of 'vendor management' became firmly established again and hardly altered in the intervening 60 years. It was summed up by Sir Robin Cater, Chairman of DCL from 1976 till 1983, who is quoted as saying 'Don't look to me for leadership; I'm only chairman of the trade co-operative.' In recent years a management committee had been formed, which did concentrate control to an extent but nowhere near sufficient to produce sharp decision taking.

As the Guinness acquisition of Bell's was being digested during August, Distillers continued to be the subject of bid rumours with James Gulliver's Argyll being linked with them. The directors realised that there was not much time and began to think about changes. As a start, they disclosed their 'secret' talks with Allied to the *Financial Times* thus giving the impression that they were seriously looking for partners to give their business a boost.

Guinness's successful bid for Bells was 258p per share amounting to £340m. The initial offer in June had been 229p. The final price was almost twice the market value before the bid was announced and many viewed this as high but it did indicate that Scotch whisky companies with good brands were worth more than they were valued by the stock market. However, Bells was a lean company and needed time to realise its potential overseas. The immediate growth prospects were certain but modest and Guinness would find it difficult to produce increased profits to justify the price paid.

James Gulliver of Argyll had been planning his attack on the DCL for over a year and was putting the final touches to his plan to make a bid when the rumours caused the DCL shares to start rising. Gulliver had been a high flyer since his brilliant university days. In his early thirties he had transformed the Fine Fare supermarket chain, part of Associated British Foods, into the first truly modern food business. Later he bought into Oriel Foods and together with Alistair Grant and David Webster proceeded to expand the company before selling out at a large profit. The three made a superb and very capable team and went on to make another fortune in Alpine, a double-glazing company. In 1982 they took over Allied Suppliers from James Goldsmith to form the Argyll Group. After the DCL affair was concluded Gulliver went on to achieve his ambition to control a large company by acquiring Safeway in the UK from the American company, and turn it into the third largest supermarket operator in this country.

Gulliver was a talented and successful businessman but he had a bit of a reputation, which *Private Eye* featured on several occasions, and this did not appeal to the very respectable and straight-laced DCL directors. In spite of the strength of the Argyll management, they were determined to look for any other solution in the search for a partner. Later, Guinness entered the scene as a bidder and the DCL people found them much more to their taste. The Scotch Whisky Association was, of course, not involved in the battle between Guinness and Argyll but DCL had a fair number of members on the Council, whereas Argyll had none. The Council chairman was John MacPhail of Highland Distilleries, the first non-DCL man to hold the post. He gathered all the independent Council members together to ask for their views on the two bidders and who might be triumphant. It was clear that he was trying to persuade us that Guinness would be a more desirable winner from the industry's point of view and that we should give support to them. There was a division of opinion and it was agreed that the SWA could not take sides even though the DCL felt that they had a right to expect their colleagues to support them.

The Argyll financing was not yet in place and a bid did not seem possible until more backing was available. DCL was over three times larger than Argyll and more time was needed. There had been talks with GEC, where Weinstock ruled supreme over a big company with a pile of cash. Part was invested in DCL and Gulliver hoped to have financial assistance for his bid. However, nothing came of this idea and something had to be done to stop the rise in DCL's shares.

It was thought wise to consult the Takeover Panel and see what could be done to dampen the premature speculation. The Panel requested that a statement be put out immediately and, after a lot of agonising over a weekend, it was decided to announce that: 'Argyll does not intend to make an offer for Distillers at the present time.' It proved to be a very confusing statement and, in the event, the opportunity to acquire Distillers was lost because of the delay. If the bid had been launched on the day of the issue of the statement on 2 September 1985, it might well have succeeded without too much trouble. The problem for Argyll was that they had to commit themselves to wait for three months before making another move.

The DCL proceeded to indulge in a flurry of activity involving changes to all parts of the organisation. Perhaps they were inspired by the case put by Allied's chairman, Sir Derrick Holden-Brown, when talking to them about a merger. In any case there was no time to lose in taking firm action if the directors were to preserve the DCL's independence. The five-man management committee was scrapped as were the committees reporting to it. Sales managements in the UK were combined and rationalised and marketing specialists employed.

One of the biggest changes involved DCL's relations with the City and the analysts. They made a two-day presentation in October 1985. Many were impressed including de Zoete & Bevan, who recommended a BUY 'in the expectation of further developments and throwing caution (for once) aside'. Certainly the results for year to March 1985 were good. The profit before tax was up 23 per cent and the interim profit to 30 September was up 54 per cent. The latter result may have been influenced by advanced shipments overseas compared with the previous year. The Interim Report stated: 'They were influenced by an exceptional upsurge in export sales which is likely to alter the normal balance of activity between the two halves of the Group's financial year'. Volume in the USA was up 20 per cent reflecting 'the acceleration of buying ahead of the increase in Federal Excise Tax'. Given the Argyll threat, it was also a reasonable defensive tactic. On balance, de Zoete commented that the analysts had had to change their opinion on seeing how strong the DCL business was after viewing the presentation. Everyone appeared to have underestimated the company, although that was understandable given the DCL's unwillingness to communicate. The shares, which had been 289p on May 31, were 426p in late October and forecast to go over 500p if any sort of bid materialised.

So far so good. The board was strengthened by the appointment of Bill Spengler as Deputy Chairman and Deputy Chief Executive and Sir Nigel Broackes, Chairman of Trafalgar House as a non-executive. Spengler had recently retired as Vice Chairman of Owens-Illinois with whom DCL had a long-standing relationship in the glass business.

Strangely, although he was Deputy Chief Executive, there is no mention of John Connell, the chairman, assuming the role of Chief Executive! All the public statements were signed simply as Chairman. A new merchant bank, Kleinwort Benson was appointed with the task of constructing a defence against the expected bid from Argyll. The active promotion by the revitalised DCL management had taken the shares to 510p on 29 November in anticipation.

On 2 December the bid was announced – for every 10 Distillers shares eight new Argyll ordinary, 10 new Argyll convertible preference and £14.50 in cash. This was equivalent to 513p per DCL share at the time of the offer. The cash alternative offered was 485p. The acceptance date was fixed for 7 January. DCL rejected the bid as inadequate and both sides embarked on a newspaper advertising campaign designed to remind shareholders of the key issue – who was going to do a better job for Scotch in the future, Argyll or Distillers. It was a choice between the incumbent management with their deep knowledge of the business and the team of three successful managers, Gulliver, Grant and Webster, who had proved themselves in several businesses.

No punches are pulled in a contested bid and a lot of nasty things are said and written. Ungentlemanly tactics are used to ruffle the opposition and their advisors. The advisors were a merchant bank, a stockbroker, an accountant, a lawyer, a public relations agency and a media advertising agency. All these people are very able and command high fees. A takeover does not come cheap even if it is an agreed one. The various documents required have to be prepared with great care to make sure that they comply with legislation and the various regulatory authorities. The bill will come to many millions of pounds and have to come out of the profit and loss account. If the bid fails it is tough to have to explain the cost to the shareholders at the end of the year. Argyll introduced an innovation by persuading the now more flexible banks to accept lower fees for underwriting if the bid failed but to expect a very much higher amount if it succeeded.

It was not until 30 December that DCL came out with their defence document issued from their Edinburgh office. This was a long delay and the timing of the mailing at the New Year holiday was not the best. It made skilful use of sales statistics and attacked Argyll as being wholly inexperienced in international marketing. Much was made of the high debt burden to be taken on by Argyll as part of the financing package. There was no mention of profits in the future.

This was a period of considerable takeover activity and one of the beneficiaries was the advertising industry. The contestants allocated large budgets and ads appeared in all the broadsheet press presumably to grab the constant attention of those who would influence the result. It seems that analysts are willing to accept £10m or £20m spent on a six or eight week campaign without comment but would heavily criticise a company spending that on a brand at the expense of a drop in profit! *The Daily Telegraph* of 2 January carried a full page Argyll ad with the headline 'ARGYLL WISHES DISTILLERS A PROSPEROUS 1986' and a graph comparing Argyll's rising share price with DCL's declining curve up to the time of the rumours in August.

The Times on 4 January ran a short piece about the possibility of a counter bid by Guinness. In fact Saunders had been pressed by various people to enter the fray but was reluctant. Guinness carried out a study, which valued Distillers at £2.7 billion or 670p per share. Olivier Roux, the Guinness financial controller seconded from consultants Bain & Co, set three conditions for a bid: it should be below 670p, the Distillers board should agree it unanimously, and the costs should be underwritten by the DCL if the bid failed. This was another innovation, which had doubtful legality.

Politicians were to take a keen interest in the battle for Distillers and the first into the press was Harry Ewing, Labour MP for Falkirk. He was concerned about the risk to employment at DCL establishments in his constituency and asked Leon Brittan, the Trade and Industry minister, to refer it to the Monopolies and Mergers Commission.

Argyll extended the closing date of its offer to 28 January having had acceptances from 2.72 per cent of Distillers shares. It already owned 1.26 per cent and so it could speak for 14.45m shares or 3.98 per cent. Then on 8 January Leon Brittan announced that the bid would not be referred to the Monopolies and Mergers Commission. Lex in the *FT* commented that Distillers price of 525p is in line with the bid and thought that Argyll might raise the terms to make sure of success and 'any thought that Distillers would fetch a price close to 600p per share must by now have been discarded'.

In mid January there was news that a stake of 1.6 per cent of Distillers had been acquired by Schenley Industries, part of the Rapid American Corporation, who were the US distributors of Dewar's. This was seen as a bargaining counter with the victor of the takeover battle. Rapid American featured later in the stock market dealings when Guinness entered the scene.

The press featured a new view on the value of Distillers in a report by stockbroker Victor MacColl of Grieveson Grant. Comparing recent takeovers in the USA, MacColl and his partner John Spicer claimed that the value of the Distillers brands was not less than £6 per share or £2.2bn. They went on to say that the current cost value of the net assets as per the accounts was 585p, which made a total value for the company of nearly £12 per share.

From the date of issue of the Listing Particulars on 17 December, there were a number of key dates under the Takeover Panel's rules. The offer might last for 60 days, which means that the DCL had until 15 February to convince their shareholders to stay with the present management. After the 46th day Argyll would not be allowed to raise its bid and they would have to make up their mind by 1 February whether or not to increase the offer. The Distillers shares rose 28p on the announcement of the bid being cleared and the price of 525p was higher than the offer. Distillers was barred from releasing fresh financial information after the 39th day and was required to bring out its latest profit estimate for the year to 31 March 1986 by then. With the prospect of an intervention by Guinness, the scene was set for an exciting few weeks.

Distillers ran ads in the press with the headline 'Sorry Argyll. You are two years too late.' Argyll countered with 'Is it surprising that Distillers Pension Fund invests in Argyll shares?' On 16 January Distillers rose 20p to 558p helped by the Grieveson, Grant & Co report and adding further pressure for an increase in the offer.

The Sunday press on 19 January ran stories about an agreed

merger of Distillers and Guinness. This was followed by further speculation on Monday, although it was obvious that the Office of Fair Trading would be interested in the market share such a group would have in the UK market. On the 20th Leon Brittan wrote to Brian Gould, the Labour shadow trade secretary, to clarify the government's policy on mergers stating that 'the Secretary of State will make references primarily (but not exclusively) on competition grounds; and in evaluating the competitive situation in individual cases, he will have regard to the international context – to the extent of competition in the home market from non-UK sources, and to the competitive position of UK companies in overseas markets.'

The same day Guinness made their long expected bid to DCL shareholders and the real battle started. Sentiment had been favouring Argyll, as the market was not convinced that the DCL management had changed sufficiently to be given support. The Distillers people seemed to have reckoned that they would fall into the hands of Argyll unless they could find a 'white knight'. Behind the scenes the talks with Guinness had been tough and had been carried out at great speed in view of Argyll's progress. Ultimately Distillers had agreed to the Guinness merger terms including the controversial devices to underwrite the Guinness costs.

The Guinness offer:

For 5 DCL shares		
8 Guinness shares	293p	23.44
Cash		7.00
		£30.44
Divided by 5	**Per share**	**609p**
Cash alternative	**Per share**	**584.8p**

The speculation was how Argyll would act in view of the fact that their bid had been cleared but there was a big risk that the Guinness one would be referred. However, the DCL directors had fixed a price at which they were prepared to sell and matching it and hoping for a clear run if Guinness were referred was a sensible tactic given that Distillers still seemed cheap.

The Argyll bid was equivalent to:

For 10 DCL shares		
8 Argyll shares	355p	28.44
10 Argyll Con Pref	112.3p	11.26
Cash		14.50
		£54.20
Divided by 10	**Per share**	**542p**
Cash alternative	**Per share**	**485p**

Ernest Saunders claimed 'if you consider the strategic importance of this business and its importance in British exports I can't imagine that any British Government will worry about one or two points of brand share in the British market.' In fact the combined market share was 35 per cent, which was well above the limit of 25 per cent fixed by the OFT.

Before the bid announcement Saunders had talks about the composition of the board of the combined group. John Connell, the chairman of Distillers was not thought to be suitable nor was Lord Iveagh, the family chairman of Guinness. Sir Thomas Risk was mentioned and ultimately agreed to chair the new company. He was clearly intending to take a keen interest in certain strategic matters and wished to see the headquarters in Scotland. He gave the impression that Scottish employment interests were to be put before those of shareholders when they conflicted. However, he agreed to serve and Saunders was glad to have this delicate issue settled except that he still had to tell John Connell. He did this over the weekend before the bid announcement on Monday 20 January.

Edinburgh was chosen for the first press conference and was attended by Saunders, David Connell, John's brother, Sir Thomas Risk and Charles Fraser. The full composition of the board of the merged company included, besides the above four: John Connell, Lord Iveagh, Olivier Roux, Vic Steel, Bill Spengler, Arthur Furer and Sir Nigel Broackes.

The key issue in the short term was the possibility of referral of the Guinness bid. Although the decision that Distillers would pay the Guinness bid costs win or lose created a diversion and brought a lot of criticism from the Argyll camp. *The Sunday Times* on 26 January suggested that Saunders may have to sell the Bell's company in order to avoid a referral. Saunders naturally wanted to hold onto Bells and his position was that the future of an international industry was at stake. However, the market still thought a referral was likely as the shares closed at 576p compared with the Guinness cash alternative of 585p.

During the week of 27 January the press ads started to appear again. The Argyll one was still emphasising the fact that their bid was the only one cleared by the OFT and clearly hoped that Guinness would be referred leaving its own bid a free run at its existing level. At the same time Argyll appealed to the Takeover Panel to ban the arrangement for Distillers to underwrite the bid costs of Guinness even if the bid failed. The appeal failed and Argyll considered legal action in the courts. Later it was realised that the legality was very doubtful and probably would have been caught by section 151 of the Companies Act 1985, which bans a company from helping to buy its own shares except in certain circumstances. An exception is when the financial assistance is given as part of a larger purpose. It was the opinion of the Guinness lawyers and counsel's advice that the exception applied in this case but the deputy director of the DTI took the opposite view and told the Takeover Panel. It is likely that the DTI's hostility to Saunders dates from the time this issue was debated.

On 29 January Argyll extended its offer until 15 February, which was the 60-day limit for the offer. However, the Guinness bid altered the timetable and the 60-day limit restarted from the date the formal Guinness bid was posted. There was a good deal of discussion about Distillers having agreed to pay the Guinness bid costs. The legality of the arrangement was being debated and Guinness gave DCL directors individual indemnity in the event of legal action against them.

The debate about referring the Guinness bid to the MMC was raging in the press. With the agreement of the Allied-Lyons board, I signed a letter to the OFT putting the case for a referral based on the combined Guinness and Distillers market share in the UK of 35 per cent. This was a distinct threat to our Teacher's brand, which had 12 per cent share of the market. Subsequently, I had a telephone conversation with one of the OFT officials, who summarised the Saunders case for no referral. He claimed that the issue was the position of Scotch in the world market and that in the UK Guinness needed to be strong in order to provide a solid platform to take on the major spirits competitors overseas. It was necessary, he said, to support one of Britain's major exporters against the fierce competition of other spirits such as Japanese whisky. I pointed out that Japanese whisky sells only in Japan and both J&B and Cutty Sark brands proved in the USA that success can be achieved without any sales in the UK. I also pointed out that about 80 per cent of Scotch was exported and that the home market was not vital as DCL had demonstrated when withdrawing Johnnie Walker from it.

Guinness were delaying the issuing of their formal offer document hoping that they would receive clearance from the OFT. Under the rules they had until 17 February to post it to shareholders. Meanwhile Argyll issued a High Court writ seeking to nullify the controversial agreement under which Distillers agreed to pay the costs of the Guinness bid. Ten City institutions were consulted about the action brought under section 151 of the Companies Act 1985 which prohibits a company from providing financial assistance for the purchase of its own shares. The writ sought to declare the agreement null and void and to secure an injunction restraining Distillers from making any payments. Opinion in the City was divided on the matter.

Argyll made an unexpected move by announcing an increased offer on 6 February. It had been thought that they would wait for a decision by the government on referral to the MMC. The increased offer was as follows:

For 10 DCL shares

11 Argyll shares	338p	37.25
10 Argyll Con Pref	109.5p	10.95
£15 cash		15.00
		£63.20
Divided by 10	**Per share**	**632p**
Cash alternative	**Per share**	**600p**

The new closing date was 27 February . The comparative Guinness offer was then valued at 599p. The new offer gave Argyll more flexibility to buy Distillers shares in the market up to the cash value of the offer as far as 15 per cent of the shares and thereafter up to the new cash alternative of 600p instead of 485p.

It was announced on 11 February that two Japanese companies had bought the Tomatin distillery. They were Takara Shuzo, the largest producer of the cheap Japanese spirit Shochu and Okura, an international trading company. Needless to say Saunders made the most of this development as it emphasised his case to the OFT about the Japanese threat. The decision about referral was imminent. The press speculation was heightened by the decisions on the friendly proposal by Imperial to acquire United Biscuits (UB) and the hostile bid for Imperial by Hanson. The former was referred and the latter was cleared! This seemed to suggest that Guinness might be referred leaving Argyll to go ahead and acquire Distillers as their bid had an unconditional clearance. There was a suggestion, however, that a clearance can be withdrawn as happened in the case of the Beecham bid for Glaxo in the early 1970s. It was cleared only to be referred later after the emergence of Boots as a rival contender.

In the event it was announced on 14 February that the Guinness bid was to be referred. Both Guinness and Distillers complained that this left the way open for Argyll and denied Distillers shareholders a choice. On the news Distillers rose 10p to 620p in the market and Argyll were up 13p at 353p valuing Distillers shares at 652p. Most of the press assumed that Argyll would win but were of the opinion that Guinness/Saunders would have made a better job of building up the DCL brands than Argyll/Gulliver. However, the logic of the Imperial decisions was being followed and it seemed unlikely that Distillers shareholders would wish to wait for six months until the MMC had reported, preferring to accept the Argyll offer. Meanwhile, the timetable reverted to the position before Guinness made its offer. Day 39 was 19 February and was the last chance for DCL to publish defensive information with closure 21 days later. The first closing date was named as 27 February in Argyll's recent increased offer.

Distillers' directors were determined to go on fighting the Argyll bid. There was talk in the press of another 'white knight' but it did not prove to be a serious suggestion. An Argyll ad addressed to the shareholders claimed that 'We obviously value your company more than your directors do.' And quoted the Guinness lapsed offer of 604p and Argyll's of 641p reminding them that the closing date was 27 February.

There was speculation on 19 February that Guinness might find a way to make a fresh bid, which would not be referred. In the Imperial/United Biscuits case, the bid was referred but they then proposed that UB would bid for Imperial and sell off Golden Wonder Crisps, thus reducing the combined share of the snacks market. In the same fashion, Guinness/DCL could sell off some brands and reduce their market share to the maximum 25 per cent.

Guinness announced that it had abandoned its bid for Distillers and the MMC said that it would not, therefore, be looking into the proposed merger. The next thought canvassed was for Distillers to bid for Guinness but doubt was expressed about the value of Distillers paper (share value - would the institutions accept it?) The idea did not survive long but there was much discussion about how Guinness could dispose of UK market share without having to sell Bells.

The Wall Street Journal reported on 20 February that the Takeover Panel had ruled that the ultimate closing date for the Argyll bid would be 14 March. The same day Guinness announced a fresh offer for Distillers, which it hoped, would not be referred like the last one. At the same time Argyll increased its stake in Distillers to 10 per cent and said it would do anything to win. The new Guinness bid involved selling five brands with a UK market share of roughly 10 per cent. They were the secondary brands John Barr, Buchanan Blend, Claymore, The Real Mackenzie and one time brand leader Haig Gold Label. Claymore with a share of 5.91 per cent produced a net profit of only £187,000 and the others were equally unprofitable. The OFT had been asked to clear the new offer as speedily as possible.

The new Guinness offer was as follows:

For 3 DCL shares		
5 Guinness shares	301p	15.05
£5.16 cash		5.16
		£20.21
Divided by 3	**Per share**	**674p**
Cash alternative	**Per share**	**630.3p**

There was some critical comment on this new offer and Alastair Grant, Managing Director of Argyll, was quoted in *The Glasgow Herald* as saying 'If the Government allows this to happen it opens the door to any amount of corporate gerrymandering to avoid a Monopolies reference.' While the market share of sales in the UK would be reduced to a level acceptable to the OFT, it could easily be increased later by introducing a new brand onto the UK market. Furthermore, the new group would have 37 per cent of the output of new whisky. The opinion in the press was that the new Guinness offer radically altered the takeover rules and reflected the system in the USA, where companies proposing a merger were required to give binding undertakings to divest operations, which conflicted with competition principles. Some wondered if the authority of the OFT was not being undermined.

Lord Spens of Henry Ansbacher, and advisor to Bells during the Guinness bid for the company, wrote to the *Financial Times* on 21

February criticising the decision to sell off The Real Mackenzie brand. Guinness had given an assurance that the brand would be developed and employment would be secured. As Lord Spens pointed out, The Real Mackenzie accounted for 5 per cent of Bell's production and its sale would threaten some of the jobs at Bell's bottling plant. He posed the question 'Should assurances and undertakings given in a takeover battle count for nothing so soon after the event?' He thought that the Office of Fair Trading must consider this point in its further deliberations on the merits of the present Guinness/Distillers situation. In fact the bottling continued to be carried out by Distillers for their brands and The Real Mackenzie by Bells. However, the production director reckoned at the time that the DCL plant at Leven, which bottled Claymore, could also handle Mackenzie thus reducing employment at Bell's plant.

The movements in the share prices of the two bidders since the Guinness second offer narrowed the gap between them on 21 February. The Guinness offer looked like this:

For 3 DCL shares		
5 Guinness shares	280p	14.00
£5.16 cash		5.16
		£19.16
Divided by 3	**Per share**	**638.6p**

And the Argyll one:

For 10 DCL shares		
11 Argyll shares	342p	37.63
10 Argyll Con Pref	109.5p	10.95
£15 cash		15.00
		£63.58
Divided by 10	**Per share**	**635.8p**

Prompted by Argyll, the Stock Exchange questioned Morgan Grenfell about its market support operations in the Distillers battle. Under the rules quoted companies must seek shareholder approval when undertaking an investment, which may give rise to a commitment greater than 25 per cent of capital and reserves. Morgan Grenfell, acting for Guinness, had recently bought £70m worth of Distillers shares, while having an indemnity agreement to cover any losses, as was customary practice. As the net worth of Guinness was calculated at £264m, the limit had been reached. The Stock Exchange said it would consider the matter.

On 28 February Argyll extended its offer until 20 March. Distiller's shareholders were still biding their time as acceptances totalled only 2.77 per cent, although Argyll now owned 14.21 per cent with shares already owned and bought. Both sides were embarked on market support operations. These involved Guinness and Argyll arranging with others to purchase their shares and to provide indemnities against loss. In addition, each was buying Distillers shares in the market whenever they were offered. Argyll kept slightly ahead of Guinness and by this time about 23 per cent of Distillers shares were owned by or committed to the two rival bidders.

On 6 March the High Court rejected Argyll's allegation that the original Guinness bid had been wrongly set aside by the chairman of the MMC acting alone and without reference to the full Commission. However, Argyll intimated that they would appeal. The appeal was turned down on 14 March and Argyll said they would not pursue the matter further. At the same time Guinness filed lawsuits against Argyll alleging injurious falsehood and defamation in advertisements. At the end of March the Takeover Panel brought out a new set of rules governing the use of advertising during takeover battles. Many institutions had criticised what they saw as a waste of money and some ads were actionable. In future ads would require to be vetted by the Panel before publication and the subject matter would be severely restricted.

The new bid by Guinness, about which there was so much fuss, was cleared by the government on 21 March on the basis that there was a firm contract to sell brands equivalent to 10 per cent market share to

Whyte & Mackay. On the same day Argyll announced an increased offer. This was the final offer and was combined with a large market operation to buy £700m worth of Distillers shares. The details were:

For 100 DCL shares		
125 Argyll shares	340p	425.00
100 Argyll Pref	114p	114.00
£162.75 cash		162.75
		£701.75
Divided by 100	**Per share**	**701.75p**

The new cash alternative was 660p compared with the Guinness cash offer of 630p. Argyll's offer was due to close on 16 April. Guinness said it would not be increasing its offer and extended the closing date to 18 April. There was little point in either party issuing more shares, as this would only depreciate the bidders share price in the market. The way was open for the battle to move to the stock market, where each side sought to pick up Distillers shares and also to boost its own share price by encouraging others to buy the shares and thus enhancing the value of the offer. Those carrying out the buying operations were usually compensated by indemnities against losses or fees. One restriction, under the takeover rules, is that it is not permitted to offer more than the cash alternative.

As time went on Guinness shares moved up and its offer improved and Distillers shares followed a little behind. Each looked keenly at the rising level of acceptances but buying in the market was restricted by the rise in Distillers above the cash alternative offer. Guinness announced on 6 April that it controlled 19.5 per cent against Argyll 17.4 per cent. However, Guinness had a higher level of acceptances and it seemed to be favoured by the shareholders. Both sides lobbied the institutional shareholders in order to persuade them of the abilities of the respective management teams. Guinness seemed to have the edge in view of their greater experience in brand marketing but Argyll men had perhaps a little more entrepreneurial flair. Advertisements were appearing every day in all the broadsheets and even Distillers placed some ads reminding shareholders that their board recommended the Guinness offer.

The *Sunday Express* on 13 April backed Gulliver 'through thick and thin' on the basis of his proven record of building three superb businesses. Likewise *The Sunday Telegraph* backed Gulliver for his management ability and financial performance, while acknowledging that Saunders was a strong chief executive and ran a fine company. On Monday 14 April Robert Martin in *The Glasgow Herald* said Distillers shareholders should back Argyll. He preferred the Argyll team to the Guinness one simply because it has a proven record and Saunders and his men, able as they were, had still to perform. On the other hand *The Times* came out in support of Guinness on 14 April and predicted that Argyll would lose the battle.

Argyll announced on 14 April that its offer would remain open until 18 April, the same closing date as Guinness. Its merchant bank Morgan Grenfell said it had bought more Distillers shares and had raised the stake of Guinness and its associates to 11.6 per cent. Argyll's merchant bank Samuel Montagu bought more Argyll shares and said that it had fully disclosed all its support operations on behalf of Argyll but claimed that even more support had been mustered for Guinness shares in such a way that it did not need to be disclosed.

Guinness revealed on 16 April that it had acceptances of 16.8 per cent and in total controlled 31.8 per cent of Distillers. Argyll had only 2.87 per cent the previous day and victory seemed almost certain for Guinness. By the next day Guinness claimed it spoke for 46 per cent of Distillers, including acceptances of 31.3 per cent. By mid-afternoon on the 18th Guinness had secured victory and Argyll had conceded defeat. Johnathan Guinness in his *Requiem for a Family Business* suggested that the final thrust was the purchase of 10 million Distillers shares on 17 April by Bank Leu. 'When the block came on offer, Samuel Montagu, on Argyll's behalf, at once offered the 660p they were permitted to bid.' This was the limit being the amount of the alternative cash offer. Guinness and its supporters were limited to their cash offer of 630p but the block was secured at a price of 700p.

The takeover of Distillers was a major event in the history of Scotch whisky and it was also notable in the British industrial scene. It was the largest acquisition at that time in spite of the fact that Guinness was so much smaller than its prey. It had been a considerable effort for all concerned and succeeded because the City institutions backed the management team at Guinness led by Ernest Saunders. Reviewing the press reports, the impression remains of a well conducted campaign by Argyll with each move calculated to advance the bid step by step. On the other hand, Guinness had little time for preparation but had greater forces at its disposal. Its advisors were some of the best available and they were big and had some strong characters assigned to the job. However, it is not always clear that they acted in a co-ordinated fashion. Olivier Roux, Ward and Morgan Grenfell seemed to push Saunders at times, when he had not had time to think things through, with the result that he was not able to assess the consequences of all the moves. This must have been the case with the market support operations, which were to result in criminal charges later for some of the Guinness team and their supporters.

The immediate task after the successful acquisition of Distillers was to deal with all the Guinness shares bought in the market by its friends to support the price. These people did not expect to make a loss and Guinness had, in a number of cases, agreed to cover any losses. If the Guinness price had fallen these losses would have been considerable and, potentially, could have brought the company down. Further efforts had to be made to support the price and it must have been touch and go.

In addition, Guinness, and banks acting in concert with Guinness, had purchased Distillers shares, which were assented to the Guinness offer. A formal proposal was put to shareholders on 23 May for the purchase by the company of 90m shares or 9.8 per cent of the Guinness equity at a cost of £275m and for these shares to be cancelled. This purchase helped to stabilise the Guinness share price just as Argyll were selling their Guinness shares amounting to14.4 per cent of Distillers.

The next crisis occurred when Saunders decided that he could not work with the board structure envisaged in the offer documents. On 14 July Guinness confirmed reports that Ernest Saunders would succeed the Earl of Iveagh as chairman, combining that role with that of chief executive. As *The Times* of 15 July reported 'This statement detonated a small underground nuclear explosion in the City'. Saunders had a meeting with the Governor of the Bank of England at which he probably explained the thinking behind the decision to abandon the holding company board proposed in the listing particulars of the Guinness offer. Saunders had concluded that it was the duty of the board to serve the best interests of the shareholders and that he and his team had to have a more direct control over the DCL operations in view of the problems to be solved. The result was that Sir Thomas Risk, Charles Fraser and the Distillers directors were told that they were not wanted. In spite of the fuss Saunders was adamant that the Guinness management team had to have direct control over the DCL operations if the profits forecast during the bid were to be delivered.

After much discussion it was agreed that four new and respected non-executive directors would be appointed with influence at least equivalent to that of a non-executive chairman. Norman Macfarlane was asked to collect a group of Scottish businessman, who would be willing to join the board and act as a check on Saunders as well as giving the Scottish flavour promised at the outset. One of those he approached was Campbell Christie, the leader of the Scottish TUC. He revealed the invitation early in 1999 as he was nearing retirement. The case for the appointment was to establish better employee relations in the whisky industry. Confidentially he consulted the important key figures in the trades union movement and received wholehearted support. He accepted but when it was announced, the opposition from the Scottish TUC movement was so great that he had to resign within a month and never attended a board meeting.

The new structure was put to a Guinness shareholders meeting on 11 September and was given massive support. Ernest Saunders was to be Chairman and Chief Executive and the full board approved by the shareholders was:

Executive	**Non-Executive**
Ernest Saunders	The Earl of Iveagh
Olivier Roux	Dr Arthur Furer
Victor Steel	Anthony Greener
Brian Baldock	Hon Johnathan Guinness
Shaun Dowling	Sir Norman Macfarlane
Edward Guinness	Ian MacLaurin
Sir David Plastow	Thomas Ward

Very rapidly the changes in the DCL management were implemented and Guinness began to sell off surplus DCL assets. Things seemed to be returning to normal leaving the management with the major task of improving the profitability of the new group. The lull did not last long and was rudely interrupted when DTI inspectors arrived at the Guinness headquarters on 1 December to carry out an investigation. Olivier Roux the finance director, who had been seconded from consultants Bain & Co, decided to reveal some of the actions during the bid period and this led to Saunders being dismissed and Norman Macfarlane being appointed Chairman for a couple of years. Norman I knew well and admired his success, with his brother Hamish, in building a successful packaging business, which supplied the Scotch whisky industry. Anthony Tennant was recruited from Grand Metropolitan to be chief executive and he later became chairman of the group. He was able to set it on its feet and all the problems left over from the DTI investigation and the court cases against Saunders and others that followed were left behind.

The Scotch whisky business of Guinness, now called United Distillers (UD), was again able to exert its considerable influence on the market place. By this time, however, the competition was much stronger. Allied-Lyons had acquired Hiram Walker with its valuable brands, including Ballantine's; Grand Metropolitan, through their spirit company; International Distillers and Vintners (IDV), were a powerful force with J&B and Smirnoff Vodka; and Seagrams with its major North American business supported by Chivas Regal completed the powerful competition. These four were the biggest spirit businesses in the world and the scene was set for a battle royal in the world markets. In addition, Allied-Lyons had become associated with Suntory, the largest Japanese whisky producer and dominant in their home market.

In the early and mid nineties the world spirit markets declined considerably and in particular the US market suffered most. Some comfort was taken from the good performance in Europe, where Allied, IDV and UD benefited from increased demand for their brands. Guinness was a little more vulnerable to declining spirit sales than the others because it had a narrow range of products, whereas the others operated businesses in other sectors as well as marketing a broader range of alcoholic products.

The result was another move to rationalise the spirits industry when Grand Met and Guinness decided to merge and create Diageo. This deal went through without a murmur and thus gave the new company a dominance without comparison in the business. It had a major share of the Scotch whisky market with two of the top three brands, Johnnie Walker and J&B, and also owned two of the three best white spirit brands in Smirnoff and Gordon's gin. Only Ballantine's and Bacardi rum are in the same league. It is doubtful if a similar company can be created from the remaining competitors, although that will not stop some trying. The best strategy will be to concentrate on putting together a company strong financially but with a wider range of products in categories where they dominate with equally strong brands. So, of the four majors, Guinness, Allied, Grand Met and Seagram, only three were left. Seagram sold their business to concentrate on their other interest: entertainment. The buyers were Pernod-Ricard of France and Diageo with the former taking the Scotch whisky businesses and Diageo the rum and US brands.

CHAPTER 9

The Formation of Allied Distillers

The Group Environment

We have seen how the 1960s produced several large national breweries from a series of mergers and acquisitions. The largest of these was Bass followed by Ind Coope Tetley Ansell. ICTA as it was dubbed was the result of a three-way merger of Bass's old Burton-on-Trent rival, Ind Coope & Allsop, Tetley Walker of the north of England and Ansells of Birmingham. Shortly afterwards the name of the group was thankfully changed to Allied Breweries.

These new groups looked on the face if it to be powerful and full of potential for the future. However, the beer market was static and the mergers were a means of adjusting to the changed situation by producing economies of scale and creating a broader capital base for extending investments in other drink categories. Cost savings brought profit growth and more options for future investment. The focus was still on the UK market but later the world stage beckoned.

Allied adopted these ideas and pursued them with some vigour under successive chairmen. They already had a growing wholesale and retail wine trade through the Victoria Wine off licence chain and the Grants of St James's imported wine business. Victoria Wine was dominant in London and developing nationally but Grants was quite small, apart from supplying Victoria Wine, although it had a good range and a healthy growth rate from a small base.

This was a time for building brands and it was thought that branding was the way forward in the wine business. It did not prove to be an easy task, because the two essentials were not there, a sufficient quantity of any one wine to supply the demand and a high margin to provide cash for advertising. In the 1960s California and Australia had not reached the levels of production they now enjoy and European vineyards were small and ownership was mostly splintered. It was possible to buy and blend under a single label but the controls provided by the appellation laws meant that only the vin ordinaire wines were available in quantity and they were the low quality ones. These wines are in a commodity market where competitive pricing is the order of the day. Brands were launched but failed to take off. Those that survived did not last the course and disappeared eventually through lack of advertising.

Reputation, quality and availability of the best wines can build a national wine business but the time-scale is long and distributing low volumes is expensive. This makes the economics of the business unattractive and Allied turned again to acquisition to solve the problem. By good fortune Showerings, Vine Products and Whiteways were in a similar position and had been eyeing a tie-up with one of the larger groups. Showerings shot to fame when the brilliant owners invented and launched Babycham in the early fifties and made fortunes for the four families. With a single product they felt vulnerable and had embarked on a series of acquisitions taking in Vine Products, the major manufacture of British sherry and port type wines and two cider companies, Gaymers and Whiteways.

There was little growth in these products and they saw an opportunity to acquire John Harvey & Sons of Bristol, which they succeeded in doing after an abortive first attempt. They began to shake up this old established business with its traditional attitudes increasing profitability and achieving considerable growth in the USA for Harvey's Bristol Cream brand. Having seen what could be done in applying aggressive management to the traditional wine trade, Showerings felt that it was worth a go at one of the slow-moving brewers! Allied was the target and a merger was arranged and agreed.

The style of the management in brewery companies looks from the outside rather laid back and comfortable but underneath this façade are some of the country's most able and forward looking managers. In most cases decisions are delegated and initiative was encouraged. The Showering business was managed aggressively but most decisions were taken at the top and they had been extraordinarily successful. In Allied the three constituent breweries and the wine business had a good working relationship and a degree of autonomy. In Showerings by contrast the four family board members were dominant and the managers took their orders from them. So far they had been astute but in a wider field it was doubtful if their system would work.

At any rate there was no chance of this happening as became obvious when the integration process was started. It was a marriage of two different cultures, the 'consensus' and the 'do what you're told' methods. The situation was complicated as each side really thought that they were taking over the other with the result that sparks began to fly! I was just being introduced to senior management at this time and it proved an exciting baptism. Major enterprises are rarely built without such problems arising and Allied was no exception. These were the days before high salaries but Allied were good at motivating, delegating and giving opportunities for promotion, whereas Showerings had built their success with long-serving, loyal and competent local staff. The situation was eventually resolved with the formation of the three divisions: beer; wines and spirits and international. The Showerings became responsible for wines and spirits and everyone seemed to accept the plan and settled down to run the business again. Tighter management benefited the wine and spirit division and the companies within it were able to look to expanding their markets at home and abroad.

The larger group with greater resources grew impressively for the next five years and began to be regarded as a broadly based company with growth potential in the world market. It was the second largest drinks business in the country and was strong in non-beer drinks in the UK through Babycham and Harvey's Bristol Cream brands. It also had strength in imported wines, as Grants were, by this time, the largest importers. The new divisional structure was sensible and gave each company a chance to define its aims and adopt appropriate strategies for achieving them. The managements were able to fix their priorities and develop their businesses within their particular sectors. No longer was an extension to a brewery given priority over the purchase of a new wine-bottling machine in the capital budgets. Each capital project stood on its own and if it met the investment criteria then it would go ahead.

The formation of the three dedicated divisions provided an opportunity to redeploy various subsidiaries and put them in the right place. Among the companies involved were three Scotch whisky producers, one in Harveys and two in the brewery. By good fortune I found myself given the task of bringing these operations together and shaping a unified business. This was a piece of luck as I had been involved as a financial advisor for a consortium Scotch whisky company in which Allied had a 30 per cent interest and, therefore, had some practical knowledge of the industry. I was also resident in Scotland running Victoria Wine and our family business had been owners of Glen Elgin distillery, although before my time. I was delighted to have a new and constructive role, as I was becoming very bored with retailing with very little chance for shaping policy. The task was made easy for me as the brewery and Harveys were quite glad to be relieved of the diversion of looking after these small operations. Within six months the opportunity arose to acquire yet another small Scotch whisky company giving us four quite different businesses each with its own management.

The New Stewarts

Stewart & Son of Dundee was based in Dundee and was owned by Harveys who had bought it as a diversification move prior to being acquired by Showerings. It was founded there in 1830 and became a listed company in 1926. In the early 1920s it found itself in financial difficulties. The then chairman, Sir Alexander Stewart, is alleged to have sold whisky stocks twice fraudulently on a temporary basis in order to tide the company over the difficulty. It is thought that he later committed suicide. The company was rescued by a group of new investors. In 1956 its ordinary shares were quoted in London and Dundee and at that time it had a capital employed of £240,260. The chairman was LJ Russell with E (Ted) J Neilson as managing director. Ted was the uncle of Jim Ford, who ran Courvoisier for Allied in the

1980s. The secretary was M (May) M Torbet, who was still there in 1969 and helped in the integration process for a year before retiring. The company had an attractive blend, Stewarts Cream of the Barley, which was the leading brand in Northern Ireland.

Glen Rossie Distillers operated out of Liverpool engaged in bulk exports to the USA, where it was bottled as Glen Rossie, and supplying Victoria Wine with a low-priced Scotch. It also supplied Guyana rum to Nova Scotia and Newfoundland where London Dock was a cult brand outselling Bacardi! It was originally a subsidiary of Joshua Tetley & Sons, one of the breweries forming the beer division. The brewery invested in Scotch whisky fillings well in excess of its needs and made some profits by reselling the surplus to other blenders.

The third company was Curtis Distillery Company and had also been a quoted public company although a subsidiary of Cannon Brewery Company, another constituent of the beer division. It had owned and operated the Mile End Distillery producing London Dry Gin but it had long been closed and bulk gin was purchased from other distillers. Its Curtis gin had a listing with the state monopoly in Sweden and sold some small quantities in export markets. In addition it blended and exported low-priced Scotch; some bottled but mostly sold in bulk.

The fourth was David Sandeman & Sons operating out of Glasgow and engaged in the export trade for low-priced Scotch. In addition it had a thriving whisky broking business, which took advantage of the post war shortage of stocks among the smaller blenders, buying and selling in its own right or on commission. Woodhall Trust, a mini-conglomerate, which had also owned the long-established Samuel Dow, whose export trade had been incorporated into David Sandeman, owned it.

Shaping the New Business

The four locations of these businesses were the first problem to tackle, as none was large enough to survive on its own. Fortunately Stewarts had a modern blending and bottling plant in Dundee and adequate office accommodation. Glen Rossie moved quickly to Dundee with no difficulty thanks to the planning and execution of Derrick Fillingham, who became the production director of the enlarged company. The blending and bottling for Curtis and Sandeman was removed to Dundee from outside bottlers with a consequent saving in costs and improved productivity. A sales office was retained in London to handle all the export trade and the Glasgow office remained to handle the broking business as most of the contacts were in the city.

The blending of the personnel was a little trickier but it was important to maintain continuity with customers and the people were very experienced. Reg Price had been managing director of Stewarts and was appointed joint MD of the new company. He did some export travel but was mainly concerned with the home trade and Northern Ireland. The MD of Curtis was a maverick character, Louis de A'Borg, a very British gentleman of Maltese origin. He travelled to Europe and South America and spoke several languages, including French and Spanish. He was also appointed a joint MD. The remaining members of the management team slotted in wonderfully well. Gordon Black, the Stewart blender and stock controller, was one of the most experienced in the industry and was a most valuable member of the new board. To complete the team it was fortunate that John Miller, who had been Finance Director of Sandeman, was available and he moved to Dundee to take charge of the finances and office activities.

We all settled down to build the business in what we discovered was a most competitive market. Louis was the most experienced and I learned a lot from him in the early stages. He had great charm but it was sometimes difficult to accept the credibility of some of his stories. He claimed to have been responsible for Charles Forte when he was interned during the war and to have arranged for his release inferring a close relationship. On another occasion I was asked by a friend on the golf course who this man de A'Borg was who had been a spy during the war! It turned out that Louis had been chatting to a *FT* journalist about his secret service work and the *FT* had published the tale. Immediately the authorities had slapped a 'D' notice on the story and this seemed to add authenticity to Louis's claim. It also provided a nice news story for a few days.

Louis visited Colombia once a year and, always an innovator, decided to apply the promotional budget for the market to donations to the favourite charities of the wife of the president. As a result he made friends with government officials, who would sometimes arrange for the liquor monopoly to give him orders for bulk Scotch. It was not a very secure way to build a business but I suppose we enjoyed some useful trade for a while. The government awarded him two medals for his (our!) charitable donations but the orders eventually dried up. On the occasion of the second award Louis was under some pressure from me about the market performance. I think my personal relationship with him took a dive when, in order to deflect me from my line of attack, he came out with 'I've just been awarded another decoration (the Order of something or other) by the Colombian Government.' I was, of course, meant to interrupt my discourse and offer congratulations and a celebratory lunch. Being a little annoyed and thinking that they had decided to placate Louis with an award and given the order to someone else, I responded with 'Louis, you're collecting the wrong orders.'

I really felt he should be contributing more. He had caused me some considerable trouble when I discovered suddenly one day that the Scotch Whisky Association was taking action against us for false labelling of whisky in his South American markets. I had prepared a stout defence on his behalf while admitting that we had not policed the actions of our customers sufficiently well. I was willing to recommend that we sign a legal document promising to 'behave'.

When I was appointed to Stewarts, Derrick Holden-Brown was the divisional MD and I reported to him. It was a pleasant relationship as it had been in the early 60s in Grants. In the meantime, however, Keith Showering, who was not very interested in a small operation like Stewarts and never made contact or offered to see me, succeeded him. He and his Uncle Francis, unknown to me until afterwards, stirred up a rumpus when I submitted the recommendation and took the matter out of my hands. They endeavoured to persuade the SWA that we should not be asked to sign the undertaking. In the end they failed and the matter was passed back to me for completion. It was reasonable in view of the efforts the SWA made to protect the good name of Scotch, and to let a member company break the rules with impunity would have ruined the chances of obtaining convictions in future. I learned much later that I had been blamed for letting Louis off the hook and not dismissing him. This I thought would not have been justified. As it was, Louis had a real roasting from me, which he did not enjoy and I had reported my action to Keith but was ignored. In the event, I suppose I was lucky to be appointed to Teachers! Louis never really settled after that and left to take up another appointment.

The profits of the combined businesses were around £200K but a lot came from bulk business overseas and whisky broking. This was marginal and did not produce a good return on the stock investment. The business did not own a distillery and, therefore, new fillings had to be purchased for cash at full prices. It was obvious that, if the industry had surplus stocks with prices cut, there would be little or no profit in bulk exports or in the broking market. The industry had always written off interest on capital, which financed its stocks and so the book cost was fictitiously low. This was a wise policy but it meant that the resale price often did not take account of this cost. The result was that there was rarely sufficient cash realised to replace the stock sold and to cover the effect of inflation. The practice has long depressed the price to the consumer, which is good news for them but not for the health of the industry or the economy.

It became clear that a twin strategy was needed to build the business if we were to at least maintain existing profits and give the company a chance to grow over time. The industry had surplus stock in the early 1970s and margins for bulk were low. It was decided that we would continue with our bulk business but minimise our cost base so that we would be competitive and make a reasonable margin. We were fortunate to have a very efficient blending and bottling operation, which had one of the best rates of productivity and lowest cost per case produced. In addition we deliberately did not purchase new whisky fillings to meet all our needs, thus saving some of the cost of financing.

The other strategic aim was to build our brands from their small bases in Northern Ireland and Eastern Canada for Cream of the Barley and in Newfoundland where London Dock rum had a dominant position. The potential was limited by the size of these markets but, nevertheless, we managed to double sales in the first few years. It was a useful lesson in the value of market leadership in growing sales and also locking out the competition. The longer-term growth would have to come from the larger markets where the market leaders would be able to contain our efforts. However, being aware of this danger, we decided to pursue the policy but to choose our target markets carefully in places where the competition was otherwise engaged and would not see our tiny operation as a threat.

Not having a distillery gave us the opportunity to claim that we were not tied to using the whisky from our own tied distilleries to keep production at an economic level. We were able to choose the very best for our blend, which was acknowledged to be excellent. Also, because we were cash buyers, we were popular among both the malt and grain distillers. There was enough competition to enable us to negotiate good discounts for new fillings. Gordon Black was our lead man in this effort but we also gave him support as a team by making our presence felt on all possible occasions and establishing our credibility and letting it be known that we were serious players in the industry. One of our wheezes was to turn up in force at the next AGM of the Scotch Whisky Association and each of us to ask a number of pertinent questions. This meeting was usually conducted in a formal manner with little or no comment from the floor. That day we were certainly noticed!

I remember going to see one of the doyens of the industry to try to persuade him to let us have some new fillings in order to gives us a wider choice for our blend. He was George Rattray, then a non-family managing director of Macdonald & Muir. Gordon had said that he had been unsuccessful in obtaining any fillings from the company in the past and I thought a new face might produce a sympathetic hearing. George explained that they did not sell fillings to outsiders but eventually yielded to my pleading by giving me 25 hogsheads each of Glen

Moray and Glenmorangie. This order probably kept us going for a few days and Gordon was right afterall!

In the course of our discussion on the future of the industry George advised me there would never be another successful new brand in the market and so I left thinking that if he was right my colleagues and I were wasting our time. This attitude was quite common and particularly so in the dominant Distillers Company. They controlled about 70 per cent of the industry at that time and could not expect to increase market share profitably. Their tactic was to discourage new initiatives and to block efforts by small companies to expand distribution both at home and abroad.

Canada the Start of 20 Years of Travel

My first overseas trip after joining Stewarts in 1969 was to Nova Scotia and Newfoundland to find out what was happening with London Dock. I was accompanied by Derrick Fillingham, who had handled the production of the London Dock brand at Glen Rossie Distillers in Liverpool. So far as we could find out no one had visited these markets for about twenty years and yet the business was extremely good. London Dock rum was a leading brand in Nova Scotia and the outright leader in Newfoundland. We were curious to find out why we were so successful.

In Halifax we met a charming elderly lady, whose husband had been the agent before his death some years previously and she had simply inherited the agency but was not able to promote the brand. She was well connected and it seems that her friend, the Liquor Commission chairman, had given the brand his support to help her in spite of the fact that he had not met the owners. The great man, a leading lawyer in the city, gave us an audience and advised us to find a proper agent, who could promote the brand and relieve him of his obligation to his old friend's widow. As rum is important in the Nova Scotia market we could see some prospect of growth and gave him an assurance that we would act on his advice.

Halifax is in some ways like Glasgow. It is a major port with a wonderful deep water harbour and we were made to feel quite at home as there was a fine drizzle falling during our stay. We then set off for St John's, Newfoundland, in the early evening of 20 November 1970 in a Vanguard aircraft. This was the equipment used by British European Airways and it was used extensively on the Glasgow to London service. The weather was not good and was deteriorating. The captain warned us that we might be delayed and we did not know at the time that St John's had a notorious record for fog and sometimes passengers were stuck there for days.

Sure enough the weather became worse and bad news awaited us when we landed at Stephenville. It is on the west coast of the island, whereas St John's is on the east some 500 miles away. We were informed that our flight was being terminated at Stephenville and we would be put up in a hotel overnight and either be flown out the next morning or put on a bus if the airport at St John's was still fogbound. This left us with a dilemma as we had a meeting scheduled with the chairman of the Board of Liquor Control the next morning and our schedule was extremely tight for the remainder of our trip. Moreover, appointments with these powerful men, who ran the provincial liquor monopolies, were not easy to arrange. By chance we met up with two young men equally keen to reach St John's for the next day and we agreed to rent a car together and drive over-night. The weather prospects were not good but we set off in an ancient Dodge with power steering and brakes, which neither Derrick nor I was familiar with.

The young men took the first two turns at driving and I was last at the wheel after about four hours. By this time I was half asleep and when I started to drive I found that all I could see were dozens of little lights dancing before my eyes. It was not long before the rather anxious young men took over again and drove the rest of the way to St John's. We had a brief stop at Gander airport, which was still being used as a stopover on the Atlantic route, although the jets, with their longer range, were beginning to take over. It was magic to be at Gander as it had become famous during WWII as a staging post for American bombers being ferried across to Europe.

The journey was really scary because the fog kept swirling across the road and one never knew when a moose or caribou might run out in front of us. Nevertheless, we arrived in St John's having completed the journey in 10 hours. After a shower we presented ourselves at the Liquor Control office five minutes early. The chairman and his staff were astonished to see us as they all knew that the airport had been closed since early the previous day. I believe our effort did us a lot of good and established our credibility without the effort we were anticipating. Liquor monopoly staff never liked new people and tended to make things a little difficult in order to test them out. There was none of that for us and our business received their full support from then on.

London Dock in Newfoundland we discovered was a cult brand. The consumer preference was strong and had been sustained over many years without too much encouragement. Some years later, when I was a non-executive director of the Clyde Port Authority, I attended a world port conference as one of the Clyde's representatives. By luck I was seated for lunch next to the CEO of the St John's Harbour Board and mentioned my connection with London Dock. He suddenly lit up and talked about the brand more enthusiastically than I did. He told me that one Christmas stocks of the brand ran so low there was a possibility of running out. Apparently the chamber of commerce raised the matter at one of their meetings to see what could be done about the shortage. The crisis passed without a complete disaster but everyone had to be careful until the next shipment arrived!

It was no wonder that once we began to give some support to London Dock that we found the sales began to increase and it reached a higher plateau. There was really no demand outside the Atlantic Provinces and as we grew in size it became more difficult to devote much time to the brand. Eventually the Liquor Commission asked if we would agree to hand it over to them for local bottling leaving us with the supply of the rum spirit. This we happily did and London Dock survives into the 21st century.

Canada became a priority for our efforts and we introduced Cream of the Barley to Ontario with the help of the wonderful Les Lyons and also to British Columbia. Les had had a successful career in the motor industry and had taken early retirement to start an agency business. He made good progress in collecting various brands including an imported beer described to me as a licence to print money it was so popular. He taught us a lot about how to deal with the liquor monopolies and it was a joy to see him operating on the various calls we made together. He had real style and was an elegant salesman. He became a good friend in retirement after he moved out to Calgary.

At this time I met up with Tom Fogden, who had not long retired from being managing director of IDV in Canada. He gave me a very helpful background of the trade emphasising the need for regular contact with the outlets to verify that your brand was being given display and was never out of stock. He related the classic method of selling into bars. As everything was controlled by the provincial monopoly, you could not take an order but had to persuade the manager to stock your brand. In a bar the best method of doing this was to appear at opening time when the barman was setting up the spirits on the optics. If your brand was not there you would say to the barman that you really felt poorly and must have a Cream of the Barley, a Teacher's or whatever your brand was. He was then obliged to go down to the cellar and bring up a bottle and, of course, it was there for the day. If he had none in stock, you would urge him to place an order. As you can imagine, this was very labour intensive and it was difficult to persuade a sales agent to spend time doing that when his reward in commission was very small for a developing brand. Nevertheless, Les stuck to the task and made some useful progress.

British Columbia started well but the local agent was too impatient and over time we had to abandon the market. We had long and very fruitful talks with a well established company in San Francisco with a view to starting in California. The company was Balfour Guthrie, who wished to expand their trading operations into imported liquor. They had been a substantial company in the late 19th century when they were a major supplier to the men prospecting for gold in the north west. They were owned by a British company but a change in top management of the group caused them to abandon the project. That was a disappointment to our two teams, because we reckoned we had a very practical plan to introduce Cream of the Barley to the San

Francisco Bay area and sustain a suitable effort over time. We met the new boss but he turned out to be young and ambitious for quick results and we were politely shown the door. I suppose the compensation for this setback was that I became captivated by San Francisco and tasted abalone steaks for the first time American style! Later I tried them when on holiday in Japan with my wife Fiona and discovered that the shell fish, a great delicacy, was extremely tough to eat and sold at 'market price'. The dinner cost so much that we spent the rest of the holiday eating noodle soup for lunch in workers restaurants! In California they batter the creature until it is tender.

The European Continent

Another of our important customers was the famous French retail wine chain of Nicolas. We supplied own label Scotch and it was profitable business. All of us played a part in servicing their needs and I went to visit occasionally with our sales team. I was stopped in my tracks one day when one of our young executives, Tom Cotterill, said he would like me to address the Nicola annual sales conference "in French"! I am totally useless at any foreign language, although, like many, I did mandatory French at school. Tom reassured me that all would be well and he would write out what I should say. Having rehearsed the text and read a translation, I duly delivered the speech. I suppose it was worth making the effort to gain goodwill but I wasn't entirely confident that the French were not trying to have a bit of fun. Afterwards Tom seemed impressed and I could not think why. "Where did you acquire that perfect accent?" he said. I then realised that our French teacher, Mr Shaw, at school had done a good job without much talent to work with. I think it was on that occasion that we had dinner with a wealthy young man who was a son of the owner. He talked a lot about the restaurants in Paris and left us with our months hanging open when he described eating in one where the bill was £25 per head. At that time we were used to an expensive meal costing about £5!

We had another French importer for Cream of the Barley, the Camus cognac company, but we found them difficult to motivate, although our brand did have a place but behind their cognac, which they had to work hard at to do the business. France was also one of the few markets to sell Curtis Scotch bottled in Scotland and the importer was the family cognac business of Jacques Hardy. He was an engaging character and tried hard with our brand and managed to find some loyal customers willing to take a good Scotch at a competitive price. He was a keen fisherman and Derrick Fillingham, himself no mean exponent of the art, arranged an annual visit for Jacques and friends to fish on the Tay. As you will gather, we developed friendships with many of our overseas customers and this made tiring trips overseas quite bearable.

Another customer for Curtis was the Swedish monopoly where Curtis gin had a listing. The story of how this was obtained was buried in history but it was good business fostered by a delightful agent who had been a Davis Cup tennis player in his younger days. He had influence and regularly played tennis with the old Swedish King and was clearly well connected. This was probably responsible for the listing originally.

In Norway there was one of the classical old-fashioned agents who had been trained by his father and sent to all the principal producer areas of the world and acquired a fund of knowledge about the products he acted for. He was Arne Kolby and was the perfect gentleman, a man of integrity and well respected by the Norwegian monopoly as well as his trade contemporaries. He contracted Alzheimer's disease in retirement and died in 2002. I still keep in touch with his wife as I do with a few other widows and occasionally see them on overseas trips. They were all such nice people as well as being good and energetic agents. I am always curious to know if the modern system on selling overseas is any more efficient but am unlikely to be able to compare the two!

We were able to build a reasonable business in Denmark for both Curtis and Stewarts but it was never going to be large in such a competitive market. Like other Scandinavian countries, Denmark was a big consumer of akvavit and Scotch was largely stocked for tourists and wealthy Danes who liked to buy at the lowest price available. However, we shipped a fair number of containers over the years.

The Nordic markets were a priority for us because they were comparatively small and we could cover them with limited manpower. They were not important for the big brands and we could apply some innovative ideas to them without being noticed too soon by the top managements of the large companies. This led us to complete our listings in the northern countries by seeking a listing with the Finnish Liquor Monopoly where selling was next to impossible. No displays of products appeared in the liquor stores and very limited advertising was allowed. For us this was impossibly expensive and so we had to find someone who would devote some time to obtaining a listing with our backing and be prepared to work hard to build distribution among the stores. After quite a short time we found a delightful man, Martti Pokela, who with his wife Marjatta ran a small agency business. She had inherited it from her father and Martti helped her part-time, spending the rest of his time on music. He was a famous exponent of Finnish folk music and had a grant from the government to research old songs from the past. He was a master of the flatbed string instrument called a kantela, similar to the zither but with only five strings. He with Marjatta and their daughter Eveliina made many recordings of delightful songs and tunes. The voices sounded like the angels, they were so pure and tuneful!

We were fortunate in gaining a listing and in order to encourage the support of the monopoly we agreed to take on the British agency for Finlandia vodka, which was beginning to appear on the international market. The monopoly export manager was not well versed in marketing and we had some frustrating exchanges about how they must tackle the job of creating awareness among consumers so that they would ask for the brand. He and his bosses assumed that, as we were owned by a large brewery with many pubs, all we had to do was to stock all our pubs with a case and we would sell thousands of bottles. Oddly enough the same principal did not apply to the Finnish liquor stores for Stewarts Scotch! The business did not survive for long although all involved on both sides put in a considerable effort.

Italy was an important development market for Cream of the Barley. Sales of Scotch were growing and we were fortunate to have as our importers the firm of Illva di Saronno, which produced the world famous almond drink Ameretto di Saronno. They had an active import division but it needed constant attention in order to maintain a high profile for Cream of the Barley in the minds of their salesmen. On one occasion, Simon Sanders, one of our bright young executives, fluent in Italian, decided that it was imperative that he addressed the annual sales conference although he had pressing priorities in other markets. He solved the problem by flying to Milan, addressing the conference and flying back the same day.

Canada, Ireland, Britain, Scandinavia, France and Italy were the mainstay of our sales for our small brands and gradually the business began to grow. However, progress was slow in the face of stiff competition. The large brands enjoyed the main share of the growing export trade in the larger markets where they were firmly established and had plenty of funds to support their marketing efforts.

Company Performance

One of the rather awesome tasks of managing directors in the division was to attend and report your company's bid for advertising expenditure as part of the budgetary process. Francis Showering chaired these meetings and he had around him the accountant and other divisional experts to support him. Basically his aim was to avoid wasting money on fruitless schemes and he wielded a sturdy axe. His methods were rather arbitrary and if you were not careful you would be left with inadequate promotional funds. At one meeting when I was quite new he tried to slash the Stewart advertising and I resisted. This prompted him to remark, 'Mr Blanche, if you cannot do with less you shouldn't be running this company'. Taking leave of my senses, I responded by saying that it was a matter of record that we had increased our gross profit after advertising consistently over the previous three years thus adequately justifying the expenditure. No one had dared to contradict Francis before. Happily he backed off but he set the gossips buzzing in Shepton Mallet afterwards when it was thought that either things would not be so difficult in future or I would be out of a job!

On another occasion I turned up about five minutes early for the advertising meeting to find no one in the anteroom. Thinking they must have started early, I knocked on the door and went straight into the boardroom. Everyone was sitting around the table and all went quiet as I entered. I walked right round the room looking for a seat but there was none and it was only then I realised that this was a board meeting obviously called before the Advertising one. I could only apologise and walk out. Not one word was uttered by anyone else!

The seventies was a time when business planning came into vogue and, given that we had a tough job, we reckoned that at least we should define our aims and set a clear direction for our activities. Our first plan was prepared in the early seventies before the spiralling inflation brought about by the oil crisis of 1973. The flow from the UK's North Sea oilfields was desperately small when OPEC imposed a massive increase in price exceeding $30 per barrel at one point from a $5–$10 range. The world economy was thrown into disarray and the UK suffered more than most. Inflation averaged over 15 per cent between 1970 and 1980 and touched 25 per cent in 1974. The stock market collapsed and the FT 30 Index fell to 147 similar to its level in 1945. There were constant demands for wage increases to match constantly increasing prices in the shops. In 1974 Edward Heath's government clashed with the miner's union over wage claims and when he called a General Election was defeated narrowly. During this period many families were purchasing a whole year's supply of food in order to avoid steeply rising prices. At one point industry was put on a three-day week to conserve coal stocks for the power stations.

The results for the first five-year plan were reasonably good. Operating profit exceeded the target and our brand Cream of the Barley increased in volume by 78 per cent and was 19 per cent above target. However, the return on capital employed was well below target at 10 per cent largely due to the competitive pricing of the dominant company in the industry, The Distillers Company. The DCL deliberately depressed prices in the UK in order to keep growing brands in check. This meant that those companies, which had a high proportion of their sales in that market, found it difficult to generate funds from profits to invest in an increase in maturing stocks to meet growth. Continuing low margins were not making future investment very attractive and by the mid 1970s it was clear that a revised plan was overdue. It was time to look for the acquisitions envisaged in the 'Concept of a Third Force' which I presented in 1971 in order to improve the position by increasing the scale of the operation.

The 10 per cent return on capital was not attractive but some of the opportunities for acquisition were not a lot better. Practically none was available to buy at a reasonable price. Whyte & Mackay was bought by young Hugh Fraser for a return on capital of 5 per cent and, although it was expanded under various owners over the next 25 years, it never improved its profitability. We considered Long John but it seemed to have the same problems as Stewarts, although much bigger. The group eventually acquired it after I retired and had a real gem among its assets, a modern grain distillery, which in time would enable Allied Distillers to close the much older Dumbarton grain plant. The overheads and head-count in a small business were too high in relation to the performance and yet the people were needed for the effort required to make progress. The results were slow to come through and it was clear that we needed a bigger business. Later when Teachers joined us we were able to establish a major position in the Scotch whisky industry which we could expand by further acquisition.

Slow and steady progress in the export business is all right for a private company but that is not what the stock market expects from a quoted company like Allied. Stewarts had to play a part in the group effort. We were doing all the right things by building an expertise, making contacts, beginning to ship small quantities and gradually persuading consumers to try our brands. The analysts, however, were always on to Allied to set higher and higher profit targets and managements struggled to respond with short-term results from long term activities. This was impossible but analysts regarded acquisitions as 'OK' for producing profit growth. They were not concerned with good fits and successful integration. As long as the profits grew they were quite relaxed. However, if acquisitions dried up and profits were slowing from existing business, they began to press again. It is always worth remembering that buying another company requires the same effort in the new operation in order to show improved performance across all the measures if the enlarged company is to succeed.

William Teacher & Sons

Acquisition policies were in vogue and Allied had already established a good track record. We had a clear idea what we were looking for and were capable of recognising an opportunity when it came along. All we needed was the luck to find one. Luck took the form of the family business of Wm Teacher & Sons Limited, a long established distiller. They were in need of a capital injection to fuel the expansion of their brand that had reached a new plateau. Investing in ever higher whisky stocks had reduced their cash flow and put them into debt. Seeking further capital from outside would have meant giving up the family control of the business. Far better to choose a partner yourself than to be exposed to the threat of an unwelcome takeover in the future. The company had been founded in 1840 and remained in private hands until it was floated on the UK Stock market in 1948. Even after this major step, the various families, descended from William Teacher the founder, retained a majority of the shares. Thus, they were able to offer Allied the whole of their family holdings leaving the board with the simple task of making a reasonable bid for the balance of the shares. They fitted Allied like a glove and together, with Harveys, gave the wine and spirit division greater power in the market for premium drinks. Teachers quickly became a happy addition with the whole-hearted support of the family members who worked in the business.

The flotation in 1948 had been an immediate success in a stock market where the industry offered very few investment choices. At the time it was in a dynamic growth phase and not many opportunities like it were available in any industry. The shortage of Scotch during WWII left a huge unsatisfied demand and supply was not to catch up until the late sixties. At that point production had outstripped demand and there was strong downward pressure on prices as a result. Teacher's trade was still expanding but margins were depressed particularly in the UK, Teacher's main market. It was difficult, therefore, for the company to produce sufficient cash flow to fuel its growth. This brought the controlling families – Teacher, Bergius, Dunlop and Anderson – to a critical decision point. Typical of this united group, they concluded that they must sell the business to preserve its future and also to preserve their accumulated wealth built up over several generations through hard work and astute decisions.

The top management was made up essentially of family members, who took all the principal decisions. They did promote competent non-family executives, who helped to provide stability and enabled the family directors to exercise their flair for promoting their business worldwide. The key people after WWII were Ronald Teacher, Adam Bergius, Walter Bergius and George Dunlop. Each had a different talent and they made a superb team. The important thing to note is that they were all competent and family. No family member was allowed into the business unless he (no women) had something to contribute and was willing to devote himself to the hard work involved. This probably was a key factor in their success as a family business.

The Teacher's Highland Cream brand was extremely successful in the British market and particularly in the south east of England. This is where the early giants Walkers, Buchanan's Black & White and Dewar's also made their name but lost market share to the newcomers Teacher's, Bell's and latterly Famous Grouse. When a company has over 60 per cent of a drinks market, which is what DCL had in the UK, complacency and bureaucracy can be dangerous. Saving money on advertising, one of the reasons given for the proposed merger of Walkers and Buchanans early in the century, and sales force costs can affect sales and prove disastrous. All these factors played a part in the DCL's loss of market share and in addition, production and financial people dominated the company's management for many years.

When Long John came into the Group at a much later date it might be argued, with hindsight, that it would have been cheaper to buy it earlier when the opportunity arose. On the other hand it would have been an equally slow process to build the business and the commitment would have diverted the group from other more profitable projects. Long John would have been a distraction but Teachers was exactly right. It had a strong brand and the task was to build wider distribution overseas and extract a higher level of profit from it. It proved a real money-spinner.

Teachers joined Allied in late 1976 and began to invest in much-needed stock and new plant for their bottling hall. In a way, the availability of capital long rationed in the family business took away the natural caution of the management, although the investment was well managed. The integration of family and Allied management was successful with Adam Bergius on the Allied Board and George Dunlop at Showerings Vine Products and Whiteways (wine & spirit division). I joined the Teacher's board and relinquished the chairmanship of Stewart in favour of Adam Bergius with me as MD. Although the management styles were different, it did not matter much as Teachers continued to run their own business with Brian McGrath, a director of Allied, keeping a benevolent eye on things.

Changing the Culture

After a couple of years, Francis Showering began to feel the need for an injection of trained marketing people into the Teacher management to give more thrust to the promotion of the brand. After all, the Showerings had brought a sharper focus and greater thrust to Harveys when they took over and so why not with Teachers. Advertising and promotion was handled in a traditional manner without the fuss of the modern-type formal presentation by the agency of its proposal and Francis's views caused a little tension. This increased when he insisted on the appointment of an executive from Shepton Mallet, Nairne Hill, as marketing director. Nairne was rightly a stickler for using disciplined modern techniques and this proved a bit of a cultural shock to Teacher's management used to using their instinctive flair in this area. The new arrangement did not work well and it clearly concerned Francis. No one else seemed to be able to resolve the conflict and it was perhaps inevitable, albeit a little sad, that some changes would be made. The Teacher people knew their own minds and Allied's philosophy was to allow new acquisitions to run their own business but this can only work if there is a reciprocal effort on the part of the company acquired to dovetail with the management needs of a large operation. I do not think that the Teacher people fully realised the need to adapt in this way.

I was not involved in any of this and had no idea what was going on. All I knew was that I had a sudden telephone call one day in March 1979 from Francis asking if I would agree to become Managing Director of Teachers. I was hesitant because I knew that the company was essentially an extension of the four Teacher dynasties, Teacher, Bergius, Dunlop and Anderson and that they were all reasonable people with the best interests of the business in mind. It must surely be possible to sort out the problems. In the event, having consulted Derrick Holden-Brown and Brian McGrath, it was clear that they wanted me to do it and I agreed. It was a thrilling promotion but it brought to an end an exciting ten years with a lot left undone. The Stewarts team worked well together and it was a joy to be part of it. How would things work out in my new role? Teachers were one of the industry leaders and were ten times the size of Stewarts. When things had settled, I mentioned to DHB that Fiona, my wife, had asked if my new salary would be ten times the old one and that I had hesitated to suggest this to Francis! I remember approaching the office each morning for weeks with butterflies in my stomach and puzzling how to take a grip of this awesome task thrust upon me at a few weeks' notice.

There must have been some anxious moments among the staff too about the possibility of major changes after the change to non-executive status of the older generation, namely Adam Bergius and George Dunlop. They had made a good team and had expanded the business considerably. They left a marvellous inheritance but there was the daunting task of dealing with an entirely new set of market conditions. Fortunately I was known to most of the management and they were generous in their willingness to work with me. The next five years proved to be the most exciting for me and I hope for all concerned and was to lead to a Scotch whisky group, which became the number two in the industry. The 'Third Force' concept was overtaken a few years later as a result of even more dramatic events in the industry, which fitted the concept and produced even greater rewards than anticipated.

It is quite difficult to take charge of a company at only three weeks' notice and make a difference in a fast-moving market without demotivating most of the staff along the way. At Stewarts I had about three months to meet staff and think about how I would approach the job. It is also difficult to know what is going on in order to take decisions about the changes required. The Teacher management was willing to make the effort to change and they only needed a lead. My method for solving the decision on strategic direction and communication problems quickly was to bring together with me the three most senior managers to help to communicate to both group level and also with the Teacher managers and staff. They were John Erwin, Robbie Dunlop and Nairne Hill. The four of us met regularly and gradually things began to happen and everyone settled down to dealing with business problems. It worked reasonably well and was accepted as a means of supporting managers in what they were trying to do. The four of us became known as 'The Gang of Four', a reference, I like to think affectionate, to that other Gang of Four, who ran China during the Cultural Revolution!

John Erwin was a very experienced manager and one of the few non-family members of the board. He knew the home trade like the back of his hand but had never travelled abroad. He had been appointed Deputy Managing Director, which helped the family to accept the changes and give the group the reassurance that there was someone knowledgeable to keep an eye on me in case it went wrong! We both worked well together and I, therefore, decided that we would share the responsibility by giving him the job of watching over the home trade business, which was a vital source of our profit for the company. This left me with more time to devote to the export trade where there was much to be done and growth prospects were greater. Adam Bergius had done a marvellous job over the years in increasing the business. With his natural flair, energy and enthusiasm he had taken Teacher's to most places in the world. The platform had been created and it was up to us to build on it.

Improving performance

Although the brand was then ranked number two in the British market, its real strength lay in the south east of England. Along with Bell's it enjoyed an easy premium status, the highest prices on the shelf and over 90 per cent weighted distribution. The result was that we were able to take price increases on a regular basis without finding much resistance. The sales team was well managed and was expanded and strengthened considerably by David Boswell the sales director. I much enjoyed attending their annual conferences and admiring abundant skills of the salesmen which I did not have.

David had established a good rapport with the key UK customers and claimed that he should not invite them to Glasgow to meet me, as they would only expect an extra discount. This was a sensitive area in the market as apart from Bells and ourselves everyone else offered generous discounts to gain distribution in the large supermarkets. Teacher's had a major position in Tesco and Sainsbury's due to its strong consumer franchise in the South East.

These buyers gave us a higher price than many of our UK customers including our own pubs and shops. Their distribution and shelf space were also better, because they earned more profit by featuring Teacher's rather than other brands. This was an argument that the traditional management in our pub group was not ready to accept and resulted in regular fruitless discussions. We did not mind favouring group companies in price but did expect our brands in return to be featured rather more strongly.

Prices in the UK became rather more competitive in later years and we had problems with the odd customer who cut the shelf price below our other stockists. The biggest sinner was the Co-op who were selling Teacher's to consumers at below cost. We naturally protested on behalf of our brand image and our other customers who were reluctant to continue stocking if we could not solve the problem. We then countered by refusing to supply the Co-op, as we were entitled to do under the law at that time. Harveys were in exactly the same position and had also refused to supply. This resulted in a high level meeting with the Co-op top management and happily the situation was resolved.

An illustration of the strength of the Teacher image suddenly hit the press one day when Michael Fagen was cleared of stealing a bottle of wine from Buckingham Palace. The *Daily Mail* reported 'Fagen was arrested after entering the Queen's bedroom and sitting on her bed when he climbed into the Palace a second time.' Fagen told the court that he had a reason for shinning up a drainpipe into the Palace at 11.30pm on 7 June 1982. He was quoted as saying, 'I wanted to show how easy it was to get in. I wanted to prove the Queen wasn't in a very safe position. I was worried about her.' The Queen had calmly chatted with him until the security people arrived and Fagen was taken away. His mother remarked to the press that it was ridiculous to accuse Michael of stealing wine. He didn't like it. Teacher's was his drink! The next day JAK, the cartoonist, had a cartoon of the Queen in her nightgown and crown putting out a bottle of Teacher's and a glass at the front door and saying to the saluting guard 'It saves Mr Fagen the trouble of climbing five flights of stairs!'

On arrival at Teachers I discovered the big programme of investment in whisky stocks and machinery. After the years of struggling to find additional working capital, it must have been a joy not to have to worry. It was available from group simply by asking. There was a close watch on capital expenditure but little or no interest was taken in stock building. It was not something that brewery companies were used to monitoring.

My background as an accountant had made me conscious of the importance of return on capital as a measure of performance in a Scotch whisky company and it was fairly obvious that increasing maturing stocks, which would not be sold for at least five years, would dent the results. From my earliest involvement in Scotch for the group in our consortium company, Wm Grant & Sons (Standfast) Ltd, I had sought to influence this ratio. It was a simple matter to cut the increases in investment and thus cut the interest bill considerably. The important point to remember was that if sales did meet forecasts you would want the stock investment you had cut. A balance had to be struck and ways of covering a shortage found. I soon learned that forecasts did not always turn out as the sales people had hoped and began to relate them directly to the stock filling programme with an input from all parties with the opportunity to revise during the financial year if trends showed we were wrong.

Combined with price increases helped by high inflation and the containment of financial costs by reducing the pace of replacement of machinery and increases in stocks we were able to produce substantial increases in profits for the first few years. The rest of the division was struggling and Teacher's was the darling of Francis from then on. This was a fortunate outcome after the rather traumatic management changes. As I said to Philip Shelbourne, a non-executive director of Allied, when he was sent up to find out how we had produced these results, 'the company had it in it and it was only a matter of disclosing its real profit potential'. It was also fortunate at this time that Raymond Miquel, Managing Director of Bells was also keen to improve his profits and pursued similar policies. He could so easily have undercut us like DCL would have done in the same situation and increased his market share. But his company was quoted on the stock exchange and an improving profit record was good for the share price.

Demand had been strong up to the 1970s but it began to decline and by 1984 it had dropped 17 per cent in five years after a decade of growth. I started at Teachers at the same time as Margaret Thatcher came to Downing Street. I was never a great fan of hers because of her fiscal and financial policies in her first year which made life much more difficult for us. Inflation climbed once more and peaked at 18 per cent accompanied by high interest rates. VAT almost doubled within a short period and the exchange rate rose to $2.40 from something like $1.50. These burdens made things really difficult for export companies as inflated costs combined with a strong currency made it impossible to retain the benefit of any price increases particularly if we were fairly weak in the market place. Overseas, Johnnie Walker was dominant everywhere and in the US, Cutty Sark and J&B held the premium spots in the market. The strong position in the British market, therefore, was our saviour. As we learned later in

Brazil, it was possible to make money under inflationary conditions as long as you were able to index the prices and hold the costs down. It was a tricky business but profitable if you were careful in setting prices and keeping costs below the inflation rate.

Expanding the Effort Overseas

The pace of travel overseas increased and I took a leading role in this activity in order to find out the quality and dedication of the distributors who served us. Normally business travel is expensive as trips are arranged at short notice and flexibility is necessary so that plans can be changed en route. The travel budget increased and I saw less of Fiona and the family. It was all very necessary and I needed to catch up with the problems quickly. The Teacher's brand was in trouble in the USA and the company began to put a lot of pressure on Scheiflin, the importers. They had had the brand for many years and at one time it was the leader in the market after the end of prohibition. However, times were changing and the new post-war brands, J&B and Cutty Sark, had overtaken the longer established names owned by DCL. The relationship with Scheiflin was a cosy one and the families of both companies were very friendly. The new management at Teachers was treated with courtesy but was not encouraged to change very much. We were regularly given lectures on the peculiar problems of the US market and not any great hope for the future.

The US Market

Keith Showering, who by now had become Group Chairman, called me one day to say that he had heard that the Bacardi company were interested in taking on Teacher's in the States and suggested I go and see them. This seemed too good to be true but worth a try as Bacardi was the largest selling spirit brand in the market. I went to see Bacardi and met Bill Walker, their president. This was the start of a good relationship and as so often happens in these cases we became friends and trusted each other. I also met with some of the Bacardi clan and discovered that Bill was the only non-Cuban in the senior management of the US Company. This was to be significant later.

Bacardi Imports Inc, responsible for the US market, had one dominant brand, which accounted for 99 per cent of the profits. Bacardi Rum was the largest selling spirit in the USA and sold around the world. Its worldwide sales were probably in excess of 20m cases. The Bacardi family owned the business, although two of the companies in their group had a small stock exchange listing, presumably to allow those who wished to cash in some of their fortune to do so. The family tree ran to several thousand all descended from Cuban ancestors. When Castro and his communists took over Cuba the family moved their business to Puerto Rico and built a new distillery. They then began to take it international and export the brand to many new markets. I can remember around 1950 my Aunt Isabel producing a bottle and saying, 'how would you like to try this new white rum, it's called Ron Bacardi'. Thirty years later it dominated the international spirits market. The family wealth multiplied many times and the current generation thought it was a licence to print money. Indeed it had become just that and would continue to be if properly looked after. Another twenty years on it remains the world's largest selling brand. All the people we met in Miami in the company were courteous, well motivated and very efficient in their jobs. They were responsible for the largest market for Bacardi and understood very clearly that nothing less than a 120 per cent effort was required of them to maintain the brand's position.

Bacardi planned to broaden its range of drinks and wanted the Teacher's brand to add to its programme of diversification. They saw this as a means of improving growth in earnings and hedging against risks to volume achievements from reduced consumer consumption and increased liquor taxes. They already had some unknown European brands and had recently bought the well-known Californian wine brand Buena Vista. Teacher's was to be the leader in the portfolio and they recognised it as a genuine quality brand. They had looked at the Scotch market with a view to finding a brand they could build into their portfolio and had concluded that Teacher's was very suitable as it had not been sullied by price-cutting or other cheap tactics. It was unspoilt, had preserved its reputation but was going nowhere. They knew it was lagging in the market and calculated that their superior marketing skills could grow the volume in a reasonable timescale. For Teachers the opportunity was too good to miss and we were willing partners. The transfer of Teachers to Bacardi was done smoothly but we fell out with Scheiflin as Keith and Francis were not willing to pay any compensation to them in view of their poor record. I would have been inclined to make a sizeable gesture in lieu of cancelling our relationship. I suppose it was a good decision, as the litigious Americans did not bring an action against us.

Bill Walker, the president, had been asked to join Bacardi after a spell in handling their advertising. Their respect for his skills was such that they wanted him all to themselves. He was a tremendous asset to their decision making and improved and professionalised their marketing effort. Typical of the Cubans, they were very grateful and rewarded him well. He never retired but continued to advise them until well into his seventies. By then he decided he had had enough and went to join his wife Jane who had relocated to her hometown Austin, Texas when he became non-executive. Until then she had supported him wonderfully in his busy life. Fiona and I visited them both in retirement and it was good to see them enjoying a more relaxed existance. Sadly Bill did not survive very long for he died within about three or four years. He had been a dedicated smoker all his life and appreciated his Bacardi and tonic preferably in dark bars with Jane.

We set to work with Bacardi Imports Inc, the US company and their team led by Edwin Nielsen, Chairman of the Board and CEO and African gamehunter, Luis Lasa, Vice Chairman of the Board and Bill's predecessor a real character who admitted to fracturing the English language whenever he spoke, Bill Walker, President, COO and member of the executive committee and African gamehunter, Luis Echarte, Assistant to the President, Robert White, Senior VP Financial and Legal Secretary and General Legal Counsel member of the executive committee, Richard (Dick) Wardell, VP General Sales Manager, Angel Fernadez, VP Marketing, Steven Naclerio, Assistant General Legal

Counsel, Eduardo Sardina, Manager Venture Group, Thomas Valdes, Advertising Manager. You will notice the rather grand job titles given to these people. They were, however, expressive and there was no doubt about the area of responsibility of each one. It is also possible to be able to define clearly the seniority of each executive. For example, both Bill Walker and Luis Echarte were chief operating officers by rank but Bill was clearly senior to Luis, as he was COO of Bacardi Imports Inc and Luis of one of the subsidiaries.

It was an impressive team and it was exciting to work with them. All our top Teacher management made a point of keeping in regular contact with the Bacardi people in Miami. Bill Bergius and I attended their sales conference in Puerto Rico in 1980 and addressed the meeting and were well received. Bill Walker gave the key address in his quiet but very effective style. He was an excellent exponent of the English language. On this occasion he wanted to guard against complacency and invented the cry 'Now we're No 1 and we've only just begun.' To those who told him the brand had 100 per cent distribution, which it had, he said 'No, we do not have all pack-sizes in every outlet!'

Crisis in Brazil

I was appointed MD of Teachers in late March 1979 and spent about four months finding out all about the operations in Glasgow, at the distilleries and meeting the UK sales force. However, I had not yet seen the Teacher subsidiary in Brazil and kept thinking it was time I went to see it. It was a small profit contributor and there were other more pressing tasks at home before I started to venture overseas. That attitude was swept out of the window one morning. When I arrived at the office I was told 'the Brazilian company has run out of money'. I had a vision of this being an open-ended drain on the group's cash and it would suddenly become a major issue for the Allied board with yours truly being consigned to the wastepaper basket! I had been asked to approve of sums of cash to be remitted to Brazil a couple of times over the previous three months and this, I was told happened from time to time to meet increasing working capital needs in an inflationary environment. This time, however, they wanted £500,000 and this really needed urgent local attention.

Scotch was one of the first premium products to achieve worldwide distribution. It first followed the Empire and gradually appealed to foreigners who travelled and took the taste back home. It offered reliability and sophistication because it was imported but scarce. Its authenticity depended on its quality which in turn is guaranteed by the 'Bottled in Scotland' statement on the label. This is still perceived as the real thing in order to distinguish it from the many unknown locally bottled Scotches now sold in dozens of countries. A premium brand will not normally want to undermine its authenticity and reputation by bottling locally.

This is fine in open markets but if import controls make it virtually impossible to become established in a market, there is little point in wasting time with more than a modest sales effort. Import controls come in two main forms. There may be a strict and small quota based either on price and volume or import taxes may be so high that the consumer price is beyond reason. A careful study of the controls in each country will determine what approach is best. Often Scotch whisky is shipped in bulk and more gallons can be imported for a quota based on value and sometimes there is a smaller import tax on bulk imports. This means that together with the lower shipping and local bottling costs, the consumer price will come within range of the domestic products.

Local bottling provides employment and investment and the purchase of bottles and caps locally adds to the economic value of the business making it more welcome than having to fork out foreign currency for the expensive luxury of 'Bottled in Scotland' (bis) Scotch. The highest quality standards used for bottling in Scotland can easily be introduced to the local operation and the resultant product can be every bit as good as 'bis'. Selling at a competitive price will produce higher sales. If it becomes popular the lack of the 'imported' cachet may not matter.

Wm Teacher & Sons Brazil SA

Looking for new markets in the 1970s, Teachers considered Brazil, which is one of the world's largest economies but found the import controls impossible. Importation of blended Scotch in bulk was not permitted but it was possible to ship the malt and grain separately as raw materials! In 1964 306,000 gallons were imported mostly in bulk and much of it was malt, which was then blended with local spirit to produce what was termed an 'admix'. This product could not be called Scotch whisky but it found a ready market with those who wanted something with a taste of Scotch but at a low price. This type of business had little lasting value and because of the low selling price, the margin of profit was tiny. The volume of 'bis' was very small and Teachers concluded that the small market potential did not justify the cost of the selling effort. However, they did find some local partners who had an idea worth trying. They would set up a dedicated Teacher's bottling plant with modern equipment and following the high standards practised by the Teacher's plant in Glasgow. The brand could then be offered as the real thing.

The Brazilian economy was not in a healthy state for a foreigner to set up business and yet the market was there. Economic growth was high due to the abundance of natural resources both mineral and agricultural. Exports were very healthy but so was the import bill and many categories of goods were restricted as well as Scotch. Overheating was a constant problem and inflation was in the hundreds per annum. It seems that this problem was endemic as it had been around since the mid 19th century when foreign trade had begun to grow steadily. To make matters worse, the government decided to introduce a number of expensive capital projects and funded them from foreign borrowing. This put pressure on the currency and exacerbated the inflation problem due to the large interest bill on the external debt.

The decision to go ahead was a brave one but the attraction was the growing number of consumers who had an increasing disposable income and a quality Scotch at a reasonable price would have a good chance of becoming a profitable business and maybe even a dominant market share. After all the Brazilians were spirit drinkers consuming over 40 million cases of Cachaca each year. Cachaca is distilled from cane juice and sold at a low price. Something special would surely appeal to the growing number of middle class consumers. The project was started with the help of a lawyer called Gamma, who introduced the local partners, the Rabinowitz brothers. They were importers and, therefore, understood the myriad regulations involved. They were convinced that a quality 'bis' Scotch would be a viable business and they proved extremely helpful in setting up a local company with Teachers supplying most of the capital.

The project was typical of the innovative approach of the Teacher families over the generations. The present one led by Adam Bergius and George Dunlop was no exception. Adam had flair and had opened up many overseas markets and established good relationships with some very able importers. His over-riding consideration was to inject quality into every action to match the quality of the product.

A suitable site was found in Nova Friburgo, in an area settled by Swiss immigrants, for a bottling plant with a source of good water for reducing the bulk whisky to bottling strength and good access to quality bottling staff. The partners recruited an administrative staff in Rio and a production manager called Jiulio Dessante. He was given a small share in the equity and this seemed to go to his head as he became very uncooperative and tended to go his own way. Teacher's technical staff in Glasgow supervised the setting up of the plant and the installation of equipment. Great care was taken to make sure that the Nova Friburgo plant achieved the same high standards in the blending, reduction, bottling and packaging as the company's Craigpark plant in Glasgow. Production quality checks were carried out through regular visits by Glasgow staff. Later it became evident that an executive from Scotland should be resident in Brazil to supervise the local management and at the same time to become familiar with the Brazilian business practices and problems.

The marketing aim was to present Teacher's Scotch bottled in Brazil as an authentic Scotch. It was of course but as it was bottled locally the consumer needed to be convinced of this. It had to be appreciated that it was as good as the 'bis' product but with a price advantage. The cost savings were not in quality but in lower rates for transportation, import taxes and local labour costs. In the event the market soon invented a new category to distinguish Teacher's from 'bis' brands by calling it a 'Nacional' Scotch. This was a slight disadvantage but simply made it more necessary to convince everyone that it was as good as 'bis'.

The selling campaign was an instant success and prompted competitors to follow the idea. However, Teacher's had the advantage in being first in the market and the others were not brave enough to bottle any of their famous brands locally in the same way. Later Bell's, a direct competitor in the UK market, did follow suit but by that time there was plenty of room and indeed a need for some competition to help to expand the category. The dominant company in the industry, The Distillers Company, did nothing, although they could have taken a brand like Dewar's and enjoyed a share of the market.

The young man who was sent out to represent the company had little experience in general management having been a regional sales manager with the UK sales force. He applied himself nobly to the task but his lack of financial 'know-how' was a severe disadvantage in a market suffering from inflation, which could reach 20 per cent per month! Moreover, he was not able to control the actions of the sometimes devious local partners, who had their own agenda. By the time I came on the scene the financial situation was out of control and no one locally seemed to understand what was happening. The high inflation required to be fed with ever increasing amounts of working capital, which was not being generated by the sales revenue. There was a nine month gap between the first payment of importing costs and the ultimate payment for goods by the retail customers. Credit to customers was often six months but the cost of these terms of credit was not being recovered in the selling price. This is a problem in many markets and it became a crisis for Teachers with inflation so high.

As well as the regular remittances of cash from Glasgow the financial controller in Rio borrowed from the banks but did not seem to be able to convince the sales people that the price should be raised to cover the cost. The banks in refusing to lend any more money had precipitated the present crisis. Although there were other priorities at the time, this one chose itself as number one and I decided to add a visit to Brazil onto my already planned trip to New York to visit Scheiflin for the first time. I set off on my first visit to the company with the only other person in Teachers who had current knowledge of the operations in Brazil, Jack Oliver. He was a very intelligent and experienced export director whose judgement I respected. However, his PPE at Oxford had not provided him with financial 'know-how' and he had not previously been given the authority to order changes in the local management in spite of the fact that he was very wary of the partners.

Teacher Brazil Reborn

On arrival we quickly concluded that a change in general manager was essential and set about the difficult task of finding someone with knowledge of the Brazilian market, who was fluent in the language and could relate to Teachers and what it was trying to do. It was not easy and few candidates were available or willing to risk a change for a somewhat insecure future. Luckily one proved able to fit the job spec and he was Ken Stephen, an Aberdonian, who had spent 25 years in Brazil with J&P Coats and Cargill. He lacked financial experience but he was a self-sufficient manager and we reckoned he could help us to stabilise and improve control of the company's operations. He had a keen wit and was always coming out with some penetrating comment. I remember some of us were discussing foreign investors in Brazil and the failure of Kentucky Fried Chicken was mentioned. Well says Ken, it's not surprising as no one in Brazil eats chicken unless someone has died or the chicken has! It is a little different now.

Ken proved to be a tough but sensitive operator and thoroughly honest. He began to root out some of the bad apples in the staff, some of whom were feathering their own nest. Moreover, he was capable of standing up to our partners while listening to their often very sensible suggestions. The sales force was overhauled and at last there was a chance to shape some strategic aims for the brand now that we had someone who could interpret the market situation for us and be confident that he could carry out new policies and enable us to build on the excellent start made in setting up in Brazil and producing a quality product.

Two further improvements were made to the management inspired by Ken. Jiulio Dessante was persuaded to move on and in his place a young Brazilian engineer, Thalis Kerr Pinheiro was appointed. He fitted in immediately and came to Glasgow for training, and thereafter, became an important member of the management team. In order to deal with the continuing financial management problems we had a stroke of good fortune one day when Ken met up with a Chartered Accountant, Gervase Shorter, who had experience in Brazil and was fluent in Portuguese. Knowing of our desperate need for top rate financial management, Ken persuaded him to join us after consulting me by telephone. It was a risk for Gervase as it had been for Ken to join our rather shaky organisation.

Admittedly the operation had been under capitalised but the expectation was that it would become self-financing in time. There was obviously a limit to these cash injections and we remained concerned that the business may not have a future in view of the fact that inflation continued at astronomic levels. Happily Gervase was able to provide the right financial guidance and the operation was put on a more stable footing in a few months. The result was that the underlying strength of the business was disclosed and remarkably the profitability improved from a loss of £300,000 to a profit of £3 million in a matter of two years. We were able to look and plan ahead, to promote the brand and, with a management team that understood the market and the economy, to implement a number of ideas for expansion of the business.

Innovative Marketing

The first task was to put some money into advertising, which would give the distributors and retailers some support for their efforts and help to expand the brand franchise. Fortunately Brazil was almost unique at the time in allowing the use of TV for spirits and the question was, could we use the medium effectively? We had good luck again in finding an agency with imagination and the ability to persuade us that a campaign could improve sales volume. Teachers were already the undisputed leaders in Scotch whisky and this gave us the opportunity to expand our market sector and take advantage of a growing affluent society. Those with increasing disposable income were potential targets to be weaned away from the native spirit Cachaca. Its sales of 40 million cases dwarfed those of Scotch by about 99:1.

The campaign proposed by the agency was not unique but was new to Brazil and met our objective precisely. Imported 'Bottled in Scotland' Scotch was the prestige drink but it was horrendously expensive and thus sold only in small quantities. Most of the consumption was purchased duty free. Scotch bottled in Brazil styled 'Nacional' Scotch was perceived as somewhat inferior. Our task was to convince our consumers that Teacher's was authentic and that it was the same product and quality as that sold in Scotland. In other words, it was the brand guarantee that was important and the bottling location was irrelevant.

The TV commercial featured Ken Stephen, an authentic Scot, dressed in full Highland Dress. He stood beside a log fire in his Scottish castle and explained the merits of Teacher's in fluent Portuguese spoken with his Aberdeen accent! It was an instant success and Ken became a media star overnight. The brand's sales increased by over 25 per cent and provided the company with an increasing profit trend. A reorganisation of the sales force helped to exploit the opportunity presented by this extra exposure and was a distinct improvement on the experiment with the Bacardi Brazilian company, who acted as our sales agents for a while. That arrangement was not a success and we found, as we did when they acted for us in the United States, that when the pressure was on their main brand they tended to give it priority. Ours would be presented to customers if the salesmen had the time.

Our next project was to widen the range of goods handled and thus make greater use of the sales and production capacity. By far the largest sector of the whisky market (not solely Scotch) was the 'admix' category. Of course it could not be described as Scotch whisky but it had the flavour and taste of Scotch and was an acceptable product for those who did not wish to pay a higher price for the real thing. We decided we had to be represented in this category and the 'Wall Street' brand was introduced in due course. Alongside the whisky other local spirits such as gin and vodka were added and gave the company the chance to become a bigger supplier of goods to the main retailers and increase the time our salesman spent with the buyers. They could devote more of this precious time to the merits of the Teacher's brand, which was such a good profit earner both for us and the retailer.

Diplomatic Activity

One of the limiting factors to a higher volume of Teacher's was the import quota system operated by the government over a range of goods. They were anxious to prevent the import bill rising too fast and resulting in an adverse affect on the balance of payments. However, we were adding to the economy of the country by sourcing many of our materials locally and providing additional employment and our expansion plans strengthened our case. Therefore, we thought it worthwhile lobbying the government in Brasilia for additional import licences.

The British Ambassador was very helpful and arranged to take us to meet with the minister of agriculture. It was an interesting day and I was reminded of the days one read about in history when merchants sought an audience with the king. It would take forever to reach the 'presence' involving moving from one anteroom to another until at last you reached the throne room. It was a sophisticated form of queuing and had the advantage of separating visitors who might be rivals or be tempted to discuss plotting against the monarch if they had common interests. In addition, at the ministry, each room was warmer than the one before so that, by the time we reached the minister's room, we were sweating profusely. One suspected that it was all a ploy to make the visitors feel ill at ease and at a slight disadvantage in the discussion! Our delegation consisted of the Ambassador, myself and Ken and we were received cordially and having been rehearsed by the Ambassador presented our case emphasising the advantages for Brazil as well as stating our requirements clearly and concisely. Whether or not our mission did any good is impossible to say. The minister promised to speak to his officials and politely indicated that the meeting was at an end. Some years later we had another meeting with the Ambassador and it was refreshing to find that in foreign countries our diplomatic service was both accessible and helpful. How much more difficult it is to obtain an audience with even a very junior minister in the UK.

'J T Tachino' and Opportunity missed

As a means to further expansion in Brazil and adding some excitement to our British marketing efforts, we decided to introduce a brand of Cachaca in Europe. The white spirit sector of the market was enjoying explosive growth led by vodka and white rum. If Cachaca were successful, it would give our group another growth brand for the future and a stake in the growing sector of the market. There is very little that is new in distilled spirits but now and again someone succeeds in branding a local drink in the international market. Since WWII this has happened with vodka and then Caribbean white rum. Two brands have resulted: Smirnoff Vodka, produced anywhere and Bacardi white rum, bottled anywhere.

Like vodka and white rum, Cachaca has a strong heritage but it is different from the other two in that it is distilled from sugar cane juice. Vodka is distilled from grain or other materials and white rum from molasses, a by-product of the sugar making process. Cachaca, therefore, has a unique taste as well as a unique provenance. The Teacher's production people led by Mike Cowman, who was an Oxford chemistry graduate, and the marketing team led by Hew Evans co-operated in putting together a new product project, which was taken to test market in Glasgow and created quite a stir in the trade. It was not an easy task to launch not only a new brand but also a new category. It took Bacardi at least twenty years to establish itself as a new product category when rum previously had meant dark rum only. They had determination and sustained their effort over a long period. The investment in sales and advertising can be considerable but it can be very profitable in the long run.

It was not surprising that our new branded drink, 'J T Tachino', came to the notice of the Bacardi company management. It was a threat to them albeit a small one in the short term. Nevertheless they reckoned that some response was required. They redoubled their sales effort in Glasgow and their two senior international officers approached the wine and spirit divisional chairman, Michael Jackaman, and myself for a discussion. We were taken out for a very nice lunch in a quiet restaurant in London and were subjected to a very professional charm offensive. It was suggested that 'J T Tachino' would take years to develop, cost a lot of money in the process and be a high-risk project. We would be far better to drop the whole idea and redouble our efforts in selling the Bacardi brand! Sadly, Allied did not have the patience to at least give it a try after I retired and so we shall never know if a wonderful opportunity was missed. It is perhaps a sad commentary on the constraint put upon quoted companies by a stock market devoted to regular profit growth on a quarterly basis. As I am completing this story I hear that Diageo (formed from Guiness, DCL and Grand Metropolitan) have launched a Cachaca with a budget of £22m so perhaps we shall be able to see we did lose a valuable opportunity. I wish I had been ten years younger because we had the product and the team to have a chance of succeeding.

Ken and Gervase retired in Brazil but sadly Ken died in 2006 and is greatly missed as a friend. I am sure I gave him a hard time in his job but he responded brilliantly if often in an unconventional way. These two can be well satisfied with their work. I know it was appreciated by our then chairman, Sir Derrick Holden-Brown. Ken devoted himself to the game of golf with his new wife Genete and Gervase, keener on intellectual pursuits, does translation work for foreign companies and has begun to write novels. The Brazilian company also provided a good foundation for the Allied Domecq business in the country.

Progress in the US?

To return to the United States, Bacardi set to work with a will. The lines of distribution were overhauled without losing any support from state distributors and wholesalers all of whom welcomed some fresh impetus behind the brand. With Bill Walker's marketing expertise we all felt very confident that his contacts and knowledge would find us a theme that would successfully reach the consumer and persuade him to buy. The US market was too large for us to go national in the most expensive media but there are ways of sectioning the market and testing and gradually widening the effort. Fortunately, Teacher's reputation was intact and the brand was not tarnished in any way by discounting or other short-term schemes. The advertising worked out well and the sales force applied themselves to the task of translating this good start into real progress. No one thought we could expect speedy results but all of us looked for some clear and sustained movement in the volume to encourage greater efforts and justify the time of the highly professional sales and management team.

The expected progress did not materialise and, in spite of an increased effort, Bacardi began to reassess the marketing plan. I think they were very surprised and a little embarrassed that their skills could not crack the problem. At this stage, I suppose if we had said we would put up $10m for a national campaign, they would have jumped at the offer and set to with renewed effort. Needless to say, this was never an option and the best that they could suggest was a discounting plan to motivate the state distributors and justify the time of their salesmen. Teacher's at that time was one of Allied-Lyons's only two premium brands with a presence in the international market and we declined to accept such a move in such an important market and lose the untarnished image earned over several decades without any payback. Bacardi made it very clear that they saw no other course of action and the result was we parted company rather sadly. Later on when we owned Ballantine's it was a different matter because we could position Teacher's as a value brand with Ballantine's as the premium.

Why did this project fail? The principal contributing factor was that the growth had gone out of the market and indeed in the first 12 months of our relationship with Bacardi the sales of Scotch in the USA fell by 24 per cent. This was an unprecedented drop and was repeated in other spirit sectors albeit at lower levels of decline. The Bacardi brand did not escape the trend and it was expected to continue for some years. Shipments of Scotch declined 44 per cent in the ten years from 1978 to 1988 and by a further 37 per cent in the next ten years. By 1998 France had become the top market with USA falling to second. The US consumer had started to adopt a healthier lifestyle and distilled spirits were considered to be a danger to health. Mineral water became very popular and soft drinks continued to grow. There was also a change in fashion. Liquor was old hat and wine started to take its place and grow quite fast but overall the consumption of alcohol declined and has continued to do so. I suppose there was little chance of a revival of a traditional brand in these circumstances and the Teacher's management was not ready to give up an image, which is a necessary ingredient for a premium brand.

Due to the market decline, Bacardi also decided that they must redouble their efforts for their main brand as it was their major profit earner. As one of our colleagues, John Watkins, said at the time, 'it's the mother brand not just for Bacardi Imports Inc but to the family as a whole'. The family was not going to be happy to see the company spend a lot of time and money on another brand that did not produce profit every year. With some of us having had the experience of trying to build Cream of the Barley from scratch it became evident that a team running a major brand did not have the attitude suitable for taking on something smaller. The work is different although no less skilful but the rewards in the short term, i.e. the annual bonus, are not so attractive! The same applies to large companies with many large brands. Top managements will generally be unable to apply themselves to dealing with small brands. They will either sell them or ignore them and allow them to wither.

We were left to reflect on the failure of our change to Bacardi after so much effort and hopes for a break through in an important market. But this was not to be and all we had to take away were some anecdotes and memories of our experiences. On one of my visits to the US with Nairne Hill we decided to make a flying visit to New York to deal with an advertising decision on the spot. The visit was to be short and for one purpose only and I considered that we should try to minimise the cost by taking one of the many bargain offers on return flights available at that time mainly for tourists. The tickets were of the no change variety but the price at £250 was attractive. We had a successful meeting with the advertising agency and Nairne and I returned to our hotel about 6pm New York time for a relaxing drink. I decided to call our group chairman, Keith Showering, who was taking a keen interest in our efforts to revive our business in the States. A few rude words were spoken about the time it was taking for the switchboard at Allied House to answer our call. I think it took me fully three or four minutes to realise that there would be no one in the office at 11pm London time! This was one of the few times when I was able to identify jet lag so clearly. So often one is unaware of its effect on a businessman travelling across time zones from one office meeting to another.

Anyway we set off the next morning for London and Glasgow on our Pan Am flight from JFK. All went well until we were within an hour of London, when the captain announced that Heathrow was closed due to a heavy fall of snow and we were diverting to Frankfurt. He confidently anticipated that the delay would be only about a couple of hours. We landed mid-morning and waited on the aircraft patiently for the word that the snow had been cleared at Heathrow. After several announcements over the next six or seven hours, we were told that there was no prospect of being able to land at London that evening and we were being de-planed and given accommodation overnight. Frankfurt is a busy business centre and it was clear that rooms would be difficult to find for all the passengers of a Boeing 747.

Nairne and I found ourselves in a virtual scrum in front of a reception counter of a hotel that was being renovated and had been brought into service at short notice. Rooms were going to have to be shared if you were lucky enough to reach the front desk before they had all gone. Nairne, with commendable initiative, found us a taxi and we set off for the airport hotel, which had rooms and we spent a comfortable night after having phoned our rather anxious wives.

We had been summoned to join the others at 7am at the airport and we boarded the 747 again at about eight o'clock. London was still under snow but it would not be long now before we were on our way said the captain. Four hours later we were still there and it was Friday. It looked as if our weekend would be spent in Frankfurt airport with only burgers for sustenance. I suddenly remembered that there was a KLM flight from Amsterdam to Glasgow in the late afternoon as I had used it on visits to Holland to avoid Heathrow. By chance I had glanced at the departures board as we joined our Pan Am plane and had seen a KLM flight posted for Amsterdam about one o'clock. On the spur of the moment we decided to abandon our Pan Am flight and try for tickets to Glasgow via Amsterdam. Happily there was room on the flights and we were back in Glasgow in the evening. We had no possibility of having our baggage off-loaded and so we simply told the cabin staff we were off. It turned up a few days later none the worse.

A low cost visit to New York turned out to be very expensive and was a lesson for business travellers, who have to move fast. It is probably better to pay more and have flexibility and less disruption to the travel schedule. The frustrating thing about our diversion was that, if we had been on a British Airways flight, we would have diverted to Prestwick an hour from our homes. On the other hand, it is possible that the airline would not have let us off the aircraft and insisted on us continuing to London. I often wonder if walking off an aircraft sitting at the gate and abandoning your luggage would have been allowed in the days after 11 September and particularly after the disaster at Lockerbie to Pan Am flight 103. The chances are we would have been arrested! Pan Am was a fine airline but sadly it never recovered from the PA103 incident.

Canada

This was an important market and successful one for our brand. A company in the Hiram Walker group, Meagher's Distillery of Montreal, handled it. The president was an engaging character, Gerry Levesque. He was a powerhouse and was well liked by all in the trade including the officials of the provincial Liquor Boards. His name Levesque is French for bishop and he used to leave his friends with a little hand sign imitating crossing not himself but you! Canada was one of the first markets to be opened up for Scotch and, being a Commonwealth country, it was a welcome import. However, like the USA, the consumption declined and it fell out of the top market list. Teacher's had done quite well and enjoyed a top five position in a market dominated by DCL, J&B and Ballantine's, owned by Hiram Walker. It was difficult to be sure that Hiram Walker gave sufficient support to the sales effort for our brand and there seemed to me to be a need for a stronger thrust behind it. I felt that this would be an opportunity to try to bring all the Allied brands under the same roof with a dedicated sales team who knew the market. Doing this from scratch was not an option but with Hiram Walker as a partner it would make sense. Listings with the provincial monopolies was the important and obviously essential element in marketing liquor in Canada and working with a competitor was not such a risk if they were friendly and wanting to outpace the competition.

It is perhaps worth going over the project as it is an example of the sort of problem that faces exporters, who do not have a big enough portfolio to justify their own sales and marketing organisation in the larger markets. The Canadian market was restricted by provincial control of the importing and retailing of liquor and it was fiercely competitive. Moreover, Hiram Walker (Ballantine's), International Distillers & Vintners (J&B) and The Distillers Company (Johnnie Walker) dominated the Scotch whisky business. They had a broad portfolio of brands and a series of strong experienced sales forces. Teachers had some advantage in the support of Hiram Walker as long as we were not challenging Ballantine's, the market leader. The Meagher's Distillery Limited was owned by Corby Distilleries Limited, which in turn was 52 per cent controlled by Hiram Walker. Meagher's earned most of its profit from Canadian spirits and imported wines. It had an import portfolio, which included Teacher's Scotch, Beefeater London Dry Gin and Moet & Chandon. Beefeater was a big brand and its chairman, Norman Burrough, was on the Corby board. It, therefore, received a lot of attention from the Meagher's management. Another company in the Corby group handled Courvoisier Cognac, the market leader.

In order to bring greater priority to Allied brands, it was clear that we needed our own dedicated team of salesmen. Two of our brands, Teacher's and Harvey's, were big enough to contribute substantially to the cost but we needed more brands. Harveys, by coincidence, were dissatisfied with their agents, IDV, and agreed to look at the possibilities and the other smaller brands joined in. The main task was to persuade Hiram Walker that they could have all our brands if they were willing to enter into a joint venture and contribute some of their own non-competing brands. Meagher's would have to lose Teacher's but Corby could be the home for the joint venture, thus keeping it separate from the main part of Hiram Walker.

I therefore decided to approach Roger Lachappelle, President and CEO of Corby Distilleries, which owned Meagher's to suggest setting up a separate operation to handle Allied's brands if they could be brought together. Roger was a delightful character whom I had met on several occasions. He talked incessantly and I had always found it difficult to get a word in edgeways! I thought long and hard as to how I could gain his attention for long enough to enable him to take in the significance of what I was proposing. Eventually I wrote a one page summary of what I had in mind and then recorded it on my portable dictating machine the night before my meeting with him.

The next morning, after our greetings and enquiries about our colleagues, I invited him to listen to an idea and turned on my machine. He was all attention and never said a word until it was finished. He had in a few minutes understood what I was on about and liked the idea of attracting to his operation more Allied business. He suggested I put the idea with his support to his boss Cliff Hatch Jr. I was in any case going to see Cliff in Windsor and when I put the proposal I found him very receptive. Happily the more difficult task of persuading the other Allied companies to join in turned out to be much easier than I had thought it would be. The result was Wm Mara Company jointly owned by Corby and Allied-Lyons. This joint venture was overtaken months later by Allied acquiring the whole Hiram Walker group. Wm Mara was useful when trying to persuade the competition authorities to agree to the acquisition of Hiram Walker by a foreign company.

Australia and Pacific

Australia was the other Commonwealth country, which was an early market to import Scotch. It has continued to be an important contributor to the export business in spite of some decline and the tendency for Australian wholesalers and retailers to cut prices. Teacher's had done well over the years thanks to the work of the importer and distributor, Tucker & Co. When I went there for the first time I was greeted by Tim Halstead, their managing director, who was one of the old school of agents rather like Arne Kolby in Norway. He was a nice, courteous outgoing character and made sure that his principals were always well received on their visits. You were entertained and shown around the market to meet customers. If business had to be discussed it was done as quickly as possible so as to leave plenty of time for the golf course or whatever else you wanted to do. If you went away happy and trusting that a good job was being done, then that was success for both principal and agent. That left him to meet the next one and so on. However, you could never be sure that the effort demonstrated on your visit was kept up when you left.

Tuckers had been dedicated to Teacher's over the years and had established the brand in the Eastern states where the market was, particularly in New South Wales. When Allied took a substantial stake in the Australian brewery group Castlemaine Toohey there was pressure in 1982 for the brand to be transferred to their wine & spirit company based in Melbourne. I was against this and so was Tucker naturally enough. After all they had done the work and were selling Teacher's at a premium in a market that was devoted to low prices. Even some of the bigger brands were discounting in order to achieve volume, although not profit. With much effort I persuaded Tim to agree that we could appoint Castlemaine as the Australian importers while Tucker remained distributors in New South Wales where about 75 per cent of the sales were made. This avoided an edict from on high to change and preserved our position in the most important area of the market. Tucker's profitability was preserved and gave Castlemaine the opportunity of demonstrating their abilities by growing the other areas if they were any good, which I doubted. In the event, Castlemaine failed to make any headway and started to persuade us to discount the brand. We refused and they decided unilaterally to withdraw sales support for the brand just before we embarked on a TV advertising campaign. Not content with this heinous crime they proceeded to give us an ultimatum saying we must discount or we could withdraw the brand. Needless to say we declined and left them to think about it. The next event in the saga was the matter was referred by the Castlemaine group chief executive to our group chairman, Derrick Holden-Brown and I was summoned to the presence to explain, with the implication that the crime was ours not theirs. I remember being very angry, explaining the situation and saying that the Castlemaine actions had been quite the worst of any agent in our experience. Derrick, always the master conciliator, calmed me down by replying that of course there are always two sides to any argument. There were further efforts by Castlemaine to retain the brand but there was no way our team would be able to trust them in the future and we happily transferred the full responsibility back to Tuckers.

Under the management of a new generation headed by Robert Hirst, Teacher's made further progress and was performing better than other major brands. The premium price policy we had held to enabled us to support our brand and provide a good profit incentive for Tuckers. No other Allied brand did well in Australia and this was further evidence of the benefit of having a determined and dedicated distributor. The same result can be achieved by having your own company but the effort has to be equally strong.

Japan

Our brands sold in other markets in the Pacific area but there was no outstanding opportunity except perhaps Japan. This market had been very restricted for years due to the discriminatory excise taxes on imported spirits. Japan had a thriving domestic spirit sector mostly cheap schochu and the very creditable Japanese whisky made to a high standard and consisting of local Japanese whisky blended with Scotch malt. The locally produced products enjoyed a preferential lower rate of excise duty and the Scotch Whisky Association had been pressing for the abolition of this practice as it contravened various international agreements. These efforts were beginning to pay off and all the big Scotch brands were taking a closer interest in the market. Teachers had been successful in persuading one of the largest Japanese trading companies, Marubene, to take on the distribution of our brand and had negotiated a fairly tight contract.

The terms were starting to look very costly for us and I doubted if we could sustain the investment required over the years without any real progress in growing volume. I set off to see if it was possible to renegotiate thinking that, with the Japanese reputation for tough dealing, there was not much hope. Imagine my surprise when they immediately agreed to put the contract aside as it was not now appropriate in the light of market conditions. It turned out that Japanese companies saw contracts as simply an expression of intention and did not feel bound by them if circumstances changed.

During this first visit my two colleagues and I were escorted everywhere by a bright young man who spoke perfect English and insisted on giving us all western nicknames. Any attempt by us to make complimentary references to Japanese culture or offer a few words in Japanese were met by a very frosty response. They wished to penetrate our culture and keep us at a distance regarding theirs. I was quite tired of travelling by this time and the attentions of this guy began to annoy me intensely. He was with us all the time and kept us going from morning till night bringing a fresh team out in the evening in order to keep up the pace.

We were taken around numerous bars, all of which seemed to be in ten storey buildings in narrow back streets. Each bar we visited had Teacher's as its sole drink. It was a Teacher's bar. I discovered that the deal was a year's contract for which we had to pay up front a fee for the exclusivity, which left us at best with a break-even at the end. The likelihood was that some other brand would come along and offer a higher fee and we would not be able to renew. The advantage was supposed to be the ability to create awareness and trial among consumers and gradually the brand would be in demand. I had one drink, Teacher's and water and found to my horror that the water was heavily chlorinated and the drink tasted foul and certainly would not endear consumers to our brand. Fortunately we were able to persuade the Marubene management that a different strategy was worth considering.

Much later Suntory, the giant Japanese whisky company, did a share exchange deal with Allied. They acted for Harveys and Hiram Walker's Ballantine's. Ballantine's was the lead brand and it is probable that by now Teacher's is no longer in the market. We made an attempt to introduce Stewarts to the market and with the help of a friend shipped a few containers including an exclusive Scotch for one of the major hotels in Tokyo.

Other Travels

In my first year at Teachers I managed to visit seven overseas markets and set some changes in hand. Progress was being made in USA, Canada and Brazil but the European markets were not very satisfactory and obviously needed more attention. I was able to devote more time to the continental markets although I never visited the smaller ones as there was never time with all the commitments at group and the various essential management meetings in the company. I did however go to Malta on holiday one year and met a delightful man Alfred Manduca, a long-serving agent of Teacher's. The story goes that his father met Ronald Teacher, a past chairman of the company during the war when Ronald was in the navy. They got talking and Manduca senior said one day as they were enjoying some shooting of birds, not Germans, that he owned half the island. Ronald responded by saying that he owned half the Scotch whisky industry. The Manducas became the Teacher's agents and were extremely loyal and successful in a limited market.

An Allied Spirits Group

Teachers and Stewarts were now working in tandem and we were able to cover the whole spectrum of the industry with brands to offer in most Scotch categories. When United Rum Merchants was added, we could offer four spirits having set up Nicholson's gin distillery in Glasgow about the same time. We were keen to extend the range to cognac and vodka, drinks that we could understand and which would compensate for the decline in spirits consumption by having a wider range. We had a look at a small cognac business but it proved unattractive and when Hiram Walker joined us there was Courvoisier, a leading brand.

Later we tried to buy the prestigious Janneau Armagnac. We saw cognac or armagnac as a logical addition and Janneau was the only brand with an international presence likely to be available. We had been approached by a French bank to see if we were interested and immediately made contact. I had trained with a demobilised serviceman apprentice, John Drylie, who did a three-year apprenticeship in accountancy compared with my five-year one having come straight from school. John had qualified and immediately took a post in Paris. He had been shot down during the war and had been sheltered by the maquis until escaping and loved France. I called him and asked if he would help us with an investigation into the Janneau company and particularly their financial profile. We had several meetings with the family accompanied by Michael Jackaman and established a very good relationship. They were keen for us to make an offer and there was no one else in sight. The only problem as we saw it was that Martell, one of the leading cognac houses had a 30 per cent holding in the family company, and we expressed some doubt that they would sell to us. Pierre, the head of the family, was quite confident that he would persuade them and we agreed that he should try. Predictably, they refused and planned to buy the company themselves. That was the end of that one although I did have some contact with Pierre afterwards, as he had been intrigued at my name. Apparently he had had a girlfriend in his youth called Violette Blanche and he was determined to show me her house! I never did see it but had a pleasant exchange with him.

We did manage to secure a vodka when we became involved with Stolichnaya. Teacher's had a rather privileged position in the Soviet Union at the time, as we were the preferred brand in the exclusive shops reserved for politicians, diplomats and civil servants. The business was good and had been looked after very well by Ronnie Anderson, one of the original Teacher family directors. He introduced me to the head of the Soviet import organisation, Mr Kairuk, and I signed a contract to distribute Stolichnaya in the UK. Later I signed a new agreement with his boss, which gave us a better status within the organisation. Afterwards he gave us a celebratory lunch in one of Moscow's best restaurants but we had no vodka with it. Gorbachev had recently introduced a measure to cut down alcohol consumption by decreeing that no alcoholic drink could be consumed before 2 pm. This was followed by a renewal signed by Mike Cowman who later became MD of Teachers. It will be obvious that the Soviets loved bits of paper with autographs, as they seemed to give them greater status with their political superiors.

On another visit by contrast we were invited to see round the distillery in Moscow and were plied with a series of vodkas in the sample room. Our hosts were clearly enjoying the opportunity to drink without restriction and were intent on drinking us under the table. We resisted as politely as possible and survived for another day. The distillery was a wonderful old building dating from the late 19th century. The machinery looked as if it might have been installed at that time and it was very much under utilised. We discovered that the spirit was first distilled in Ukraine and brought to Moscow and redistilled. This was to avoid redundancy but it also perhaps compensated for the slightly inefficient plant and thus maintained the high quality of the drink, which is distilled from grain.

After my retirement the contract was terminated after some useful progress. There was frustration on the part of the Soviets that we were not progressing fast enough and on our part because whenever we put in an order for more containers they were out of stock. The Soviets had the wonderfully naïve attitude that they need not build a reserve stock ready for shipping but would only produce the vodka when an order came in. The shipping lead time alone was six weeks and the production cycle could be months in addition. Happily Allied regained the brand and have also gained the distribution for the United States. The privatised Russian company is now geared to servicing overseas markets.

Taking an unconventional route we cast our eyes at Inchcape and did an investigation into the possibility of making a bid. Inchcape was an international trader with some overseas agencies in spirits but was in many other businesses. The attraction was their knowledge of many foreign markets and profitable opportunities in them. It could be our distribution arm and could perhaps help our brands to grow. We might even set up joint ventures with other European and North American brand owners. The figures did not stack up and the idea was dropped. However, Inchcape went on to sell off a lot of peripheral businesses and concentrate on overseas distribution of brands in a single sector. They chose cars not spirits.

Allied faced the prospect of striving for years to build a big enough international spirits business which could make money and have growth prospects. We were in the right position to take part in a second major restructuring of the Scotch whisky industry and ready in all respects to make a move. The group had a policy of not making contested bids for other companies for the simple reason that that type of acquisition usually meant paying too much and diluting the shareholders return. Teachers came to us and terms were agreed amicably resulting in a seamless change of ownership with benefit to both sets of shareholders and staff alike. It seemed that it was unlikely to happen again. This view was immediately changed when an opportunity presented itself to acquire Hiram Walker.

Hiram Walker and Ballantine's

Hiram Walker was quite a different animal. The Hatch family, who had built a powerful liquor business over three generations, controlled it. They started in distilling in a small way and gradually acquired bigger businesses until they ranked among the largest in North America. Their brands included Canadian Club whisky, Courvoisier cognac, Ballantine's Scotch, Kahlua coffee liqueur, Tia Maria coffee liqueur and a host of drinks peculiar to the Canadian and US markets. Among the smaller brands is Maker's Mark bourbon, a small volume but high quality product.

The Hatchs are very much an establishment family, who had enjoyed a successful and stimulating life-style as a result of a series of astute investments in the liquor business. Their ambitions were to continue to pursue a stable but growing activity in a field they knew inside out, while taking opportunities to acquire good businesses at a reasonable price without major risk. Stability was a key element in their approach to their business and this suited them and their employees. The full story of the events leading to the acquisition has been told earlier and suffice to say full management control was achieved at the end of 1987 when Olympia & York agreed to sell their 49 per cent of the equity to Allied. The way was open to rationalise its management with that of Allied Vintners.

By this time I was nearing retirement and I was offered the non-executive chairmanship of the new Scotch company to be called Allied Distillers. I was delighted to remain close to the new company as I had been involved, together with others, in building and expanding the Allied spirit business for 18 years from the development of the 'third force' concept to its final creation. At this point the chairman asked me to set up an Allied operation to promote investment and trade with the communist countries particularly the Soviet Union and China. So I set about putting a small team together to bring us to the notice of the ministries in Moscow and Beijing.

David Jarvis from Harveys was appointed managing director of Allied Distillers and took on the tricky task of integrating the Teacher group and Ballantines. The Teacher companies had been used to controlling all activities from distilling through to selling worldwide, whereas Ballantines in Dumbarton were responsible only for production. Their marketing and selling was carried out by a separate office in London, which reported directly to the Canadian management. The Dumbarton people were the experts in Scotch whisky and were left to run the business with little interference. The sales operation in London handled all the Hiram Walker brands but unlike Teacher's, a similar operation at Horsham, it reported directly to the CEO of Hiram Walker in Canada.

Fortunately David Jarvis was an able and strong manager and it was not long before full integration was achieved in the management, which was a nice blend of the Teacher and Ballantine people. Thereafter, administration and blending and bottling activities were concentrated in Dumbarton resulting in significant cost savings. The facilities in Dumbarton were the Hiram Walker office, grain distillery, small bottling hall and the modern facility at Kilmalid, just outside the town. In addition Teachers had the United Rum Merchants bottling plant in Dumbarton.

Kilmalid was a large site with a lot of spare land and was ideal for accommodating all the activities, except distilling. A major investment would have been required to achieve this concentration but the improvements in unit costs and overall efficiency would have been well justified. In addition, the distillery at Dumbarton could have been closed within a short time when the Long John distillery in Glasgow was acquired from Whitbread. A considerable area of land would have been freed for redevelopment, including a strategic site in the centre of the town. This site might well have attracted government finance in the same way as Greenock and thus have transformed a run-down town into a thriving community. The opportunity was missed at the time but ten years later in January 1999 it was announced that the plan to concentrate on Kilmalid would be adopted.

Nevertheless, the company made excellent progress and became a major earner for Allied-Lyons in the next few years. Among its numerous achievements was the granting of the Queen's Award for Export 1994 marking the transformation into the second largest Scotch whisky company in the industry. It was a fitting tribute to the efforts of the people in the business, who had coped with an extraordinary level of change.

Scotland the What?

Often there was fun in the business and one such experience gave us all much enjoyment. We discovered Ken Stephen had been at school with one of a maverick trio namely Buff Hardie. They sang a song in their review called 'Save Us Our Glens'. The words were not about the famous geographical features of Scotland but referred to the distilleries, Glenlivet, Glendronach, etc. I wrote thanking them for the free advertising and sent a case of our Glendronach single malt. The result was that we had several riotous gatherings together and eventually came up with their very own whisky 'The Auchterturra' from an 18-year old cask of our Ardmore single malt, which is situated near Kennethmont, a wonderful dram! The product was named after their mythical village, Auchterturra, which was said to be half way between Kennethmont and Rhyney.

Becoming a Communist!

My own adventures in the USSR and China is another story but it turned out to be extremely interesting and provided an opportunity to meet a wide range of people in these countries which were trying to join the wider trading world. I was fortunate in bringing into the operation two excellent colleagues, Godfrey Linnett and Jim Hubner. The progress we made in creating a strong awareness of Allied-Lyons would not have been possible without their contribution. In addition, for a short while we had some expert advice on the food industry from Hugh Bidwell who became Lord Mayor of London during his spell with us. He brought a fresh mind to the problems and helped us to enjoy ourselves with his sense of fun. We found that the Soviets were inexperienced and everything had to be done through the ministries in Moscow where the ministers, diplomats and civil servants were reluctant to take decisions. There was also little or no legal infrastructure and property rights were non existent. However there were opportunities both for trade and investment and the introduction of Baskin Robbins ice cream was an early success. We tried to lay down a principle of minimum investment with maximum involvement in trade and learned a lot from people in other industries whom we met frequently.

I had time for China before retirement and discovered that trade with the Chinese was much more developed; we were dealing with people who as nation are natural traders. Joint ventures were the normal method used and of course finding the right partners and then establishing a common interest was a tricky business requiring a lot of patience. It would take time and a medium to long-term commitment to a sustained effort to achieve results. I am not sure if Allied was ready for that and even now such efforts are restricted to India which Teachers started to set up in the mid 1980s and is only now producing results. Fortunately new managements have recognised the opportunities and in time China will no doubt follow.

CHAPTER 10

Epilogue

Peter Blance was a fishing skipper and farmer and descended from a family that had lived in Shetland for over 300 years and maybe since the time of William the Conqueror. He was in a sense the first of the recent family to engage in the spirit business having been caught smuggling in 1866. His son, grandson and great-grandson continued in spirits and distilling all their careers albeit in a more legitimate role. A few years ago a group of people, with myself as a small shareholder, attempted to start the first distillery in Shetland thus adding yet another dimension to the economy. Sadly the task was beyond the financial resources available to the promoters but the challenge is still there.

Having been retired for many years after over 30 years in the industry, I was strangely excited about this venture. It follows the success of the Welsh Whisky Company and another in Cape Breton where the Glenora Distillery operates and is the only single malt distillery in North America. Jon, Mark and Robo have started the Easy Drinking Whisky Company to produce blends that are pleasant to taste and are sold in an informal and humorous package. A number of others are innovating in a similar manner and a new area of activity in the industry is appearing. Rather like the advent of micro breweries, small Scotch whisky distilleries have arrived and, if properly capitalised, could become established and play a major role in the further growth of the industry.

As a consequence of the restructuring of the industry many new opportunities for smaller companies are available to create a viable presence in the market. The large groups will rarely spend time on small brand/market opportunities, as it diverts resources from supporting their major brands. They are constantly under pressure from the stock markets to improve performance and the best way to do this is to increase the market share of their key products. All three of the majors are using this strategy, although one hopes that somewhere they are building other products for the long term. This is where a new Shetland Distillery has a chance to make its mark by developing a unique position better suited to fulfilling the demand disclosed by changing consumer tastes.

I wonder what Grandfather John would have thought about these developments? Maybe he would regret that he did not think of it himself. On the other hand he would have found it impossible to gain acceptance for the idea in an economy still dominated by the landlords and merchants who made money from fishing in Shetland. At that time the local government was controlled by the merchant class and did not have the vision of the present day council. Today government policy encourages initiatives of this sort and the economy of the islands is now very broadly based as a result. The task of establishing a new distillery would not be an easy one but if the management is both skilful and determined and it can provide novelty and innovative ideas then it will have a chance of success. If the project can earn the goodwill of the trade here and overseas, it stands a good chance of succeeding. It is a wonderful opportunity for Shetland to have the prospect of an entirely new industrial activity, which could bring new wealth and job prospects not only from distilling but also by attracting many more visitors. It is worthy of support.

Quite rightly the various public bodies in Shetland with funds at their disposal are willing to support ventures of this kind with substantial funds. They will have the tricky task of keeping a watchful eye on progress to make sure that the public funds are being used wisely and that plans are being carried out with energy and imagination. At the same time they will need to avoid inhibiting the actions of management by a too heavy-handed and bureaucratic approach. The management in turn should realise the responsibility they will bear in using these funds for the benefit of the economy of the islands. Although I have no primary interest in these projects, I am keen that these principles are followed and I imagine I shall find it difficult not to voice opinions from time to time!

Grandfather John was born in Shetland in poor circumstances but like all islanders, the family was careful to make sure that their children took advantage of any educational facilities available to them. Fortunately schools began to appear in Shetland in the late 19th century to take the place of the itinerant teachers of the earlier periods. John and his siblings benefited from these educational facilities when they moved to Edinburgh and established themselves in gainful occupations. John struggled to build a business and bring it through a world war and in the process lost seven of his ten children and one of his two wives. The effort is more than likely to have shortened his life but he seemed to have remained an optimist to the end.

The Guinness Trials

The Guinness bid story dragged on for a decade in another direction with the conviction of some of the participants for illegal share trading. In 1990 Ernest Saunders was convicted of conspiracy, false accounting and theft in connection with a share support operation and served a third of his five year sentence at Ford Open Prison. There was some speculation that he had claimed to have had Alzheimer's disease during the trial and was treated more leniently as a result. After his release he showed no signs of the illness and he became known as the only person who had recovered from Alzheimer's. His son, in his book *Nightmare – The Ernest Saunders Story*, said that the story was pure invention by the press and was entirely untrue. However, after the judgement by the European Court of Human Rights in 1994 one of his advisors said at a press conference that the doctor who had diagnosed the disease 'admitted publicly that he had got it wrong'!

Saunders never gave up trying to clear his name. I had thought that he was unlucky to find himself charged with these offences in connection with his leadership of the battle for Distillers. The 1985 Companies Act had applied stricter rules about dealing in your own shares and gave the Department of Trade and Industry powers to compel witnesses to give evidence. The interpretation of the Act was debatable and some years earlier his actions would have been within the law and were common City practice. He had been reluctant to enter the fray in the first place but had been urged on by Distillers and his advisors. As Argyll had the initiative, he was obliged to move fast and there must have been little time for him to make cool judgements on the various stages of the Guinness bid. Olivier Roux and others constantly pressed him for immediate decisions on a daily basis in the fast moving train of events.

When the Department of Trade investigators suddenly appeared in the Guinness office in 1986 he was required under the law to answer a broad range of questions and had no right to remain silent and no opportunity to challenge the inspectors' findings. This evidence was handed over to the prosecution and it was crucial in bringing about a conviction. In addition the media coverage meant that the jurors would know who he was and there was some pressure to find a scapegoat for the departure from what was regarded as a proper and acceptable conduct of takeovers in a City community conscious of the harm to its supposedly good reputation.

Along with Saunders, several others were convicted including Sir Jack Lyons, Gerald Ronson and Tony Parnes. Olivier Roux, who was seconded to Guinness as Finance Director decided to talk to the DTI and was never charged. He would have applied the greatest pressure on Saunders during the battle as he was trusted by him, having been specially brought in to sort out the restructuring of Distillers as quickly as possible in order to achieve an immediate improvement in profits and deal with the huge mountain of shares bought by the firms who had helped to prop up the Guinness share price and raise the value of the bid.

In 1994 the European Commission of Human Rights found in favour of Saunders in regard to the DTI evidence saying that he was 'in effect compelled to incriminate himself' and that this incriminating material was a 'not insignificant part of the evidence against him at his trial'. A year later the Court of Appeal in London upheld the 1990 convictions and this led Saunders to bring the matter to the European Court of Human Rights in December 1996, which ruled that the admission of the DTI evidence was 'a remarkable departure from one of the basic principles of fair procedure'. The court did not suggest that he should have been acquitted but Saunders claimed a partial victory in his quest to clear his name

Developments in Scotch

In the years since my active participation in the Scotch whisky industry much has happened to both the Allied-Lyons group and the industry itself. The group became Allied Domecq with the acquisition of the Domecq businesses in Spain and Mexico thus broadening the base of the operation so that it has the most diverse range of alcoholic products of all the majors. Furthermore Allied Distillers increased in size by acquiring other companies and thus maintained its position as the second largest Scotch whisky company in the industry.

The largest is now known as Diageo and is the combination of The Distillers Company, taken over by Guinness in that famous battle of the 1980s, and Grand Metropolitan, which owned International Distillers and Vintners, itself an international major. This brought the two largest Scotch whisky brands, Johnnie Walker and J&B into the same stable. In addition this group owns an impressive range of other spirits including Smirnoff Vodka, Gordons Gin and Captain Morgan Rum. It is doubtful if any other company can rival Diageo for size, although many have made similar statements in the past only to be proved wrong in 20 years time! However, competition authorities in the USA and the European Union are becoming ever more determined to stop large international companies from gaining a dominant share of market. They insisted on a series of concessions before agreeing to the Diageo merger, the principal one being that the new group would require to sell their Dewar's Scotch brand, which is a big seller in the US. It was sold to Bacardi and so that company managed to find their Scotch after all; 14 years after dropping Teacher's. They might have been better to stick to the job we gave them then but perhaps that is just a dose of sour grapes!

The fourth major of the 1980s, Seagrams, was swallowed up by Diageo and Pernod-Ricard of France, who became number three. A large proportion of the international spirits market came under the control of three companies, Diageo, Allied Domecq and Pernod-Ricard, two of them British and the other French. It is notable that none of the US companies can rival them although Bacardi is bidding to match them with the acquisition of Dewar's and Martini vermouth and Grey Goose premium vodka, which they bought for $2bn in 2004. The Bacardi range of rums continues to grow and vie with Smirnoff vodka for the number one position in the international spirits market.

The Demise of Allied Domecq (formerly Allied-Lyons)

Allied Domecq had said in the past that it intended to take part in the process of rationalising the industry either by acquiring other companies or brands or being acquired itself by another company in the same business. This led to press speculation that Pernod Ricard might consider making a bid. After a few years of talk that is exactly what happened. Pernod was slightly smaller but they joined up with another company of similar size and ambition to them, Fortune Brands of the United States. Both are keen to acquire more spirit brands in order to increase the scale of their operations and thus reduce the unit costs of marketing and distribution.

Allied had few opportunities to acquire others as those that are compatible, such as Bacardi, are tightly controlled by founding families. Pernod is one such company and an agreed bid would not have been possible. Even if Pernod had been a willing seller, the addition of the Pernod portfolio would not have increased growth prospects very much. Allied's core brands are all top quality premium products and doing well, whereas the Pernod range is less buoyant. The Pernod and Ricard pastis brands (aniseed products) are sold mostly in France and have long achieved maximum penetration. Martell cognac competes directly with Allied's Courvoisier and Pernod's Chivas Scotch whisky may have reached a plateau but could perhaps introduce brand extensions. The Pernod wine business, largely Jacob's Creek, is in the low-priced category with most of its sales in the UK. But looking at a combination from Period's point of view, there is no doubt that those brands they will retain will greatly strengthen their business. They will be able to enjoy an attractive cash flow from Chivas without too much investment in marketing or in building whisky stocks. Pernod and Ricard brands will continue to offer regular strong cash flows as they are really part of French culture and fairly secure.

The best option for Allied would have been to join with Bacardi and its iconic rum giving it the ability to take on Diageo. Bacardi has acquired Dewar's Scotch in recent years a big seller in the States where Allied's share of the Scotch market is poor. However, Bacardi is controlled by a series of families descended from the founders and who enjoy the financial benefits of a big cash generating business. Until family shareholders in companies, like Bacardi, want to realise capital there is little prospect of an agreed or hostile bid being launched. As Allied's shareholdings are very widely spread and a high proportion is held by financial institutions, the shareholders are mainly short-term holders and they are always open to realising their shares if a very attractive offer appears. The Allied management has astutely created a good value for the group and the Pernod offer was cleverly negotiated by both sides making sure as far as possible that the interests of all stakeholders were catered for. Thus Allied has achieved its objective of taking part in the industry rationalising process but at the expense of extinction. Allied's story is one of nearly 50 years of sustained growth by acquisition and has come to an end. The company will disappear but its brands will continue to give satisfaction to millions of consumers under new owners. Also I hope that the management teams built up to manage the company will find new and exciting roles. It makes no sense to discard good people, who can contribute enormously to improving performance. The skill in integrating two companies is to motivate the people to play a part in a larger team.

The management of large corporations is now in the hands of a different breed of executive geared to responding to the pressures of the institutional investors, who are not always long-term shareholders. As they hold shares for pension funds and private investors, they are more concerned with short to medium-term profits. They will move on to another profit opportunity without a thought. Recently some businessmen have become openly critical of these institutions claiming that there was a crying need for long-term holders of company shares allowing managements to build their companies on more solid foundations. Having served on the Allied board when it was under attack from a predator on two occasions and repelled them both times, I wonder how my old colleagues would have responded to the challenges presented to the current management!

Growth Prospects for Scotch?

I have speculated, more for fun than with serious intentions, on the continuation of the Scotch whisky industry for the next 30–40 years. As we have seen in the last 30 years living habits have changed and the pace may well increase. Methods of travel will develop and space will no doubt be explored by many people. The way of life may preclude the drinking of alcohol altogether, as everyone becomes conscious of the recipe for a healthy way of life. Who knows? More likely some things will remain constant and change will be restrained by slower economic growth.

One of the key issues that needs to be addressed urgently is to find ways to improve the economic performance of the under-developed countries. They must have access to western markets and be able to contain the influence and the control major companies have over them in their rush to extract mineral resources, for their own benefit mostly. Here Shetland has already shown the way in the agreements it negotiated with the oil companies. Brazil has also succeeded in managing its resources for the benefit of its population with the result that a growing middle class has produced increased spending power and lo and behold – a growing Scotch whisky market! India too is well on the way to matching some of the developed economies. Indian and Chinese economies are catching up and with Brazil they will provide growth opportunities for Scotch whisky in the foreseeable future.

The Core Brand Philosophy

Most of the large international groups operating in food and drink have been slimming down their brand portfolios in order to concentrate marketing funds on those brands that have wide distribution and high margins. This makes sense as increases in volume will produce a faster rate of profit growth and be a more effective use of marketing spend.

This policy will produce results provided there is an effective method adopted for monitoring the performance. Managements, in their determination to make the policy work, may lose sight of the point where extra spend does not produce the desired improvement. There will be an optimum point and recognising it will be important so that funds can be diverted to other projects.

A second proviso is that the core brand policy for managing existing brands should be accompanied by research into new opportunities and the development of new brands. After all, pharmaceutical companies would not survive without research and development investment to find new drugs. Even in the mature spirits market there are still ideas waiting for someone to pick them up and run with them. A good example is cachaca mentioned in the previous chapter, which was not pursued by Allied but has recently been taken up by another company. In this regard there comes to mind Victor Borge's lovely story of his uncle who invented a soft drink called 'Two Up'. It did not succeed but he persevered with 'Three', 'Four', 'Five' and then 'Six Up' all of which failed!

Bibliography

Donaldson, Gordon, *Shetland Life Under Earl Patrick*, Oliver and Boyd, 1958

Barnard, Alfred, *The Whisky Distilleries of the United Kingdom 1887*, Famedram Publishers Ltd, 1983

Bianco, Anthony, *The Reichmanns*, Times Books, 1997

Carter, W Hodding, *A Viking Voyage*, Ebury Press, 2001

Craig, H. Charles, *Scotch Whisky Industry Record*, Index Publishing Ltd, 1994

Fenton, Alexander, *The Northern Isles: Orkney and Shetland*, John Donald Publishers Ltd, 1997

Flinn, Derek, *Travellers in a Bygone Shetland*, Scottish Academic Press Ltd, 1989

Guinness, Jonathan, *Requiem for a Family Business*, Macmillan, 1997

Halcrow, A., *The Sail Fishermen of Shetland*, Shetland Times Ltd, 1994

Howarth, David, *The Shetland Bus*, TBS The Book Service Ltd, 1967

Kochan, N. and Pym, H., *The Guinness Affair*, Christopher Helm Publishers Ltd, 1987

Liv Kjorsvik Schei, *The Shetland Story*, Batsford Ltd, 1991

Linklater, Eric, *Orkney and Shetland*, Robert Hale Ltd, 1990

Livingstone, W. P., *Shetland and the Shetlanders*, T. Nelson, 1948

Lockhart, Sir Robert Bruce, *Scotch The Whisky of Scotland*, The Bodley Head Ltd, 1959

McCulloch, John Herries, *Old Shetland!* Shetland Times Ltd, 1969

McDowall, R. J. S., *The Whiskies of Scotland*, John Murray, 1968

Monopolies and Mergers Commission – Elders IXL Ltd and Allied-Lyons PLC

Morrison, Ian, *The North Sea Earls*, Gentry Books, 1973

Mowat, Farley, *The Alban Quest*, Wiedenfeld & Nicolson, 1999

Moss, Michael S. and Hume, John R., *The Making of Scotch Whisky*, James & James (Publishers) Ltd, 1981

Nicolson, James R., *Traditional Life in Shetland*, Robert Hale Ltd, 1978

Nicolson, James R., *Shetland (Islands)*, David & Charles PLC, 1984

Pugh, Peter, *Is Guinness Good For You?* Financial Training Pubns, 1987

Robson, Adam, *The Saga of a Ship: 'The Earl of Zetland'*, Shetland Times Ltd, 1982

Ross, James R., *Whisky*, Routledge and Kegan Paul Books, 1970

Saunders, James, *Nightmare – The Ernest Saunders Story*, Arrow Books Ltd, 1989

Smith, Hance D., *The Making of Modern Shetland*, Shetland Times Ltd, 1977

Smith, Hance D., *Shetland Life and Trade 1550-1914*, John Donald Publishers Ltd, 1984

Tabraham, Chris (ed.) *The Ancient Monuments of Shetland*, HMSO, 1993

Weir, R. B. *The History of the Distillers Company 1877–1939*, Clarendon Press, 1995

Appendix

OUTPUT AND STOCK COVER (m original litres of alcohol)

Year	Output				Sales	Stocks				Surplus
	Grain	Malt	pf gls	Lpa		Actual	Estim	Cover	Requd	
1850			12	30	27	46	46	2	44	2
1851			10	27	24	50	50	2	44	5
1852			10	26	21	54	54	2	44	10
1853			10	27	24	58	58	2	47	10
1854			10	26	21	63	63	2	50	12
1855			11	29	27	65	65	2	56	9
1856			11	29	24	70	70	2	62	8
1857			13	32	33	70	70	2	62	8
1858			13	35	30	75	75	2	62	13
1859			13	33	33	76	76	2	56	19
1860			13	35	30	81	81	2	59	21
1861			11	29	27	83	83	2	68	15
1862			13	32	33	83	83	2	68	15
1863			13	34	36	82	82	2	71	11
1864			14	36	33	85	85	2	68	17
1865			15	38	38	84	84	2	59	25
1866			13	34	30	88	88	2	53	35
1867			12	31	30	89	89	2	50	39
1868			11	29	24	94	94	2	56	38
1869			12	32	27	99	99	2	62	37
1870			14	36	30	106	106	2	62	44
1871			15	38	33	111	111	2	65	46
1872			14	36	30	117	117	2	74	43
1873			16	41	36	123	123	2	74	49
1874			17	44	38	128	128	2	80	48
1875			16	42	36	135	135	2	92	43
1876			18	46	44	136	136	2	92	44
1877			18	47	47	136	136	2	86	50
1878			19	49	44	140	140	2	80	60
1879			17	45	41	144	144	2	80	64
1880			17	43	38	148	148	2	83	66
1881			17	44	41	151	151	2	86	65
1882			19	50	41	159	159	2	89	70
1883			19	50	44	165	165	2	95	70
1884			20	52	44	173	173	2	89	84
1885			21	53	50	176	176	3	115	61
1886			18	47	38	184	184	3	121	63
1887			17	45	38	191	191	3	130	61

OUTPUT AND STOCK COVER (m original litres of alcohol)

Year	Output				Sales	Stocks				Surplus
	Grain	Malt	pf gls	Lpa		Actual	Estim	Cover	Requd	
1888			18	47	38	200	200	3	142	58
1889			19	49	44	204	204	3	142	62
1890			20	52	47	209	209	3	142	67
1891			21	55	50	213	213	3	139	74
1892			20	53	44	221	221	3	145	76
1893			20	52	47	226	226	3	151	75
1894			22	56	47	235	235	3	169	66
1895			22	58	50	242	242	3	160	82
1896			25	64	53	253	253	3	180	72
1897			29	74	65	262	262	3	115	146
1898			34	87	41	308	308	3	219	89
1899			36	93	74	327	327	4	281	46
1900			32	83	71	338	338	4	272	66
1901			30	78	74	343	343	4	263	79
1902			30	78	71	349	349	4	251	98
1903			26	67	65	352	352	4	248	103
1904			27	70	62	360	360	4	243	117
1905			25	65	65	360	360	4	237	124
1906			24	62	59	363	363	4	222	141
1907			25	64	62	365	365	4	207	158
1908			23	59	56	368	368	4	207	161
1909			24	63	59	372	372	4	207	165
1910			22	58	44	386	386	4	231	155
1911			20	52	47	390	390	4	251	139
1912			24	61	56	395	395	4	260	135
1913			24	63	59	399	399	4	272	127
1914			28	73	68	404	404	4	272	131
1915			27	70	68	406	406	4	272	133
1916			27	69	65	410	410	4	272	138
1917			28	73	71	412	412	4	278	134
1918			15	38	68	382	382	4	284	98
1919			13	34	68	349	349	4	287	62
1920			23	58	65	342	342	4	290	52
1921			29	76	77	341	341	4	284	57
1922			25	64	74	331	331	4	269	62
1923			27	70	71	330	330	4	251	79
1924			27	71	68	333	333	4	234	100
1925			27	71	71	333	333	4	213	120
1926			26	67	59	342	342	5	243	99
1927			17	43	53	331	331	5	225	106
1928			19	49	50	330	330	5	198	132
1929			21	53	50	333	333	5	178	156

OUTPUT AND STOCK COVER (m original litres of alcohol)

Year	Output				Sales	Stocks				Surplus
	Grain	Malt	pf gls	Lpa		Actual	Estim	Cover	Requd	
1930			21	54	47	340	340	5	169	171
1931			16	41	41	340	340	5	172	168
1932			9	24	36	328	328	5	195	133
1933			6	15	24	320	320	5	231	89
1934			13	34	30	324	324	5	244	80
1935			17	44	38	330	330	5	248	82
1936			20	53	44	338	338	5	251	87
1937			25	64	59	343	343	5	233	110
1938			25	65	59	349	349	5	206	142
1939			38	98	43	383	404	5	196	186
1940			14	36	42	397	397	5	180	216
1941			8	21	48	370	370	5	164	206
1942			2	5	41	334	334	5	157	177
1943			1	4	33	305	305	5	157	148
1944			0	0	33	272	272	5	157	115
1945			10	25	27	271	271	5	172	99
1946			14	37	31	277	277	5	184	93
1947			8	21	34	209	264	5	194	14
1948			19	50	33	227	281	5	212	15
1949			25	65	33	314	314	5	233	81
Year	**Output**				**Sales**	**Stocks**				**Surplus**
	Grain	**Malt**	**% Tot**	**Total**		**Actual**	**Estim**	**Cover**	**Requd**	
1950	40	30	43	70	42	291	342	5	253	38
1951	43	33	43	76	43	322	375	5	276	46
1952	45	33	42	78	44	356	409	5	302	54
1953	36	32	47	68	51	382	426	5	327	55
1954	50	35	41	85	53	410	458	5	358	52
1955	61	39	39	100	62	447	496	5	388	59
1956	66	41	38	107	66	483	537	5	427	56
1957	76	47	38	123	71	535	590	5	471	64
1958	82	53	39	135	76	590	649	5	517	73
1959	89	58	39	147	84	647	712	5	565	82
1960	109	65	37	174	92	721	794	6	778	-57
1961	120	69	37	189	105	799	878	6	837	-38
1962	139	70	33	209	114	883	973	6	937	-54
1963	161	75	32	236	122	987	1087	6	1007	-20
1964	201	85	30	286	133	1123	1240	6	1100	23
1965	232	102	31	334	147	1302	1428	6	1207	95
1966	238	116	33	354	158	1486	1624	6	1303	183

OUTPUT AND STOCK COVER (m original litres of alcohol)

Year	Output				Sales	Stocks				Surplus
	Grain	Malt	% Tot	Total		Actual	Estim	Cover	Requd	
1967	193	133	41	326	163	1643	1787	6	1432	211
1968	174	124	42	298	215	1753	1870	6	1544	209
1969	200	144	42	344	192	1888	2022	6	1684	204
1970	222	149	40	371	226	2044	2167	6	1802	242
1971	228	160	41	388	254	2200	2302	6	1903	297
1972	259	176	40	435	253	2421	2483	6	2054	367
1973	272	199	42	471	292	2600	2662	6	2155	445
1974	262	214	45	476	327	2734	2811	7	2568	166
1975	215	179	45	394	332	2813	2873	7	2606	207
1976	195	167	46	362	344	2848	2891	7	2603	245
1977	222	171	44	393	355	2844	2929	7	2591	253
1978	250	209	46	459	404	2932	2985	7	2528	404
1979	255	204	44	459	394	3035	3050	7	2486	549
1980	238	178	43	416	375	3084	3091	7	2467	617
1981	158	110	41	268	365	2934	2994	7	2466	468
1982	151	97	39	248	370	2830	2872	7	2453	377
1983	146	93	39	239	340	2744	2771	7	2462	282
1984	154	99	39	253	343	2662	2680	7	2451	211
1985	156	105	40	261	340	2598	2601	7	2445	153
1986	161	104	39	265	352	2453	2514	7	2461	-8
1987	174	116	40	290	356	2438	2448	7	2468	-30
1988	192	138	42	330	364	2433	2414	7	2470	-37
1989	218	167	43	385	357	2473	2442	7	2475	-2
1990	236	193	45	429	350	2543	2522	7	2510	33
1991	231	186	45	417	333	2604	2606	7	2532	72
1992	217	166	43	383	334	2629	2655	7	2571	58
1993	210	141	40	351	368	2655	2638	7	2589	66
1994	208	146	41	354	363	2662	2629	7	2620	42
1995	236	158	40	394	366	2647	2657	7	2624	23
1996	259	170	40	429	361	2722	2725	7	2644	78
1997	278	193	41	471	385	2848	2810	7	2642	206
1998	258	185	42	443	354	2905	2899	7	2674	231
1999	235	160	41	395	374	2946	2921	7	2687	259
2000	205	141	41	346	386	2939	2881	7	2691	248
2001	208	140	40	348	395	2926	2835	7	2687	239
2002	219	151	41	370	370	2935	2835	7	2710	225
2003	229	147	39	376	381	2948	2829	7	2724	224
2004	229	147	39	377	383	2823	2823	7	2737	86
2005	230	147	39	377	385	2815	2815	7	2751	64
2006	230	148	39	378	387	2805	2805	7	2765	41
2007	242	155	39	397	389	2813	2813	7	2778	34
2008	254	163	39	416	391	2838	2838	7	2792	46

OUTPUT AND STOCK COVER (m original litres of alcohol)

Year	Output				Sales	Stocks				Surplus
	Grain	Malt	% Tot	Total		Actual	Estim	Cover	Requd	
2009	266	171	39	437	393	2883	2883	7	2806	76
2010	266	171	39	437	395	2925	2925	7	2820	105
2011	266	171	39	437	397	2965	2965	7	2834	131
2012	266	171	39	437	399	3004	3004	7	2849	155
2013	266	171	39	437	401	3040	3040	7	2863	177
2014	266	171	39	437	403	3074	3074	7	2877	197
2015	266	171	39	437	405	3107	3107	7	2892	215
2016	267	171	39	438	407	3138	3138	7	2906	232
2017	268	172	39	439	409	3169	3169	7	2921	248
2018	268	172	39	441	411	3198	3198	7	2935	263
2019	269	173	39	442	413	3227	3227	7	2950	277
2020	270	173	39	443	415	3254	3254	7	2965	290
2021	270	174	39	444	417	3281	3281	7	2979	302
2022	271	174	39	445	419	3307	3307	7	2994	312
2023	272	174	39	446	421	3331	3331	7	3009	322
2024	272	175	39	447	423	3355	3355	7	3024	331
2025	273	175	39	448	426	3378	3378	7	3039	338
2026	274	176	39	449	428	3400	3400	7	3055	345
2027	274	176	39	451	430	3420	3420	7	3070	350
2028	275	177	39	452	432	3440	3440	7	3085	355
2029	276	177	39	453	434	3458	3458	7	3101	358
2030	277	178	39	455	436	3477	3477	7	3116	361
2031	279	179	39	457	439	3496	3496	7	3132	364
2032	280	180	39	460	441	3515	3515	7	3147	367
2033	281	181	39	462	443	3534	3534	7	3163	371
2034	283	182	39	464	445	3553	3553	7	3179	374
2035	284	182	39	467	447	3572	3572	7	3195	377
2036	286	183	39	469	450	3592	3592	7	3211	381
2037	287	184	39	471	452	3611	3611	7	3227	384
2038	288	185	39	474	454	3630	3630	7	3243	387
2039	290	186	39	476	456	3650	3650	7	3259	391
2040	291	187	39	478	459	3670	3670	7	3276	394
2041	293	188	39	481	461	3689	3689	7	3292	397
2042	294	189	39	483	463	3709	3709	7	3308	401
2043	296	190	39	486	466	3729	3729	7	3325	404
2044	297	191	39	488	468	3749	3749			
2045	299	192	39	490	470	3770	3770			
2046	300	193	39	493	473	3790	3790			
2047	302	194	39	495	475	3810	3810			
2048	303	195	39	498	477	3831	3831			
2049	305	196	39	500	480	3851	3851			
2050	306	197	39	503	482	3872	3872			

Index